American Architecture

American Architecture

A Field Guide to the Most Important Examples

William Dudley Hunt, Jr.

HARPER & ROW, PUBLISHERS, New York
Cambridge, Philadelphia, San Francisco, London
Mexico City, São Paulo, Sydney

FIRST EDITION

Designer: Abigail Sturges

Library of Congress Cataloging in Publication Data

Hunt, William Dudley.
 American architecture, a field guide to the most important examples.

 Includes index.
 1. Architecture—United States—Guide-books. 2. United
States—Description and travel—Guide-books.   I. Title.
NA705.H85   1983   917.3′04927   83–47535
ISBN 0–06–015219–2   84 85 86 87 88 10 9 8 7 6 5 4 3 2 1
ISBN 0–06–091077–1 (pbk.) 84 85 86 87 88 10 9 8 7 6 5 4 3 2 1

Contents

NEW ENGLAND STATES   1

MIDDLE ATLANTIC STATES   45

SOUTHEASTERN STATES   107

MIDWESTERN STATES   175

ROCKY MOUNTAIN STATES   241

SOUTHWESTERN STATES   261

PACIFIC STATES   287

List of Illustrations

Acknowledgments

American Architecture is the result of several years of research that included the study of hundreds of guides, histories, and other books, magazines, archives, visits to actual locations and return trips to check early drafts. Hundreds of individuals, including architects, editors, writers, critics and people who simply like and enjoy architecture, were consulted. The buildings included and those considered the most important were selected on the basis of the research and the many valuable suggestions received.

It is impossible to list all of the people who helped in the long process of putting the book together, researching facts, checking draft manuscripts, discovering photographs, criticizing the writing, making suggestions. However a few must be named: Robbin Reynolds and Diane Foster who, very early, were convinced of the need for the book; the author's son, architect-to-be Stephen Hunt, who performed several difficult tasks; American Institute of Architects librarian Stephanie Byrnes, who made sure the author stayed busy by supplying references and other assistance; Harper & Row editor Cass Canfield, Jr., who believed in the book from the beginning and who was a constant source of encouragement; and the author's wife, Gwen, who performed many chores authors hate and put off, including the typing of early drafts until a new word processor was employed, a fierce taskmaster that greatly simplified the assembly of myriads of little pieces of information in some semblance of order.

William Dudley Hunt, Jr.

Introduction

This book is intended for all people who are interested in the architectural, historical and sociological heritage of the most important United States buildings. It has been designed to be truly portable, fitting easily into a pocket, purse or automobile glove compartment. It has been organized and written to be easily used by people en route to, or visiting, buildings.

ORGANIZATION

The book is organized by regions, beginning with the New England states and ending with the Pacific states. Within regions, the organization is by states, alphabetically, and within states by major cities, also alphabetically. Immediately following the major cities are trips in various directions. For example, after the entry New York City, an entry entitled New York City Vicinity (N, via George Washington Bridge & US 9W) outlines a trip ending in Newburgh, N.Y. After this entry, a note indicates that locations not far north of Newburgh are included in the entry entitled Albany Vicinity (S, via US 9). Within cities, towns and other locations, the effort has been made to list buildings in a logical, concise manner, in walking tours whenever that mode seems practical; in other cases, by automobile, subway or other means of transportation. However, there is no reason why a walking or other type of tour must begin with the first building listed in a city or other location. A person in a certain location might wish to locate that position in the guide and proceed in either direction. Similarly, a traveler in an intermediate location along one of the trips outside major cities might proceed in either direction.

Short introductions at the beginning of entries for the states contain fundamental information on major factors that deeply affect architecture—history, geography, geology, climate, building materials. Also mentioned are cities and other localities of more than ordinary architectural interest.

BUILDINGS

The attempt has been made to include the most important American buildings, from pre-Columbian structures of the ancestors of the Indians to the latest modern examples. The very finest of all buildings, architecturally, are indicated by a symbol (•). These are examples that a traveler with very limited time might choose to see. Other very important architectural examples are noted in the text by "fine," "very fine," or other similar adjectives. Also included are examples that have architectural merit and others of interest for historical, sociological or other reasons. In many locations, including some small towns, "Interesting buildings include . . . ," or words to that effect, are used to indicate that interesting examples other than those listed are to be found. Most of the buildings listed are open to the public at certain times and under certain circumstances. These are indicated by the symbol (*). Fees, ranging from nominal amounts to several dollars, are charged for entry to many of the buildings. Both hours of admission and fees are very changeable. For that reason, fearing instant obsolescence, neither are cited in this book. No maps are included, for similar reasons, and because of the impossibility of making them large and accurate enough for genuine usefulness. Large cities and many smaller cities and towns have visitor or tourist information centers from which reliable maps and information on fees, hours and other subjects may be readily obtained. For those who find their appetite for enjoyment of architecture whetted by this book, extensive, detailed guidebooks are available for most important cities and some states.

ARCHITECTURAL STYLES

Some people, including some architects, wish that the subject of architectural styles would simply fade away. However, styles provide a useful way to classify and study buildings and may considerably enhance the enjoyment of architecture. This is not the place for a detailed discussion of this subject, which can be overpoweringly complicated. However, some mention of major American styles should be of interest.

PRE-COLUMBIAN ARCHITECTURE
Adobe, stone and earth cliff dwellings, pueblos and other structures of the ancestors of present-day Indians have survived from the era before Christopher Columbus arrived in America, 1492, while other early structures of more perishable materials have not (see photos on pp. 246, 268 bottom, and 270 top).

COLONIAL ARCHITECTURE
In the earliest settlements by Europeans, the colonists built structures much like those they had known in their homelands, later adapting them to the demands of the frontier, climate, and so on. Thus, there is no single "Colonial" style, but several, including that of the English, as in New England Colonial (pp. 17, 19, 20), mostly derived from Gothic architecture in England; French Colonial (p. 127); Spanish Colonial (pp. 265 and 268 top), derived from Baroque architecture in Spain. Other Colonial architecture includes that of the Dutch, Germans, Swedes, and other settlers. Other styles were also imported from Europe, including Jacobean, named for English King James I (p. 167).

GEORGIAN ARCHITECTURE

Derived from architecture prevalent in England during reigns of George I, II, III, and to an extent, IV. From about 1700 to 1790, first solidly established style in United States. Simple, elegant, symmetrical buildings, often of brick or brick with stone trim, usually without free-standing columns (pp. 56, 64, 96, 149, 150).

CLASSIC REVIVAL ARCHITECTURE

Although also popular in England, believed to be the first attempt to establish an American style; based on the rational principles of Classic Greece and Rome. Considerably more elaborate than Georgian examples, buildings usually have columns, forms and details derived from, or sometimes almost replicas of, ancient buildings of Classic Greece and Rome. Prevalent from about 1770 to 1850, the style is often subdivided into Greek Revival, based on Greek architecture (pp. 83, 100, 132, 133, 137, 138) and Roman Revival, especially the buildings of Thomas Jefferson, based on Roman examples (pp 161 and 162). Another less prevalent style during this period was the Federal, sometimes called Adam for four brothers who were noted English furniture designers of the era. The Federal style is similar to the Georgian, but is characterized by very light, delicate forms and ornament (pp. 12, 23, 25).

GOTHIC REVIVAL ARCHITECTURE

Popular in Europe as well as in the United States from about 1800 to 1890, style based on emotional, imaginative principles and forms of Gothic architecture of the Middle Ages. Characterized by use of pointed arches and vaults and other Gothic forms (pp. 50, 75, 80, 82 right, 87).

ECLECTIC ARCHITECTURE

Beginning about 1820 and extending well into the 20th century, architects designed buildings in many styles other than Classic or Gothic Revival, a state of affairs collectively known as eclecticism. Some architects chose a given style for each building, while others took elements from a number of styles combining them in sometimes imaginative, sometimes unfortunate, ways. Styles from any place and any era were utilized. Thus, there were revivals of Italian Renaissance (pp. 16 and 39 top) and Second Empire derived from era of Napoleon III (p. 52), as well as Egyptian, Queen Anne, Georgian and others, including even revivals of revivals such as Classic. One of the most important styles was Romanesque Revival, especially in the buildings of Henry Hobson Richardson, exemplified by use of early medieval round arches and vaults (pp. 15 and 104). Another was Victorian Gothic Revival (p. 98 top). Other important style eras were Beaux Arts, based on the historical classic training of American architects at the famous school in Paris (pp. 78 and 79 bottom); Stick, expressing wood-framed structures (pp. 292 top and 293); and Shingle (p. 39 bottom).

MODERN ARCHITECTURE

Generally taken to mean the type of architecture, beginning in the late 19th century, that attempted to discard the forms of traditional styles, use the latest structural systems such as iron and steel skeleton framing, eliminate or subdue ornament and produce functional buildings that expressed their functions and engineering. The modern movement began about the same time in Europe and in the United States, especially in the early work of the members of the so-called Chicago School—William LeBaron Jenney, Holabird and Roche, Burnham and Root and Louis Sullivan. Their work, in what is sometimes called the Commercial style, paved the way for future developments (pp. 70, 177–179, 217). Later, many other architects, most notably Frank Lloyd Wright, continued the movement (pp. 180 bottom, 185, 236, and others). Other noted architects made pioneering efforts, including the so-called International style of Howe and Lescaze (p. 98 bottom), Walter Gropius (pp. 24 and 27), Richard Neutra (pp. 296 and 298), Ludwig Mies van der Rohe (pp. 180 top, 182, 1 4). Some architects, influenced by the style of a 1925 Paris exposition, popularly called Art Deco, or sometimes modernistic or Moderne, designed buildings with geometric, often zig-zag, ornament (p. 77 right).

A large number of architects have designed fine modern buildings in the relatively recent past (pp. 29, 72, 76, 99, 105, 181, 186, 202, 238, 243, 294, 303, 314, and others). In more recent years, various phases of modern architecture have been called expressionism (p. 160), brutalism (p. 13), along with formalism, and many others. Recently, several movements have arisen, all sometimes included under the name post-modernism. This is an unfortunate choice of language since, in their use of distorted pseudo-historic forms and decoration, these buildings cannot seriously be considered ahead of their time. Many of the buildings have also been seriously criticized for their seemingly senseless two-dimensional forms and their disregard of building functions, needs of users, and their sites and surroundings. And their architects have been criticized for ignoring important architectural principles and responsibilities in order to satisfy their own whims or egos. In spite of all of the "post-modernist" ballyhoo, a great many other American architects continue to produce some of the finest architecture in the world.

New
England
States

Connecticut

Early inhabitants Indians of several tribes, including Mohican, Pequot. First explored and claimed by Dutch, 1614, led by Adriaen Block; no permanent settlement made. First English permanent settlement: Windsor, 1633. Connecticut Colony, also called River Colony, chartered by England, 1662; New Haven Colony, 1638; two colonies united, 1665. Became fifth state, Jan. 9, 1788. Today: Important manufacturing, retailing, and tourist industries; also major financial industry, especially insurance.

Land Regions: E to W, Eastern New England Uplands; Coastal Lowlands; Connecticut Valley Lowland; Western New England Upland; in extreme NW, small Taconic section.

Climate: Temperate, no extremely high or low temperatures; moderate precipitation.

Major Building Materials: Timber, especially hardwoods; sand and gravel; clay; stone.

Architecture: Rich and varied, from Colonial era to present, including some of finest U.S. examples, in many locations, especially in Hartford and vicinity; New Haven and vicinity. Also note smaller towns such as Litchfield, New Canaan, Ridgefield.

HARTFORD

Interesting buildings include: *State Capitol (1878; later alt.), Capitol Hill; architect: Richard Upjohn; Gothic Revival by famous architect. Not far: *Old State House (1796; later alt.; rest.), 800 Main St; architect: Charles Bulfinch; architect, rest.: Roger Clark; fine Federal by famous architect. Behind State House: interesting modern *Constitution Plaza (1964), architect: Charles Dubose; landscape architects: Sasaki, Dawson & DeMay. Also: *Harriet Beecher Stowe House (1871; rest.), 73 Forest Ave; once home of author of *Uncle Tom's Cabin* and other abolitionist books. *Armsmear, the Samuel Colt House (1857; later alt.), 80 Wethersfield Ave; Eclectic Victorian; once home of inventor of Colt revolver, now Episcopal Women's Home. *Nook Farm, the Mark Twain House (1874; later alt. & addit.; rest.), 351 Farmington Ave; architect: Edward T. Potter; Victorian; once home of famous author; interior ornament by noted designer Louis Comfort Tiffany. Few blocks: modern *Aetna Life & Casualty Computer Center (1972), 151 Farmington Ave; architects: Kevin Roche & John Dinkeloo. Near junction of US 44 & St. 189,

*Unitarian Meeting House (1964), 50 Bloomfield Ave; architect: Victor Lundy; interesting modern church by noted architect. Few miles farther, via St. 189: BLOOMFIELD. Fine modern *Connecticut General Life Insurance Co. South Building (1957) and North Building, originally Emhart Manufacturing Co. (1963), 900–50 Cottage Grove Rd; architects: Skidmore, Owings & Merrill. Approx. 9 mi NE of Hartford, via US 44A: MANCHESTER. *Timothy Cheney House (about 1780; later alt. & addit.). Approx. 12 mi E of Manchester, via US 44A & St. 31: COVENTRY. *Nathan Hale House (1756; rest.); once family home of Revolutionary War patriot hanged by British.

Hartford Vicinity *(N, via US I-91).* Approx. 6 mi: WINDSOR. Interesting buildings include, on Palisado Ave, *First Congregational Church (1794; later alt. & addit.); at no. 96, gambrel-roofed Colonial *Lt. Walter Fyler House (1640; addit. 1765; rest.); at no. 778, *Oliver Ellsworth House (1740; addit. about 1785), once home of third U.S. chief justice. Also: *Joseph Loomis House (1640; later alt. & addit.), Batchelder Rd, now part of Loomis Institute. Approx. 10 mi NW of Windsor, via US I-91 & St. 20: EAST GRANBY. Nearby, infamous *Newgate Prison (1773; later alt. & addit.). Approx. 8 mi N of Windsor, via St. 159: WINDSOR LOCKS. Interesting old houses here. Approx. 5 mi N of Windsor Locks, via St. 75: SUFFIELD. Main St, *Hatheway House (1760; addit. 1795; rest.), *Dr. Alexander King House (1764; rest.).

Hartford Vicinity *(SE, via St. 2).* Approx. 25 mi: COLCHESTER. Interesting buildings include: *Foote House (1702; rest.), on The Green; very small Colonial house; moved here. Approx. 15 mi farther: NORWICH. Interesting buildings include: *Leffingwell Inn (1675; later alt. & addit.; rest.), once owned by founder of city, Thomas Leffingwell. On Rockwell St, at no. 42, *Dr. John D. Rockwell House (1818; later alt. & addit.); at no. 44, *Nathaniel Backus House (1750; later alt. & addit.), once home of another founder; moved here. Also: *Little Plain Hist. Dist. Approx. 10 mi NW of Norwich, via St. 87: LEBANON. Interesting buildings include number connected with famous Trumbull family. Around *The Common: *Gov. Jonathan Trumbull House (1740; later alt. & addit.; rest.), once home of first state governor and birthplace of his grandson, John Trumbull, famous painter of *The Declaration of Independence* and other patriotic works; *First Congregational Church (1809; part. dest. 1938; rebuilt & rest. 1954), architect: John Trumbull; Jonathan Trumbull House (1769; later alt.), once home of first and second state governor of name; Welles House (1712; later alt. & addit.), birthplace of William Williams, signer of Declaration of Independence.

Hartford Vicinity *(SE, via US I-91 & St. 9).* Approx. 4 mi: WETHERSFIELD. Interesting buildings include: *Buttolph-Williams House (1686; later alt.; rest.), 249 Broad St; fine New England

Colonial; interesting kitchen. On Main St: at no. 203, *Silas Deane House (1766; rest.), large mansion; at no. 211, *Joseph Webby House (1678; addit. 1752; rest.), fine Georgian; at no. 215, *Isaac Stevens House (1789; rest.). Approx. 12 mi farther: MIDDLETOWN. Interesting buildings include, on High St, *Wesleyan University buildings: at no. 301, Greek Revival *Richard Alsop House, now Davison Art Center (1838; later alt.), probable architect: Ithiel Town. Across street, same architect's fine Greek Revival *Samuel Russell House, now Honors College (1829; later alt. & addit.); at no. 327, Gothic Revival *Davison House (1845; later alt.). On Wyllys Ave, *Wesleyan Center of the Arts (1973), architects: Kevin Roche & John Dinkeloo; interesting modern complex for arts, music and drama. On Main St, *Gen. Joseph K. F. Mansfield House (1807; later alt.). Approx. 10 mi SE of Middletown, via St. 9 & 9A: HADDAM. Interesting buildings include: *Thankful Arnold House (1795; later alt. & addit.), Haddam Green. Approx. 4 mi farther, via St. 9A & 82: EAST HADDAM. Interesting buildings include: *Gillette Castle (1919), State Park, fantastic 24-room house built by noted actor and playwright William Gillette. Approx. 3 mi N of East Haddam, via St. 149: MOODUS. *Amasa Day House (1816; rest.), the Green; Greek Revival. Approx. 7 mi S of East Haddam, via St. 9A & 82: DEEP RIVER. *Deacon Ezra Southworth House, also known as Old Stone House (1840; later alt. & addit.), S Main St. Approx. 4 mi SE of Deep River, via St. 9: ESSEX. Interesting buildings include: *Pratt House (about 1750), 20 West Ave; also *Pratt Smithy.

Hartford Vicinity *(SW, via US 6).* Approx. 13 mi, via US 6 & St. 10: FARMINGTON. Interesting buildings include: *Stanley-Whitman House (about 1664; later alt. & addit.; rest.), 37 High St; architect, rest.: J. Frederick Kelly; very fine wood-frame New England Colonial; fine gardens. ••**First Church of Christ,** Congregational (1772; later alt.; rest.), Main St; architect: Judah Woodruff; fine Colonial. *Alfred A. Pope House, now Hill-Stead Museum (1900), Farmington Ave; architect: Stanford White; fine mansion by famous architect; interesting art and furniture collections. Approx. 8 mi SW of Farmington, via St. 10, US 6 & St. 69: BRISTOL. *Miles Lewis House, now American Clock & Watch Museum (1801; later alt. & addit.), 100 Maple St.

Hartford Vicinity *(W, via US 44/202).* Approx. 6 mi: WEST HARTFORD. *Noah Webster Birthplace (1700–20; later alt.), 227 S. Main St; once home of famous dictionary author. Approx. 10 mi farther: AVON. *Congregational Church (1819; later alt.), 6 W. Main St; architect: David Hoadley. Approx. 5 mi N of Avon, via US 202: SIMSBURY. Interesting buildings include: *Capt. Elisha Phelps House (1771; addit. 1879; later alt.), 800 Hopmeadow St; once tavern & inn; now museum. Approx. 23 mi SW of Avon, via US 202, LITCHFIELD, beautifully preserved old New England town. Interesting buildings include: in Hist. Dist. around and near

*Village Green (bounded by North, East, South & West sts), *First Congregational Church (1829; later alt. & addit.; rest.), probable architect: Levi Newell; architect, rest.: Richard H. Dana, Jr.; fine example; moved to another location and back to original site. Other houses of interest around or near The Green include: on South St, Oliver Wolcott, Sr. House (1753; later alt. & addit.), once home of signer of Declaration of Independence, and state governor; Wolcott's father was also state governor; lead statue of King George III hauled from New York City and melted here to make bullets. *Oliver Wolcott, Jr. House (1799; addit. 1817; later alt.), once home of another state governor, son of Oliver senior. *Tapping Reeve House (1774; rest.) and *Law School (1784; rest.), believed to be first law school in U.S.; Benedict Arnold and John C. Calhoun students here. Also of interest: taverns, bank, apothecary shop.

NEW HAVEN

Interesting buildings include, on The Green, three early churches: *Trinity Church, Episcopal, (1814; later alt. & addit.), architect: Ithiel Town; fine Gothic Revival, now much altered; by famous architect; *First Church of Christ, Congregational, also known as Center Church, (1814; later alt.), architect: Ithiel Town, perhaps with aid of Asher Benjamin; fine Georgian; *United Church, Congregational, also known as Old North Church (1815; later alt.), supervised by architect David Hoadley; fine Georgian. Interesting modern buildings by noted architects Kevin Roche & John Dinkeloo include: *Knights of Columbus Building (1970), 1 Columbus Plaza; *Veterans Memorial Coliseum (1972), bet. N. Frontage Rd & Church, George & Orange sts. At *Yale University, interesting buildings include: Colonial *Connecticut Hall (1752; later alt. & addit.), Elm St; oldest building on campus; also number of Eclectic buildings, mostly Victorian and Gothic Revival and unusual number of very fine modern buildings by famous architects. Among them: **Yale Art Gallery Addition** (1953), 1111 Chapel St; architect: Louis Kahn; original building (1928); architect: Egerton Swartwout. Across street, at Chapel & High sts: **Yale Center for British Art** (1977), architect: Louis Kahn, completed after his death by architects Pellechia & Meyers. **Art and Architecture Building** (1963; interior burned 1969; renov.), 180 York St; architect: Paul Rudolph. *Beinecke Rare Book and Manuscript Library (1963), High & Wall sts; architects: Skidmore, Owings & Merrill. Nearby, interesting, *Grove Street Cemetery Gates (1848), 227 Grove St; architect: Henry Austin; Eclectic Egyptian Revival entrance to cemetery where many famous people buried. *Othniel C. Marsh House (1880), 360 Prospect St; architect: J. Cleveland Cady; redstone mansion; once home of famous, and America's first, paleontologist. Other very fine modern university buildings include: *Stiles and Morse colleges (1962), Broadway & Tower Pkwy; architect: Eero Saarinen. ●●**D. S. Ingalls Hockey Rink** (1958), 73 Sachem St; architect: Eero Saarinen. Nearby, Eclectic *James Dwight Dana House (1849; later alt.), 24 Hillhouse Ave; architect: Henry Austin; once home of famous geologist and zoologist. On Yale Upper Campus, two very fine modern buildings by famous architect Philip Johnson: ●●**Kline Biology Tower** (1966), Hillhouse Ave, and *Kline Geology Tower (1963), 210 Whitney Ave. On outskirts of city: *Pardee-Morris House (1685; burned & rebuilt 1799), 325 Lighthouse Rd.

New Haven Vicinity *(N, via US 5)*. Approx. 5 mi: HAMDEN. *Jonathan Dickerman House (1770; later alt. & addit.), Mt. Carmel Ave. Approx. 5 mi farther: WALLINGFORD. Interesting buildings include: *Nehemiah Royce House (1672; later alt. & addit.; rest.), 538 N. Main St; *Samuel Parsons House (1759; addit. 1855; later alt.), 180 N. Main St; once tavern and stagecoach station. At *Choate-Rosemary Hall School, Christian St, interesting modern *Paul Mellon Arts Center (1971), architect: I. M. Pei; *Upper Campus (1972), architect: James Stewart Polshek. Approx. 5 mi farther: MERIDEN. Interesting buildings include: *Moses Andrews House (1760; later alt. & addit.), 424 Main St.

New Haven Vicinity *(E, via Boston Post Rd, US 1 or Conn. Tpk)*. Approx. 15 mi: GUILFORD. In well-preserved old village, interesting buildings include: *Henry Whitfield House (1640; later alt.; rest.), Whitfield St; architect, rest.: J. Frederick Kelly; believed to be oldest stone house in New England; interesting herb garden; once served as church, meeting hall and fort. On Boston St, at no. 84, *George Hyland House (1660; later alt. & addit.), New England Colonial; at no. 161, *Thomas Griswold House (1735; later alt.), New England Colonial saltbox; interesting outbuildings. Approx. 5 mi farther: MADISON. *Nathaniel Allis House (1739; later alt. & addit.), 853 Boston Post Rd. Approx. 4 mi farther: CLINTON. *Stanton House (about 1789; later alt.), 63 E. Main St; interesting reprod. of old Stanton country store. Approx. 12 mi farther: OLD LYME. Interesting buildings include: ●●**First Congregational Church** (1817; burned 1907; reconst. 1909), Lyme St; fine example. *Florence Griswold House (1817; later alt.), Boston Post Rd; fine Greek Revival. Nearby, in EAST LYME, *Thomas Lee House (about 1660; later alt. & addit.; rest.), Shore Rd; fine New England Colonial saltbox. Approx. 14 mi E of Old Lyme, via St. 156: WATERFORD. *Edward Stephen Harkness Mansion (1904), Harkness Memorial Park; Eclectic Italianate. Approx. 4 mi past Waterford, via St. 156: NEW LONDON. Interesting buildings include: *Joshua Hempsted House (1678; addit. 1728; rest.), 11 Hempsted St; *Nathaniel Shaw House (1756; partially burned 1781; reconst.; later alt. & addit.), 11 Blinman St; Federal *Deshon-Allyn House (1829), 613 Williams St. Also of interest: *U.S. Coast Guard Academy. Approx. 8 mi E of New

London, via US 1: MYSTIC. *Capt. George Denison House (1717; rest.), Pequot-Sepos Rd. Nearby, via St. 27, *Mystic Seaport, fascinating reconst. & rest. mid-19th century whaling and coastal shipping town. Interesting buildings include: *Samuel Buckingham House (1768); *Thomas Greenman House (1842); *Edwards House (about 1815); fanciful Gothic Revival *New York Yacht Club (1845), moved here from Oyster Bay, N.Y.; architect: Alexander Jackson Davis. Also of interest, ships, including: whaler *Charles W. Morgan; training ship *Joseph Conrad. Also of interest nearby: *Mystic Marinelife Aquarium. Approx. 4 mi E of Mystic, via US 1: STONINGTON. Interesting buildings include: *Congregational Church (1829; later alt. & addit.), Main & Elm sts; Greek Revival.

New Haven Vicinity *(SW, via Boston Post Rd, US 1, or Conn. Tpk)*. Approx. 11 mi: MILFORD. *First United Church of Christ, Congregational (1824; later alt. & addit.), W. Main & W. River sts; architect: David Hoadley; fine example by noted architect. *Col. Stephen Ford House (about 1705; later alt.), 142 W. Main St; once tavern; original taproom. *Eells-Stow House (1684; later alt. & addit.; rest.), 34 High St. Approx. 4 mi farther: STRATFORD. Interesting buildings include: *Capt. David Judson House (1723; later alt.), 967 Academy Hill; museum adjoining. Also of interest near here: *American Shakespeare Theater. Approx. 6 mi farther: BRIDGEPORT. *Capt. John Brooks House (1788; rest.), 199 Pembroke St. Also of interest: *P. T. Barnum Museum, 820 Main St. Approx. 5 mi farther: FAIRFIELD, well-preserved old town. Number of interesting buildings include: on Green, *Town Hall (1794; later alt. & addit.; rest.); *Sun Tavern (1780; later alt. & addit.). Approx. 9 mi farther: NORWALK. *Lockwood-Matthews Mansion (1868; later alt.), 295 West Ave; architect: Detlef Lienau; large ornate house. Approx. 5 mi NW of Norwalk, via St. 123: NEW CANAAN. Interesting buildings include: Georgian *Hanford-Silliman House (about 1764; later alt.), 33 Oenoke Ridge Rd. Nearby, *John Rogers Studio (1877), once home and studio of noted sculptor; number of his works here. *First Presbyterian Church (1970), 178 Oenoke Ridge Rd; architect: Philip Ives; interesting modern example, built in front of 1899 mansion. Many other fine modern buildings, all of them private, some of them designed by noted architects for themselves including: •**Philip Johnson House** (1949), Pavilion (1962) and Gallery (1965), famous modern "glass house"; other buildings on site. Also: Eliot Noyes House (1954); Marcel Breuer House (1947). Approx. 4 mi SW of Norwalk, via US 1: DARIEN. *Bates-Scofield House (about 1737; later alt.), 45 Old Kings Hwy. Approx. 5 mi farther: STAMFORD. Interesting buildings include: *Hoyt-Barnum House (about 1690; later alt.), 713 Bedford St. Not far: *First Presbyterian Church (1958), 1101 Bedford St; architect: Wallace K. Harrison; assoc. architects: Sherwood, Mills & Smith; fascinating modern church by noted architect; enclosed with thousands of pieces of glass of many colors produced by Gabriel Loire; sometimes called "Fish Church" because of its shape derived from fish, early Christian symbol. Approx. 7 mi farther: GREENWICH. *Gen. Israel Putnam Cottage (about 1720; later alt. & addit.), 243 E. Putnam Ave; originally Timothy Knapp Tavern; here Revolutionary War general escaped British, 1779. Just W of Greenwich: COS COB. *Bush-Holley House (about 1685; later alt.; rest.), 39 Strickland Rd.

New Haven Vicinity *(NW, via St. 34 & US I-84)*. Approx. 30 mi: DANBURY. *St. John House (about 1750; later alt.) and *Barnum House (1780; later alt.), both at 43 Main St; now Scott-Fanton Museum. Approx. 15 mi N of Danbury, via US 7/202: NEW MILFORD. *Knapp House (1815), 1 Old Albany Post Rd. Approx. 14 mi E of New Milford, via St. 67 & 317: WOODBURY. *The Glebe House (1690; addit. 1750), Hollow Rd; here Samuel Seabury was elected first American Episcopal bishop, 1783.

Maine

Early inhabitants Indians of Abnaki and Etchemin tribes. Believed to have been first explored by Vikings, led by Leif Ericson, c. 1000; later by Italian John Cabot, leading English expedition, about 1498. Number of French explorations, late 16th and early 17th centuries. First permanent English settlement believed to have been near present-day Saco, 1623. First chartered English city in America: York, 1641, originally Gorgeana, named for owner of state, Ferdinando Gorges. After disputes, Massachusetts bought state from his heirs, 1677, for about $6,000. Battles of French and Indian Wars fought here; at end of wars, treaty of 1763 ended French claims to area. Became twenty-third state, Mar. 15, 1820.

Land Regions: E to W, Coastal Lowlands; Eastern New England Upland; White Mountains.

Climate: Cold winters; cool summers; moderate precipitation; snowfall heavy.

Major Building Materials: Lumber, primarily softwoods, some hardwoods; sand and gravel; stone.

Architecture: Rich and varied; number of fine examples for relatively small state.

AUGUSTA

Interesting buildings include: *State House, or Capitol (1832; addit. 1911), State & Capitol sts; architect: Charles Bulfinch; architect, addit.: G. Henri Desmond; Classic Revival; part built from designs of famous Boston architect; completed some 80 years later. *James G. Blaine House (about 1830; later alt. & addit.), State & Capitol sts; Classic Revival; once home of Speaker of U.S. House of Representatives, now residence of state governor. *Ft. Western (1754; rest.), Bowman St; architect: Gershom Flagg; log building built for protection during French and Indian Wars. Approx. 24 mi N, via US 201: WINSLOW. *Ft. Halifax Blockhouse (1754; rest.); architects: Gen. John Winslow & Capt. William Lithgow; log blockhouse.

Augusta Vicinity *(S, via US 201 or I-95).* Approx. 2 mi: HALLOWELL. Gage Block (1846; later alt.), 106–114 Second St; early frame row houses. Approx. 14 mi S of Hallowell, via US I-95 & St. 197: RICHMOND. Interesting buildings include: Thomas Jefferson Southard Block (1882), 25 Front St; cast-iron front. Approx. 2 mi from Richmond, via St. 128: DRESDEN. *Pownalborough Courthouse (1761; rest.); architect: Gershom Flagg; wood-frame Colonial. Not far: wood-frame Bowman-Carney House (about 1761); by same architect.

BANGOR

*Symphony House (1833; later alt. & addit.), 166 Union St; architect: Richard Upjohn. *Grand Army of the Republic House, originally Thomas Hill House (about 1834; later alt.).

Bangor Vicinity *(SE & E, via US 1A & 1).* Approx. 25 mi: ELLSWORTH. Interesting buildings include: *Woodlawn, the Col. John Black House (1827), W. Main St; Georgian. Few miles, via St. 3, *Stanwood Homestead (1850), set in 40-acre bird sanctuary, "Birdsacre." Also of interest, approx. 10 mi SE, via St. 3, *Acadia Nat. Park. Approx. 43 mi E of Ellsworth: COLUMBIA FALLS. *Judge Thomas Ruggles House (about 1818; rest.), Main St; architect: Aaron Sherman; wood-frame, extremely fine exterior and interior wood details. Approx. 15 mi farther: MACHIAS. *Burnham Tavern (1770; later alt. & addit.), High & Free sts. Also of interest, approx. 38 mi NE, via US 1 & St. 189, near LUBEC, *Roosevelt Campobello International Park, for many years home of Pres. Franklin Delano Roosevelt.

Bangor Vicinity *(SW, via US 1A).* Approx. 38 mi: BELFAST. Interesting buildings include: *First Church (1818; later alt. & addit.), Church & Spring sts; architect: Samuel French; unusual tower. Approx. 20 mi farther: CAMDEN. *Old Conway House

(1768; rest.), Conway Rd. Approx. 6 mi farther: ROCKLAND.
*Farnsworth House (1840; alter alt. & addit.), 19 Elm St; Greek
Revival. Also see: Portland Vicinity (NE, via US 1).

PORTLAND

Interesting buildings include: *Wadsworth-Longfellow House
(1785; later alt. & addit.), 487 Congress St; boyhood home of
famous poet Henry Wadsworth Longfellow. *H. L. McClellan–D.
M. Sweat Mansion, now Portland Museum of Art, (1801; later
alt. & addit.), 111 High St; architect: John Kimball, Sr.; probable
architect, front portico: Alexander Parris; fine Federal. *Charles
Q. Clapp House, now School of Fine and Applied Art (1833; later
alt. & addit.), 97 Spring St. Hunnewell-Shepley House, now Portland Club (1805; later alt.; addit. 1922); architect: Alexander Parris; architect, alt. & addit.: John Calvin Stephens. *First Parish
Church, Unitarian (1825), 425 Congress St; architect: John Mus-
sey. *Victoria Mansion, the Morse-Libby House (1863; rest.), 109
Danforth St; architect: Henry Austin, fine Victorian. Also: *Park
St Block (1835); *Spring Street Hist. Dist. Approx. 3 mi W, via
Congress St: STROUDSBURG. *George Tate House (1755; rest.),
1270 Westbrook St; fine Colonial.

Portland Vicinity *(N, via Maine Tpk).* Approx. 26 mi, via Maine
Tpk & St. 26, near POLAND SPRINGS, *Sabathday Lake Shaker
Village. Interesting buildings include: *Meetinghouse (1794) and
more than dozen others.

Portland Vicinity *(NE, via US 1).* Approx. 23 mi: BRUNSWICK.
*Harriet Beecher Stowe House (1805; later remod.), 63 Federal
St; here author wrote *Uncle Tom's Cabin.* At *Bowdoin College,
interesting buildings include: *Massachusetts Hall (1803; later
alt. & addit.); architects: Aaron Melcher & Capt. John Dunlap;
oldest building on campus. Also at Bowdoin: modern *Coles Tower (1964); architect: Hugh Stubbins. Approx. 8 mi farther: BATH.
Interesting buildings include: *Winter Street Congregational
Church, now Bath Marine Museum (1848; later alt.), 880 Washington St; architect: Anthony Coombs Raymons; architect, 1890
alt.: John Calvin Stevens; Gothic Revivial. At 963 Washington St,
main building of museum, *Harold M. Sewall House (1844; later
alt. & addit.); architect, 1902 addit.: Addison Mizner; Greek Revival. *U.S. Custom House & Post Office (1858; later alt. &
addit.), 25 Front St; architect: Ammi B. Young; architect, addit.:
James Knox Taylor. Approx. 11 mi farther: WISCASSET. Interesting buildings include: *Nickels-Sortwell House (1812; rest.),
Main & Federal sts; fine Federal, fine details. *Lincoln Co.
Courthouse (1824), facing fine Village Green. *Lincoln Co. Jail
(1811), Federal St. Few miles from Wiscasset, via St. 27, near
NORTH EDGECOMBE. *Ft. Edgecombe (1890), part. rest., part. rebuilt log stockade and blockhouse. Approx. 6 mi farther: DAMAR-

ISCOTTA. *Chapman-Hall House (1754; rest.), Main & Church sts; typical New England farmhouse of era. Approx. 4 mi S of Damariscotta, via St. 129, *Old Walpole Meeting House (1772; rest.). Approx. 7 mi farther: *Colonial Pemaquid Village. Approx. 8 mi NE of Damariscotta, via US 1: WALDOBORO. Nearby, off St. 32, *German Lutheran Church (1772; moved here 1795; rest.). Also see: Bangor Vicinity SE & E, via US 1A (1).

Portland Vicinity *(SE, via US I-95).* Approx. 21 mi: KENNE-BUNK. *Wedding Cake House, the George W. Bourne House (1826; later alt.), Summer St; simple wood-frame example, noted for intricacy of Gothic Revival woodwork. Other interesting buildings in nearby KENNEBUNKPORT. Approx. 8 mi farther: KITTERY POINT. **••Lady Pepperrell House** (1760; later alt. & addit.; rest.), St. 103; fine Georgian. Nearby, Sparhawk House (1742); William Pepperrell House (1683; later alt. & addit.). Few miles farther, *Ft. McClary (1690; addit. 1812; rebuilt 1845; part. rebuilt and rest.). Approx. 5 mi NE of Kittery Point, via St. 103: YORK. Interesting buildings include: *York Co. Gaol, or Jail (1653; later alt. & addit.), Lindsay St. Across street: *Jefferd's Tavern (1750; moved here), Lindsay St; *Emerson-Wilcox House (about 1740; later alt. & addit.), once tavern, post office. On Southside Rd, *Elizabeth Perkins House (1686; later alt. & addit.). Approx. 8 mi NW of Kittery, via St. 91 & 4: S. BERWICK. *Capt. Theodore Jewett House (1774; later alt. & addit.), 101 Portland St; birthplace of novelist Sarah Orme Jewett. Approx. 3 mi S, via St. 236, *Jonathan Hamilton House (1788; later alt. & addit.; rest.).

Portland Vicinity *(NW, via US 302).* Approx. 25 mi: S. CASCO. *Nathaniel Hawthorne House (1812; later alt. & addit.), Raymond Cape Rd; boyhood home of famous author.

Massachusetts

Early inhabitants Indians of several tribes, including Massachusett, Mohican. Believed to have been first explored by Vikings, led by Leif Ericson, c. 1000; Italian John Cabot, for English, believed to have visited about 1498. Frenchman Samuel de Champlain drew maps of coast, 1606. First permanent English settlement, by Pilgrims: Plymouth Colony, 1620. Chartered by English king, Puritans joined colonists at Salem, founded about 1627. In 1630, Puritans founded Boston, Massachusetts Bay Colony. Many Indian attacks until 1668. Charters revoked, 1684; with other N colonies, became Dominion of New England, 1686. Two colonies merged, 1691; given new charter. Sir William Phipps first royal governor, 1692. French and Indian Wars, waged in area, ended with British victory, 1763, ending French claims. Colonists began resistance to British tax laws, 1764; Stamp Act of 1765 increased resistance and led to Boston Massacre, 1770, in which several colonists were killed by British soldiers. In protest of taxes, Americans dumped tea into harbor, 1773, in Boston Tea Party. American Revolution began, at Lexington and Concord, 1775; troops of Gen. George Washington defeated British, 1776, driving them out of Boston; fighting then moved S of state for remainder of war. Became sixth state, Feb. 6, 1788. Today: Major industrial state, with important manufacturing, seafood and tourist industries; also major cultural, educational and research center.

Land Regions: From E to W, Coastal Lowlands; Eastern New England Upland; Connecticut Valley Lowland; Western New England Upland (Berkshire Hills); Berkshire Valley; Taconic Mountains.

Climate: Moderate in E portion with fairly cold winters and fairly cool summers; colder in W portion, summer and winter; moderate precipitation, with more snow in areas farther from coast.

Major Building Materials: Timber, hardwoods and softwoods; granite; limestone; marble; sand and gravel.

Massachusetts State House—Federal (Wayne Andrews)

Boston City Hall—Modern
(Massachusetts Department of Commerce and Development)

Architecture: State like treasure house of fine buildings from earliest Colonial era to present; one of most important states architecturally and historically. Fine buildings, many among finest of U.S. examples, in many locations including Boston and vicinity, especially Salem, Concord and other nearby towns; Cambridge; New Bedford and vicinity, especially Nantucket; Springfield vicinity, especially Deerfield; also in number of other small towns.

BOSTON

City full of fine, important architecture, especially of the 18th–20th centuries, by great number of famous or noted architects.

DOWNTOWN

Interesting buildings include: ●*State House (1798; later alt. & addit.), architect: Charles Bulfinch; architect, 1895 addit.: Charles E. Brigham; architects, 1917 addit.: Chapman, Sturgis & Andrews; very fine Federal by famous Boston architect, considered first professional American architect. Not far:
●*First Harrison Gray Otis House (1796; later alt. & addit.), 141 Cambridge St; architect: Charles Bulfinch; very fine house, one of three by architect for city mayor, later U.S. senator. Nearby, ●*Old West Church, now branch of Boston Public Library (1809; later alt. & addit.; rest.), 131 Cambridge St; architect: Asher Benjamin. Not far: *State Service Center (begun 1971), bet. Cambridge, Staniford, Merrimac & New Chardon sts; architects: Paul Rudolph, with M. A. Dyer; Desmond & Lord; Shepley, Bulfinch, Richardson & Abbott; fine modern governmental complex. Not far: ●*City Hall (1969), Government Center Sq; architects: Kall-

mann, McKinnell & Knowles; Campbell, Aldrich & Nulty; structural engineer: William LeMessurier; very fine sculptural modern building. Nearby, *Sears Crescent (1841; later alt. & addit.; renov.), architect: Alexander Parris; architect, renov.: F. A. Stahl. Also nearby, *Old State House (1713; rebuilt 1748; later alt. & addit.; rest.), State & Washington sts; architect, rest: George A. Clough. Not far: *New England Merchants National Bank (1969), 28 State St; architect: Edward Larrabee Barnes; interesting modern high-rise offices. Not far: *Faneuil Hall (1742; burned 1761; rebuilt 1763; later alt., addit. & renov.), Dock Sq; architect: John Smibert; architect, 1806 alt. & addit.: Charles Bulfinch; architect, 1978 renov.: Benjamin Thompson. *Quincy Market (1826; later alt., addit. & renov.), architect: Alexander Parris; architect, renov.: Benjamin Thompson; fascinating early shopping complex, beautifully renov. Few blocks away: *Paul Revere House (about 1676; later alt. & addit.; rest.), 19 North Sq; architect, rest.: Joseph Everett Chandler; wood-frame Colonial; once home of famous silversmith, designer and patriot. Next door, at no. 29, *Moses Pierce-Hichborn House (1680; later alt. & addit.; rest.), architect, rest.: C. R. Strickland; brick Colonial. Not far: *Christ Church, Episcopal, also known as Old North Church (1723; later alt. & addit.; rest.), 193 Salem St; architect, 1806 alt.: Charles Bulfinch; architects, rest.: R. Clipston Sturgis & Henry C. Ross. At 401 Hanover St, *St. Stephen's Catholic Church, also known as New North Church (1804; later alt. & addit.), architect: Charles Bulfinch, although not considered one of his best designs; only surviving church in city by famous architect. At 32 Atlantic Ave, facing Boston Harbor, *Lewis Wharf (1840; later alt. & addit.; renov. 1972), architect, renov.: Carl Koch; interesting modern renov. of old granite warehouse into waterfront residential, office, shopping and restaurant complex. Few blocks away, at Central Wharf, Atlantic Ave & Central St, *New England Aquarium (1971), architects: Cambridge Seven; interesting modern building; exciting exhibits. Farther down avenue: *Federal Reserve Building (1978), 600 Atlantic Ave; architect: Hugh Stubbins; fine modern government offices by noted architect. At State & India sts, *U.S. Custom House (1847; remod. 1913), architect: Ammi B. Young; architects, remod.: Peabody & Stearns; city's first skyscraper; fine views of harbor and city from observation platform. Not far: *Old South Meeting House (1730; later alt. & addit.; rest.), Washington & Milk sts; architect: Robert Twelves. Across street: *Boston Five Cents Savings Bank (1972), 10 School St; architects: Kallmann & McKinnell; interesting small modern example. At 45 School St, *Old City Hall (1865; later alt. & addit.; renov. 1972), architects: Gridley J. F. Bryant & Arthur Gilman; architects, renov.: Anderson, Notter & Finegold; fine Eclectic Second Empire; renov. into office building. Nearby, •*King's Chapel (1754; later alt. & addit.), 58 Tremont St; architect: Peter Harrison; fine Georgian by famous early self-taught architect; very fine interiors. Not far:

BEACON HILL

Famous part of city, now Hist. Dist. Interesting buildings include: *Park Street Church (1810; later alt. & addit.), Tremont & Park sts; architect: Peter Banner. *St. Paul's Cathedral (1819; later alt. & addit.), 136 Tremont St; architect: Alexander Parris; architects, 1923 addit.: Cram & Ferguson; first Greek Revival in city. Also of interest nearby: *Boston Common. Fine houses along Beacon St include: at no. 40, *Nathan Appleton House, now Women's City Club (1818; later alt. & addit.), probable architect: Alexander Parris. At no. 45, Third Harrison Gray Otis House (1806; later alt. & addit.), architect: Charles Bulfinch. At no. 55, *Ward-Prescott House, now known as Headquarters House (1808; later alt. & addit.), Federal. Nearby, other interesting houses by Bulfinch and Parris on Chestnut St. Nearby, on Mt. Vernon St. At no. 55: *Rose Standish Nichols House (about 1810; later alt. & addit.), architect: Charles Bulfinch; Federal. At no. 85: Second Harrison Gray Otis House (1800; later alt. & addit.), architect: Charles Bulfinch. Nearby: *Louisburg Sq; fascinating bow-front row houses (1834–47); also of interest: *Public Garden. Not far: *Massachusetts General Hospital (1820; later alt. & addit.), Fruit & Blossom sts; architect: Charles Bulfinch; architects, addit: Shepley, Rutan & Coolidge and successor firm, Coolidge, Shepley, Bulfinch & Abbott; original building now known as Bulfinch Pavilion in honor of its famous architect.

BACK BAY

Largest district in city. Interesting buildings include: *Arlington Street Church (1861), Arlington & Boylston sts; architect: Arthur Gilman. *First Baptist Church, originally New Brattle Square Church (1872; later alt. & addit.; never completed), Clarendon St & Commonwealth Ave; architect: Henry Hobson Richardson; fine example by famous architect; very much overshadowed, however, by his nearby masterpiece: ••**Trinity Church** (1877; later alt. &

Trinity Church—Romanesque Revival
(Massachusetts Historical Commission)

Boston Public Library—Eclectic Italian Renaissance Revival
(Library of Congress)

addit.; rest.), Copley Sq; architect: Henry Hobson Richardson; architects, 1897 addit.: Shepley, Rutan & Coolidge; architect, 1938 alt.: Charles D. Maginnis; magnificent Romanesque Revival by famous architect; considered one of finest U.S. buildings. Across Copley Sq: ●*Boston Public Library (1895; addit. 1972), architects: McKim, Mead & White; architects, 1972 addit.: Philip Johnson & John Burgee; assoc. architects: Architects Design Group; Eclectic Italian Renaissance Revival by famous firm; considered masterpiece of U.S. architecture; modern addition by famous architect. Also at Copley Sq: *John Hancock Building (1976), architect: I. M. Pei; modern high-rise glass office building, contrasting mightily with its neighbors. Also of interest: *Copley Sq, redesigned, 1970; landscape architect: Hideo Sasaki. Not far: modern *Christian Science Center (1972), Huntington & Massachusetts aves; architect: I. M. Pei; assoc. architects: Cossuta & Ponti. Nearby, *First Church of Christ, Scientist (1894; addit. 1904), architect: Charles S. Brigham; assoc. architect: Solon S. Beman; Romanesque Revival with Eclectic Roman Revival dome added. Not far: *Fenway Court, now known as Isabella Stewart Gardner Art Museum (1903; later alt. & addit.), 280 The Fenway; architect: Edward H. Sears; Eclectic Italian Villa Revival. At 465 Huntington Ave: *Museum of Fine Arts (1909; later alt. & addit.), architect: Guy Lowell; architect, 1981 addit.: I. M. Pei; Eclectic Beaux Arts; modern addit. Not far: interesting buildings of *Dorchester Nat. Hist. Site; fine, modern Francis A. Countway Library (1965), Harvard Medical School, 10 Shattuck St; architect: Hugh Stubbins. Just across Charles River from city, via Charlestown Bridge: CHARLESTOWN. *U.S. Naval Shipyard. Interesting buildings here and most famous American ship, *U.S.S. *Constitution,* usually known as *Old Ironsides.*

Boston Vicinity *(N & NE, via US I-95 or US 1).* Approx. 11 mi: SAUGUS. Interesting buildings include: *Scotch-Boardman House (about 1686), Howard St; New England Colonial; named for Scottish prisoners who lived here while forced to work in nearby *Saugus Ironworks, now Nat. Hist. Site. *Ironmaster's House (1646; rest.); New England Colonial. Also: reconst. of first successful Colonial ironworks; architects, reconst.: Perry, Shaw & Hepburn. Approx. 5 mi farther: WAKEFIELD. *Col. James Hartshorne House (1681; later alt. & addit.; rest.), 41 Church St. Approx. 5 mi farther: DANVERS. Interesting buildings include: *Glen Magna Mansion (about 1690; later alt. & addit.; rest.), Glen Magna Estate; architect, 1895 alt. & addit.: Herbert Browne; fine Eclectic. On grounds: *Elias Haskett Derby Summerhouse (1793; later alt. & addit.), architect: Samuel McIntire; fine Federal by famous early architect; fine fence designed by architect; moved here. Also: *Jeremiah Page House (1754; later alt. & addit.), 11 Page St; *Rebecca Nurse House (1678; later alt. & addit.; rest.), 149 Pine St; once home of woman hanged as witch, 1692; *Judge Samuel Holton House (about 1670; later alt. & addit.), 171 Holton St. In nearby DANVERSPORT, *Samuel Fowler House (1810); fine Federal; once home of Revolutionary War patriot. Approx. 3 mi farther: MIDDLETON. *Capt. Andrew Fuller House (1750; later alt. & addit.), 47 King St. Approx. 3 mi farther: TOPSFIELD. **Parson Joseph Capen House** (1683; rest.), 1 Howlett St; New England Colonial; considered one of finest U.S. buildings of any era. Approx. 13 mi farther: NEWBURYPORT. Interesting buildings include: *Caleb Cushing House (about 1808), 98 High St; fine Federal; *Old Gaol, or Jail (1744; later alt. &

Parson Joseph Capen House—New England Colonial (Wayne Andrews)

addit.), Vernon & Auburn sts. Approx. 3 mi E, via High Rd:
NEWBURY. Interesting buildings include: on High Rd, at no. 4,
*Swett-Ilsley House (about 1670; later alt. & addit.); at no. 16,
*Tristam Coffin House (about 1651; later alt. & addit.); at no. 39,
*Short House (about 1732; later alt. & addit.; rest.). Also see:
Boston Vicinity (NE, via St. 1A; NW, via US I-93 or St. 28).

Boston Vicinity *(NE, via St. 1A).* Approx. 3 mi: WINTHROP.
*Deane Winthrop House (1637; later alt. & addit.), 40 Shirley St.
Nearby: CHELSEA. *Gov. Bellingham-Samuel Cary House (1659;
later alt. & addit.), 34 Parker St. Approx. 4 mi farther: LYNN.
Interesting buildings include: *Hyde-Mills House (1838; later alt.
& addit.), 125 Green St; interesting Greek Revival double house:
Nearby: SWAMPSCOTT. Interesting buildings include: *John Hum-
phrey House (1634; later alt. & addit.), 99 Paradise Rd; one of
oldest wooden houses in U.S. Approx. 2 mi farther: SALEM. Delightful old town, founded 1626, noted for fine architecture as well
as for 17th-century witchcraft trials. Interesting buildings include:
on Essex St, at no. 128, •*Gardner-Pingree House** (1805), architect: Samuel McIntire; very fine Federal with fine woodwork by
famous Salem architect; now part of Essex Institute as is no. 126
next door, *Crowninshield-Bentley House (1727; later alt. & addit.; rest.); Georgian; moved here. Also part of Institute, at no.
132, *John Ward House (1684; rest.); at no. 310½, *Judge Jonathan Corwin House, also known as The Witch House (about 1642;
rest.), once scene of witchcraft examinations by judge; at no. 318,
*Judge Nathaniel Ropes Mansion (1719; later alt. & addit.). On
Chestnut St, one of most beautiful in U.S., in Hist. Dist.: no. 9,
Hamilton Hall (1807; later alt. & addit.), architect: Samuel
McIntire; fine Federal; private, as are other fine examples here.
At 18 Broad St, *Col. Timothy Pickering Mansion (1651; later
alt. & addit.); Colonial with later Gothic Revival details; once
home of U.S. secretary of state under presidents Washington and
John Adams. Not far, at 80 Federal St: •*Pierce-Nichols House**
(1782), architect: Samuel McIntire; very fine late Georgian or
early Federal with fine woodwork by famous architect; owned by
Essex Institute. At 54 Turner St, *John Turner House, also known
as House of the Seven Gables (1668; later alt. & addit.), named
for famous novel by Nathaniel Hawthorne; on grounds: *Hawthorne House (1750), birthplace of novelist; moved here; *Hathaway House (1682); *Retire Beckwith House (1682). At 21 High
St, *Gedney House (1655; later alt. & addit.). On Clifton Ave,
*Pioneer Village, reconst. buildings of earliest era. On Derby St,
*Salem Maritime Nat. Hist. Site. Interesting buildings include:
fine Federal *Gen. Benjamin Hawkes House (1801), architect:
Samuel McIntire; other fine buildings of era when city was important seaport. Approx. 2 mi E of Salem, via St. 1A & 114: MAR-
BLEHEAD. Interesting buildings include: *Col. Jeremiah Lee Man-
sion (1768; rest.), 161 Washington St; New England Colonial;
fine interior paneling. *King Hooper House (1728; later alt. &

John Whipple House—New England Colonial
(Massachusetts Historical Commission)

addit.), 8 Hooper St. *Old Gun, or Artillery, House (about 1800), 45 Elm St. *Old Powder House (1775), Green St. Approx. 4 mi N of Salem, via St. 1A, BEVERLY. Interesting buildings include: *John Balch House (1638; later alt. & addit.), 448 Cabot St; early New England Colonial; one of oldest U.S. wood-frame houses. *John Cabot House (1781), 117 Cabot St; imposing Georgian. *Rev. John Hale House (1694; later alt.), 39 Hale St. Hexagonal *Powder House (about 1805), Powder House Hill. Approx. 15 mi NE of Beverly, via St. 128: GLOUCESTER. Interesting buildings include: *Capt. Elias David House (1804), 27 Pleasant St; Federal. *Sargent-Murray-Gilman-Hough House (1768), 49 Middle St; Georgian; once home of Rev. John Murray, founder of Universalism. *Fitz Hugh Lane House (1850), Rogers St; Gothic Revival. Approx. 3 mi N of Gloucester, via St. 127A: ROCKPORT. Interesting buildings include: *Old Castle (1678; later alt. & addit.), Old Castle Lane; *Sewall-Scripture House (1832; later alt. & addit.), 40 King St. Approx. 4 mi N of Beverly, via St. 1A: WENHAM. *Claflin-Richards House (about 1664), Town Center. Approx. 15 mi NW of Gloucester, via St. 133: IPSWICH. Interesting buildings include: *John Heard House (1795; later alt. & addit.), 40 S. Main St; **John Whipple House** (1640; later alt. & addit.; rest.), 53 S. Main St; very fine New England Colonial; considered one of finest U.S. buildings. *Emerson-Howard House (1648; later alt. & addit.), 41 Turkey Shore Rd. Approx. 4 mi farther: ROWLEY. Interesting buildings include: *Platts-Bradstreet House (1677; later alt. & addit.), Main St; *Chaplin-Clark-Williams House (about 1671; later alt. & addit.), 109 Haverhill St. Also see: Boston Vicinity (N & NE, via US I-95 or 1).

Boston Vicinity *(SE, via St. 3 or 3A).* Approx. 2 mi: QUINCY. Interesting buildings include: ●**Crane Memorial Library** (1883), architect: Henry Hobson Richardson; very fine Romanesque Revival by famous architect. *Adams Mansion and Garden (1731; later alt. & addit.), 135 Adams St; New England Colonial; home of Adams family for many generations. On grounds: *Woodshed (1799), moved here; *Adams Mansion Library (1870), architect: Edward C. Cabot. *John Adams Birthplace (1681; rest.), 133 Franklin St. *John Quincy Adams Birthplace (1663; rest.), 141 Franklin St. *United First Parish Church, also known as Church of the Presidents (1828; later alt. & addit.), 1306 Hancock St; architect: Alexander Parris; both presidents Adams worshiped here and are buried in cemetery. At 20 Muirhead St, *Col. Josiah Quincy House (1770; later alt. & addit.). At 34 Butler Rd, *Quincy House (1706; later alt. & addit.), once home of Dorothy Quincy, wife of John Hancock. Just W of Quincy: MILTON. Interesting buildings include: *Capt. Robert Bennet Forbes House (1833; later alt. & addit.), 215 Adams St; architect: Isaiah Rogers; Greek Revival. Just S of Quincy: BRAINTREE. *Gen. Sylvanus Thayer Birthplace (1720; rest.), once home of "father" of the U.S. Military Academy in West Point, N.Y. Nearby: EAST WEYMOUTH. *Abigail Adams Birthplace (1685), North & Norton sts; once home of wife of President John Adams. Just W of East Weymouth, via St. 3A: HINGHAM. Interesting buildings include: ●**Old Ship Meeting House,** also known as Old Ship Church (1681; later alt. & addit.; rest.), 107 Main St; architect, rest.: Edgar T. P. Walker; Gothic; considered one of finest U.S. buildings; only surviving 17th-century New England meeting house. *New North

Old Ship Meeting House—Gothic (Philip O. Swanson)

Meeting House (about 1806), North & Lincoln sts; architect: Charles Bulfinch; fine building by famous architect. *Old Ordinary (1650; later alt. & addit. rest.), 19 Lincoln St; interesting old inn. *Samuel Lincoln House (about 1741; later alt. & addit.), 182 North St. Approx. 4 mi farther, via St. 3A: COHASSET. *David Nichols House, also known as Cohasset Hist. House (about 1804; later alt. & addit.), Elm St. Approx. 5 mi farther: SCITUATE. *Cudworth House (1797; later alt. & addit.), First Parish Rd. Approx. 10 mi farther: MARSHFIELD. *Isaac Winslow House (1699; later alt. & addit.), Webster & Carswell sts; on grounds: *Daniel Webster's Law Office. Approx. 5 mi farther: DUXBURY. *John Alden House (1653; later alt. & addit.), 105 Alden St; once home of John and Priscilla Alden; built by their son Jonathan; also other buildings of Pilgrim era. Approx. 8 mi farther, via St. 3A & 3: KINGSTON. *Maj. John Bradford House (1674; later alt. & addit.), Landing Rd. Approx. 5 mi farther, PLYMOUTH, first permanent English settlement in state, founded 1626. Interesting buildings include: *William Harlow–Old Fort House (1677), 119 Sandwich St. Not far: *Harlow-Holmes House (about 1649), 8 Winter St. *Jabez Howland House (1667; later alt. & addit.; rest.), 33 Sandwich St; only house in town in which an original Pilgrim, John Howland, actually lived. *Richard Sparrow House (1640), 42 Summer St. Also of interest: *Plymouth Rock; replica of *Mayflower; *Burial Hill, where number of Pilgrims are buried. Just S of town, via St. 3A, reconst. *Plimoth Plantation on site of original settlement.

Boston Vicinity (S, via St. 138 or 24). Approx. 25 mi: NORTH EASTON. Interesting buildings include number of Romanesque Revival examples by famous architect Henry Hobson Richardson: •*Ames Memorial Library (1879; later alt.), Main St, very fine example. Nearby, *Oakes Memorial Hall (1879). Not far: *Ames Gate House (1881), very fine; main house demolished. Approx. 12 mi SE, via St. 123, 27 & 18: EAST BRIDGEWATER. *Dr. Hector Orr House (1749; later alt. & addit.) and *1791 House (1791; later alt. & addit.), both on the Old Common.

Boston Vicinity (SW, via US I-95 or 1). Adjoining city: DEDHAM. •*Jonathan Fairbanks House (1636; later alt. & addit.), East St & Eastern Ave; very fine early example; one of oldest surviving wood-frame houses in U.S. Approx. 20 mi farther, via US I-95 or 1 & St. 140: MANSFIELD. *Fisher-Richardson House (1704; later alt. & addit.; rest.), 354 Willow St. Approx. 10 mi farther, via US I-495 & 1: NORTH ATTLEBORO. *John Woodcock Garrison House (1669; later alt. & addit.), 362 N. Washington St; once tavern, inn and home of Indian fighter.

Boston Vicinity (SW, via US I-90, Massachusetts Tpk or St. 9). Adjoining city: BROOKLINE. Interesting buildings include: *John F. Kennedy Birthplace (about 1908; later alt. & addit.), 83 Beals

St; once home of president. *Edward Devotion House (about 1740; later alt. & addit.), 347 Harvard St. Adjoining Brookline: NEWTON. *Jackson House (1809; later alt. & addit.), 527 Washington St. Adjoining Newton: WELLESLEY. Interesting buildings include: on campus of *Wellesley College, modern *Jewett Art Center (1958), architect: Paul Rudolph; assoc. architects: Anderson, Beckwith & Haible; *Science Center (1979), architects: Perry, Dean, Stahl & Rogers. Approx. 45 mi from Boston: WORCESTER. Interesting buildings include: *Old Union Station (1875), architects: Van Brunt & Ware; Eclectic Victorian Gothic Revival; *Salisbury House (1835; later alt. & addit.), 61 Harvard St; Classic Revival. *Worcester Center (1971; addit. 1974), the Common; architects: Welton Becket Assoc; *Worcester Co. National Bank (1974), architects: Kevin Roche & John Dinkeloo; modern complex including shopping center, hotels, office buildings and other types. Nearby, *City Hall (1898; later alt. & addit.), architect: Richard Howland Hunt; Eclectic Italian Renaissance Revival. *Mechanics Hall (1857; rest.), 321 Main St; architect: Elbridge Boyden; another example in same style. Also: at *Clark University, fine modern *R. S. Goddard Library (1969), architect: John M. Johansen. *Plumley Village East (1971), Laurel St, off US I-290; architect: Benjamin Thompson; interesting housing development. Also see: Springfield Vicinity (E, via US I-90 or US 20). Approx. 6 mi NE of Worcester, via US I-290: SHREWSBURY. *Artemas Ward House (1728; later alt. & addit.), 786 Main St; once home of Revolutionary War general. Approx. 12 mi S of Worcester, via St. 52 & US 20: NORTH OXFORD. *Clara Barton Birthplace (1805; later alt. & addit.), Clara Barton Rd; once home of founder of American Red Cross. Approx. 6 mi SE of Worcester, via St. 140: GRAFTON. Approx. 3 mi N, via North St, *Willard House (1718; later alt. & addit.; rest.), once home and workshop where Willard Brothers made their noted grandfather clocks and banjo clocks.

Boston Vicinity *(W, via US 20).* Approx. 3 mi: WATERTOWN. Interesting buildings include: *Marshall Fowle House (about 1775; later alt. & addit.), 28 Marshall St; Provincial Congress met here, 1775. *Abraham Browne House (about 1698; later alt. & addit.), 563 Main St. Approx. 4 mi farther: WALTHAM. Interesting buildings include: **Gore Place,** the Gov. Christopher Gore Mansion (1806; later alt. & addit.; rest.), 52 Gore St; magnificent late Georgian or early Federal; considered one of finest of U.S. buildings; beautiful landscaped grounds, landscape architect: Robert Murray; original *Coach House & Stable (about 1806; rest.); *The Vale, the Theodore Lyman House (1793; later alt. & addit.), Lyman St; architect: Samuel McIntire; very fine Federal by famous early architect; interesting landscaping and outbuildings, including stable designed by architect. At *Brandeis University, interesting modern buildings include: three *Chapels (1955), Jewish, Protestant and Roman Catholic; architects: Harrison & Abra-

Gore Place—Late Georgian, or Early Federal (Wayne Andrews)

movitz; *Academic Quadrangle (1960), architects: The Architects Collaborative (TAC); *Heller-Brown Complex (1968), architect: Benjamin Thompson. Approx. 3 mi farther: WESTON. *Josiah Smith Tavern, also known as Jones House (about 1756; later alt. & addit.), 358 Boston Post Rd. Approx. 6 mi farther: SUDBURY. *Longfellow's Wayside Inn (about 1686; damaged by fire 1955; rest.), Old Boston Post Rd; name from *Tales of a Wayside Inn* by Henry Wadsworth Longfellow.

Boston Vicinity *(NW, via St. 2)*. Adjoining city: SOMERVILLE. *Old Powder House (about 1704; later alt. & addit.; rest.), Powder House Park; originally gristmill, served as powder magazine for Colonial army. Adjoining Somerville: ARLINGTON. *Jason Russell House (about 1680; later alt. & addit.), 7 Jason St; Russell and other Minutemen killed here during battles of Lexington and Concord. Adjoining Arlington: LEXINGTON. Interesting buildings include: *Buckman Tavern (about 1710; later alt. & addit.; rest.), Village Green, where Minutemen awaited British. Also: Munroe Tavern (1695; later alt. & addit.; rest.), 1332 Massachusetts Ave; used as headquarters and hospital by British. *Hancock-Clarke House (1698; later alt. & addit.; rest.), 35 Hancock St; here Samuel Adams and John Hancock awakened by Paul Revere on his famous ride, 1775. Approx. 3 mi W of Lexington, via St. 2 & Bedford Rd: LINCOLN. Interesting modern houses

Walter Gropius House—Modern (The Architects Collaborative)

include: •**Walter Gropius House** (1938), Baker Bridge Rd; architects: Walter Gropius and Marcel Breuer; very fine example by famous architects. Nearby, Marcel Breuer House (1939), architects: Gropius & Breuer. Approx. 6 mi from Lexington, via St. 2: CONCORD. Interesting buildings include number of reminders of 19th-century flowering of New England culture and literature: *Old Manse, the Rev. William Emerson House (1769; later alt. & addit.), Monument St; boyhood home of Ralph Waldo Emerson, later home of Nathaniel Hawthorne. *Ralph Waldo Emerson House (1828), Cambridge Tpk; home of famous author for almost 50 years. *Wayside, the Caleb Ball House (about 1715; later alt. & addit.), Lexington Rd. once Hawthorne's home, bought from Alcott family. Next door, *Orchard House (about 1650; later alt. & addit.), Lexington Rd.; once home of famous author Louisa May Alcott. Also of interest: reconst. of *Henry David Thoreau cabin, original of which was located at Walden Pond, short distance from town; *Antiquarian House Museum, Lexington Rd; *Minute Man Nat. Hist. Park; *Sleepy Hollow Cemetery, in which all of famous writers mentioned here are buried. Approx. 15 mi farther, via St. 2 & 110: HARVARD. *Fruitlands Museums, Prospect Hill Rd, including *Harvard Shaker Society Building (1794; later alt. & addit; rest.) and three others. Approx 7 mi SW of Harvard, via St. 110: LANCASTER. ••**First Church of Christ**, also known as Lancaster Meeting House (1816; later alt. & addit.), Village Green; architect: Charles Bulfinch; late Georgian or early Federal; considered one of finest U.S. buildings and one of famous architect's masterpieces.

Boston Vicinity *(NW, via US I-93 or St. 28)*. Approx. 8 mi: WOBURN. *Rumford House (1714), 90 Elm St; once home of Benjamin Thompson who became Count Rumford of Holy Roman Empire. *Winn Memorial Library (1878), Pleasant St; architect: Henry Hobson Richardson; fine Romanesque Revival by famous architect. Adjoining Woburn: READING. *Parker Tavern (1694; later alt. & addit.), 103 Washington St; saltbox; interesting gardens. Approx. 8 mi farther: ANDOVER. Interesting buildings include: *Deacon Amos Blanchard House (1819), 97 Main St; fine Federal. *America House (about 1830; later alt. & addit.), 147 Main St; once home of Samuel F. Smith who wrote song *America*. Approx. 4 mi farther: NORTH ANDOVER. Interesting buildings include: *Stevens-Coolidge House (about 1800; later alt. & addit.), Andover St; Federal; fine woods, lawns, gardens. *Parson Thomas Barnard House (1715; later alt. & addit.; rest.), 179 Osgood St; fine New England Colonial. Approx. 10 mi NE, via US I-495: HAVERHILL. Interesting buildings include: *The Buttonwoods, the Rev. John Ward House (about 1640; later alt. & addit.; rest.), 240 Water St; on grounds: other interesting buildings. *John Greenleaf Whittier Birthplace (1688; later alt. & addit.), 305 Whittier Rd; once home of famous poet. Approx. 12 mi farther, via US I-495: AMESBURY. Interesting buildings include:
●●**Rocky Hill Meeting House** (1785), Elm St & Portland Rd; very

First Church of Christ—Late Georgian, or Early Federal (Bill McClarin)

fine New England Colonial. *John Greenleaf Whittier House (about 1836; later alt. & addit.), 86 Friend St; last home of famous poet. *Macy-Colby House (1654; later alt. & addit.), Main St. Also see: Boston Vicinity (N & NE, via US I-95 or US 1). Approx. 35 mi SW of Amesbury, via US I-495: LOWELL. *Whistler House (1823; later alt. & addit.), 243 Worthen St; once home of famous artist James Abbott McNeill Whistler. Approx. 2 mi farther: CHELMSFORD. *Old Chelmsford Garrison House (about 1690; later alt. & addit.; rest.), Garrison Rd; early fortified example. Approx. 16 mi W, via US I-495 & St. 119: GROTON. *Gov. George Sewall Boutwell House (1851), Main St; once home of state governor and U.S. secretary of war under President Grant. Approx. 4 mi farther: TOWNSEND HARBOR. *Conant House (about 1720), South St; once tavern.

CAMBRIDGE

Interesting buildings include: M. F. Stoughton House (1883), Brattle & Ash sts; architect: Henry Hobson Richardson; fine Romanesque Revival by famous architect. *Longfellow House, also known as Vassail-Craigie-Longfellow House (1759; later alt. & addit.), 105 Brattle St; fine Georgian; once home of famous author Henry Wadsworth Longfellow, now Nat. Hist. Site. Not far: *Lee-Nichols House (about 1660; later alt. & addit.), 159 Brattle St. On Village Common: *Christ Church (1760; later alt. & ad-

Carpenter Center for the Visual Arts, Harvard University—Modern
(Harvard University)

Harvard University Graduate Center—Modern
(The Architects Collaborative)

dit.), architect: Peter Harrison, not considered among finest designs of famous early architect. At 21 Linnaean St: *Cooper-Frost-Austin House (1657; later alt. & addit.). Not far: *Harvard University. Interesting buildings in and near The Yard include fine 18th–20th-century examples by noted architects. *Wadsworth House (1727; later alt. & addit.), 1341 Massachusetts Ave; residence of Harvard presidents for more than hundred years. *Harvard Hall (1766; later alt. & addit.), architect: Thomas Dawes. ●*Sever Hall (1880; later alt. & addit.), architect: Henry Hobson Richardson; very fine Romanesque Revival. *Memorial Hall (1878; later alt. & addit.), architects: Ware & Van Brunt. Interesting modern buildings include: fine *Loeb Drama Center (1960), Brattle Stand. *Nathan Marsh Pusey Library (1975), The Yard, architect of both: Hugh Stubbins. ●*Holyoke Center (1966), Massachusetts Ave; architects: Sert, Jackson & Gourley; very fine multi-purpose building by noted architects. ●*Carpenter Center for the Visual Arts (1963), Quincy St; architects: LeCorbusier, with Sert, Jackson & Gourley; very fine building by famous Swiss-French architect. *George Gund Hall, the Harvard Graduate School of Design (1972), Quincy St; architects: Canadian John Andrews; Anderson & Baldwin. *Undergraduate Science Center (1973), Oxford & Kirkland sts; architects: Sert & Jackson. ●*Harvard Graduate Center (1950), Everett St; architects: The Architects Collaborative; very fine example. ●*F. G. Peabody

F. G. Peabody Terrace, Harvard University—Modern (Harvard University)

Terrace (1964), Memorial Dr; architects: Sert, Jackson & Gourley; very fine high-rise housing for married students. At *Massachusetts Institute of Technology, interesting modern buildings include: *Baker House (1948), 362 Memorial Dr; architect: Alvar Aalto; assoc. architects: Perry, Shaw & Hepburn; fine dormitory by famous Finnish architect. Not far: ●*Chapel (1955), Massachusetts Ave; architect: Eero Saarinen; assoc. architects: Anderson, Beckwith & Haible; very fine small building by famous architect; fine grille by noted sculptor Harry Bertoia; spire by noted sculptor Theodore Roszak. Nearby, ●*Kresge Auditorium (1955), architect: Eero Saarinen. Nearby, *Stratton Student Center (1965), architect: Eduardo Catalano. Nearby, *Hockey Rink and Field House (1980), architects: Davis & Brody.

NEW BEDFORD

Interesting buildings include: in Hist. Dist., *William J. Rotch House (1846; later alt. & addit.), 396 County St; architects: Alexander Jackson Davis & William R. Emerson; Gothic Revival; moved here. *Congregational Church, now First Unitarian Church (1838; later alt. & addit.), Union & 8th sts; architects: Alexander Jackson Davis & C. Russell Warren; Gothic Revival. Other buildings by Warren, all Greek Revival: Joseph Grinnell House (1836; later alt. & addit.), 379 County St, now St. John's Roman Catholic Convent and Academy; *Merchants' and Mechanics' Bank Building, now Fishermen's Pension Trust Building (1835; later alt.), 56–60 Water St; two buildings later joined together; *Institution for Savings (1853; later alt.), William & 2nd sts. Also: *U.S. Custom House (1837; later alt.), William & 2nd sts; architect: Robert Mills; Greek Revival by famous architect. Also of interest: *Bourne Whaling Museum.

New Bedford Vicinity *(E, via US I-195 or 6: Cape Cod).* Approx. 35 mi: SANDWICH. *Hoxie House (about 1665; rest.). Nearby, *Dexter Grist Mill (about 1654; rest.). Approx. 20 mi farther: BARNSTABLE. *William Sturgis House (1644; later alt. & addit.), Main St. Approx. 3 mi farther: YARMOUTH PORT. *Capt. Bangs Hallet House (1740; later alt. & addit.), Strawberry Lane; Greek Revival elements. *Col. John Thacher House (about 1680; later alt. & addit.), Thacher Lane. Next door, *Winslow Crocker House (about 1780; later alt. & addit.). Approx. 4 mi farther: SOUTH DENNIS. *Jericho House (1801; later alt. & addit.; rest.), Old Main St; Cape Cod type. Approx. 25 mi farther: EASTHAM. *Capt. Edward Penniman House (1868; rest.), Ft. Hill Rd; Victorian. Also of interest: *Cape Cod Nat. Seashore. Approx. 12 mi S of Eastham, via US 6 & St. 28: CHATHAM. *Old Atwood House (1752), Stage Harbor Rd; once home of novelist Joseph C. Lincoln. From nearby Hyannis, summer ferries to Nantucket and Martha's Vineyard. See: New Bedford Vicinity (SE, via ferry). Approx. 25 mi W of Chatham, via St. 28: CENTERVILLE. *Mary Lincoln House (about 1840; later alt. & addit.; rest.), 513 Main St; Cape Cod type. Approx. 5 mi SW, via Co. Rd: OSTERVILLE. *Capt. Jonathan Parker House (about 1795; later alt. & addit.), Parker Rd. Approx. 13 mi farther, via St. 28: FALMOUTH. *Julia Wood House (1750; later alt. & addit.), 55 Palmer Ave. Next door, *Conant House (about 1794; later alt. & addit.). Approx. 3

Chapel, Massachusetts Institute of Technology— Modern (Joseph W. Molitor)

mi N, via St. 28A: *Saconesset House (1678), unusual bowed roof like ship's hull. Approx. 5 mi SW of Falmouth, via Co. Rd: WOODS HOLE. Harold C. Bradley House (1912), architects: Purcell & Elmslie; early modern Prairie style house similar to those of Frank Lloyd Wright by architects once associated with him. Via ferry from Woods Hole: Martha's Vineyard and Nantucket. See: New Bedford Vicinity (SE, via ferry).

New Bedford Vicinity *(SE, via ferry).* Martha's Vineyard and Nantucket, via Woods Hole. Interesting buildings in both, including, in Martha's Vineyard: EDGARTOWN. *Thomas Cooke House (1765), Cooke St, and in NANTUCKET, *Jethro Coffin House (about 1686; rest.), Sunset Hill; architects, rest.: William Sumner Appleton & Alfred F. Shurrocks; Colonial saltbox type. Amazingly, five other Coffin family houses have survived here: Maj. Josiah Coffin House (1724), 60 Cliff Rd; Joshua Coffin House (about 1750), 52 Centre St; Coffin-Gardner House (1820), 33 Milk St; Henry Coffin House (1833), 775 Main St; *Ocean House, the Jared Coffin House (1845; later alt. & addit.), now hotel. Also: *Nantucket Athenaeum (1847; later alt. & addit.), India & Federal sts; probable architect: Frederick Coleman; Greek Revival library. *William Hadwen House, also known as Satler Memorial (1845), 96 Main St; Greek Revival. Modern examples, both private, facing Atlantic Ocean: Wislicki House (1972) and adjacent Trubeck House (1972); architects of both: Venturi & Rauch; reminiscent of 19th-century Shingle style.

New Bedford Vicinity *(NW, via US I-195 or 6).* Approx. 2 mi: NORTH DARTMOUTH. *Southeastern Massachusetts University (1972), architects: Paul Rudolph; Desmond & Lord; interesting modern buildings arranged around mall. Approx. 8 mi farther: FALL RIVER. Interesting 19th-century mills. Also of interest: *Battleship Cove, location of U.S. Navy ships *U.S.S. *Massachusetts;* *U.S.S. *Joseph Kennedy, Jr.;* *U.S.S. *Lionfish.*

SPRINGFIELD

*Linden Hall, the Alexander House (1811; later alt. & addit.), 284 State St; probable architect: Asher Benjamin; fine Federal; once home of painter Chester Harding. Approx. 11 mi N, via St. 116: S. HADLEY. *Mount Holyoke College, fine modern buildings by Hugh Stubbins blend with older examples on beautiful campus.

Springfield Vicinity *(N, via US I-91 or 5).* Approx. 20 mi: NORTHAMPTON. Interesting buildings include: on Bridge St, at no. 58, *Cornet Joseph Parsons House (1658; later alt. & addit.); at no. 46, *Isaac Damon House (1814; later alt. & addit.), architect: Isaac Damon. Also: two former homes of President Calvin Coolidge, and his law office. Approx. 2 mi NE of Northampton, via

St. 9: HADLEY. *Forty Acres, the Porter-Phelps-Huntington House (1752; later alt. & addit.), 128 River Dr; once home of Frederic Dan Huntington, first Episcopal bishop of Central New York. Approx. 5 mi farther: AMHERST. Interesting buildings include: *Nehemiah Strong House (1744; later alt. & addit.), 67 Amity St. Also: homes of authors Eugene Field, Emily Dickinson, Robert Frost and Helen Hunt Jackson. At *University of Massachusetts, fine modern: *Murray Lincoln Campus Center (1972), architects: Marcel Breuer & Herbert Beckhard; *Southwest Quadrangle (1966), architect: Hugh Stubbins; *Fine Arts Center (1974), architects: Kevin Roche & John Dinkeloo. Approx. 10 mi SE of Amherst, via St. 9: BELCHERTOWN. *Old Stone House (1827; later alt. & addit.) and Ford Annex; interesting collections including sculptures of John Rogers. Approx. 17 mi N of Northampton, via I-91 or 5: DEERFIELD. *Old Deerfield Village. Interesting buildings, mostly in Hist. Dist., in delightful Colonial setting, on Old Deerfield St or nearby, include: *Memorial Hall, originally Deerfield Academy (1797; later alt. & addit.), architect: Asher Benjamin; *First, or Brick, Church (1824; later alt. & addit.), architect: Winthrop Clapp; Ashley House (about 1730; later alt. & addit.; rest.).

Springfield Vicinity *(E, via US I-90 or 20)*. Approx. 40 mi: *Old Sturbridge Village, interesting collection of 18th- and 19th-century buildings, including houses, shops, mills, school, meetinghouse and others.

Springfield Vicinity *(W, via US I-90 or 20)*. Approx. 5 mi: WEST SPRINGFIELD. *Joshua Day House (1754; later alt. & addit.), 70 Park St; saltbox type. Approx. 55 mi farther, via US I-90 or 5 & 7: STOCKBRIDGE. Interesting buildings include: *Mission House (1739; later alt. & addit.; rest.), Main & Sergeant sts; once home of Rev. John Sergeant, early missionary; moved here. *Tranquillity, the Merwin House (about 1825; later remod.), 39 Main St. *Naumkeag Gardens, the Joseph H. Choate House (about 1885), Prospect St; architect: Stanford White; once home of U.S. ambassador to England. Approx. 2 mi W, via St. 102, *Chesterwood (1901), once home, studio and garden of famous sculptor Daniel Chester French. Approx. 12 mi N, via US 7/20: PITTSFIELD. Interesting buildings include: *William Brattle House (1762), 626 Williams St. *Caleb Goodrich House (1792; later alt. & addit.), 823 North St. On Holmes Rd, *Arrowhead (1794; later alt. & addit.), once home of famous author Herman Melville and where he wrote *Moby Dick* and other novels; originally tavern; *Holmesdale (19th century), once home of famous author Oliver Wendell Holmes. Approx. 5 mi W, via St. 20, *Hancock Shaker Village (late 18th–19th centuries; rest.), architect, rest.: Terry F. Hallock; remarkably well-preserved group of interesting buildings, including: *Round Barn (1826; later alt.); *Meeting House (1793; later alt. & addit.), moved here from Shirley, Mass.

New Hampshire

Early inhabitants Indians of several tribes, including Nashua, Ossipee, Piscataqua. First explorers unknown; explorers in early 17th century included Englishman Martin Pring, 1603; Frenchman Samuel de Champlain, 1605; Englishman Capt. John Smith, 1614. First English settlement, 1623: Rye, originally Odiorne's Point, by David Thomson; about same time, Englishman Edward Hilton founded Dover, originally Hilton's Point. Region granted to John Mason, 1629; named New Hampshire; became part of Massachusetts, 1641; separated again, 1680; made royal colony. Colonists led by John Sullivan took military supplies and equipment from British fort at New Castle, one of first armed forays of Revolution. Formed first government independent of British, Jan. 5, 1776; only original state in which no Revolutionary War battles took place. Became ninth state, June 21, 1788. Today: Important manufacturing and tourist industries.

Land Regions: SE to N, Coastal Lowlands; Eastern New England Upland; small portion of White Mountains.

Climate: Cold winters, cool summers with low humidity; moderate precipitation; snowfall heavy.

Major Building Materials: Granite; sand and gravel.

Architecture: Number of important buildings, especially early examples in Portsmouth.

CONCORD

Interesting buildings include: *State House (1819; later alt. & addit.), N. Main St; architect: Albe Cady; architects, alt. & addit.: 1866, Gridley J. F. Bryant; 1911, Peabody & Stearns; Federal; Eclectic addit. *Merrimack Co. Bank (1826; later alt. & addit.), 214 N. Main St; Federal; once law office of President Franklin Pierce, once again law offices. *Franklin Pierce House (1857), 52 S. Main St; last home of president.

Concord Vicinity *(N, via US I-93)*. Approx. 12 mi: CANTERBURY. Nearby, via St. 106, *Shaker Village (begun 1792); number of interesting buildings include: *Meetinghouse (1792), *Main Building (1793). Approx. 8 mi farther: FRANKLIN. Approx. 3 mi S, via US 3 & St. 127, *Daniel Webster Birthplace (about 1780; later alt. & addit.; rest.); once home of famous statesman. Approx. 35 mi, via US 11, 11A & St. 28: WOLFEBORO. *Clark House

(1778; later alt. & addit.; rest.), S. Main St. Approx. 20 mi, via St. 109: MOULTONBOROUGH. *Lucknow, also known as Castle of the Clouds (1913), St. 171; large mansion and outbuildings in mixture of Eclectic styles. Approx. 35 mi NE of Moultonborough, via St. 15 & 16: N. CONWAY. *Boston and Maine Railroad Station (1874; later alt. & addit.; rest.), architect: Nathaniel J. Bradlee; seemingly derived from architecture of Russia; now office building. Also of interest nearby: *White Mountains; *Franconia Notch. Approx. 30 mi NW of Conway, via US 302: BRETTON WOODS. Nearby, *Mt. Washington Hotel (1902; later alt. & addit.), architect: Charles A. Clifford; massive Eclectic Spanish Renaissance Revival; view toward Mt. Washington. Approx. 35 mi W of Moultonborough, via St. 25: RUMNEY. *Mary Baker Eddy House (mid-19th century), once home of founder of Christian Science.

Concord Vicinity *(S, via Everitt Tpk or US 3)*. Approx. 18 mi: MANCHESTER. Interesting buildings include: *Grace Episcopal Church (1860; later alt. & addit.), Lowell & Pine sts; architects: Richard Upjohn & Richard M. Upjohn; fine Gothic Revival by architect, famous for style, and his noted son. Not far: *City Hall (1846; later alt. & addit.), Elm & Market sts; architect: Edward Shaw; also Gothic Revival; intricate details and ornament. *Currier Art Gallery (1926), 192 Orange St; architect: Edward L. Tilton; Eclectic Classic Revival. *Gen. John Stark House (about 1737; later alt. & addit.; rest.), 2000 Elm St; once home of Revolutionary War hero. Only two houses in state by Frank Lloyd Wright, both private: on Heather St, at no. 233, Isadore J. Zimmerman House (1950), modern late Prairie style; at no. 117, Toufic H. Kalil House (1955), in style architect called Usonian. Also: *Amoskeag Manufacturing Co. Mills (19th century), on bank of Merrimac River. Approx. 15 mi farther: NASHUA. Contains other old mills.

Concord Vicinity *(W & SW, via US 202)*. Approx. 15 mi: HENNIKER. *James Wallace House, also known as Ocean-born Mary House (about 1750; later alt. & addit.), Bear Hill Rd; Georgian; legend that Wallace's daughter, Mary, was born on a ship boarded by pirates who gave baby silk for wedding gown. Approx. 10 mi farther, via US 202, St. 9 & St. 31: HILLSBORO LOWER VILLAGE. *Franklin Pierce House (1804; later alt. & addit.; rest.), once home of future president. Approx. 8 mi NW of town, via St. 31: WASHINGTON. Interesting 18th- and 19th-century buildings around relatively unspoiled *Village Green. Approx. 18 mi S of Hillsboro Lower Village, via US 202 & St. 123: HANCOCK. Another unspoiled *Village Green. Interesting buildings include: *Meeting House (1820; later alt. & addit.), architect: Elias Carter. Approx. 10 mi S of town, via St. 123 & US 202: PETERBOROUGH. Nearby, interesting *MacDowell Colony, established 1907 as retreat for artists, writers and composers by famous com-

poser Edward MacDowell, and still in operation. Approx. 14 mi
SE of Peterborough, via US 202 & St. 124: NEW IPSWICH. *For-
est Hall, the Charles Barrett House (1800; later alt. & addit.),
Main St; fine Federal mansion; on grounds: interesting Gothic
Revival summer house, other outbuildings. Approx. 7 mi W of
Peterborough, via St. 101, HARRISVILLE, interesting relatively un-
spoiled 19th-century mill village. Approx. 15 mi farther: KEENE.
*Wyman Tavern (1762; later alt. & addit.), 339 Main St. Approx.
35 mi NW of Keene, via St. 12: CHARLESTOWN. *St. Luke's Epis-
copal Church (1863; later alt. & addit.), Main St; architect: Rich-
ard Upjohn; architect, alt. & addit.: Richard M. Upjohn; fine
wood-frame Gothic Revival by famous architect; addit. by his son.
Approx. 6 mi E, via St. 123A: ACWORTH. Well-preserved *Village
Green; *United Church (1821; later alt. & addit.), architect: Elias
Carter.

Concord Vicinity *(NW, via US I-89).* Approx. 50 mi: HANOVER.
Interesting buildings include: on campus of *Dartmouth College,
*Reed Hall (1840; later alt. & addit.) and *Shattuck Observatory
(1854), architect of both: Ammi B. Young; *Old Dartmouth Hall
(1791; destroyed; reconst.). Modern *Leverone Field House
(1963) and *Robert C. Thompson Ice Arena and Auditorium
(1975), architects of both: Campbell & Aldrich; structural engineer of both: Pier Luigi Nervi. Approx. 10 mi SW of Hanover, via
St. 12A: PLAINFIELD. Nearby, *Aspet, the Augustus Saint-
Gaudens House (about 1800; later alt. & addit.), once home of
famous sculptor; now Nat. Hist. Site; on grounds: studio, other
outbuildings, gardens; sculptor buried here in *Temple (1926),
architects: McKim, Mead & White. Approx. 20 mi NE of Hanover, via St. 10: ORFORD. Unique group of houses, seven in row,
*Orford Row, Orford St, in late Georgian, Federal and Classic
Revival styles. Also: number of interesting buildings, approx. 12
mi farther, via St. 10, in HAVERHILL and approx. 12 mi past Haverhill, via St. 10 & US 302 in BATH.

PORTSMOUTH

Very large number of fine buildings in relatively small city of
approx. 26,000 population. Interesting buildings include: *Gov.
John Langdon House (1784; later alt. & addit.), 143 Pleasant St;
architect: Daniel Hart; architects, 1906 addit.: McKim, Mead &
White; Georgian; once home of state governor and Revolutionary
War leader. *U.S. Custom House and Post Office (1860; later alt.
& addit.), 40 Pleasant St; architect: Ammi B. Young; Eclectic
Italian Renaissance Revival; now offices. *Thomas Bailey Aldrich
House (1790), 386 Court St; once home of noted author and
model for house in his *The Story of a Bad Boy.* On Middle St, at
no. 180, Larkin-Rice House (1815; later alt. & addit.), one of
three Federal houses in row; others: at no. 160, Larkin House

(1809; later alt. & addit.); at no. 152, Langley-Boardman House (about 1800; later alt. & addit.). Also on Middle St, at no. 132, Victorian Capt. William Parrott House (about 1864; later alt. & addit.), architect: Gridley J. F. Bryant. At no. 43, *Capt. Gregory Purcell House, also known as John Paul Jones House (1758; later alt. & addit.; rest.); fine Colonial; once home of famous naval hero. At Islington St & Maplewood Ave, *Portsmouth Public Library (1809; later alt. & addit.), architect: James Nutter; late Georgian; originally Portsmouth Academy. *Portsmouth Athenaeum (1805; later alt. & addit.), Congress & Market sts; architect: Bradbury Johnson; Federal; formerly offices of N. H. Fire and Marine Insurance Co., now library. At 154 Market St, ●*Moffatt-Ladd House (1764), very fine late Georgian; very fine interior woodwork; once home of Gen. William Whipple, signer of Declaration of Independence. Nearby, on Chapel St, *St. John's Episcopal Church (1809; later alt. & addit.), architect: Alexander Parris. At 150 Daniel St, ●*Macphaedris-Warner House (1723; later alt. & addit.; rest.), very fine early Georgian; of brick, unusual in New England in this era. At 18 Court St, *John Pierce House (about 1799; later alt. & addit.), Federal. In old S end, *Strawbery Banke, original name of first settlement of city, founded 1623. Interesting and important rest. project of approx. 10 acres, bounded by Court, Marcy, Hancock, & Washington sts; approx. 30 buildings, including: Federal *Gov. Ichabod Goodwin House (1811; later alt. & addit.); *Joseph Sherburne House (1695; later alt. & addit.). At 140 Mechanic St, on bank of Piscataqua River, ●*Wentworth-Gardner House (1760; later alt. & addit.; rest.), very fine Georgian; very fine ornamental interior woodwork; once home of Royal Gov. Benning Wentworth. At 76 Northwest St, *Richard Jackson House (about 1799; later alt. & addit.; rest.), Colonial; oldest surviving house in state. Few miles SE of city: *Wentworth-Coolidge Mansion (1695; later alt. & addit.; rest.), Little Harbor Rd; 42-room Colonial; once home of Royal Gov. Benning Wentworth. Few miles farther, via St. 1A & 1B: NEW CASTLE. Interesting buildings include: *Wentworth-by-the-Sea (1874; later alt. & addit.), last surviving Victorian summer hotel on N New England coast. Nearby, at Forest Point, *Ft. Constitution, originally Ft. William and Mary (1631; later alt. & addit.). Also of interest: on Seavey Island in Piscataqua River, *Portsmouth Naval Shipyard, established 1800. Also see: Maine—Portland Vicinity (SE, via US I-95).

Portsmouth Vicinity *(SW, via US I-95 & St. 101).* Approx. 12 mi: EXETER. Interesting buildings include: *Gilman House (about 1650; later alt. & addit.), 12 Water St; once home of Brig. Gen. Peter Gilman; built as "garrison" house for protection against Indians. *Ladd-Gilman House (1721; later alt. & addit.), Water & Governor sts; once home of Nicholas Gilman, signer of Declaration of Independence. At *Phillips Exeter Academy, number of fine 18th- to 20th-century examples including: ●*Library (1971), architect: Louis I. Kahn; fine modern by famous architect. Approx. 15 mi SW of Exeter, via St. 111 & 121A: SANDOWN. *Sandown Meeting House (1774; rest.). Approx. 5 mi SE of Exeter, via St. 111A: DANVILLE. *Danville Meeting House (1760; rest.).

Portsmouth Vicinity *(NW, via Spaulding Tpk)*. Approx. 5 mi: NEWINGTON. *Town Meeting House (1712), Little Bay Rd; oldest meeting house in state; used continuously since construction; bell made by Paul Revere. Nearby, *Old Parsonage (1725); also *Carriage House. Approx. 8 mi farther: DOVER. Interesting buildings here include, at *The Woodman Institute, 182–92 Central Ave, three interesting houses: *William Damme House (about 1675), frontier "garrison" for protection from Indians; moved here; Federal *John Parker Hale House (1813); *William Woodman House (1818). Nearby, *Friends Meeting House (1768), 141 Central Ave. At 5 Hale St, *William Hale House (1805; later alt. & addit.), also known as Lafayette House, since famous French marquis was once entertained here.

Rhode Island

Early inhabitants Indians of several tribes, including Narraganset, Pequot, Wampanoag. Portuguese Miguel de Corte Real believed to have visited, 1511; explored by Italian Giovanni da Verrazano, for France, 1524; named Rhode Island; explored later by Dutchman Adriaen Block, 1614. First permanent English settlement by religious leader Roger Williams, 1636: Providence; others soon followed, Portsmouth, originally Pocasset, 1638; Newport, 1639; Warwick, 1643. Four towns united, 1647, under charter to Roger Williams; second charter granted, 1663. Indians peaceful at first but attacks soon began, ending in this area, 1676; continued in Maine and New Hampshire two more years. Colonists resisted tax and trade restriction laws of British by many acts of rebellion, including burning of ship *Liberty* at Newport, 1769. British occupied Newport, 1776, and made raids in other places, but no major battles fought here; colony first to declare independence, May 4, 1776. Became thirteenth state, May 29, 1790. Today: Important industrial state, especially manufacturing of textiles and jewelry.

Land Regions: E to W, Coastal Lowlands; Eastern New England Upland.

Climate: Relatively mild, summer and winter; moderate precipitation; moderate snow.

Major Building Materials: Granite; limestone; sand and gravel.

Architecture: Rich and varied, for small state, unusually large number of fine buildings, some among finest U.S. examples, especially Colonial and late 19th-century in Newport and Providence.

NEWPORT

Relatively small city (population about 30,000) is like museum of fine architecture of 17th through 20th centuries. Interesting buildings include: in Hist. Dist., ●●**Brick Market** (1762; rest.), Washington Sq, architect: Peter Harrison; fine Colonial example by famous early architect. *Old Colony House (1741; later alt. & addit.; rest.), Washington Sq; architect: Richard Munday; fine Georgian by noted early architect; formerly State House, or Capitol, of state. *Abraham Rodriguez House, now Newport National Bank (1740; later alt.), Washington Sq; gambrel-roofed Colonial. *Hunter House (about 1748; rest.), 54 Washington St. *Wanton-Lyman-Hazard House (about 1765; later alt. & addit.; rest.), 17 Broadway; mostly Georgian. *William Vernon House (1758), 43 Clarke St; late Georgian; wood frame, with details resembling stone. *Samuel Whitehorne House (1810; rest.), 414 Thames St. *Trinity Church (1741; later alt.), 141 Spring St; architect: Richard Munday; fine New England Colonial. ●●**Touro Synagogue** (1763), 85 Touro St; architect: Peter Harrison; Colonial masterpiece of famous architect; considered one of finest U.S. buildings. *Mawdsley-Gardner-Watson-Pitman House (about 1700), 228 Spring St. *Edward King House (1847; later alt. & addit.), Aquidneck Park, Spring St; architect: Richard Upjohn; Eclectic Italian Villa Revival by famous architect. On Bellevue Ave, number of fine buildings. At no. 50, ●●**Redwood Library** (1748; later

Touro Synagogue—Colonial (Wayne Andrews)

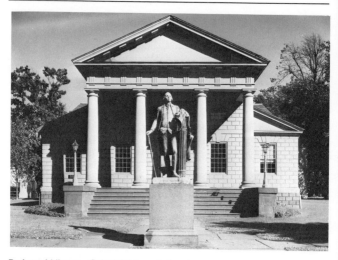

Redwood Library—Colonial (Wayne Andrews)

alt. & addit.), architect: Peter Harrison; another Colonial master-piece of famous architect; named for benefactor Abraham Red-wood, not for materials; considered one of finest U.S. buildings. At no. 76, *J. N. A. Griswold House, now Art Assoc. of Newport (1892; later alt.), architect: Richard Morris Hunt; Stick style mansion by famous architect. At no. 194, *Newport Casino, now National Tennis Hall of Fame (1881; later alt. & addit.), archi-tects: McKim, Mead & White. Continuing down avenue, other magnificent summer homes, called "cottages" by their super-wealthy owners: *Kingscote, the George Noble Jones House (1839; addit. 1881), architect: Richard Upjohn; architects, addit.: McKim, Mead & White; Victorian. *The Elms, the Edward J. Berwind House (1901), architect: Horace Trumbauer; Eclectic French Chateau Revival; once home of coal millionaire. *Cha-teau-sur-Mer, the William S. Wetmore House (1852; remod. 1874, 1914), probable architect: Seth Bradford; architects, re-mod.: 1874, Richard Morris Hunt; 1914, John Russell Pope; lav-ish Victorian; once home of China trade millionaire. *Rosecliff (1902), architects: McKim, Mead & White; modeled after Grand Trianon (1688), Versailles, France. *Marble House, the William K. Vanderbilt House (1892), architect: Richard Morris Hunt; Eclectic Beaux Arts; perhaps most lavish house in city; original furnishings. *Belcourt Castle (1894), architect: John Russell Pope; modeled after architecture of time of King Louis XIII of France. At Ochre Point & Ruggles Ave,
•*The Breakers, the Cornelius Vanderbilt House** (1895), architect: Richard Morris Hunt; Eclectic Italian Renaissance Revival; most magnificent of all Newport "cottages"; Grand Salon constructed in France, shipped here; on grounds: Eclectic Queen Anne Revival

Children's Playhouse; elaborate Carriage House and Stables at Coggeshall & Bateman aves. On Shepherd Ave, ●∗**William Watts Sherman House** (1876), architect: Henry Hobson Richardson; very fine Shingle style example by architect more famous for Romanesque Revival.

Newport Vicinity *(N, via St. 138).* Approx. 3 mi: MIDDLETOWN. ∗Whitehall (1729; rest.), Berkeley Ave; frame house of Church of England Dean (later Bishop) George Berkeley, famous philosopher. Approx. 8 mi farther: PORTSMOUTH. Nearby, via St. 114, ●∗**Portsmouth Abbey Chapel** (1961), architect: Pietro Belluschi; assoc. architects: Anderson, Beckwith & Haible; fine modern example by architect famous for church design; other fine buildings here by same architect. Approx. 5 mi N of Portsmouth, via St. 138 & 114: BRISTOL. ∗Herreshoff House (about 1800; later alt.), 142 Hope St. Approx. 18 mi SE of Portsmouth, via St. 138N & 77: LITTLE COMPTON. ∗Wilbur House (1690; later alt. & addit.; rest.), West Rd; New England Colonial; old barn here.

The Breakers—Eclectic Italian Renaissance Revival (Wayne Andrews)

William Watts Sherman House—Shingle Style (Wayne Andrews)

Newport Vicinity *(W, via St. 138).* Approx. 9 mi: JAMESTOWN. *Jamestown Windmill (1787; rest.), North Rd; interesting type with large vanes and rotating head usually associated with Holland. Approx. 14 mi farther: SAUNDERSTOWN. Nearby, on US 1, *Gilbert Stuart Birthplace (about 1750; rest.), Gilbert Stuart Rd; once home of famous portrait painter. On US 1A, Silas Casey Farm (about 1750; later alt. & addit.). Also see: Providence Vicinity (S, via US 1).

PROVIDENCE

Interesting buildings include: *State House (1901; later alt.), bet. Gaspee, Francis & Smith sts; architects: McKim, Mead & White; imposing building with huge dome. Not far: *The Arcade (1829; remod. 1980), 130 Westminster St; architects: J. C. Bucklin & Russell Warren; architect, remod.: Irving B. Haynes; fine early Greek Revival shopping center, sensitively remod. On Power St, at no. 52, ••**John Brown House** (1788; later alt. & addit.), architect: Joseph Brown; very fine Georgian; designed by noted architect for his brother. At no. 66, another fine Georgian example, Thomas Poynton Ives House (about 1811; later alt. & addit.). Not far: *Joseph Brown House (1774; later alt. & addit.), 50 S. Main St; architect: Joseph Brown; designed by architect for himself. Not far: *Gov. Stephen Hopkins House (1707; later alt. & addit.), Benefit & Hopkins sts; once home of state governor who was signer of Declaration of Independence. Bet. Prospect, Waterman & George sts: *Brown University. Interesting buildings include oldest *University Hall (1770; later alt. & addit.), architect: Joseph Brown. Nearby, University Hill Hist. Dist. At 251 N. Benefit St, *The Athenaeum (1838; alt. 1868; later alt. & addit.), architect: William Strickland; architect, 1868 alt.: J. C. Bucklin; fine Greek Revival library by famous architect, his only New England building. At 75 N. Main St, *First Baptist Church, formerly Meetinghouse (1775; later alt.), architect: Joseph Brown; very fine example, considered one of its architect's finest. Not far: at 155 N. Main St, *Old Colony House, also known as Old State House (1762; later alt. & addit.), first state capitol building. In NW section of city: *Adm. Esek Hopkins House (1756; later alt.), 97 Admiral St; once home of first commanding admiral of U.S. Navy. In SW section of city: *Betsy Williams Cottage (1773; later alt.), Roger Williams Park, once home of descendant of Roger Williams, famous religious leader and founder of Rhode Island. Approx. 10 mi NW of city, via St. 122: WOONSOCKET. Interesting 19th-century mill village and mills.

Providence Vicinity *(NE, via US 1 or I-95).* Approx. 4 mi: PAWTUCKET. *Slater Mill (1793; later alt. & addit.; rest.), Roosevelt & Slater aves; fine early New England mill. In Hist. Site, several interesting buildings, including: *John Daggett House (1685; later alt. & addit.; rest.), Slater Park. Approx. 2 mi farther: LINCOLN. *Eleazar Arnold House (about 1687; later alt.; rest.), 499 Great Rd; early Colonial stone-end Rhode Island house; clapboard front and back.

Providence Vicinity *(S, via US 1)*. Approx. 5 mi: CRANSTON. Interesting buildings include: *Gov. William Sprague House (1790; later alt. & addit.), 1351 Cranston St; large house, once home of state governor, later U.S. senator. *Job Joy House (1770; rest.), 156 Scituate Ave. Approx. 11 mi SW of Cranston, via US 1 & St. 117: ANTHONY. *Gen. Nathanael Greene House (1774; rest.), once home of Revolutionary War general. Approx. 9 mi S of Cranston, via US 1: EAST GREENWICH. Interesting buildings include: *Kent County Courthouse (1750; rest.), Main St; state constitutional convention held here, 1842. *Gen. James Mitchell Varnum House (1773; rest.), 57 Pierce St; fine mansion; fine interiors; once home of Revolutionary War general. Approx. 7 mi farther: WICKFORD. Interesting buildings, especially on or near Main St, include: *St. Paul's, or Old Narragansett, Church, Episcopal (1707; rest.), 60 Church Lane, just off Main St; fine New England Colonial. Approx. 1 mi N, via US 1, *Smith's Castle (1678; rest.). Approx. 4 mi farther: JOHNSTON. *Clemence-Irons House (about 1680; rest.), 38 George Waterman Rd; interesting stone-end house.

Vermont

Early inhabitants Indians of Abnaki, Mohican and Penacook tribes; driven out by Iroquois, early 17th century; returned to defeat Iroquois. Frenchman Samuel de Champlain probably first explorer; claimed for France, 1609. First American permanent settlement, 1724: Brattleboro, originally Ft. Dummer. Royal Gov. Benning Wentworth made many grants of land, 1749–63; New York, which also claimed area, made grants of same land to others; English ruled in favor of New York; Vermont settlers organized Green Mountain Boys who drove New Yorkers out, 1770. Lake Champlain area major battleground in French and Indian Wars; at end, 1763, French claims relinquished to British. In Revolution, Ethan Allen and Green Mountain Boys captured Ft. Ticonderoga from British, 1775. Battle of Bennington, 1777, just outside state in New York, helped end British war activities in area; Vermont declared itself independent state, renamed New Connecticut, 1777; again named Vermont later in year; remained independent 14 years. Became fourteenth state Mar. 4, 1791. During Civil War, small band of Confederate soldiers raided banks in St. Albans, farthest north action of war, 1864. Today: Important manufacturing, agricultural and tourist industries.

Land Regions: E to W, White Mountains; Western New England Upland; Green Mountains; Vermont Valley; Taconic Mountains; Champlain Valley.

Climate: Long, cold winters; short, mild summers; moderate precipitation; heavy snow.

Major Building Materials: Timber; granite; marble; slate.

Architecture: Relatively small number of fine buildings in number of locations.

BENNINGTON

Interesting buildings include: fine *First Congregational Church (1805; later alt.; rest.), Monument Ave; architect: Lavius Fillmore. In NORTH BENNINGTON, Victorian *Park-McCullough House (1865; rest.), Park & West sts; once home of John G. McCullough, governor of state. Approx. 65 mi E, via St. 9 & 30: NEWFANE. Interesting buildings, mostly around Village Green, include: fine Greek Revival *Windham County Courthouse (1826); *Newfane Inn (about 1790; later alt.).

BURLINGTON

Interesting buildings include: *First Unitarian Church (1816; later alt. & addit.), Church & Pearl sts; architect: Peter Banner; fine Georgian by noted early architect. *University of Vermont, *Billings Student Center, formerly library (1885; later alt.; rest.), architect: Henry Hobson Richardson; very fine Romanesque Revival; some furniture designed by its famous architect. Approx. 13 mi SE, via US I-89: RICHMOND. *Old Round Church, now meetinghouse (1800; later alt.), architect: William Rhoades; unusual wood-frame, actually 16-sided rather than round; central belfry.

Burlington Vicinity *(S, via US 7)*. Approx. 7 mi: SHELBURNE. *Shelburne Museum, Shelburne Rd; outstanding collection of large number of rest. 18- and 19th-century buildings and other structures, including: *Stagecoach Inn (about 1780; rest.); *Charlotte Meeting House (1840; rest.); *Vermont House (about 1790); some moved here. Approx. 12 mi farther: FERRISBURG. *Rokeby, the Robinson Homestead (1789; rest.), Quaker house; once station on "Underground Railroad" for runaway slaves. Approx. 12 mi SW of Ferrisburg, via US 7 & St. 22A: ADDISON. *Gen. John Strong House (1795; rest.), Chimney Point; fine Federal; once home of Revolutionary War general. Also see: Rutland Vicinity (N, via US 7 & St. 3).

MONTPELIER

Interesting buildings include: *State Capitol (1838; burned 1857; reconst. & addit. 1859), State St; architect: Ammi B. Young; architects, reconst. & addit.: Thomas W. Silloway, Joseph R. Richards; fine small building. Approx. 45 mi SE, via US I-89 & St. 132: STRAFFORD. *Sen. Justin Smith Morrill House (1851; rest.), Main St; architect: Sen. Morrill; charming Gothic Revival.

Montpelier Vicinity *(NE, via St. 14)*. Approx. 12 mi: CALAIS. *Kent Tavern, now museum (1832; rest.), Kent's Corner. Approx. 75 mi NE of Montpelier, via US 2 & I-91: BROWNINGTON. *Old Stone House, now museum, (1836; later alt.), originally dormitory for Orleans County Grammar School; built, almost single-handedly, by black headmaster, Rev. Alexander Twilight.

RUTLAND

Interesting buildings include: *Public Library (1856; rest.), Court & Center sts; architect: Ammi B. Young.

Rutland Vicinity *(N, via US 7 & St. 3)*. PROCTOR. *Wilson's Castle (1867), Proctor Rd; fantastic 32-room Eclectic house. Approx. 8 mi farther: BRANDON. *Stephen Douglas House (about 1805; rest.), birthplace of "Little Giant" who debated Abraham Lincoln, 1858. Approx. 30 mi farther: MIDDLEBURY. Interesting buildings include: ●*Congregational Church (1809), the Common; architect: Lavius Fillmore; very fine; considered best design by its architect. Federal *Seymour House, now Community House (1816; rest.), Main St. *Sheldon Museum (1829; later alt. & addit.), 1 Park St; originally house. At *Middlebury College, *Emma Willard House (1809; later alt. & addit.), once home of noted pioneer of education for women; now college offices.

Rutland Vicinity *(E, via US 4 & St. 100)*. Approx. 25 mi: PLYMOUTH. Charming group of small-town buildings include: *Coolidge Homestead (about 1875; rest.), boyhood home of Pres. Calvin Coolidge, sworn in as president here, 1923; *Coolidge Store (about 1835; rest.) and attached house (about 1840; rest.), where future president was born. Approx. 10 mi farther, via St. 100 & US 4: WOODSTOCK. Relatively unspoiled village. Interesting buildings include: on Elm St, *Old White Meetinghouse, the Second Congregational Church (1808; rest.); at no. 26, *Dana House (1807; rest.). Approx. 25 mi farther, via US 4 & I-91: WINDSOR. Interesting buildings include: *Old Constitution House (about 1760; rest.), originally tavern; constitution for independent state was drafted here, 1777. Approx. 25 mi S of Windsor, via US I-91 & St. 103: ROCKINGHAM. ●*Rockingham Meeting House (1800; rest.), very fine Colonial.

Middle
Atlantic
States

Delaware

Second smallest state; slightly more than 2,000 square miles. Early inhabitants Indians of Delaware and Nanticoke tribes. First exploration probably by Englishman Henry Hudson, for Dutch, 1609; later by Capt. Samuel Argall of Virginia Colony, 1610; named area for Thomas West, Lord De La Warr, royal governor of Virginia colony. First Dutch settlement, 1631: Lewes, originally Zwaanendael; destroyed by Indians. First permanent settlement by Swedes, 1638: Wilmington, originally Ft. Christina, part of New Sweden; Peter Minuit, director-general of New Amsterdam (now New York), first governor of New Sweden. Peter Stuyvesant, Dutch governor of New Netherland, founded New Castle, originally Ft. Casimir, 1651; fort captured by Swedes, 1654; all New Sweden captured by Dutch, 1655; captured by English, 1664; recaptured by Dutch, 1673; returned to England, 1674; S portion became part of Pennsylvania, 1682. Became first state, Dec. 7, 1787. Little fighting in state during Revolution or War of 1812; none during Civil War. Today: Important agricultural and manufacturing state, especially chemicals.

Land Regions: Entire state Atlantic Coastal Plain except small N Piedmont portion.

Climate: Humid; mild winters, hot summers; precipitation moderate; snowfall light.

Major Building Materials: Stone; clay; sand and gravel.

Architecture: Interesting buildings here, but not numerous in such a small state.

DOVER

Interesting buildings include, in Hist. Dist. and elsewhere: *State House (1792; later alt. & addit.; rest.), the Green; architect: Alexander Givan; Georgian; now used mostly for ceremonial purposes; other governmental functions in nearby buildings, including *Legislative Hall (1933), architect: William E. Martin. *Swedish Log House (about 1750; rest.), Delaware State Museum, 316 Governors Ave; moved to this location. Approx. 6 mi SW, via Kitts Hummock Rd: *Judge John Dickinson Mansion (1740; later alt.; rest.), Georgian; once home of noted patriot known as "Penman of the Revolution" for his many writings for cause.

Dover Vicinity *(SE, via US 113 & St. 1).* Approx. 17 mi: MILFORD. Interesting buildings include: *Parson Thorne House

(1735; later alt. & addit.; rest.), 501 N.W. Front St; brick plantation house. Approx. 19 mi farther, via St. l: LEWES. Interesting
buildings include two small houses, *Plank House (about 1700;
rest.) and *Burton-Ingram House (about 1800; rest.). Also, via
ferry from Lewes, see New Jersey—Camden Vicinity (SE, via US
30).

Dover Vicinity *(NW, via US 13).* Approx. 13 mi: SMYRNA. Interesting buildings include: *The Lindens (about 1720; later alt. &
addit.; rest.), Dutch Colonial; *Belmont Hall (1689; later alt. &
addit.; rest.), Georgian. Approx. 5 mi E, Via St. 6, *Allee House
(about 1753; rest.), brick farmhouse.

WILMINGTON

Interesting buildings include: •*Old Town Hall (1798; later alt.;
rest.), 512 Market St; architect: Pierre Bauduy; fine Georgian
example. Not far: *Grand Opera House, formerly Masonic Hall
(1871; later alt.; rest.), Market Street Mall; architects: Thomas
Dixon & Charles L. Carson; architects, rest.: Grieves, Armstrong
& Childs; interesting Eclectic French Renaissance Revival. At
Church & 7th sts, *Holy Trinity Church, also known as Old
Swedes Church (1699; later alt. & addit.; rest.). Approx. 3 mi
NW of city, via St. 52: GREENVILLE. *Hagley Museum, fascinating complex where Eleuthère Irénée Du Pont founded gunpowder-
making industry, 1802, and E. I. Du Pont de Nemours & Co.;
rest. cotton-spinning mill, powder mills, other buildings here, including mansion *Eleutherian Mills (1803; later alt. & addit.),
architect: Pierre Bauduy; fine Georgian; Du Pont family home
until 1958. Approx. 3 mi farther, *Winterthur (1839; later alt. &
addit.), fine Georgian home of Henry Francis Du Pont, now museum; fine collections of authentic early rooms from other buildings,
antiques, art; beautiful gardens; on grounds: *Garden Pavilion
(1961; later addit.), architects: Victorine & Samuel Homsey; delightful modern information and lecture center. Approx. 5 mi NE
of city, via US I-95: ARDEN. Founded early in 20th century by
group of social reformers, including noted author Upton Sinclair
who espoused socialism and single-tax theories of Henry George.
Also see: Maryland—Baltimore; Pennsylvania—Philadelphia.

Wilmington Vicinity *(SW, via US 13).* Approx. 10 mi: NEW CAS-
TLE. Interesting buildings include: in Hist. Dist., on wonderfully
preserved Green, planned by Peter Stuyvesant, Dutch governor of
New Amsterdam (now New York). Nearby, on Green, *Old
Courthouse (1732; later alt. & addit.; rest.), first capitol of state;
Old Sheriff's Office (1858; later alt.); Old Arsenal (1809; later
alt.; rest.); *Immanuel Church, Episcopal (1703; later alt. & addit.); *Old Academy (1798–1811; later alt.), now church parish
house; *Old Dutch House (about 1690; later alt. & addit.; rest.),

believed to be oldest house in state. Not far: *Amstel House (about 1707; later alt. & addit.; rest.), 2 E. 4th St. On Strand, *George Read II House (1801; rest.), fine late Georgian, designed by first owner; interesting gardens. Approx. 4 mi S, via US 13, *Buena Vista (1847; later alt. & addit.; rest.), once home of John M. Clayton, U.S. senator and secretary of war under President Zachary Taylor. Approx. 16 mi farther: ODESSA. Interesting buildings include: on Main St, Georgian *Wilson-Warner House (1769; later alt. & addit.). Next door, *Corbit-Sharp House (1774; later alt. & addit.; rest.), architect: Robert May; very fine Georgian; interesting herb garden. Approx. 1 mi N of town, via US 13, *Old Drawyers Church, Presbyterian (1773; later alt.), interesting simple Georgian.

District of Columbia

Site selected by George Washington, 1791; surveyed and planned by Maj. Pierre Charles L'Enfant; approx. 69 square mi along Potomac River, S of Maryland. City of Washington occupies entire district. Building of U.S. Capitol began, 1793. Capitol building, White House and other government buildings burned, 1814, by British during War of 1812; rebuilding began immediately. Today: major industry: Federal government and related activities.

Land Region: Atlantic Coastal Plain, not far E of Piedmont region.

Climate: Mild winters; hot, humid summers; precipitation moderate; snowfall moderate.

Architecture: Number of fine buildings, some among most important historically, and some among most important architecturally, in United States.

WASHINGTON

Nation's capital: noted for fine and interesting buildings, open spaces, landscaping and city plan designed by Major L'Enfant.

CAPITOL HILL AND VICINITY
•*U.S. Capitol (begun 1793; later alt. & addit.; burned 1814; reconst. begun 1815; later alt. & addit.; dome completed 1863; east front extended 1962), Capitol Hill; original architect: William

Thornton; followed by Stephen Hallet, George Hadfield; architect, House and Senate wings, reconst. after fire: Benjamin Henry Latrobe; architect, central portion: Charles Bulfinch; architect, present dome, House and Senate extensions: Thomas U. Walter. By any measure, architecturally, politically, historically, and symbolically, Capitol must be considered most important of American buildings; magnificent Classic Revival; on beautiful high site overlooking Mall and capital city, Capitol has continued to change and grow with nation and to reflect nation's basic principles; famous landscape architect, Frederick Law Olmsted, designed terraces. Nearby, *Supreme Court Building (1935), 1st & Capitol sts NE; architect: Cass Gilbert; late Classic Revival by noted architect. *Folger Shakespeare Library (1932), 201 E. Capitol St SE; architect: Paul Cret; consult. architect: Alexander B. Trowbridge; Beaux Arts "Moderne," with beautiful Elizabethan interior and theater. Not far: *Frederick Douglass Town House, now Museum of African Arts (about 1870; rest.), 301 A St NE; first Washington home of former slave who became noted statesman and editor. At 1411 W St SE, *Cedar Hill (about 1855; rest.), Douglass later lived here. Nearby, *Library of Congress (1886–97), 1st St NE; architects: Smithmeyer & Pelz; flamboyant exterior, even more so inside. The Mall, on Capitol Hill end, is museum-goers delight: *Botanic Gardens (1902), bet. 1st, 2nd & B sts & Maryland Av SW; architects: Bennett, Parsons & Frost; Classic Revival on Mall side, glass and steel on others. *National Air and Space Museum (1975), Independence Ave bet. 4th & 7th sts SW; architects: Hellmuth, Obata & Kassabaum; modern; interesting spaces and exhibits. *Hirshhorn Museum (1975), Independence Ave &

U.S. Capitol—Classic Revival (Joseph W. Molitor)

Smithsonian Institution—Gothic Revival (Library of Congress)

7th St SW; architects: Skidmore, Owings & Merrill; modern round building; outdoor sculpture garden. Not Far:
•*Smithsonian Institution Building** (1855; part. burned 1865; rebuilt 1867; later alt. & addit.), Jefferson Dr, bet. 9th & 12th sts; architect: James Renwick, Jr.; architect, rebuilding: Adolph Cluss; very fine, fascinating Gothic Revival by famous architect. Nearby, *Arts and Industries Building (1880; rest.), architects: Adolph Cluss & Paul Schulze; architect, rest.: Hugh Newell Jacobsen; another fascinating Smithsonian building; somewhat Romanesque Revival. *Freer Gallery of Art (1923), Jefferson Dr & 12th St SW; architect: Charles A. Platt; Beaux Arts; interesting courtyard. Across The Mall: Smithsonian buildings; undistinguished architecture, but interesting exhibits. *National Museum of Natural History (1910), architects: Hornblower & Marshall; *National Museum of History and Technology (1964), architects: McKim, Mead & White and Steinmann, Cain & White. North of Mall: *Old Post Office (1899; rest.), Pennsylvania Av & 12th St NW; architect: Willoughby J. Edbrooke; architects, rest.: MMM Design Group; Arthur Cotton Moore; Stewart Daniel Hoban; interesting Romanesque Revival; clock tower; now offices, shops, cultural center. *Ford's Theater (about 1850; rest.), 10th St bet. E & F sts, where President Abraham Lincoln was shot, 1865. Across street, *Petersen House (about 1849; rest.), President Lincoln died here. *Old Post Office, formerly Tariff Commission, now shops and offices (1839–69; rest.), bet. 7th, 8th, E & F sts NW; architect: Robert Mills, Classic Revival; not considered one of architect's best. *National Portrait Gallery, formerly Old Patent Office (1840; addit. 1853, 1856, 1867; rest.), bet. 7th, 9th & G sts

NW; architects: William P. Elliot & Ithiel Town; architect, 1853, 1856 addit.: Robert Mills; architect, 1867 addit.: Edward Clark; architects, rest.: Faulkner, Kingsbury & Stenhouse; fine Classic Revival. *National Museum of Building Arts, formerly Old Pension Building (1885; rest.), bet. 4th, 5th, F & G sts; architect: Gen. Montgomery Meigs; fascinating Eclectic Italian Renaissance Revival; marvelous interior. *D. C. Courthouse, formerly City Hall (1820–50), 4th & D sts NW; architect: George Hadfield; fine early Greek Revival. ●***National Gallery of Art** (1941; addit. 1978), Constitution Ave bet. 3rd & 7th sts NW; architect: John Russell Pope; assoc. architects: Eggers & Higgins; architect, East Wing: I. M. Pei; grandiose, almost overpowering, Eclectic Classic Revival with modern wing; superlative collections of painting, sculpture and other arts. ●***Union Station** (1908; later alt.), Massachusetts & Louisiana aves NW; architect: Daniel H. Burnham; imposing Beaux Arts by famous architect.

In Southeast. Gothic Revival *Christ Church (1805; many alt.), 620 G St SE; architect: Benjamin Henry Latrobe.

In Southwest. Interesting urban renewal area, with shopping, apartments, other buildings by well-known modern architects, including *Arena Stage (1961) and *Arena Stage II, the Kreeger Theater (1970), 6th & M sts SW; architect: Harry Weese.

WHITE HOUSE AND VICINITY

●***White House,** formerly called The President's House (begun 1792; later alt. & addit.; burned 1814; reconst. 1815; later alt. & addit.), 1600 Pennsylvania Ave NW; original, reconst. architect: James Hoban; architect, alt. & addit., 1807, 1824–29: Benjamin Henry Latrobe; landscape architect, 1849: Andrew Jackson Downing; architects, alt. & addit., 1902: McKim, Mead & White; 1952: Lorenzo Winslow; after Capitol, most important American building politically, historically and symbolically, if not architecturally. Nearby, ●***Treasury Building** (1842; alt. & addit. 1869), 1500 Pennsylvania Ave NW; architect: Robert Mills; architect, alt. & addit.: Thomas U. Walter; fine Classic Revival; considered finest of famous architect's Federal government buildings; on site ill-chosen by President Andrew Jackson, where it blocks Pennsylvania Ave vista from Capitol to White House. Nearby, *St. John's Church, also known as Church of the Presidents (1816; later alt. & addit.), 16th & H sts NW; architect: Benjamin Henry Latrobe; architect, 1883 alt. & addit.: James Renwick, Jr.; delightful, small church by famous architect; since completion, every president has worshipped here. Nearby, *Decatur House (1819; rest.), 748 Jackson Pl NW; architect: Benjamin Henry Latrobe; fine Federal; once home of Stephen Decatur, hero of War of 1812. Not far: ●***Renwick Gallery,** originally old Corcoran Gallery and formerly Court of Claims (1860; rest. 1974), Pennsylvania Ave & 17th St

NW; architect: James Renwick, Jr.; architects, rest.: John Carl Warnecke & Hugh Newell Jacobsen; fine Eclectic Second Empire; name changed to honor its famous architect. At 17th St & New York Ave NW, "new" Beaux Arts *Corcoran Gallery of Art (1897; addit. 1927); architect: Ernest Flagg; architect, addit.: Charles Platt. Not far: ●**Old Executive Office Building,** originally State, War and Navy Building (1871–88; later alt.), Pennsylvania & 17th sts NW; architect: Alfred B. Mullett; fascinating Eclectic Second Empire by supervising architect of Treasury Dept. Not far: *The Octagon House (1801; rest.), 1741 New York Ave NW; architect: William Thornton; architect, rest.: J. Everette Fauber, Jr.; fine Federal; home of President James Madison and his wife Dolley after British burned White House, 1814. Next door, modern *American Institute of Architects Headquarters (1973), 1735 New York Ave NW; architects: The Architects Collaborative (TAC). Not far: *Organization of the American States Building, originally Pan American Union (1910), Constitution Ave & 17th St NW; architects: Paul Cret & Albert Kelsey; fine Beaux Arts. Few blocks: ●*Lincoln Memorial** (1922), The Mall at 23rd St NW; architect: Henry Bacon; outstanding Eclectic Greek Revival by famous architect; shelters majestic sculpture of president by famous sculptor Daniel Chester French; marvelous Reflecting Pool (1923); architects: Henry Bacon; McKim, Mead & White. Not far, off Virginia Ave, *John F. Kennedy Center for the Performing Arts (1973), architect: Edward Durell Stone. Not far: ●*Washington Monument** (1848–85), The Mall bet. 15th & 17th sts, NW; architect: Robert Mills; spectacular Eclectic Classic Revival monument to first president designed by famous architect.

Old Executive Office Building—Eclectic Second Empire (Joseph W. Molitor)

Lincoln Memorial—Eclectic Greek Revival (M. E. Warren)

Washington Monument—Eclectic Classic Revival (Joseph W. Molitor)

Off 14th St, US I-395, near 14th Street Bridge, *Jefferson Memorial (1943); architect: John Russell Pope; assoc. architects: Eggers & Higgins; sculptor: Rudolph Evans; not considered as magnificent as Lincoln Memorial and Washington Monument, nevertheless fine Classic Revival.

GEORGETOWN AND VICINITY

Established in 1751 and thus some 50 years older than Washington, of which it is now part; noted for shops and restaurants, as well as large number of interesting buildings. Walking tour of Georgetown Hist. Dist.: *Old Stone House (1765; rest.), 3051 M St NW; believed to be oldest building in Washington. *U.S. Post Office, formerly Custom House (1857; later alt.), 1221 31st St NW; architect: Ammi B. Young; *Dumbarton House (1799; alt. & addit. 1805; rest.), 2715 Q St NW; architect, alt. & addit.: Benjamin Henry Latrobe; fine Federal or late Georgian. Nearby, another fine example of same era, Evermay (1801; later alt. & addit.), 1628 28th St. NW. Not far: *Oak Hill Chapel (1850; later alt.), Oak Hill Cemetery, 30th & R sts NW; architect: James Renwick, Jr.; small, simple Gothic Revival. *Dumbarton Oaks, now Harvard University Research Library (1801; alt. 1822; later alt. & addit.), 1703 32nd St NW; architect, 1822 alt.: Frederich Brooke; architect, later alt. & addit.: Lawrence White; fine mansion; beautiful gardens; meetings here led to establishment of United Nations; attached to main building: *Robert Woods Bliss Museum of Pre-Columbian Art (1963), architect: Philip Johnson; meticulous modern, composed of eight cylinders around central court. Not far: •**Tudor Place** (1815; later alt.), 1644 31st St NW, architect: William Thornton; magnificent private house by original architect of Capitol. Few blocks away: *St. John's Church (1809; alt. & addit. 1870 & later), Potomac & O sts NW; architect: William Thornton; architects, 1870 alt. & addit.: Starkweather & Plowman. Also of interest: old buildings at *Georgetown University; *Chesapeake & Ohio Canal. W of Georgetown: *Embassy of Federal Republic of Germany (1964), 4645 Reservoir Rd; architect: Egon Eiermann; fine, modern glass building.

Massachusetts Ave Vicinity *(E of Dupont Circle, NW on Massachusetts Ave and, to some extent, on other streets).* Large number of fine houses, mostly dating from the late 19th to early 20th centuries; many have been converted into private association offices, clubs or foreign embassies; often called "Embassy Row." On Wisconsin Ave NW, short distance to right of intersection with Massachusetts Ave, ••**Washington Cathedral,** Episcopal, The Cathedral Church of St. Peter and St. Paul (begun 1907); architects: Henry Vaughn & George Bodley; later architects: Frohman, Robb & Little; soaring, uncompleted Gothic cathedral; design and construction almost entirely according to proper medieval principles. Also see: Virginia—Alexandria Vicinity; Maryland–Washington, D.C. Vicinity (SE, via St. 5; S, via St. 210).

Maryland

Early inhabitants Indians of several tribes, including Choptank, Nanticoke, Patuxent, Wicomico. Spaniards may have explored, 16th century; explored later by Capt. John Smith, 1608. First settlement by Englishman William Claiborne at Kent Island, 1631. Granted to George Calvert, first Lord Baltimore, 1632; after his death, to his son, Cecil Calvert, second Lord Baltimore. First permanent English settlement, 1634; St. Mary's City. Colony taken from Lord Baltimore by Claiborne, 1654; returned, 1658. Mainly because of protests by colonists against Roman Catholic Calverts, became royal colony, 1691; returned to control of Protestant fourth Lord Baltimore, 1715. Resistance by colonists to tax and other British laws led to burning of tea cargo and ship *Peggy Stewart,* Annapolis, 1774; little fighting and no major battles during Revolution. Annapolis U.S. capital, 1783–84. Became seventh state, April 28, 1788. Several battles fought in state during War of 1812, including American defeat in Battle of Bladensburg, 1814; next day, British burned Capitol, White House and other government buildings in Washington; naval attack on Baltimore, same year, during which Francis Scott Key wrote *The Star-Spangled Banner;* British defeated and driven out of state. People in state of divided sympathies in Civil War, but state remained in Union. Several military actions in state, including Battle of Antietam, near Sharpsburg, 1862; Gen. Robert E. Lee's army driven back to Virginia. Today: Important manufacturing and shipping industries.

Land Regions: Atlantic Coastal Plain around Chesapeake Bay; in remainder of state, from E to W, Piedmont; Blue Ridge; Appalachian Ridge and Valley; Appalachian Plateau.

Climate: Hot summers, generally mild winters; humid; precipitation moderate; snowfall moderate in SE, heavier in W.

Major Building Materials: Timber; stone; clay; sand and gravel.

Architecture. Rich and varied, from Colonial era to present; includes some of finest U.S. buildings, especially in Annapolis; Baltimore.

ANNAPOLIS

Planned by Royal Gov. Francis Nicholson. Interesting buildings include: in Hist. Dist., ●*State House (1779; later alt. & addit.), State Circle; architect: Joseph Horatio Brown; architect, 1787

Hammond-Harwood House—Georgian (M. E. Warren)

addit.: Joseph Clark; architect, 1878 alt. & addit.: George A. Frederick; fine building, fine interiors; longest continuous use of any state capitol; for year, 1783–84, served as U.S. Capitol; on grounds: fine *Old Treasury Building (1737; later alt.; rest.). Nearby, *Government House (1868; later alt.), College Ave. Also on College Ave, *St. John's College; interesting buildings include: *McDowell Hall (about 1745; burned 1909; reconst.). Not far: ●*Chase–Lloyd House (1774; later alt.), 22 Maryland Ave; architect: William Buckland; very fine Georgian; beautiful woodwork by famous architect-joiner; built for Samuel Chase, signer of Declaration of Independence. Across street:
●*Hammond-Harwood House (1775; later alt.; rest.), 19 Maryland Ave; architect: William Buckland; considered one of finest Georgian houses in U.S., among best in any style, and its architect's masterpiece; very fine woodwork. Nearby, *William Paca House (1765; rest.), 186 Prince George St.; fine house and garden; birthplace of signer of Declaration of Independence. Also of interest: *U.S. Naval Academy. Approx. 17 mi S, via St. 2 & 255, *Tulip Hill (about 1760; later alt. & addit.), fine Georgian house. Not far away, at Herring Creek, *St. James Episcopal Church (1763; later alt.).

Annapolis Vicinity *(Eastern Shore, SW, via US 301 & 50)*. Approx. 26 mi, off US 50, on St. 662: WYE MILLS. Interesting buildings include: *Old Wye Church, originally St. Luke's Chapel, Episcopal (1722; rest.), architects, rest.: Perry, Shaw & Hepburn, small example; reconst. vestry house. Approx. 3 mi S, Wye House (about 1784; later alt. & addit.), elegant late Georgian.

Approx. 18 mi N of Wye Mills, via St. 213: CHESTERTOWN. Interesting old buildings in Hist. Dist. Approx. 11 mi S of Wye Mills, via US 50: EASTON. Interesting buildings include: *Third Haven Friends Meeting House (1683; later alt.). Approx. 10 mi W of Easton, via St. 33: ST. MICHAEL'S. *Chesapeake Bay Maritime Museum. Approx. 15 mi S of Easton, via US 50: CAMBRIDGE. Georgian *Meredith House (about 1760; rest.), Maryland Ave. Approx. 7 mi SW of Cambridge, via St. 16: CHURCH CREEK. *Old Trinity Church, Episcopal (about 1675; later alt.; rest.), fine small example. Approx. 44 mi SE of Cambridge, via US 50 & 13: PRINCESS ANNE. Interesting buildings include: *Teackle Mansion (1801; later alt. & addit.; rest.), Mansion & Prince William sts; fine Federal; fine details. Also see: Virginia—Norfolk Vicinity (NE, via US 13).

BALTIMORE

Long known for its row houses, first of which, Waterloo Row (1815; later alt.), Calvert St, were designed by famous architect Robert Mills. Interesting buildings include:
●*Basilica of the Assumption of the Virgin Mary, Roman Catholic (1806–21; alter alt. & addit.), Cathedral & Mulberry sts; architect: Benjamin Henry Latrobe; magnificent Classic Revival by famous architect; often called "Baltimore Cathedral"; considered one of finest U.S. buildings. Not far: another fine Classic Revival example, *First Unitarian Church (1818; later alt.), Charles & Franklin sts; architect: Maximilian Godefroy. At Druid Hill Ave

Basilica of the Assumption of the Virgin Mary—Classic Revival (M. E. Warren)

& Paca St, Godefroy's *St. Mary's Seminary Chapel (1808; later alt.), believed to be first Gothic Revival building in U.S. Eclectic Second Empire *City Hall (1867–75; later alt.; remod.), E. Fayette & Holliday sts; architect: George A. Frederick. At Front & Lombard sts, Federal *Carroll House (about 1812; rest.), 844 E. Pratt St; once home of Charles Carroll of Carrollton, signer of Declaration of Independence. Not far: late Georgian *Flag House (1793; rest.), once home of Mary Pickersgill, who sewed U.S. flag that flew over Ft. McHenry, 1814, when Francis Scott Key wrote *The Star-Spangled Banner.* Nearby, *Ft. McHenry (1790; later alt. & addit.), Nat. Mon. & Hist. Shrine; offshore, on British ship, Key wrote national anthem. Not far: *Inner Harbor Development, modern multipurpose complex, mostly along Pratt St at W end of Baltimore harbor; planners & landscape architects: Wallace, McHarg, Roberts & Todd. Interesting buildings include: *National Aquarium (1980), architects: Cambridge Seven; *World Trade Center (1977), architect: I. M. Pei; shops and restaurants of *Harbor Place (1981), architect: Benjamin Thompson; *Baltimore Convention Center (1979), architects: Naramore, Bain, Brady & Johanson and Cochran, Stephenson & Donkervoet; *Maryland Science Center (1976), architect: Edward Durell Stone; also houses, apartments, office buildings, hotel. Moored here: rest. *U.S.S. *Constellation,* first U.S. Navy ship to capture foreign warship; also other ships here. Not far: *Federal Hill and *Fells Point Hist. Dist. Few blocks NW, earlier redevelopment: *Charles Center; planners: David A. Wallace; Kostritsky & Potts; RTKL; includes modern apartments, office buildings and *Morris A. Mechanic Theater (1967; later alt.), architect: John M. Johansen; assoc. architects: Cochran, Stephenson & Donkervoet. In Carroll Park: ●*Mount Clare (about 1760; later alt. & addit.), fine Georgian; once home of Charles Carroll, the barrister, cousin of Charles Carroll of Carrollton. Not far: *Edgar Allan Poe House (1830; rest.), 203 Amity St; once home of famous poet and where he married his thirteen-year old cousin. At Mount Royal Ave & Cathedral St, Romanesque Revival *College of Art, Maryland Institute, formerly Mount Royal Railroad Station (1896; remod. 1966), architects: Baldwin & Pennington; architects, remod.: Cochran, Stephenson & Donkervoet; interesting building converted to new use. At *Johns Hopkins University, 34th & Charles sts, interesting old buildings include: ●*Homewood (1802; rest.), very fine Classic Revival, now university president's office. N of university, on Cold Spring Lane, off US I-83, interesting modern *Cold Spring New Town (begun 1973); architect: Moshe Safdie, noted Israeli architect of Habitat, at Expo '67, Montreal. At 4000 N. Charles St & Highfield Rd, *Highfield House (1965), architect: Ludwig Mies van der Rohe; interesting modern high-rise apartments by famous architect. At 4545 N. Charles St, Classic Revival *Evergreen (about 1850; later alt. & addit.).

Baltimore Vicinity *(N, via St. 45)*. Adjoining city: TOWSON.
•*Hampton Mansion** (1790; later alt. & addit.; rest.), Hampton
Nat. Hist. Site, 535 Hampton Lane; very fine, very large, late
Georgian manor house; fine gardens, rest. slave quarters and other
outbuildings. Approx. 8 mi N of Towson, via US 695 & 83:
COCKEYSVILLE. Modern *Noxell Building (1967), York Rd; archi-
tects: Skidmore, Owings & Merrill.

Baltimore Vicinity *(SW, via US 29)*. Approx. 20 mi: *COLUMBIA.
New town (begun 1966) with interesting modern buildings of
many types; planners: Morton Hoppenfeld; Howard Research &
Development Corp. Much earlier new town, (begun 1936) located
approx. 30 mi SW of Baltimore, via Baltimore-Washington Park-
way (US 1): *GREENBELT. planner: Clarence Stein. Approx. 10 mi
from Greenbelt, via US I-495 & 95 & St. 197: LAUREL. *Montpelier (1751; later alt. & addit.; rest.), large Georgian house; interesting woodwork.

Baltimore Vicinity *(NW, via St. 140)*. Adjoining city: PIKES-
VILLE. *Grey Rock (about 1700; later alt. & addit.), Reister-
town Rd; birthplace of John Eager Howard, Revolutionary War
general, state governor & U.S. senator. Approx. 25 mi farther:
WESTMINSTER. Georgian *Shellman House (about 1807; later alt.;
rest.); Greek Revival *Carroll Co. Courthouse (1836; later alt.).

HAGERSTOWN

Interesting buildings include: *Jonathan Hager House, also
known as "Hager's Fancy" (1740; rest.), near City Park; simple
stone house, once home of founder of city. *Miller House (1824;
rest.), 135 W. Washington St. Also of interest, approx. 10 mi S,
via St. 65, *Antietam Nat. Battlefield Site. Also see: West Virginia—Charles Town & Vicinity.

Washington, D.C. Vicinity *(SE, via St. 5)*. Approx. 55 mi: LEON-
ARDTOWN. Interesting buildings include: Georgian *Tudor Hall
(1780; later alt.; rest.). Approx. 10 mi NE of Leonardtown, approx. 3 mi past HOLLYWOOD, via St. 245, *Sotterley Mansion
(about 1730; rest.), Georgian; once home of Maryland Gov.
George Plater. Approx. 15 mi SE of Leonardtown, via St. 5: ST.
MARY'S CITY, founded 1634, by Leonard Calvert and his followers,
who landed there from ships *Ark* and *Dove*. Interesting buildings
include: in Hist. Dist., *Old State House (1676; burned 1829;
reconst. 1934); *Trinity Church, Episcopal (1829; later alt.).

Washington, D.C. Vicinity *(S, via St. 210)*. Approx. 15 mi: *Ft.
Washington (begun 1812), Nat. Park, well-preserved example; lo-
cation chosen by George Washington; designed by Maj. Pierre
Charles L'Enfant, who planned nation's capital.

New Jersey

Early inhabitants Indians, mostly of Delaware tribe. First explorer probably Italian Giovanni da Verrazano, 1524, for France; later explorations by Englishman Henry Hudson, 1609, for Dutch; Dutchman Cornelius Mey, 1614; Cape May named for him. Swedes came to S portion, 1638; driven out by Dutch, 1655. First permanent Dutch settlement, 1660: Bergen. Ceded to England, 1664; granted first to James, duke of York, who gave area to Lord John Berkeley and Sir George Carteret. Berkeley's share sold to Quakers, led by Edward Byllynge, 1674; same year divided into East Jersey and West Jersey, latter becoming first Quaker colony; another group of Quakers bought Carteret's East Jersey, 1682. After disputes and riots by colonists who disliked Quaker owners, both areas given to British, 1702; ruled by governor of New York; two capitals, Perth Amboy and Burlington. First Colonial governor, Lewis Morris, appointed 1738. Opposition to British tax and other laws led to rebellious acts, including Greenwich Tea Burning, 1774, destroying cargo of ship near Greenwich. Major battles during Revolution fought here, including battles of Trenton, 1776, Princeton, 1777, and Monmouth, 1778. Princeton served as U.S. capital, 1783, as did Trenton, 1784. Became third state, Dec. 18, 1787. Today: Important manufacturing and agricultural industries.

Land Regions: S to NW, largest, Atlantic Coastal Plain; Piedmont; New England Upland; Appalachian Ridge and Valley.

Climate: Mild; precipitation moderate; colder and greater snowfall in N areas than in S.

Major Building Materials: Stone; clay; sand and gravel.

Architecture: Number of important buildings architecturally as well as historically in many locations, especially Princeton and vicinity and Newark and vicinity.

CAMDEN

Interesting buildings include: *Pomona Hall, the Joseph Cooper, Jr. House (1726; later alt. & addit.; rest.), Euclid Ave & Park Blvd; Georgian. Dr. H. Genet Taylor House & Office (1886; later alt. & addit.), 305 Cooper St; architect: Wilson Eyre, Jr. *Walt Whitman House (about 1840), 330 Mickle St; famous poet lived here late in life. *Newton Friends Meeting House (about 1830; later alt. & addit.), Cooper near 7th St. Also see: Pennsylvania—Philadelphia & Vicinity.

Camden Vicinity *(SE, Via US 30)*. Approx. 8 mi, via US 30 & St. 41: HADDONFIELD. Interesting buildings include: on King's Hwy E, at no. 233, *Indian King Tavern (about 1750; later alt. & addit.), first state legislature met here, 1777. At no. 343, *Greenfield Hall, the John Gill IV House (1747; later alt. & addit.). Approx. 30 mi SE of Haddonfield, via St. 41, US 30 & Co. 542: BATSTO. *Batsto Village, part. rest. early 19th-century bog-iron-producing town, now State Hist. Site. Approx. 19 mi SE of Batsto, via Co. 542 & US 9: SMITHVILLE. *Smithville Hist. Towne, number of interesting 18th- and 19th-century buildings moved here. Also of interest, approx. 2 mi farther, via US 9, near OCEANVILLE, *Brigantine Nat. Wildlife Refuge. Approx. 20 mi farther: SOMERS POINT. *Richard Somers Mansion (1726; later alt. & addit.), Shore Rd & Mays Landing. Approx. 50 mi farther: CAPE MAY, charming 19th-century Victorian houses, resort hotels. Also see: via ferry, Delaware—Dover Vicinity (SE, via US 113 & St. 1).

Camden Vicinity *(SW & S, via US I-295)*. Approx. 8 mi: WOODBURY. Interesting buildings include: *Friends Meetinghouse (1722; later alt. & addit.), 120 N. Broad St. *Hunter-Lawrence House (1765; later alt. & addit.; rest.), 58 N. Broad St; once home of naval hero Capt. James Lawrence, commander of U.S.S. *Chesapeake* during War of 1812; when mortally wounded, he cried "Don't give up the ship!". *Candor Hall, also known as Ladd's Castle (1688; later alt. & addit.), 1337 Lafayette St; Dutch Colonial. *Whitall House (1748; later alt. & addit.), 100 Hessian Ave. Approx. 14 mi farther: SWEDESBORO. Interesting buildings include: *Trinity Episcopal Church (1748; later remod.), Church & Main sts; Colonial. Stratton Hall, the Dr. James Stratton House (about 1794; later renov.), King's Hwy. Approx. 25 mi farther, via US I-295 & St. 49: SALEM. Interesting buildings include: *Alexander Grant House (1721; later alt. & addit.; rest.), 83 Market St; Colonial. Approx. 10 mi farther, via Co. Rd: HANCOCKS BRIDGE. Interesting buildings include: *Judge William Hancock House (1734; later alt. & addit.), unusual zigzag lines of glazed brick on wall; behind: *Cedar Plank House (about 1640; later alt.), Swedish Colonial. Approx. 15 mi farther: GREENWICH. Interesting buildings include: *Nicholas Gibbon House (1730; later alt. & addit.; rest.), fine interior woodwork. Approx. 18 mi farther, via Co. Rd & St. 49: MILLVILLE. *David Wood House (1804; later alt. & addit.), Columbia Ave; once home of ironmaster.

NEWARK

Interesting buildings include: *First Presbyterian Church (1791; rest.), 820 Broad St; architect: Eleazar Ball; Georgian; interesting wood carvings. *Trinity Episcopal Church (1810; later alt. & addit.), Rector & Broad sts; architect: Josiah James; Greek Revival.

*South Park Presbyterian Church (1853; later alt. & addit.), Broad St & Clinton Ave; architect: John Welsh. John Sydenham House (about 1760; rest.), 720 De Graw St.

Newark Vicinity *(N New Jersey Metropolitan Area)*. Interesting buildings in surrounding towns and cities; area so built up that visitors should rely on latest maps and local directions. E of city: see New York—New York City. N & NE of Newark: RIVER EDGE (near Hackensack). ●***Ackermann-Zabriskie House,** also known as von Steuben House (about 1739; later alt. & addit.), 1209 Main St; fine Dutch Colonial; given to General von Steuben by state in appreciation of Revolutionary War service. PATERSON. *Lambert Castle (1892; later alt. & addit.), Garret Mountain; mansion modeled after Warwick Castle, England; towers and turrets. FAIRLAWN. *Radburn (1931 & later), planners: Clarence S. Stein & Henry Wright; fine early modern planned community by noted architect-planners. RAMSEY. *Old Stone House (about 1745; rest.), 536 Island Rd; Colonial. RINGWOOD. *Ringwood Manor (about 1810; later alt. & addit.; rest.), State Park; mansion in park of almost 600 acres; once home of ironmaster Martin Ryerson, of Peter Cooper and of Abram S. Hewitt.

N & NW of Newark: WEST ORANGE. *Glenmont, the Thomas A. Edison House (1887; later alt. & addit.), once home and laboratories of famous inventor, now Nat. Hist. Site; Edison and his wife buried on grounds. MONTCLAIR. Interesting buildings include: *Israel Crane House (1796; later alt. & addit.), 110 Orange St; Federal, remod. into Greek Revival. CALDWELL. *Rev. Richard F. Cleveland House (1832; later alt. & addit.), 207 Bloomfield Ave; birthplace of President Grover Cleveland. LIVINGSTON. *Deacon Thomas Force House (about 1745; later alt. & addit.; rest.), S. Livingston Ave; adjacent: old *Cookhouse. WAYNE. Interesting buildings include: *Dirck Dey Mansion (about 1740; later alt. & addit.), 199 Totowa Rd; Georgian influenced by Dutch Colonial; another of George Washington's many headquarters. *Van Riper-Hopper House (1787; later alt. & addit.), 533 Berdan Ave; Dutch Colonial. *Union Camp Building (1970), 1600 Valley Rd; architects: Schofield & Colgan; interesting modern corporate headquarters; fine landscaping. MORRISTOWN. Interesting buildings include: *Col. Jacob Ford, Jr. Mansion (1774; later alt. & addit.; rest.), 230 Morris St; imposing Georgian; yet another Washington headquarters; on grounds: *Historical Museum (1937), architect: John Russell Pope. *George Perot MacCulloch House (1810); later alt. & addit.; rest.), 45 MacCulloch Ave. Schuyler-Hamilton House (1760; later alt. & addit.; rest.), 5 Olypant Pl; Colonial; here Alexander Hamilton courted Elizabeth Schuyler, 1779–80. *Henry Wick House (about 1750; later alt. & addit.; rest.), Jockey Hollow. *Ft. Nonsense (1777; reconst.), believed to have been ordered by Washington to keep soldiers busy. STANHOPE. *Waterloo Village (mid-18th century; rest.), community founded near Morris Canal for blast furnace and refinery operations.

S & SW of Newark: ELIZABETH. Interesting buildings include: on E. Jersey St, at no. 1045, *Nathaniel Bonnell House (about 1682; later alt. & addit.; rest.). At no. 1046, *Belcher-Ogden Mansion (about 1700; later alt. & addit.; rest.), once home of John Ogden, Jr., founder of city and later of Royal Gov. Jonathan Belcher; at no. 1073, *Boxwood Hall, the Elias Boudinot House (about 1755; rest.), once home of president of American Congress under Articles of Confederation. PERTH AMBOY. Proprietary House, also known as Gov. William Franklin Mansion (about 1770; later alt. & addit.), 149 Kearney St; architect: William Pryor; once home of Royal Gov. William Franklin, son of Benjamin Franklin. NEW BRUNSWICK. Interesting buildings include: *Joyce Kilmer Birthplace (about 1885; later alt. & addit.), 17 Joyce Kilmer Ave; once home of noted poet. *Buccleuch Mansion (1739; later alt. & addit.), Buccleuch Park; Georgian. SPRINGFIELD. *Cannon Ball House, the Abraham Hutchings House (about 1750; later alt. & addit.), 126 Morris Ave; hit by cannon ball during Revolution. PLAINFIELD. *Nathaniel Drake House (1746; later alt. & addit.), 602 W. Front St; another Washington headquarters. SOMERVILLE. On Washington Pl, at no. 38, *Wallace House (1778; later alt. & addit.), George & Martha Washington lived here, 1778–79; at no. 65, *Old Dutch Parsonage, the Rev. John Frelinghuysen House (1751; later alt. & addit.), once home of founder of seminary which later became Rutgers University.

Newark Vicinity *(S, via Garden St. Pkwy)*. Approx. 35 mi: MIDDLETOWN. Interesting buildings include: *Marlpit Hall (about 1684), 137 King's Hwy; Dutch Colonial; fine interior woodwork. Approx. 25 mi farther, via pkwy & Co. Rd 524: ALLAIRE. *Deserted Village (19th century; part. rest.), State Park; old bog-iron-producing town.

TRENTON

Interesting buildings include: *State House (1792; later alt. & addit.), 121 W. State St; architect: Jonathan Doan; architects, alt. & addit.: 1846, John Notman; 1872, Samuel Sloan; 1889, Lewis Broome; 1891, James Moylan; 1900, George Poole. Nearby, *State House Hist. Dist.; *Chief Justice William Trent House, also known as Kingsbury Hall, Bloomsbury Court and Woodlawn (1719; later alt. & addit.; rest.), 539 S. Warren St; once home of state chief justice and other political leaders. *Old Barracks (1759; later alt. & addit.; rest.), S. Willow & Front sts; rare surviving Colonial military barracks. *Isaac Watson House (1708; rest.), 151 Westcott St. Also: *Mill Hill Hist. Dist. Nearby, *Alexander Douglass House (1766; later alt. & addit.), Mill Hill

Nassau Hall, Princeton University—Georgian (Library of Congress)

Park; where Gen. George Washington planned Battle of Princeton, 1777; moved here.

Trenton Vicinity *(NE, via US 206).* Approx. 10 mi: PRINCETON. Interesting buildings include, at *Princeton University:
●●*Nassau Hall,** also known as Olde North and North College (1756; part. burned; later alt. & addit.; rest.), Nassau & Witherspoon sts; architects: Robert Smith & William Shippen; architect, rest. after fire, 1802: Benjamin Henry Latrobe; architect, cupola and other addit., 1855: John Notman; very fine, famous Georgian by famous architect of Independence Hall, Philadelphia; Continental Congress met here, 1783. President's House, also known as Dean's House (about 1755; later alt. & addit.; rest.), 73 Nassau St; architect: Robert Smith; Eclectic Collegiate Gothic Revival. *Blair Hall (1897), architects: Cope & Stewardson. *Graduate School (1913) and *University Chapel (1923), architect: Ralph Adams Cram. Fine modern examples include: *Stanley P. Jadwin Hall (1969), architect: Hugh Stubbins; *Woodrow Wilson School (1965), architect: Minoru Yamasaki; *Spelman Halls (1973), architect: I. M. Pei. Other interesting buildings in Princeton include: *Dr. Absalom Bainbridge House (about 1760; later alt. & addit.; rest.), 158 Nassau St; birthplace of Commodore William Bainbridge, commander of U.S.S. *Constitution,* affectionately known as *Old Ironsides.* Morven, the Richard Stockton House (about 1755; later alt. & addit.; rest), 63 Stockton St; once home of signer of Declaration of Independence. Just S of town, via St. 583, *Stony Brook Meeting House (1727; damaged by fire 1759; rebuilt 1760; rest.), a Quaker meetinghouse, near which Battle of

Princeton was fought, 1777. Approx. 5 mi N of town, via US 206: ROCKY HILL. *Rockingham, the Judge John Berrien House (about 1735; later alt. & addit.; rest.), another headquarters of Washington; here he wrote his "Farewell Address to the Armies," 1783.

Trenton Vicinity *(SW, via US 130)*. Approx. 10 mi: BORDEN-TOWN. Interesting buildings include: Imlay-Hopkinson House (1750; later alt. & addit.), 101 Farnsworth St; once home of Francis Hopkinson, member of Continental Congress and signer of Declaration of Independence. *Gilder House (about 1745; later alt. & addit.), Crosswicks & Union sts. Approx. 15 mi farther: BURLINGTON. Interesting buildings include: *Old St. Mary's Episcopal Church (1704; later alt. & addit.), W. Broad St; architect: Robert Mills; fine example by famous architect. Nearby, *New St. Mary's Episcopal Church (1854; damaged by fire 1976; reconst. 1979), architect: Richard Upjohn; architect, reconst.: Richard Murphy; fine Gothic Revival by architect famous for style. James Fenimore Cooper House (about 1780), 457 High St; once home of famous author. *Capt. James Lawrence House (about 1696; later alt. & addit.; rest.), once home of famous naval hero of War of 1812. Few miles SW of Burlington, via Co. Rd: MOUNT HOLLY. Interesting buildings include: Burlington Co. Courthouse (1796; later alt. & addit.), High & Union sts. Also see: Camden & Vicinity.

Trenton Vicinity *(NW, via St. 31)*. Approx. 10 mi: WASHINGTON'S CROSSING. *Johnson, also known as McKonkey, Ferry House (about 1750; later alt. & addit.; rest.), State Park; where Washington's army crossed Delaware River, Christmas, 1776, for attack on Trenton. Also see: Pennsylvania—Philadelphia Vicinity (N, via St. 611). Approx. 20 mi farther: FLEMINGTON. Interesting buildings include: *Doric House (1846; rest.), 114 Main St; architect: Mahlon Fisher. *Samuel Fleming House (1756; rest.), 5 Bonnell St; small house built as inn and residence by founder of town; also known as Fleming Castle for contrast with even smaller houses usual in era.

New York

Early inhabitants Indians of number of tribes, including Cayuga, Delaware, Mohican, Mohawk, Montauk, Oneida, Onondaga, Seneca. First explorer probably Italian Giovanni da Verrazano, 1524, for France; S portion explored by Englishman Henry Hudson, 1609, for Dutch, who claimed territory and named it New Netherland; N portion explored same year by Frenchman Samuel de Champlain. First permanent Dutch settlement, 1624: Albany, originally Ft. Orange. Settled, 1625: New York City, originally New Amsterdam, by Dutch under Director-General (Gov.) Peter Minuit, who bought Manhattan from Indians for goods valued at about 60 Dutch guilders, or about $24; number of other Dutch colonies established. English sent expedition to capture New Netherland, 1664; Dutch Gov. Peter Stuyvesant surrendered it peacefully; ceded to England, 1667. N portion of region explored, 1669, by Frenchman Robert Cavelier, Sieur de La Salle; claimed for France. English and French fought for possession, during French and Indian Wars, 1689–1763; at end of wars, French claims relinquished to England. People had divided sentiments about independence. During Revolution, important battles fought here, including Oriskany and Saratoga, both 1777. Became eleventh state, July 26, 1788. New York City served as U.S. capital, 1785–90. Today: Outranks all other states in manufacturing; wholesale, retail and foreign trade; transportation; communications; finance. Major cultural and educational center. Tourism and agriculture also important.

Land Regions: Quite varied, from Long Island and Staten Island in Atlantic Coastal Plain to, from E to W, New England Upland; Appalachian Plateau; Erie-Ontario Lowland; Adirondack Upland; St. Lawrence Lowland.

Climate: Quite varied; cold winters, cool summers in Adirondack region; much milder winters, hotter summers in SE portion; precipitation also quite varied; somewhat heavy with considerable snow on SW slopes of Adirondacks and Catskills; moderate with less snow in other areas.

Major Building Materials: Iron; stone; sand and gravel.

Architecture: Rich and varied; large number of important examples architecturally and historically, from Colonial era to present. Many of finest U.S. buildings, in many locations, especially in Buffalo and New York City and vicinity.

ALBANY

Interesting buildings include: *State Capitol (1867–99; part. rest.), bet. Eagle, State & Swan sts & Washington Ave; architects: Augustus Laver & Thomas W. Fuller; successor architects: Henry Hobson Richardson; Leopold Eidlitz; Isaac G. Perry; peculiar combination of Eclectic Renaissance Revival, Romanesque Revival; very fine Senate Chambers interiors by Richardson. Across Washington Ave, *State Education Building (1912; later alt.), architect: Henry Hornbostel. Nearby, on Eagle St, *City Hall (1882; later alt.), architect: Henry Hobson Richardson; not considered one of his best designs. Also on Eagle St, *Joseph Henry Memorial Building, originally Old Albany Academy (1817; later alt.; rest.), Academy Park; architect: Philip Hooker, architect, rest.: Marcus T. Reynolds; fine Federal; named for famous physicist who taught here. At N. Pearly & Orange sts, *First Dutch Reformed Church (1799; later alt. & addit.), architect: Philip Hooker. At 9 Ten Broeck Pl, *Gen. Abraham Ten Broeck Mansion (1798; rest.), built by Revolutionary War general, later mayor of Albany. At 27 Clinton St, The Pastures, the *Gen. Philip Schuyler Mansion (1762; later alt. & addit.; rest.), fine Georgian; once home of Revolutionary War general and public official. On S. Pearl St near 1st Ave, *Historic Cherry Hill (1768; later alt. & addit.), Colonial. Across Hudson River: RENSSELAER, *Ft. Crailo (about 1704; later alt.), Riverside Ave; fine manor house built by Hendrick Van Rensselaer. *St. Anthony-on-Hudson, originally Beverwyck (1840; later alt.), Washington St; another Van Rensselaer house, now monastery. Approx. 25 mi S, via St. 9W: COXSACKIE. *Bronck Museum, collection of rest. early buildings, including *Pieter Bronck House (1663; later alt.; rest.); a "Declaration of Independence" was issued in town, 1775.

Albany Vicinity *(N, via US 4).* Approx. 5 mi: TROY. Interesting buildings in *Fifth Ave–Fulton St Hist. Dist. *Hart-Cluett Mansion (1827), 59 2nd St; Classic Revival; fine carriage house and gardens. *Julia Howard Bush Memorial Center, originally First Presbyterian Church (1876; later alt. & addit.), *Russell Sage College, Congress & 1st sts; architect: James Dakin; fine Greek Revival; now concert and lecture hall. Approx. 6 mi farther: VAN SCHAICK ISLAND. *Anthony Van Schaick Mansion (1735; later alt.); approx. 2 mi farther: WATERFORD. *Hugh White House (1830; later alt.), 2 Museum Lane; architect: Joshua Clark. Approx. 10 mi farther: STILLWATER. *John Neilson House (1775; rest.), Saratoga Nat. Hist. Park. Approx. 5 mi E of Stillwater, via St. 67: SCHAGHTICOKE. Georgian *Johannes Knickerbocker Mansion (about 1765). Approx. 8 mi farther: SCHUYERVILLE. *Gen. Philip Schuyler House (1777), Hist. Park. Approx. 12 mi W of Schuylerville, via St. 29: SARATOGA SPRINGS. Interesting buildings include: Yaddo, the Spencer Trask Mansion (1893; later alt.

& addit.), Union Ave; Eclectic Tudor Revival; architect: William Halsey Wood; imposing house, landscaped grounds; since 1926, retreat for great number of famous artists and writers. Approx. 13 mi N of Schuylerville, via US 4: FT. EDWARD. *Old Fort House (1777; rest.), 27 Broadway. Also of interest, approx. 15 mi NW of Ft. Edward: *LAKE GEORGE. Also see: Plattsburgh Vicinity.

Albany Vicinity *(S, via US 9).* Approx. 20 mi: KINDERHOOK. Federal *House of History, the James Vanderpoll House (1810; rest.), 16 Broad St; architect: Barnabas Waterman; in village cemetery, grave of President Martin Van Buren. Nearby, via St. 9H, Dutch Colonial *Van Alen House (1737; rest.). Approx. 15 mi farther, off St. 9G: HUDSON. *Olana, the Frederick E. Church House (1874; addit. 1890), architect: Calvert Vaux; fascinating Eclectic mansion, somewhat Moorish or Persian, on magnificent site overlooking Hudson River; once home, studio and gallery of famous painter, a leader of the "Hudson River School," who contributed to its design; original furnishings and many of Church's paintings. Also: old houses of Front & Lower Warren sts and *Parade Hill Hist. Dist. Approx. 9 mi SW of Hudson, via St. 9G: GERMANTOWN. Georgian *Clermont (1782; later alt. & addit.), Clermont State Park; once home of noted public official and diplomat Robert Livingston who, with James Monroe, made Louisiana Purchase; first successful steamboat, *Clermont,* was named for estate by Robert Fulton who was aided and financed by Livingston. Approx. 20 mi S of Hudson, via US 9: RED HOOK. Federal *Maizefield, the David Van Ness House (1797; later alt. & addit.), 75 W. Market St. Also of interest, approx. 3 mi S of Red Hook, *Old Rhinebeck Aerodrome, with antique planes and occasional air shows. Across the Hudson River from Red Hook, approx. 10 mi: KINGSTON. Number of interesting buildings here, in *Clinton Ave Hist. Dist. and elsewhere, including: *Senate House (1676; burned by British & rebuilt; rest.), 312 Fair St; first state senate met here, 1777; adjacent: Museum (1927); first state governor, George Clinton, buried in adjoining cemetery. *Chapter House, also known as John Tappan House (1696; rest.), Crown & Green sts. Few miles S, via US 209, Dutch Colonial *Bevier House (about 1710; rest.). Approx. 3 mi SW of Kingston, via US 209: HURLEY. In Hist. Dist. of town, originally named Nieuw Dorp, interesting early Dutch Colonial houses include: *Jan Van Deusen House (1725; later alt.). Also see: New York City Vicinity (N, via US 9; N, via George Washington Bridge & US 9W).

Albany Vicinity *(NW, via US I-90 or St. 5).* Approx. 30 mi: AMSTERDAM. *Guy Park Manor (1773; burned, rebuilt same year; later alt. & addit.), 366 W. Main St; once home of Sir Guy Johnson, superintendent of Indian Affairs. Approx. 3 mi farther: FT. JOHNSON. Nearby, via St. 5, *Old Ft. Johnson, originally Mount Johnson (1749; later alt. & addit.), once home of superintendent of Indian Affairs, Sir William Johnson, uncle and father-in-law of Sir Guy; interesting old miller's house, store and outdoor privy.

Approx. 12 mi NW of Ft. Johnson, via St. 5 & 30A: JOHNSTOWN. Fine Georgian *Johnson Hall (1763; later alt. & addit.; rest.), 139 Hall Ave; built, and probably designed, by Sir William Johnson, who is buried in St. John's Cemetery here. Approx. 20 mi W of Ft. Johnson, via US I-90 or St. 5: ST. JOHNSVILLE. Nearby, on St. 5, *Ft. Klock (1750; later alt. & addit.; rest.), built by Johannes Klock; other interesting rest. buildings here. Approx. 11 mi farther: LITTLE FALLS. Nearby, *Gen. Nicholas Herkimer House (1764; rest.), once home of Revolutionary War general. Approx. 40 mi S of Little Falls, via St. 5 & 28: COOPERSTOWN. About 1 mi N, via St. 80, *Farmers' Museum and Village Crossroads, interesting reconst. & rest. 18th- and 19th-century buildings; most moved here from other locations, including *Joseph Lippitt Farmhouse (1797; rest.), tavern, church, country store, school and other buildings. Across highway, *Fenimore House Museum, Main St. Also of interest, in town, *National Baseball Hall of Fame. About 10 mi N, in Glimmerglass State Park,

•*Hyde Hall, the George Hyde Clarke House (1817; later alt. & addit.; rest.), architect: Philip Hooker; very fine Classic Revival mansion by noted architect. Also see: Syracuse Vicinity (E, via US I-90 or St. 5).

BINGHAMTON

Interesting modern buildings include: *First-City National Bank (1972), 2 Court St; architect: Ulrich Franzen; beside Chenango River. S of city, via St. 434, *State University of New York; master plan architects: Moore & Hutchins; modern *Science Complex (1974), architects: Davis, Brody.

Binghamton Vicinity *(W, via St. 17)*. Approx. 23 mi: OWEGO. Victorian *Tioga County Courthouse (1872; later alt.), The Green; architect: M. F. Howes. Approx. 35 mi farther: ELMIRA. *Mark Twain Study (1872), *Elmira College, small cottage used several summers by famous writer; moved here; writer buried in Woodlawn Cemetery here. Approx. 25 mi N of Elmira, via St. 14: WATKINS GLEN. Greek Revival *John Ireland Manor House (1833; rest.), in Yorker's Yankee Village. Approx. 32 mi N of Elmira, via St. 13: ITHACA. *Cornell University, interesting buildings include two modern examples on Tower Rd, *Bradfield Agronomy Building (1968) and *Veterinary Medicine Research Laboratory (1973); architect of both: Ulrich Franzen.

BUFFALO

Interesting buildings include: •*Guaranty Building (1896; later alt.; rest. 1983), Church & Pearl sts; architects: Dankmar Adler & Louis Sullivan; architects, rest.: Cannon Design; de Polo/Dunbar; very fine early modern office building designed by Sullivan,

**Guaranty Building—
Early Modern**
(Wayne Andrews)

famous modern pioneer; very fine ornament; considered one of finest U.S. buildings. Across street, at Pearl & Erie sts; *St. Paul's Episcopal Cathedral (1815; later alt. & addit.; damaged by fire, rest. 1888), architect: Richard Upjohn; architect, rest.: R. W. Gibson; very fine Gothic Revival by famous architect. Not far: *Ellicott Square Building (1896; later alt.), architect: Daniel Burnham. At 1285 Elmwood Ave, *Albright-Knox Art Gallery (1906; addit. 1962), architect: Edward B. Green; architects, addit.: Skidmore, Owings & Merrill; Eclectic Classic Revival building; fine modern addition. Also of interest nearby: *Delaware Park (1870), planners: Frederick Law Olmsted & Calvert Vaux; one of number of parks in city by famous landscape architect and architect who also designed interconnecting parkways. At 641 Delaware Ave, *Ansley Wilcox House (about 1838; addit. about 1895; rest.), architect, addit.: George Cary; Greek Revival; Theodore Roosevelt sworn in as president here after assassination of President William McKinley at Buffalo Pan-American Exposition, 1901. Frank Lloyd Wright's magnificent Larkin Building (1903) on Seneca St was demolished, 1950; he designed several fine Prairie style houses here, all private, including:
●*Darwin D. Martin House (1904), 125 Jewett Pkwy. Barton House (1903), 118 Summit Ave; Heath House (1905), 76 Soldiers Place; Davidson House (1908), 57 Tillinghast Pl.

Buffalo Vicinity *(N, via St. 70).* Approx. 22 mi: LOCKPORT. *Col. William Moulton Bond House (1825; rest.), 143 Ontario St; Classic Revival, *Outwater-Scott House (1860; later alt.), 215 Niagara St. Adjacent: *Washington Hunt Law Office (1835), once used by governor of state.

Buffalo Vicinity *(NW, via US I-190).* Approx. 20 mi: NIAGARA FALLS. Interesting modern buildings, including: *Convention Center (1974), 4th St & Rainbow Center; architects: Philip Johnson & John Burgee. *Winter Garden (1977), Rainbow Blvd; architects: Victor Gruen Assoc. Also: *Rainbow Center Mall; *Earl W. Brydges Public Library (1974), architect: Paul Rudolph. Also of interest: falls, including Niagara, American, Horseshoe, Canadian. Approx. 13 mi farther: YOUNGSTOWN. *Old Ft. Niagara (1726; later addit.; rest.), State Park.

NEW YORK CITY

Divided into five boroughs: Manhattan, the Bronx, Brooklyn, Queens and Richmond (Staten Island). World center of fine architecture, presented here by boroughs and, in case of Manhattan, by major areas. Walking tours feasible in some areas, such as Midtown or Downtown Manhattan; in some areas, widely separated examples make transportation by subway, bus or taxi more convenient. Along the way, many city scenes and happenings, often as fascinating as the architecture.

UPPER MANHATTAN

Dominated by: *Central Park (1859; later alt. & addit.), bet. 5th Ave, Central Park W, 59th & 110 sts; planners: Frederick Law Olmsted & Calvert Vaux; wonderful park without equal in U.S.; by famous landscape architect and architect; approx. 840 acres with many kinds of attractions; divides Upper Manhattan into Upper East Side and Upper West Side.

Manhattan—Upper East Side. Large number of interesting buildings, especially houses of several styles. Finest examples, somewhat scattered, include: *Abigail Adams Smith House, 421 E. 61st St, bet. York & 1st aves; now Colonial Dames of America Club (1799; later alt.; rest.); simple Georgian; stable converted to home of daughter of President John Adams. Not far: *Treadwell Farms Hist. Dist., bet. 2nd & 3rd aves & 61st & 62nd sts; almost uniform houses built 1870. On and near 5th Ave, great art museums include: *Frick Collection, formerly Henry Clay Frick House (1914; remod. 1935; later addit.), 1 E. 70th St. just off 5th Ave; architects: Carrère & Hastings; architect, remod.: John Russell Pope; Eclectic Renaissance Revival; fine interior, glass-roofed courtyard. Few blocks away: •*Whitney Museum of American Art (1966), 945 Madison Ave at 75th St; architects: Marcel Breuer &

Solomon R. Guggenheim Museum—Modern
(Guggenheim Museum, Robert E. Mates)

Hamilton P. Smith; fascinating modern concrete building; upper floors cantilevered over moat, entrance bridge; interesting art collections. A few blocks away: ●●**Metropolitan Museum of Art** (1880; addit. 1888, 1895, 1902, 1906, 1965, 1980), in Central Park, facing 5th Ave bet. 80th & 84th sts; architects: Calvert Vaux & Jacob Wrey Mould; architects, addit.: 1888, Theodore Weston; 1895, Richard Morris Hunt; 1902, Richard Howland Hunt; 1906, McKim, Mead & White; 1965, Brown, Lawford & Forbes; 1980, Kevin Roche & John Dinkeloo, fascinating "grande dame" of U.S. art museums; hodge-podge of styles ranging from Eclectic Renaissance Revival to ultra-modern; art collections without peer in U.S. or almost anywhere. Few blocks up avenue: ●●**Solomon R. Guggenheim Museum** (1959), 1071 5th Ave bet. 88th & 89th sts; architect: Frank Lloyd Wright; magnificent modern building by famous architect; considered masterpiece of his later career and one of finest U.S. buildings; unusual inverted cone shape; interior spiral ramp for viewing art which is almost overcome by art of building itself. Few blocks up avenue: *International Center of Photography (1914; later alt. & addit.), 5th Ave & 94th St; architects: Delano & Aldrich; Eclectic Georgian Revival; originally home of Willard Straight. Many fine houses in area, mostly private, include those in *Henderson Place Hist. Dist., E. 86th St bet. York & East End aves; delightful, small Eclectic Queen Anne Revival houses (about 1885). In Carl Schurz Park at 88th St, *Gracie Mansion (1799; later alt. & addit.; rest.), official residence of mayor of city. In Harlem, interesting sights include few that are architectural: *St. Nicholas Hist. Dist. bet. 7th & 8th aves, 138th & 139th Sts, Striver's Row; fine row houses, many by famous firm of McKim, Mead & White. In East

Harlem, *1199 Plaza (1975), 1st Ave bet. 107th & 111th sts; architects: Hodne & Stageberg; modern complex of high- and low-rise apartments. At Madison Ave & E. 121st St, *Watchtower (about 1857), architect: James Bogardus; interesting iron structure by architect of many iron-front buildings in city and elsewhere.

Manhattan—Upper West Side. Interesting area of city; the few important buildings include: *Lincoln Center for the Performing Arts (1959–68), bet. Columbus & Amsterdam aves, W. 62nd & 66th sts; director of architecture: Wallace K. Harrison; interesting modern cultural complex; buildings by noted architects, arranged around court, include: *Avery Fisher Hall, originally Philharmonic Hall (1962; remod. 1976), architect: Max Abramovitz; architect, remod.: Philip Johnson; *New York State Theater (1964), architects: Philip Johnson & Richard Foster; *Metropolitan Opera House (1966), architect: Wallace K. Harrison; *Vivian Beaumont Theater (1965), architect: Eero Saarinen; *Juilliard School of Music (1968), architects: Pietro Belluschi & Eduardo Catalano; Westerman & Miller. ●*The Dakota (1884; later alt.), 1 W. 72nd St & Central Park W; architect: Henry J. Hardenbergh; very interesting first luxury apartment in city; name came from its distant location, which seemed as far away as Dakota Territory; now co-op; gained unwanted notoriety with murder of Beatle John Lennon, 1980; other interesting apartment buildings in vicinity. At Manhattan Square, Central Park W, *American Museum of Natural History (1877; later alt. & addit.), architect: J. C. Cady; architects, addit.: 1935, Trowbridge & Livingston; 1936, John Russell Pope; very fine scientific collections. In Morningside Heights area of city, NW of Central Park:
●*Cathedral Church of St. John the Divine (begun 1892), Amsterdam Ave near W. 112th St; architects, 1892–1911: Heins & LaFarge; 1911–42, Cram & Ferguson, 1966–, Adams & Woodbridge; very fine church, largest in modern times; originally designed as Byzantine Romanesque Revival, changed to Gothic Revival by Ralph Adams Cram; magnificent interior. Nearby, *Columbia University, Amsterdam Ave bet. 114th & 120th sts; fine and interesting buildings include: ●*Low Memorial Library (1897; later alt.), architects: McKim, Mead & White; very fine Eclectic example by famous firm; now administration offices. Nearby, by same architects: Eclectic Renaissance Revival *Avery Hall (1912; later alt.), occupied by School of Architecture and Avery Library, largest architectural library in U.S. Also: *St. Paul's Chapel (1904), architects: Howell & Stokes. N of Morningside Heights, in Hamilton Heights: Federal *Hamilton Grange (1802; rest.), 287 Convent Ave; architect: John McComb, Jr.; last home of famous statesman Alexander Hamilton; moved here. N of Hamilton Heights, interesting buildings include: *Chapel of the Intercession (1914), Trinity Cemetery, Broadway & W. 155th St; architects: Cram, Goodhue & Ferguson; very large, fine Gothic

Rockefeller Center—Modern (Thomas Airviews)

Revival example on site overlooking Hudson River. Not far: *Morris-Jumel Mansion (about 1765; alt. 1810; later alt.), Edgecomb Ave & W. 160th St; summer home of Loyalist, or Tory, Robert Morris; later Washington's headquarters, 1776; alt. to Federal style. At Broadway & W. 175th St: flamboyant Moorish style *Loew's 175th Street Theater; architect: Thomas Lamb. Also of interest: fine *George Washington Bridge (1931; later alt.), engineer: Othmar Ammann; consult. architect: Cass Gilbert; interesting modern: *Bus Station (1963), designed by famous Italian engineer Pier Luigi Nervi. In *Fort Tryon Park, off Riverside Dr, *The Cloisters (1938; later alt. & addit.), architect: Charles Collens; architects, alt. & addit.: Brown, Lawford & Forbes; medieval collections of Metropolitan Museum of Art, including portions of authentic medieval monasteries and chapels. Not far: ●*Dyckman House (1783), 4881 Broadway & 204th St; fine Dutch Colonial example; some original furnishings; lone surviving 18th-century farmhouse in city.

MANHATTAN—MIDTOWN

Interesting buildings include: ●***Rockefeller Center** (1931–40), bet. 5th Ave, Ave of Americas, 48th & 51st sts; architects: Reinhard & Hofmeister; Corbett, Harrison & MacMurray; Hood & Fouilhoux; marvelous complex of buildings clustered around interesting plaza; first important complex of its kind; office buildings, interesting shops, restaurants, ice-skating rink, *Radio City Music Hall, home of famous Rockettes, *RCA Building observation deck and other attractions. Not far: ●***CBS Building** (1965), 51 W. 52nd St at Ave of Americas; architect: Eero Saarinen; fine modern, only high-rise office building by famous architect; interesting, elegant restaurant completely designed by architect's firm. Nearby ●***Museum of Modern Art** (1939; alt, & addit. 1951 & 1964; addit. 1982), 11 W. 53rd St, bet. 5th Ave & Ave of Americas; architects: Philip Goodwin & Edward Durell Stone; architect, 1951 & 1964 alt. & addit.: Philip Johnson; architect, 1983 addit.: Cesar Pelli; fine modern building thought to be first designed to display its collections properly; sculpture garden; attached: Museum Tower Apartments (1983), architect: Cesar Pelli. Not far: *Plaza Hotel (1907; later alt.), just off 5th Ave bet. 58th & 59th sts, facing the Plaza; architect: Henry J. Hardenbergh; elegant hotel, somewhat Eclectic French Renaissance Revival. At Madison Ave & 55th St, so-called post-modern *AT&T Corporate Headquarters (1983), architects: Philip Johnson & John Burgee; high-rise offices with Eclectic columns, roof and other details. At 1 W. 54th St & 5th Ave, fine Eclectic Italian Renaissance Revival University Club (1899; later alt.), architects: McKim, Mead & White. At 1 W. 53rd St & 5th Ave, fine Eclectic Gothic Revival *St. Thomas Church, Episcopal (1914; later alt.), architects: Cram, Goodhue & Ferguson. Just down the street, at 3 E. 53rd just off 5th Ave, delightful little *Paley Park (1967), landscape architects: Zion & Breen. Not far: ●***St. Patrick's Cathedral, Roman Catholic** (1858–79), 5th to Madison aves bet. 50th & 51st sts; architect: James Renwick; very fine, imposing Gothic Revival

St. Patrick's Cathedral—
Gothic Revival (Library of Congress)

(Left) **Seagram Building—Modern** (Joseph W. Molitor)
(Right) **Lever House—Modern** (Joseph W. Molitor)

example by famous architect; interesting *Lady Chapel (1906), architect: Charles T. Matthews. Nearby, *Villard Houses (1886; later alt.), Madison Ave bet. 50th & 51st Sts; architects: McKim, Mead & White; fine Eclectic Italian Renaissance Revival townhouses converted to offices and entrance and public rooms of *Helmsley Palace Hotel (1980); architects: Emery Roth & Sons. Not far: *St. Bartholomew's Church, Episcopal (1919; later alt.), Park Ave bet. 50th & 51st sts; architect: Bertram G. Goodhue; Eclectic Byzantine Revival. Just up avenue: •*Seagram Building (1958), 375 Park Ave bet. 52nd & 53rd sts; architects: Ludwig Mies van der Rohe & Philip Johnson; assoc. architects: Kahn & Jacobs; very fine modern office building, his first, by famous architect; open plaza; elegant restaurant interior and furnishings designed by Johnson; considered one of finest U.S. buildings. Across avenue: Racquet and Tennis Club (1918; later alt.), 370 Park Ave bet. 52nd & 53rd sts; architects: McKim, Mead & White; another Eclectic Italian Renaissance Revival example by famous firm. A block away: •*Lever House (1952), 390 5th Ave bet. 53rd & 54th sts; architects: Skidmore, Owings & Merrill; very fine office building by famous firm; pioneered open site and glass curtain wall; considered one of finest U.S. buildings. Not far: •*Citicorp (1977), Lexington Ave bet. 53rd & 54th sts; architect: Hugh Stubbins; more recent very fine office building; multi-level interior court with shops, restaurants, open space, landscaping; filled with

(Left) **Daily News Building—Early Modern** (Joseph W. Molitor)
(Right) **Chrysler Building—Art Deco** (Wurts Brothers)

people and activities from early morning until late at night. Not far: *Greenacre Park (1971), 217 E. 51st St bet. 2nd & 3rd aves; landscape architect: Hideo Sasaki. Not far: *Turtle Bay Hist. Dist., 226–246 E. 49th St and 227–247 E. 48th St bet. 2nd & 3rd aves; rows of houses (about 1865; remod. 1920); common path and gardens between. Not far: ●●**United Nations Headquarters** (1953), United Nations Plaza, 1st Ave bet. 42nd & 48th sts; architects: international committee, chairman: Wallace K. Harrison (U.S.); 13 other members, including LeCorbusier (France), Oscar Niemeyer (Brazil), Sven Markelius (Sweden); interesting modern complex of buildings; landscaped grounds; interesting works of art. On other side of Plaza and nearby, number of modern office, apartment and other types of buildings, including: *One United Nations Plaza (1976), 44th St & 1st Ave; architects: Kevin Roche & John Dinkeloo. Nearby, ●●**Ford Foundation Building** (1967), 320 E. 43rd St bet. 1st & 2nd aves; architects: Kevin Roche & John Dinkeloo; landscape architect: Daniel Kiley; very fine modern building by noted architects; offices arranged around beautifully landscaped atrium. Not far: ●●**Daily News Building** (1930; addit. 1958), 220 E. 42nd St; architects: Raymond M. Hood & John Mead Howells; architects, addit.: Harrison & Abramovitz; fine early modern skyscraper by noted architects. Not far, another example of same era: ●●**Chrysler Building** (1930; later alt.), 405 Lexington Ave bet. 42nd & 43rd sts; architect: William Van Alen;

Grand Central Station—Eclectic Beaux Arts (Library of Congress)

fine Art Deco example by noted architect; fine lobby and details. Next block: ●***Grand Central Station** (1903–1913; later alt.), 42nd St bet. Lexington & Vanderbilt aves; architects: Warren & Wetmore; Reed & Stem; very fine Eclectic Beaux Arts; marvelous vaulted ceiling over main waiting room, upper level. Few blocks away: *****Sniffen Court** (about 1855; later alt.), 152 E. 36th St bet. 3rd & Lexington aves; interesting group of Romanesque Revival carriage houses. Not far: ●*****Empire State Building** (1931; later alt.), 350 5th Ave bet. 33rd & 34th sts; architects: Shreve, Lamb & Harmon; very fine early modern skyscraper, tallest in world for 40 years; striking tower and ever-popular observation platforms offering wonderful views of city, rivers and harbor. Not far: ●*****Morgan Library** (1907; addit. 1928, 1960, 1977), 33 E. 36th St bet. Madison & Park aves; architects: McKim, Mead & White; architects, addit.: 1928, Benjamin W. Morris; 1960, Alexander Perry Morgan; 1970, Platt, Wyckoff & Coles; Eclectic Italian Renaissance Revival gem; fine collection of books, manuscripts and prints. Not far: ●*****New York Public Library** (1898–1911), 5th Ave bet. 40th & 42nd sts; architects: Carrère & Hastings; magnificent Eclectic Beaux Arts by noted architects, considered among finest examples of style and era and one of finest U.S. buildings. Directly behind: *****Bryant Park**. Across from park: *****American Radiator Building** (1924; later alt.), 40 W. 40th St; architect: Raymond Hood; interesting black and gold colored, inside and out, example by famous architect. Not far: ●*****Manufacturers Hanover Trust** (1954), 510 5th Ave at 43rd St; architects: Skidmore, Owings & Merrill; very fine, small modern bank; glass window wall reveals interior, including vault. About 5

**Empire State Building—
Early Modern**
(Wurts Brothers)

**New York Public
Library—
Eclectic Beaux Arts**
(Library of Congress)

blocks away, interesting early modern office building:
•*Old McGraw-Hill Building, now Group Health Insurance, (1931; later alt.), 330 W. 42nd St bet. 8th & 9th aves; architects: Raymond M. Hood, with Godley & Fouilhoux. Also of interest, few blocks away, at W. 46th St & Hudson River Pier 86: aircraft carrier U.S.S. *Intrepid*. Approx. 8 blocks S, *General Post Office (1913; later alt), 8th Ave bet. 31st & 33rd sts; architects: McKim, Mead & White; Eclectic Classic Revival. Few blocks:
•*Starrett-Lehigh Building (1931; later alt.), bet. 26th & 27th sts & 11th & 12th aves; architects: Russell G. & Walter F. Cory; assoc. architect: Yatsuo Matsui; fine early modern industrial building; pioneered bands of glass windows. Not far:
•*Flatiron Building, originally Fuller Building (1903; later alt.), bet. Broadway & 5th Ave, 22nd & 23rd sts; architect: D. H. Burnham & Co.; interesting Eclectic office building by famous architect; name changed to reflect triangular shape required by site. Not far: *Theodore Roosevelt House (1848; later remod.; rest.), 28 E. 20th St bet. Broadway & Park Ave; birthplace of U.S. president. Across from *Gramercy Park Hist. Dist., bet. Irving Pl & Park Ave, two fine houses: Players Club (1845; later remod. & alt.), 16 Gramercy Park S; architect, remod.: Stanford White; once home of famous actor Edwin Booth; National Arts Club (1874; later alt.), architect: Calvert Vaux; once home of Samuel J. Tilden, governor of state and unsuccessful U.S. presidential candidate.

LOWER MANHATTAN
Number of communities here; among them, Greenwich Village, now Hist. Dist., and Financial Dist. Many things to do and sights

**Grace Church—
Gothic Revival**
(Library of Congress)

New York City Hall—Eclectic (Wayne Andrews)

to be seen in the Village, including one-time homes of famous artists, writers and others. Other interesting architectural examples include: *Memorial Arch (1892), Washington Square Park, architects: McKim, Mead & White.
●*Jefferson Market Library, originally Jefferson Market Courthouse (1877; remod. 1967), 425 Ave of Americas at W. 10th St; architect: Frederick C. Withers; architect, remod.: Giorgio Cavaglieri; fascinating, colorful high Victorian building, lovingly remod. into library. Not far, just outside Village, ●*Grace Church, Episcopal (1846; later alt.), 800 Broadway at E. 10th St; architect: James Renwick, Jr.; magnificent Gothic Revival by famous architect noted for that style. Few blocks E: *St. Mark's in the Bouwerie, Hist. Dist. (1799; addit. 1828; 1854; part. burned 1978), 2nd Ave & E. 10th St; architect: Ithiel Town; Georgian, Greek Revival steeple; built on site of chapel of Gov. Peter Stuyvesant who is buried beneath church; in Dist., interesting Federal houses. Not far: *Old Merchant's House, also known as Seabury Tredwell House (1832), possible architect: Minard Lafever. Few blocks away: ●*Bayard Building, originally Condict Building (1898; later alt.), 65 Bleecker St at Bond St; architect: Louis Sullivan; very fine early modern office building by famous architect, his only example in city. In SoHo district, (So)uth of (Ho)uston St, in *Cast Iron Hist. Dist., wonderful collection of cast-iron front buildings bet. Broadway & W. Broadway, Houston & Canal sts; many have been demolished; survivors include very fine: ●*Haughwout Building (1857; later alt.), 488–92 Broadway at Broome St; architect: J. P. Gaynor.

Financial Dist. walking tour might include: ●*City Hall (1812;

(Left) **Woolworth Building—Eclectic Gothic Revival** (Joseph W. Molitor)
(Right) **Trinity Church—Gothic Revival** (Wurts Brothers)

rest. 1909; rest. 1956), City Hall Park bet. Broadway & Park
Row; architects: John McComb, Jr. & Joseph François Mangin;
architects, rest.: 1909, Grosvenor Atterbury; 1956, Shreve, Lamb
& Harmon; very fine, amazing mixture of Georgian, Federal,
Eclectic French Renaissance. Nearby, interesting buildings of several eras. Also of interest, nearby, *South Street Seaport; magnificent *Brooklyn Bridge (1869–83), engineers: John Augustus
Roebling, Washington A. Roebling. Nearby,
●*Woolworth Building** (1913; later alt.), 233 Broadway at Park Pl;
architect: Cass Gilbert; fine Eclectic Gothic Revival skyscraper,
tallest in world for about 17 years. Nearby, *St. Paul's Chapel
(1766; tower addit. 1794; later alt. & addit.), Broadway bet. Vesey & Fulton sts; architect: Thomas McBean; tower architect,
James C. Lawrence; fine Georgian example; only surviving Colonial church in city. Short distance: *World Trade Center (1966–
80), Church St bet. Vesey & Liberty sts; architects: Minoru Yamasaki and Emery Roth & Sons; two almost identical 110-story,
1,350-foot modern towers; fine restaurant on top of one, observation platforms on other, offering spectacular views of city, rivers,
harbors and vicinity. Nearby, three fine high-rise buildings, all by
Skidmore, Owings & Merrill: *One Liberty Plaza (1972), 165
Broadway; *Marine Midland Building (1968), 140 Broadway;
*Chase Manhattan Bank (1961), 1 Chase Manhattan Plaza.
Along Wall St, number of interesting buildings include: at no. 26,
●*Federal Hall National Memorial,** formerly Subtreasury Build-
ing, originally U.S. Customs House (1842; later alt.; rest.), archi-

tects: Town & Davis; architect, alt.: John Frazee; very fine Greek Revival building; considered one of finest of its era; George Washington took oath as first president on spot where statue of him, by James Quincy Adams Ward, stands today. Not far:

●*Trinity Church (1846; chapel, 1913; addit. 1966), Broadway & Wall sts; architect: Richard Upjohn; architect, chapel: Thomas Nash; architects, addit.: Adams & Woodbridge; magnificent Gothic Revival; considered its architect's masterpiece and one of finest U.S. buildings. Not far: *U.S. Custom House (1909; later alt.; rest.), Bowling Green bet. Broadway & Whitehall St; architect: Cass Gilbert; interesting Eclectic Beaux Arts; interesting exterior sculptures, *Four Continents,* by famous sculptor Daniel Chester French, interior murals by noted painter Reginald Marsh. Nearby, *Fraunces Tavern (originally built 1719; destroyed; reconst. 1907), 54 Pearl St; Washington delivered famous "Farewell Address" in original building, 1783. Also of interest, nearby, *Battery Park; *Staten Island Ferry; in harbor, *Statue of Liberty (1884), sculptor: Frederic Bartholdi; engineer: Gustave Eiffel; architect, base: Richard Morris Hunt.

THE BRONX

N & E of Manhattan. Interesting buildings include: At *College of Mount Saint Vincent, W. 261st St & Palisade Ave, *Library, formerly named Fonthill Castle (1852; later alt.), resembles medieval fort. Nearby, on Henry Hudson Pkwy, two fine, small Gothic Revival churches, by famous architects, at W. 252nd St: *Christ Church (1866), architect: Richard Upjohn; and at W. 249th St, *Riverdale Presbyterian Church (1863), architect: James Renwick, Jr. At 675 253rd St & Sycamore Ave, fine Federal Wave Hill (1830; later alt. & addit.). Not far: *Van Cortlandt Mansion (1748; later alt.), Van Cortlandt Park, Broadway & W. 246th St;

Federal Hall National Memorial—Greek Revival (Joseph W. Molitor)

fine stone Georgian country house; fine interior and furnishings. Not far: Valentine-Varian House (1775; later alt.), Bainbridge Ave bet. Van Cortlandt Ave & E. 208th St; fine stone house, once home of Isaac Varian, mayor of New York City. In *Poe Park, Grand Concourse & Kingsbridge Rd, *Poe Cottage (1816; rest.), once home of famous poet Edgar Allan Poe; moved here. At *New York University, W. 180th St & University Blvd, interesting buildings include: *Gould Library (1900; later alt.), architects: McKim, Mead & White; fine Eclectic Classic Revival. Also by same architects: *Hall of Fame (1900); *Cornelius Baker Hall of Philosophy (1912; later alt.); *Hall of Languages (1894; later alt.). Modern examples include: *Technology Building and Begrisch Lecture Hall (1964), architect: Marcel Breuer; assoc. architect: Hamilton P. Smith.

At New York Zoological Park, the *"Bronx Zoo," Bronx Pelham & Bronx River pkwys, interesting buildings include modern *World of Birds Building (1972) and *World of Darkness Building (1969); architect of both: Morris Ketchum, Jr. Nearby, in Bronx Park, *New York Botanical Garden, *Conservatory (1900; rest.), architect: William R. Cobb; architect, rest.: Edward Larrabee Barnes. At 1200 Waters Pl, near intersect. of Hutchinson River Pkwy & Westchester Ave, Bronx Developmental Center (1977), architect: Richard Meier; interesting modern treatment center. At Pelham Bay Park, on Shore Rd, *Bartow-Pell Mansion (1675; badly damaged about 1776; rebuilt 1790; remod. about 1845; rest. 1914), probable architect, 1845 remod.: Minard Lafever; large house, once home of Pells, lords of the Manor of Pelham.

BROOKLYN

Interesting buildings include many fine 19th-century houses in fashionable Brooklyn Heights Hist. Dist. just S of magnificent *Brooklyn Bridge (1869–83), bridge engineers: John Augustus Roebling & Washington A. Roebling. Row houses in *Cobble Hill Hist. Dist., originally called Punkiesberg, just S of Brooklyn Heights. In various locations scattered around borough: *Borough Hall, formerly City Hall (1851; cupola 1898; later alt.), 209 Joralemon St at Court & Fulton sts; architect: Gamaliel King; architects, cupola: C. W. & A. A. Houghton; Greek Revival; Victorian cupola. At 5th Ave & 25th St, *Gatehouse (1861), Green Wood Cemetery; architect: Richard M. Upjohn; fantastic Gothic Revival. *Reformed Protestant Dutch Church (1796; later alt. & addit.), Church & Flatbush aves; architect: Thomas Fardon. *Peter Lefferts House (1777–83; rest.), Prospect Park, bet. Flatbush & Parkside aves & Prospect Park W & SW; simple farmhouse moved here. Also interesting: marvelous *Prospect Park (1872), planners: Frederick Law Olmsted & Calvert Vaux. Also of interest: *Verrazano-Narrows Bridge (1964), engineer: Othmar H. Ammann; *Brooklyn Botanic Garden.

QUEENS

Interesting buildings, widely scattered, include: *John F. Kennedy International Airport, formerly Idlewild (begun 1942), Van Wyck Expwy & Southern Pkwy; modern complex of individual airline terminals and other buildings by number of noted architects, on large, landscaped site, include: ••*TWA Flight Center** (1962), architect: Eero Saarinen; very fine modern building by famous architect; noted for soaring roof and interesting interior forms and spaces. At Jamaica Ave & 150th St, *King Mansion (1730; addit. 1755; addit. 1806; rest.), once home of statesman Rufus King and of his son, John Alsop King, governor of state. At 37–01 Bowne Ave bet. 37th & 38th sts, *John Bowne House (1661; rest.), once home of man jailed and tried by Dutch Gov. Peter Stuyvesant for holding Quaker meetings here; acquittal milestone in establishment of religious freedom in colony. Also of interest: surviving buildings of 1939 and 1964 world's fairs, Flushing Meadow Park, off Grand Central Pkwy. Nearby, *U.S. Tennis Center; *Shea Stadium.

RICHMOND (Staten Island)

Borough one of most historic areas of city; reached by Staten Island Ferry from Battery Park in Manhattan, Verrazano-Narrows Bridge from SW Brooklyn, or bridges from Bayonne, Elizabeth or Perth Amboy, N.J. Interesting buildings, mostly widely separated, include: near ferry terminal, Eclectic *Borough Hall (1906; later alt.) and *Richmond Co. Courthouse (1919; later alt.); architects of both: Carrère & Hastings. Not far: amazing collection, ••*Sailors' Snug Harbor,** now called Snug Harbor Cultural Center, Richmond Terr, bet. Tysen St & Kissell Ave; five very fine interconnected Greek Revival buildings (1831–80; later alt.), domed administration building (1832; later alt.), chapel (about 1854; later alt.), and other buildings; architects: Minard Lafever, Martin E. Thompson, possibly others; established as home for old seamen retired from sea. At end of Verrazano-Narrows Bridge, old *Ft. Weed (about 1840; later alt.), Ft. Wadsworth, S end of Bay St. On Richmond Rd, at no. 1476 bet. Norden St & Forest Rd, *Biliou-Stilwell-Perine House (1662; addit. 1680, 1760, 1790, 1830), sprawling house; original portion only survivor on island from New Netherland era. At intersect., S end of Richmond & Authur Kill rds, *Richmondtown Restoration: interesting 17th- to 19th-century buildings in rest. & reconst. of town, founded 1685 as "Cocclestown," include: very fine Dutch Colonial *Lake-Tysen House (about 1740; rest.), moved here from nearby; *Voorlezer House (about 1695; rest.), reputed to be oldest surviving schoolhouse in U.S. At 76 Old Amboy Rd bet. Pacific & Richmond aves, *St. Alban's Episcopal Church (about 1855; later alt.), architect: Richard Upjohn; charming, small wood-frame Gothic Revival. Near S tip of island, *Billopp House, also known as Conference House (1680; later alt.; rest.), interesting stone house in which conference was held, 1776, by Benjamin Franklin, John Adams and Edward Rutledge with British Admiral Lord Richard Howe, in early attempt to end Revolution.

New York City Vicinity *(N, via George Washington Bridge & US 9W)*. Approx. 20 mi: TAPPAN. Dutch Colonial *John DeWint House, also known as George Washington Masonic Shrine (1700; later alt.), 20 Livingston St; Washington's headquarters, 1780 & 1783. Nearby, British Maj. John André was tried and hanged for spy activities for Benedict Arnold. Approx. 30 mi farther: WEST POINT. Interesting buildings and grounds of *U.S. Military Academy. Nearby, on Constitution Island, *Henry Warner House (about 1800; addit. 1836). Approx. 12 mi farther: NEWBURGH. *Jonathan Hasbrouck House, also known as Washington's headquarters (1750; later alt. & addit.; rest.), Liberty & Washington sts; used by general, 1782–83. *David Crawford House (1831; later alt.), 189 Montgomery St. Approx. 5 mi SW of Newburgh, via St. 94: VAILS GATE. *Gen. Henry Knox Headquarters (1754; later alt.), once used by Revolutionary War hero; also used by Gen. Horatio Gates and Gen. Nathanael Greene. Approx. 30 mi SW of Newburgh, via US I-84 & St. 17: GOSHEN. *Orange Co. Government Center (1970), 265 Main St; architect: Paul Rudolph; assoc. architect: Peter B. Barbone; modern courthouse and office complex by noted architect. Approx. 10 mi SE of Goshen, via St. 17: MONROE. *Old Museum Village of Smith's Clove; interesting collection of rest. or reconst. buildings of 19th century and earlier. Approx. 15 mi SW of Monroe, via St. 17 & 94: WARWICK. *1810 House (1810; later alt.), 80 Main St. *Old Shingle House (1764; later alt.), Forester Ave; interesting saltbox. Approx. 20 mi N of Newburgh, via US I-87: NEW PALTZ. *Huguenot State Hist. Dist.; number of interesting rest. houses including: *Jean Hasbrouck House (1814; later alt.). Approx. 8 mi NE of New Paltz, via St. 299 & US 9W: WEST PARK. *John Burroughs House (1873; burned; reconst.), once home of famous naturalist. Approx. 1 mi: *Slabsides (1896), rustic retreat built by naturalist. Also see: Albany Vicinity (S, via US 9).

New York City Vicinity *(N, via St. 22)*. Approx. 20 mi: SCARSDALE. *Wayside Cottage (about 1725; rest.), 1039 Post Rd (St. 22), once inn. Approx. 5 mi farther: NORTH WHITE PLAINS. *Elijah Miller House, another Washington's headquarters (about 1730; later alt.), Virginia Rd; used by general during Battle of White Plains, 1776, and later. Approx. 18 mi farther: KATONAH. *John Jay House (about 1800; addit. 1922), once home of famous public official and first U.S. Supreme Court Chief Justice. Approx. 6 mi farther: NORTH SALEM. *Baptist Church (1878; later alt.), architect: J. A. Wood; fine Gothic Revival.

New York City Vicinity *(N, via US 9)*. Approx. 15 mi: YONKERS. **Philipse Manor (about 1682; addit. about 1745; rest.), Warbur-

Lyndhurst—Gothic Revival
(Wayne Andrews)

ton Ave & Dock St; fine early mansion, once home of Frederick Philipse. Not far, at 511 Warburton Ave, modern *Hudson River Museum (1968), Trevor Park; architects: Sherwood, Mills & Smith. Approx. 10 mi farther: TARRYTOWN. ●*Lyndhurst (1838; addit. 1865; rest.), 635 S. Broadway; architect: Alexander Jackson Davis; very fine Gothic Revival house; once home of noted financier Jay Gould; by famous architect. Not far: *Sunnyside (1835–47; rest.), W. Sunnyside Lane; fanciful Gothic Revival; once home of famous author Washington Irving. Approx. 1 mi farther: NORTH TARRYTOWN. Nearby, just off US 9, *Upper Mills, the Philipsburg Manor (about 1683; later alt. & addit.; rest.), once belonged to Frederick Philipse; interesting old house with gristmill, and other buildings, dam and pond. Not far, on US 9, *Old Dutch Church (1684–97; rest.), Sleepy Hollow; with cemetery in which Irving and other famous people are buried. Approx. 8 mi farther, off US 9, near CROTON-ON-HUDSON.

●*Van Cortlandt Manor (about 1680; later alt. & addit.; rest.), fine Dutch Colonial; interesting rest. *Ferry House and Reconst. *Ferry House Kitchen. Approx. 14 mi N, via St. 9D: GARRISON. *Boscobel, the Staats Morris Dyckman Mansion (1805; later alt. & addit.; rest.), moved here from just downriver; *Dick's Castle (1911; later alt.), concrete "Moorish castle." Approx. 11 mi farther, via St. 9D: BEACON. Dutch Colonial *Madame Brett House (1709; later alt.), 50 Van Nydeck Rd. Approx. 17 mi N, via St. 9D & US 9: POUGHKEEPSIE. *Gov. George Clinton House (about 1765; later alt.), 549 Main St. Approx. 6 mi farther: HYDE PARK. Just S, *Franklin D. Roosevelt House (about 1826; later alt.; & addit.), large mansion birthplace and home of president; he and wife, Eleanor, buried in Rose Garden. Just N of Hyde Park, *Frederick Vanderbilt Mansion (1898), architects: McKim, Mead & White; imposing Eclectic Italian Renaissance Revival by famous firm. Approx. 4 mi farther: STAATSBURG. *Ogden Mills House (1832; remod. 1895), architect, remod.: Stanford White; now museum and State Park. Also see: Albany Vicinity (S, via US 9).

New York City Vicinity *(NE, via US I-95).* Approx. 10 mi: NEW
ROCHELLE. *Thomas Paine Cottage (about 1800; later alt.), Paine
& North aves; once home of famous author of pamphlets in favor of
American independence. Nearby, at 989 North Ave, *Paine Memo-
rial Building (1922); interesting exhibits. Approx. 6 mi farther
RYE. *Square House (about 1700; rest.), Purchase St & Boston
Post Rd. Approx. 3 mi farther: PORT CHESTER. Georgian *Abra-
ham Bush Home (about 1750; later alt.), 479 King St, John Lyon
Park; headquarters of Gen. Israel Putnam, 1777–78. Approx. 1 mi
W of Port Chester: PURCHASE. *Manhattanville College, *Ophir
Hall, formerly Reid Hall (about 1864; burned, reconst. 1888; addit.
1912), architects, addit.: McKim, Mead and White; huge, 84-room
Eclectic mansion with chapel and coach house; now college administration building. Not far: modern *State University of New York
(1971–78), architect, master plan and several fine buildings: Edward Larrabee Barnes; also fine buildings by Paul Rudolph, Gunnar Birkerts, Philip Johnson & John Burgee, The Architects Collaborative (TAC), others.

New York City Vicinity *(Northern Long Island, E, via St. 25A).*
Approx. 14 mi: KINGS POINT. *U.S. Merchant Marine Academy.
Approx. 3 mi farther: ROSLYN. *Grist Mill (1744; rest.); *Tea
House-Museum (about 1700; later alt.); Federal *Valentine House,
now Village Hall (about 1800; later alt. & addit.), 1 Paper Mill Rd.
Approx. 8 mi farther, off St. 25A, via St. 106: OYSTER BAY. Approx.
4 mi E, *Sagamore Hill, the *Theodore Roosevelt House (1885;
later alt. & addit.), architects: Lamb & Rich; once summer home of
president, now Hist. Site. Nearby, *Old Orchard Museum, once
home of Theodore Roosevelt, Jr. Also of interest, approx. 2 mi
toward town, on E. Main St, *Roosevelt Bird Sanctuary and Trail-
side Museum. Nearby, *Young Memorial Cemetery, in which president is buried. In town: *Raynham Hall, the Samuel Townsend
House (1738; addit. 1851; rest.), 20 W. Main St; Samuel's son,
Robert, was partially responsible for discovery of plot against West
Point by Benedict Arnold and Major André and for capture of latter. Approx. 9 mi farther; HUNTINGTON. *Thomas Powell House
(about 1663; later alt. & addit.), 434 Park Ave. *David Conklin
House (about 1750; later alt.), 2 High St; New England saltbox.
Short distance away: HUNTINGTON STATION. *Walt Whitman
House (about 1810; later alt.), 246 Walt Whitman Rd; birthplace
of famous poet. Approx. 3 mi farther: CENTERPORT. *Eagle's Nest,
the William K. Vanderbilt Mansion, now museum (1930; later alt.),
Little Neck Rd; Eclectic Spanish-Moroccan Revival. Approx. 10
mi, via St. 25A & 25: SMITHTOWN. *Caleb Smith House (about
1819; rest.). Approx. 8 mi farther: SETAUKET. Interesting old buildings include: *Caroline Church of Brookhaven (1729; rest.), Main
St at The Green. *Thompson House (about 1700; later alt. & addit.; rest.), N. Country Rd; saltbox. Nearby: EAST SETAUKET. Another saltbox, *Sherwood-Jayne House (1730; later alt. & addit.),
Old Post Rd. Approx. 15 mi farther: WADING RIVER. *Fram

House, now Wading River Hist. Soc. (about 1810; later alt.), N. Country Rd. Approx. 20 mi farther: CUTCHOGUE. *Old House (1649; later alt. & addit.; rest.), The Green; interesting New England Colonial; moved here 1660. Approx. 6 mi farther: SOUTHOLD. Interesting old buildings include: *Southold Hist. Soc. Museum, with late 19th-century house, barn, tool house and buttery. Approx. 10 mi farther: ORIENT. On Village Lane, *Orange Webb House (about 1740; later alt.), originally inn; moved here. Another old inn: *Village House (about 1790; rest.). Approx. 15 mi S of Orient, via St. 25 & 114 & ferries: SAG HARBOR. From here tour may continue back to city along southern route (see below).

New York City Vicinity *(Southern Long Island, E, via St. 27 & 27A)*. Approx. 24 mi, via St. 27 & Broadway: LAWRENCE. Fine Georgian *Rock Hall (1767; later alt. & addit.; rest.), 199 Broadway. Approx. 20 mi, via Broadway, St. 25 & Meadowbrook Pkwy: OLD WESTBURY. *Westbury House, the John S. Phipps House (1906; later alt.), Old Westbury Rd; architect: George Crawley; impressive Eclectic Georgian Revival example set in *Old Westbury Gardens, 100 acres of beautifully landscaped gardens, forests, lakes, pools, terraces. Approx. 14 mi E, via St. 24: OLD BETHPAGE. *Old Bethpage Village, interesting collection of rest. and reconst. late 18th- and early 19th-century buildings, including houses, shops, churches, other types; some moved here. Approx. 12 mi SE, via St. 24, 109 & 27: WEST BAY SHORE. *Sagitikos Manor (1692; later alt. & addit.). Approx. 13 mi farther, via St. 27A: SAYVILLE. *Matthew Edwards House (about 1785; later alt.), Edwards St & Collins Ave; moved here. Approx. 12 mi farther: SHIRLEY. *Manor of St. George (late 17th century; later alt. & addit.), Smith's Pt; in 127-acre park. Approx. 26 mi farther: SOUTHAMPTON. Interesting buildings include: *Captain Rogers House, now Southampton Hist. Museum (1843; later alt.), 17 Meeting House Lane; on grounds: old school, country store, barns. On Main St, *Elias Pelletreau Silversmith Shop (about 1750; later alt.); *Thomas Halsey House (1648; rest.), saltbox. Approx. 6 mi farther: BRIDGEHAMPTON. Nearby, on St. 27, *William Corwith House (about 1775; later alt. & addit.), once served as church; *Sayrelands (1734; later alt.). Approx. 6 mi farther: EAST HAMPTON. Interesting buildings include: *Home Sweet Home (1660; later alt.), 14 James Lane, Village Green; saltbox; birthplace of John Howard Payne, composer of song for which house named. Next door, *Mulford House (about 1670; later alt.). *Clinton Academy, now museum (1784; later alt.), Main St. Approx. 6 mi NW of East Hampton, via St. 114: SAG HARBOR. Interesting old buildings include: *Customs House (about 1785; rest.), Main & Garden sts; built by Henry Packer Dering, customs official and postmaster. *Old Whalers', or First Presbyterian, Church (1844; rest.), architect: Minard Lafever; charming Eclectic Egyptian Revival, unbelievably of wood, with details of other Eclectic styles; steeple, shaped like sailor's spyglass, destroyed in

1938 hurricane. Lafever also designed nearby *Benjamin Hunt-
ting House, now Suffolk County Whaling Museum (1845; later
alt.), Main St; wood-frame Greek Revival, style for which architect was noted. Approx. 15 mi N of Sag Harbor, via St. 114,
ferries & St. 25: ORIENT. From here tour may be continued back
to city along northern route. See: New York City Vicinity (Northern Long Island, E, via St. 25A).

PLATTSBURGH

Interesting buildings include: *Kent–De Lord House (1797; remod.). Also of interest, W of city, *Adirondack Mountains; S of
city, *Ausable Chasm; *Lake Champlain.

Plattsburgh Vicinity *(W, via St. 3)*. SARANAC LAKE. *Robert
Louis Stevenson Cottage (about 1885), Stevenson Lane; once
home of famous writer. Approx. 10 mi SE, via St. 86, LAKE PLAC-
ID. Noted winter resort, modern *Olympic Village (1980), architects: Hellmuth, Obata & Kassabaum. Just S of town, via St. 73,
*John Brown Farm (1855; rest.), once home of abolitionist buried
here.

Plattsburgh Vicinity *(S, via St. 22)*. Approx. 58 mi: CROWN
POINT. Nearby, in IRONVILLE, Federal *Penfield House (1828;
later alt. & addit.), ruins of British *Ft. Crown Point (1759);
French *Ft. St. Frederick (1731). Approx. 7 mi farther, via St. 74:
TICONDEROGA. *Ft. Ticonderoga (begun 1755; reconst.).

ROCHESTER

Interesting buildings include: *Campbell-Whittlesey House
(1836; rest.), 123 S. Fitzhugh St; fine Greek Revival. *Woodside,
the Silas O. Smith House (1840), 485 East Ave; architect: Alfred
Mason; fine Greek Revival. *George Eastman House (1905; later
alt. & addit.), 900 East Ave; once home of famous inventor and
industrialist, now museum of photography; on grounds: *George
Eastman Birthplace (about 1830); moved here from Waterville,
N.Y. *Stone-Tolan House (about 1780; rest.), 2370 East Ave;
once tavern, inn. At 17 Madison St, *Susan B. Anthony House
(about 1850; later alt.), once home of famous leader of women's
suffrage movement. At 11 Livingston Park, *Hervey Ely House
(1837; later alt.), architect: Hugh Hastings. At 220 S. Winton Rd,
•*First Unitarian Church (1963), architect: Louis I. Kahn; very
fine modern by famous architect. Also, SW of city, via St. 15 &
Jefferson Rd, fine modern buildings of *Rochester Institute of
Technology; architects of various buildings: Anderson, Beckwith
& Haible; Cougan & Balestiere; Edward Larrabee Barnes; Kevin

Roche & John Dinkeloo; Hugh Stubbins; Harry Weese. Adjacent: *National Technical Institute for the Deaf (1975), Jefferson Rd & John St, architect: Hugh Stubbins; fine modern institution.

Rochester Vicinity *(E, via St. 31).* Approx. 27 mi: PALMYRA. *Joseph Smith House (1823; later alt.), Stafford Rd; once home of founder of Church of Jesus Christ of Latter-Day Saints (Mormons); church founded here. Approx. 15 mi farther: LYONS. *Wayne Co. Hist. Soc. Museum, originally sheriff's house, office, jail (1854; later alt. & addit.), 21 Butternut St.

Rochester Vicinity *(SE, via US I-490 & I-90, St. 332).* Approx. 30 mi: CANANDAIGUA. Interesting buildings include: *Gideon Granger House (1816; later alt. & addit.; rest.), 295 Main St; Federal; once home of U.S. postmaster general, and of his son, Francis, who also served in this position. Approx. 15 mi E, via US 20: GENEVA. Interesting buildings include: in Hist. Dist., Federal *Prouty-Chew House (1825; later alt. & addit.; rest.), 543 S. Main St. Approx. 1 mi E of town, via St. 96A, *Rose Hill (1839; rest.), very fine Greek Revival. Approx. 15 mi S of Geneva, via St. 14; DRESDEN. *Robert G. Ingersoll Mem. House (about 1825; later alt. & addit.), birthplace of noted lawyer and orator. Approx. 6 mi E, via St. 54; PENN YANN. *Oliver Mansion (1852; later alt.), 200 Main St.

Rochester Vicinity *(SW, via US I-490 & St. 19).* Approx. 30 mi: LE ROY. *Herman Le Roy House (1817; later alt. & addit.), 22 E Main St; once home of man for whom town named. Approx. 20 mi farther, via St. 19: WARSAW. Seth M. Gates House (1824; later alt.), 15 Perry Ave; once home of noted abolitionist. Approx. 12 mi farther: CASTILE. Victorian *Henry Cumming House, also known as Castile Hist. House (1865; later alt. & addit.), 17 E. Park Rd. *Mary Jemison Log Cabin (about 1800), Letchworth State Park, once home of white woman married to Indian chief.

Rochester Vicinity *(W, via St. 104).* Approx. 35 mi: ALBION. Greek Revival *Tousley-Church House (about 1845; rest.), 249 N. Main St. Not far: CHILDS. Number of cobblestone buildings here include: *Church (1834; rest.); *Ward House (about 1840; rest.); *School (1849; rest.).

SYRACUSE

Interesting buildings include, on campus of *Syracuse University, University Ave; oldest building, *Hall of Languages (1873; remod. 1980), architect: Horatio Nelson White; architects, remod.: Architectural Resources; Sargent, Webster & Folley; Eclectic Second Empire Revival, modernized interior; fine modern *S. I.

Newhouse School of Public Communications, First Building (1964), architect: I. M. Pei; assoc. architects: King & King; Second Building (1973), architects: Skidmore, Owings, & Merrill. At 401 Harrison St, ●∗**Everson Museum of Art** (1968), architect: I. M. Pei; very fine modern example. Approx. 20 mi SE of Syracuse, vai St. 92: CAZENOVIA. Interesting buildings in Hist. Dist. Approx. 40 mi SE of Syracuse, via US I-81: CORTLAND. Victorian ∗John Suggett House (about 1868; later alt.), 25 Homer Ave.

Syracuse Vicinity *(N, via US I-81).* Approx. 65 mi: WATERTOWN. Eclectic Queen Anne ∗Edwin Paddock House (1874; later alt.), 228 Washington St. Approx. 8 mi SW of Watertown, via St. 3: SACKET'S HARBOR. ∗Pickering-Beach House (1817; later alt.), 503 W. Main St, adjacent to ∗Sacket's Harbor Battlefield State Park. Approx. 25 mi N of Watertown, via US I-81 & St. 12: ALEXANDRIA BAY. Unfinished ∗Boldt Castle (begun 1897), Heart Island. Approx. 35 mi NE of Alexandria Bay, via St. 12: OGDENSBURG. ∗Frederick Remington Art Memorial Museum (1810; later alt.), 303 Washington St; fine collection of works of famous artist. Also see: Albany Vicinity (NW, via US I-90 or St. 5).

Syracuse Vicinity *(E, via US I-90 or St. 5).* Approx. 50 mi: UTICA. Interesting buildings include:
●∗**Munson-Williams-Proctor Institute** (1960), 310 Genesee St; architect: Philip Johnson; very fine modern art museum by famous architect; on grounds: Eclectic Italianate ∗Fountain Elms, the James Williams House (1852; rest.), now part of Institute. Approx. 18 mi N of Utica, via St. 12: REMSEN. ∗Baron von Steuben Memorial, with reprod. of ∗Steuben Cabin (about 1794; reconst.), once home of Revolutionary War general; his grave here. Approx. 25 mi farther, via St. 12 & 26 & 12D: CONSTABLEVILLE. ∗Constable Hall (1819; rest.), limestone mansion modeled after house in Ireland.

Syracuse Vicinity *(SW, via St. 5).* Approx. 28 mi: AUBURN. Interesting buildings include: Greek Revival ∗Theodore Willard Case Mansion (1836; later alt.), 203 Genesee St. ∗William H. Seward House (1816; later alt.), 33 South St; once home of Lincoln's secretary of state, who was instrumental in purchase of Alaska. ∗Harriet Tubman House (about 1845; later alt.), 180 South St; once home of noted Negro activist and station for Underground Railroad for runaway slaves. ∗Millard Fillmore Memorial Cabin (1791; later alt.), Washington St; similar to cabin in which president born; moved here. SE of town, via St. 38A, reconst. ∗Owasco Indian Village, Emerson Park. Approx. 15 mi farther: SENECA FALLS. Ecelctic Italianate ∗Becker House (1823; later alt. & addit.), 55 Cayuga St. Also see: Rochester Vicinity (E, via St. 31); Albany Vicinity (NW, via US I-90 or St. 5).

Pennsylvania

Early inhabitants Indians of several tribes, including Delaware, Nanticoke, Shawnee, Susquehanna. Englishman Henry Hudson first explored and claimed for Dutch, 1609; later exploration by Dutchman Cornelius Hendricksen, 1615. Swedes made first permanent settlements, including Tinicum Island, near Philadelphia, 1643. Captured by Dutch, under Peter Stuyvesant, 1655; captured by English, 1664, and controlled by duke of York; granted to William Penn, 1681; taken from Penn, 1692; restored to him, 1694; after Penn died, 1718, his family governed until 1775. Number of important battles of French and Indian Wars fought in area; war ended 1763; Ottawa Indian Chief Pontiac defeated by British in Battle of Bushy Run that year. Philadelphia location of first Continental Congress, 1774, and second, beginning 1775; Declaration of Independence adopted here, 1776. Later that year, for safety from British troops, Congress moved to Baltimore, Md., for short time, back to Philadelphia, then to Lancaster, and later to York, Pa., where Articles of Confederation were drafted, 1777; after British withdrawal, 1778, Congress returned to Philadelphia. Became second state, Dec. 12, 1787. Constitutional Convention met in Philadelphia, 1787; city U.S. Capital, 1790–1800. Today: Major manufacturing, agricultural and mining industries; Philadelphia major historical, cultural and educational center.

Land Regions: From E to W, Atlantic Coastal Plain; Piedmont; New England Upland; Blue Ridge; Appalachian Ridge and Valley; Appalachian Plateau; Erie Lowland.

Climate: Cold winters, warm summers; precipitation moderate; snowfall quite heavy in N and W portions, much less in S and E.

Major Building Materials: Iron; limestone; clay; sand and gravel.

Architecture: Rich and varied, including some of most important U.S. buildings architecturally and historically; fine examples in many locations, especially Philadelphia and vicinity and Pittsburgh and vicinity.

ERIE

Interesting buildings include: *Old Customs House, originally U.S. Bank of Erie, (1839; rest.), 409 State St; architect: William Kelly; fine Greek Revival. Not far: *Commodore Oliver Hazard Perry Memorial House, originally Dickson Tavern (1809; rest.),

201 French St; served as headquarters for Perry during War of 1812. Also of interest, nearby, replica of Perry's ship, *Niagara*. Approx. 15 mi SE, via US 29: WATERFORD. *Amos Judson House (1820; later alt.), 31 High St, on site of destroyed French Ft. Le Boeuf. Approx. 25 mi S of Erie, via US I-79: MEADVILLE. *Allegheny College, *Bentley Hall (1820–35), architect: Rev. Timothy Alden; fine building, partially New England Colonial and Georgian. On Terrace St, *Baldwin-Reynolds House (1843; later alt. & addit.), once home of U.S. Congressman and Supreme Court Justice Henry Baldwin. Approx. 30 mi S of Meadville, via US I-79 & St. 965: MERCER. *Magoffin House (1821; later alt. & addit.), 119 S. Pitt St.

HARRISBURG

Interesting buildings include: *State Capitol (1906), Capitol Hill, State & 3rd sts; architect: J. M. Huston; Eclectic Italian Renaissance Revival. On Front St, at no. 401 N, *William Maclay Mansion (1791; later alt. & addit.), once home of one of first U.S. senators. At no. 219 S, Georgian *John Harris Mansion (1766; later alt. & addit.), once home of founder of city. At 2800 Valley Rd, *Olivetti Corp. of America Factory (1970), architect: Louis I. Kahn; fine modern by famous architect. Approx. 85 mi NW, via US 322: BOALSBURG. *Boal Mansion (1789; later alt. & addit.), fine interior woodwork; on grounds: *Columbus Family Chapel (17th century), brought here, 1919, from Spain, where it had belonged to family of Christopher Columbus.

Harrisburg Vicinity *(N, via US 11)*. Approx. 55 mi: NORTHUMBERLAND. Georgian *Joseph Priestley House (1794; rest.), 472 Priestley Ave; once home of famous English scientist who discovered oxygen. Approx. 10 mi farther: DANVILLE. Georgian Gen. William Montgomery House (1792; later alt. & addit.), Bloom St.

Harrisburg Vicinity *(E, via US 322)*. Approx. 30 mi: CORNWALL. Interesting buildings include: *Cornwall Furnace (1742; remod. 1846). Approx. 15 mi NE, via St. 419: WOMELSDORF. *Conrad Weiser House (1729; later alt. & addit.), once home of noted German pioneer. Approx. 9 mi farther, off US 322: LITITZ. Interesting buildings include: *Johannes Mueller House (1792; rest.), 137 Main St; also several other Moravian examples. Approx. 5 mi father: EPHRATA. Interesting buildings include: at *Ephrata Cloister, 632 W. Main St, founded by German Seventh-Day Adventists, *Chapel (1741; rest.); *Sisters House (1743; rest.); *Academy (1837; rest.). Also see: Harrisburg Vicinity (SE, via St. 283).

Harrisburg Vicinity *(SE, via St. 283)*. Approx. 37 mi: LANCASTER. Interesting buildings include: *Hans Herr House (1719;

rest.), Willow St; German-Swiss example; once Mennonite meetinghouse. *Wheatland (1828; later alt.), Marietta Ave; last home of President James Buchanan. *Rock Ford (1793; rest.), S. Duke St; once home of Revolutionary War Gen. Edward Hand. Approx. 4 mi NE, via US 222: LANDIS VALLEY. *Pennsylvania Farm Museum, collection of 19th-century buildings. Approx. 3 mi E, via St. 462, *Amish Homestead (1750; later alt.), with farm buildings. Approx. 6 mi E, via US 30, *Amish Farm (1805; later alt.). Short distance farther, via St. 340, *Plain and Fancy Farm, another Amish example.

Harrisburg Vicinity *(SE, via US I-83).* Approx. 25 mi: YORK. Served as U.S. Capital, 1777–78, during British occupation of Philadelphia. Interesting buildings include: on Market St, at no. 152 E, Victorian *Bonham House (about 1870; later alt. & addit.). At no. 157 W, half-timbered *Golden Plough Tavern (about 1741; later alt. & addit.; rest.) attached to stone *Gen. Horatio Gates House (1751; later alt. & addit.; rest.); behind: *Barnet Bobb Log House (1812; rest.), moved here. Approx. 32 mi SW of York, via US 30 (approx. 40 mi SW of Harrisburg, via US 15): GETTYSBURG. Interesting buildings include: *Wills House, now called Lincoln Room Museum (1849; rest.), Lincoln Sq; where president completed writing famous Gettysburg Address, 1863. *Rev. Alexander Dobbin House (1776; later alt. & addit.), 89 Steinwehr Ave; used as hospital during Battle of Gettysburg. *Jennie Wade House (about 1860; later alt. & addit.), Baltimore St; where Jennie Wade was killed, only civilian fatally shot in bloody battle that produced 51,000 casualties; nearby, *Farnsworth House (about 1860), from which fatal shot was fired. SW of town: private President Dwight David Eisenhower Farm. Also of interest: *Gettysburg Nat. Mil. Park, where decisive Civil War battle was fought; includes about 3,200 acres of approx. 25-square-mile battlefield.

PHILADELPHIA

City founded by William Penn; plan by Thomas Holme early grid pattern with two major axial streets, Broad and High, now called Market, with grand central square at their intersection, now location of City Hall; four other great squares at corners of original plan. City like a museum of fine architecture from Colonial times to present. Walking tour: ••**Independence Hall,** originally State House (1732–48; tower 1753; later alt.; tower rebuilt 1828; later alt. & addit.; rest.), Nat. Hist. Park, Chestnut St bet. 5th & 6th sts; architects: Edmund Woolley & Andrew Hamilton; architect, 1828 tower: William Strickland; architects, alt. & addit.: Robert Mills; John Haviland; architects, rest.: T. Mellon Rogers; Horace Sellars; very fine Georgian building and major historical example, where great events took place, including adoption of Declaration

Independence Hall—Georgian (Library of Congress)

of Independence; considered one of finest U.S. buildings. Flanking: *Congress Hall (1789; later alt.), first U.S. Congress met here (1790–1800); later County Courthouse. *Old City Hall (1791), first used for U.S. Supreme Court (1791–1800). In Independence Mall bet. Chestnut & Market sts, *Liberty Bell Pavilion (1974), architects: Mitchell & Giurgola; famous *Liberty Bell. Nearby, ●*Second Bank of the United States (1824; later alt.), 420 Chestnut St bet. 4th & 5th sts; architect: William Strickland; very fine Greek Revival by famous architect; at one time used as U.S. Customs House, now portrait gallery. Nearby, *Carpenters' Hall (1775; later alt.), Chestnut St bet. 3rd & 4th sts; architect: Robert Smith, of famed Carpenters' Company, members of which designed and built most of fine 18th-century and many of 19th-century buildings in city. Not far: *First Bank of the United States (1795; later alt. & addit.), 120 S. 3rd St; architect: Samuel Blodgett, Jr.; architect, 1891 addit: James H. Windrim. Nearby, *Philadelphia Exchange, also known as Merchants' Exchange (1835; later alt.; rest.), Dock & 3rd sts; architect: William Strickland; architect, alt.: Louis Hickman; very fine Greek Revival commercial building by famous architect. Nearby, *St. Joseph's Church (1733; later alt. & addit.), 321 Willings Alley; oldest Roman Catholic church in city. Interesting houses nearby include: *Bishop White House (1786; rest.), 309 Walnut St; once home of chaplain of Continental Congress and U.S. Senate; *Dilworth-Todd-Moylan House (1777; rest.), 343 Walnut St; once home of Dolley Todd, who later married James Madison. About three blocks away: ●***Christ Church,** Episcopal (1727–44; tower, steeple, 1754; later alt.), N. 2nd St bet. Market & Arch sts; possible architect: James Porteus; architects, tower & steeple: John Harrison & Robert Smith; very fine Georgian church. Not far: *Betsy Ross House (early 18th century; rest.), 239 Arch St; where first American flag was supposedly made. Nearby, *Friends Meetinghouse, also known as Arch Street Meetinghouse (1811; later alt. & addit.), Arch & 4th sts; architect: Owen Biddle; architects, addit.: Cope & Lippincott. *Free Quaker Meetinghouse (1783), Arch & 5th sts. Elfreth's Alley Hist. Dist., 100 block of Cherry St, unusual block of 17th- and 18th-century houses. In area: interesting cast-iron-front buildings. Nearby, *St. George's Church (1769; later alt.), 235 N. 4th St; oldest U.S. Methodist church. Also of interest: U.S.S. *Olympia* at Pier 3, Delaware River.

Just S of Park area, *Society Hill. Interesting buildings include: *St. Paul's Church (1761; alt. 1830), 225 S. 3rd St; architect, alt.: William Strickland. *Samuel Powel House (1765; later alt; rest.), 244 S. 3rd St; fine Georgian. Modern *Society Hill Apartments & Townhouses (1964), Locust bet. 2nd & 3rd sts; architect: I. M. Pei. *Man Full of Trouble Inn (1759; rest.) and *Benjamin Paschall House (1760; rest.), 127 S. 2nd St; oldest surviving tavern and inn in city. *St. Peter's Church (1761; steeple 1842), S. 3rd & Pine sts; architects: Robert Smith & John Kearsley; architect, steeple: William Strickland. *Third Presbyterian Church (1767; later alt. & addit.; rest.), Pine St bet. 4th & 5th sts; architect: Robert Smith; architect, 1857 alt.: John Fraser. Federal *Hill-Physick-Keith House (1786; later alt. & addit.; rest.), 321 S. 4th St; once home of Dr. Philip Syng Physick, noted early surgeon. *St. Mary's Church (1763; later alt. & addit.), Spruce & S. 4th sts; architect, 1811 addit.: Charles Johnson. Just W of Society Hill, interesting buildings include: *The Athenaeum of Philadelphia (1845; later alt.), 219 S. 6th St, across from Washington Square; architect: John Notman; interesting Italianate library with Classic Revival interior. Georgian Reynolds-Morris House (1787; later alt.), 225 S. 8th St. *Walnut Street Theater (1809; later alt. & addit.), Walnut & 9th sts; architects, alt. & addit.: 1828, John Haviland; about 1850, Joseph Hoxie & Stephen Button; 1903, Willis Hale; 1920, William H. Lee; 1970, John Dickey & Bryan Loving; believed to be oldest continuously operated theater in U.S. *Pennsylvania Hospital (E wing about 1755; W wing about 1796; central pavilion 1794–1805), Pine St bet. 8th & 9th sts; architect, wings: Samuel Rhoads; architect, pavilion: David Evans, Jr.; fine Federal example. Not far: *Academy of Music (1855; later alt.), Broad & Locust sts; architects: Napoleon LeBrun & Gustave Runge; simple exterior hides opulent Eclectic Baroque Revival interior. Few blocks away: *St. Mark's Church (1851; later alt. & addit.), 1625 Locust St; architect: John Notman; fine Gothic Revival by noted architect. Few blocks away: ●***Pennsylvania Academy of Arts** (1876; rest.), Broad & Cherry sts; architects: Frank Furness & George W. Hewitt; fascinating

**Pennsylvania Academy
of Arts—Victorian**
(Lawrence S. Williams)

high Victorian building, masterpiece of Furness, winner of Congressional Medal of Honor during Civil War; considered one of finest U.S. buildings. Not far: ●✱**City Hall** (1872–1901; later alt. & addit.), Penn Square, Market & Broad sts; architect: John McArthur, Jr.; assoc. architect: Thomas U. Walter; very fine Eclectic Second Empire Revival; interesting sculptural ornament and 27-ton, 37-foot bronze sculpture of William Penn on top of tower; sculptor: Alexander Milne Calder. Nearby, modern buildings of ✱Penn Center (1965–75), director of planning: Edmund N. Bacon. Few blocks away: ●✱**Philadelphia Savings Fund Society Building** (1932), Market & S. 12th sts; architects: Howe & Lescaze; very fine early modern skyscraper, considered one of finest U.S. buildings. Not far: ✱INA tower (1975), Arch & 17th sts; architects: Mitchell & Giurgola; interesting modern office building designed

**Philadelphia Savings
Fund Society Building—
Early Modern**
(Lawrence S. Williams)

for solar control. At 530 N. 7th St, *Edgar Allen Poe House (about 1800; rest.), once home of famous author.

On both sides of Schuykill River, *Fairmount Park. Interesting buildings include: *Philadelphia Museum of Art (1916–28), Benjamin Franklin Pkwy; architects: Zantzinger, Borie & Medary; Horace Trumbauer; imposing Eclectic Classic Revival; fine collections. Nearby, ●*Fairmount Waterworks (1812–22; later alt. & addit.), near Fairmount Ave; engineer: Frederick C. Graff; fine Greek Revival buildings. Nearby, fine houses include: *Lemon Hill (about 1770; rest.), near Sedgeley Dr; late Georgian; once home of Revolution financier Robert Morris. On Mt. Pleasant Dr, *Mount Pleasant (1762; rest.), very fine Georgian; outstanding American Chippendale furniture; interesting outbuildings. Not far: *Laurel Hill (1748–60; later alt.), Randolph Rd; another fine Georgian example. Georgian *Woodford (about 1735; later alt. & addit.; rest.), off 33rd & Dauphin sts. Nearby, *Strawberry Mansion (1798; later alt. & addit.; rest.), Georgian with later Classic Revival wings. *Strawberry Mansion Bridge, also known as The Trolley (about 1895), engineer: Samuel Smedley. Across bridge: *Memorial Hall (1875; later alt.), N. Concourse & 42nd St; architect: Herman Schwarzman; Eclectic example built for 1876 Centennial Exposition. Nearby, houses include: *Cedar Grove (about 1735; later alt. & addit.), Cedar Grove Extension; stone farmhouse; moved here. *Sweetbriar (1797; rest.), Sweetbriar Extension; early Federal. *Letitia Court House (1713; later alt. & addit.; rest.), off Girard Ave above 34th St; one of oldest houses in city; moved here. *Solitude (1785; rest.), E side of *Philadelphia Zoological Gardens.

S of Fairmount Park: *University of Pennsylvania. Interesting buildings include: *Furness Building, originally Library (1888; later alt. & addit.), 34th St bet. Walnut & Pine sts; architects: Furness & Evans; architect, 1931 addit.: Robert McGoodwin; very fine Victorian; named for its famous architect.

●*Alfred Newman Richards Medical Research Building (1961)

Alfred Newman Richards Medical Research Building—Modern
(University of Pennsylvania Archives)

and Biology Laboratory (1964), Hamilton Walk; architect: Louis I. Kahn; very fine modern building, considered its architect's masterpiece and one of finest buildings in U.S. Not far: *The Woodlands (about 1742; alt. & addit. 1788; later alt.), Woodland Ave & 40th St; architect, 1788 alt. & addit.: Andrew Hamilton; simple farmhouse transformed into very fine Federal mansion; now Woodlands Cemetery offices; on grounds: fine old barn. S of university: *John Bartram House (1655; later alt. & addit.), 54th St & Eastwick Ave; once home of famous first native American botanist; interesting gardens. Some distance S, *Ft. Mifflin (begun 1798; later addit.; part. rest.), Ft. Mifflin Rd; planner: Pierre Charles L'Enfant, who planned Washington, D.C.

NW PHILADELPHIA, GERMANTOWN

Settled by Dutch, 1683; interesting, fine buildings include: in Hist. Dist., on Germantown Ave, at no. 4650, *Loudoun (1801; addit. 1830), remod. to Greek Revival. At nos. 5208, 5214 and 5218, *Germantown Hist. Society Museum includes *Baynton House (1802; later alt.), *Conyngham-Hacker House (1745; later addit.; rest.), *Howell House (about 1770; later alt. & addit.; rest.). At no. 5267, very fine *Grumblethorpe (1744; later alt. & addit.; rest.). At no. 5442, *Deshler-Perot-Morris House (1772; rest.), George Washington once lived here part of 1793 and 1794. At Vernon Park, *Vernon (about 1740; later alt. & addit.). At no. 6019, ●*Green Tree Tavern (1748; later alt.), now parish house of First Methodist Church; fine old example. At no. 6026, ●●*Wyck (about 1690 & 1720; alt. & addit. 1824), two small houses connected and redesigned 1824 by famous architect William Strickland; very fine example. At no. 6401, ●*Cliveden (1767; later alt. & addit.; rest.), architects: Jacob Knorr & Benjamin Chew; very fine Georgian; once summer home of U.S. Chief Justice Chew. At no. 6430, *Upsala (about 1755; later alt. & addit.; rest.), fine

Founder's Hall, Girard College—Greek Revival (Wayne Andrews)

Federal. At Windrim & Courtland sts, *Stenton (1734; later alt. & addit.), once home of James Logan, William Penn's secretary and later chief justice of state.

NE PHILADELPHIA

Interesting buildings widely scattered, including *Friends Guild House Apartments (1964), 711 Spring Garden St; architects: Venturi & Rauch; Cope & Lippincott; designed by Robert Venturi; both building and its architect somewhat controversial. At *Girard College, ●*Founder's Hall (1833–47), Girard & Corinthian aves; architect: Thomas U. Walter; magnificent Greek Revival by famous architect; considered one of finest U.S. buildings; also here, four dormitories by Walter. On Castor Ave bet. Bristol & Cayuga sts, Carl Mackley Houses (1933), architects: Alfred Kastner & Oscar Stonorov and W. Pope Barney; interesting modern housing around central courts.

S PHILADELPHIA

*U.S. Naval Asylum Home (1833; later alt.), Gray's Ferry Rd; architect: William Strickland; interesting Classic Revival by famous architect. *Gloria Dei, also known as Old Swedes', Church (1698; later alt. & addit.), architects: John Smart & John Buett; architect, 1845 alt.: Samuel Sloan; survivor of early Swedish settlement; now Episcopal church.

Philadelphia Vicinity *(N, via St. 611).* Approx. 11 mi: ELKINS PARK. ●*Beth Sholom Synagogue (1959), Old York Rd (St. 611 & Foxcroft Rd); very fine modern; architect: Frank Lloyd Wright. Approx 10 mi farther: HORSHAM. *Graeme Park (1722; later alt.; rest.), County Line Rd; interesting stone country house, originally built as malt house by Colonial Gov. Sir William Keith; interesting grounds and barn. Approx. 12 mi from Horsham, via St. 611 & US 202: DOYLESTOWN. *Fonthill (1910), E. Court St; interesting concrete house like chateau; built by Dr. Henry C. Mercer, tile and pottery manufacturer. Nearby, primitive-appearing *Pottery. Approx. 10 mi from Doylestown, via US 202: NEW HOPE. Interesting buildings include: *Parry Mansion (about 1785; rest.), Main St. Approx. 15 mi NW of New Hope, via St. 32, River Rd: ERWINNA. *John J. Stover House (about 1810; later alt. & addit.; rest.); also here: *Stover-Myer Mill (1800; rest.). Also of interest, approx. 8 mi S of New Hope, via St. 32, *Washington Crossing State Park, where general and army crossed Delaware River, Christmas, 1776.

Philadelphia Vicinity *(NE, via US 13).* Approx. 13 mi: ●*Andalusia (1798; remod. 1836), on banks of Delaware River; architect, remod.: Thomas U. Walter; house remod. into very fine Greek Revival by famous architect; fine furnishings, sculpture, grounds, outbuildings; once home of noted banker Nicholas Biddle. Approx. 12 mi farther, near TULLYTOWN, *Pennsbury Manor

(1683–99; destroyed; reconst. 1946), William Penn's great mansion reconst.; fine furnishings, gardens, outbuildings. Approx. 10 mi farther: FALLSINGTON. Number of early buildings include: *Burges-Lippincott House (1780; rest.); *Stage Coach Tavern (18th century; later alt. & addit.).

Philadelphia Vicinity *(SW, via US 13)*. Approx. 15 mi: NORWOOD. *Morton Mortonson House (about 1750; rest.), E. Winona Ave, Norwood Municipal Park; gambrel-roofed brick. Approx. 1 mi farther: PROSPECT PARK. *Morton House (about 1654; addit. about 1698; rest.), 100 Lincoln Ave; Swedish log cabin. Approx. 5 mi farther: CHESTER. Interesting buildings include: *Caleb Pusey House (1683; rest.), 100 Race St. Also see: Delaware—Wilmington.

Philadelphia Vicinity *(W, via St. 3)*. Approx. 8 mi: HAVERTOWN. *Lawrence Cabin (about 1725; later alt.), Karakung Dr; one-room log cabin. Approx. 3 mi farther: BROOMALL. *Thomas Massey House (1696; later alt. & addit.; rest.), Lawrence & Springhouse rds. Approx. 12 mi farther: WEST CHESTER. *David Townsend House (about 1795; later alt. & addit.), 225 N. Matlack St. Approx. 10 mi, via US 202 & 1: CHADDS FORD. *Barnes-Brinton House (about 1770; later alt.), once home of ferryman and inn. At *Brandywine Battlefield State Park, rest. or reconst. buildings include headquarters of Washington and of Lafayette. Also of interest, approx. 5 mi W of Philadelphia, via US 1, beautiful *Longwood Gardens.

Philadelphia Vicinity *(W, via US 30)*. Approx. 10 mi: BRYN MAWR. Interesting buildings at *Bryn Mawr College include *Erdman Dormitories (1965), architect: Louis I. Kahn; very fine modern by famous architect. Approx. 1 mi farther: ROSEMONT. *Ashbridge House (1769; later alt. & addit.), Montgomery Ave; Colonial. Approx. 7 mi farther, S of Wayne: RADNOR. *St. David's Church (1718; later alt. & addit.), very small Colonial example built by Welsh immigrants; Revolutionary War Gen. "Mad" Anthony Wayne buried in cemetery.

Philadelphia Vicinity *(NW, via US 422)*. Approx. 23 mi, via US 422 & 202, SW of Norristown: KING OF PRUSSIA. *King of Prussia Inn (1709; later alt. & addit.). Approx. 7 mi SW, via St. 23, *Valley Forge State Park and *Valley Forge Nat. Hist. Park, rest. and reconst. camp of Washington's army, 1777–78; interesting buildings include: *Washington's Headquarters (about 1758; rest.), stable, soldiers' huts, school, others. Just W of Norristown, via St. 363: AUDUBON. *Mill Grove (1762; rest.), Audubon Wildlife Sanctuary, once home of famous artist and naturalist John James Audubon. Approx. 8 mi NW of Norristown, via US 422: TRAPPE. *Augustus Church (1743; later alt.), oldest Lutheran church in U.S.; built by Muhlenberg family: clergymen, noted patriots and soldiers. Approx. 11 mi farther: POTTSTOWN. *Pottsgrove Mansion (1754; rest.), W. King St; architect, rest.: G. Edwin Brumbaugh; fine Georgian built by John Potts, wealthy ironmaster and founder of town. Approx. 5 mi farther: DOUGLASSVILLE. *Mouns Jones House (1716; later alt.), built by Swedish immigrant. Approx. 4 mi farther: BAUMSTOWN. *Daniel Boone House (about 1730; rest.), once home of famous frontiersman, on site of cabin in which he was born. Approx. 6 mi S, via St. 345: *HOPEWELL VILLAGE. Interesting rest. iron-making community, now Nat. Hist. Site; furnace (1771; rest.), ironmaster's house, barn.

Philadelphia Vicinity *(NW, via St. 309)*. Approx. 15 mi: FORT WASHINGTON. *Hope Lodge (1723; later alt.; rest.), very fine Georgian mansion. Approx. 40 mi farther: ALLENTOWN. *Trout Hall (1770; later alt.; rest.), 414 Walnut St; architect, rest.: Benjamin L. Walbert, III; fine Georgian. Approx. 5 mi NE, via US 22: BETHLEHEM. *Historic Bethlehem, founded in early 1740s by Moravians, German religious sect. Interesting buildings, some rest., here include: along W. Church St, *Central Moravian Church (1806); *Gemeinhaus, or Community House, (1743), now museum; *Old Chapel (1751); *Single Brothers House (1748). Approx. 10 mi farther: EASTON. *George Taylor House (1757; later alt.), Ferry & H sts; once home of member of Continental Congress and signer of Declaration of Independence. *Jacob Mixwell House (1833; later alt.), 101 S. 4th St. Approx. 6 mi NW, via St. 45: NAZARETH. Interesting Moravian buildings include: *Rev. George Whitefield House (1740–55; later alt.), 210 E. Center St; now museum. *Gray House (1740; later alt.), E. Center & New sts; oldest U.S. Moravian building. Approx. 2 mi NW of Allentown, via St. 145: CATASAUQUA. *George Taylor House (1768; rest.), patriot's summer home. Approx. 3 mi farther: EGYPT. *Troxell-Steckel House (1756; rest.), Reliance St; interesting old barn. Approx. 27 mi NW, via St. 145 & 248 & US 209, JIM THORPE, named for famous Indian athlete. *Asa Packer Mansion (1862), Packer Hill; Eclectic Italianate.

PITTSBURGH

Interesting buildings include: *Robert Neal Log House (about 1887; rest.), Schenley Park. At *Duquesne University: *Richard King Mellon Hall of Science (1970), architect: Ludwig Mies van der Rohe; fine modern example by famous architect; modern *Student Union (1967), architect: Paul Schweiker. Few blocks away: ●*Allegheny Co. Courthouse and Jail (1888), 436 Grant St; architect: Henry Hobson Richardson; magnificent Romanesque Revival; considered one of finest U.S. buildings and one of its

**Allegheny County Courthouse
and Jail—Romanesque Revival**
(Joseph W. Molitor)

famous architect's masterpieces. Just up street: *U.S. Steel Building (1970), 600 Grant St; architects: Harrison, Abramovitz & Abbe; fine modern office building; considered one of noted architects' best. Not far, interesting earlier modern office building by Harrison & Abramovitz: *Alcoa Building (1952), William Penn Pl, across from Mellon Square; sheathed with stamped aluminum curtain wall panels. Some blocks away: *Gateway Center, bet. Liberty Ave & Ft. Duquesne Blvd; landscape architects: Clarke & Rapuano; open space almost surrounded by interesting modern office towers. By same landscape architects, adjacent *Point State Park, *Ft. Pitt Blockhouse (1764; rest.). Across Monongahela River, near Mt. Washington, *Chatham Village (1936), planners: Clarence S. Stein & Henry Wright, Sr.; architects: Ingham & Boyd; interesting residential town by noted planners. Approx. 50 mi E of Pittsburgh, via US 22 & 119: INDIANA. *Croylands (1813; later alt.), once home of Civil War Gen. Harry White; *Pioneer Log House (about 1840; rest.), moved here. Approx. 45 mi from Indiana, via US 422: ALTOONA. *Elias Baker House (about 1845; later alt.), 3500 Baker Blvd; architect: Robert Cary Long, Jr.; fine Greek Revival mansion.

Pittsburgh Vicinity *(SE, via US I-76, Pennsylvania Tpk)*. Approx. 45 mi via US I-76 & 119: WEST OVERTON. *Henry Clay Frick Birthplace (about 1845), springhouse, once home of noted industrialist; *Abraham Overhold House (1838; rest.). Approx. 15 mi SE of West Overton, via US 119, St. 711 & 381, near MILL RUN: ●*Fallingwater (1937; later alt. & addit.; rest.), architect: Frank Lloyd Wright; magnificent modern house, originally residence of Edgar J. Kaufmann, Sr.; built over Bear Run waterfall; considered one of finest U.S buildings and one of its famous architect's masterpieces. Nearby *Visitors' Center (1981), architects:

Paul Mayen; Curry, Martin & Highberger. Approx. 65 mi from Fallingwater, via St. 553 & US I-76 (approx. 95 mi from Pittsburgh, via US I-76): BEDFORD. Interesting old buildings in *Bedford Village.

Pittsburgh Vicinity *(S, via St. 15).* Approx. 30 mi, near: PERRYOPOLIS. *George Washington's Grist Mill (1776). Approx 7 mi farther: BROWNSVILLE. *Nemacolin Castle (about 1785; later alt. & addit.), Front St; 22-room house; tower and battlements. Approx. 7 mi S of Brownsville, via US 40: SEARIGHTS. Searights Toll House (1831). Another toll house of same era located at ADDISON, approx. 25 mi SE of Searights, via US 40.

Pittsburgh Vicinity *(SW, via US I-79).* Approx. 30 mi: WASHINGTON. Number of interesting buildings include, at *Washington & Jefferson College, *Administration Building (1793; later alt. & addit.); *Old Main (about 1836; later alt. & addit.). Also: Greek Revival *Dr. Francis LeMoyne House (1812; later alt.), 49 E. Marden St; once home of noted abolitionist. *David Bradford House (1788; later alt.; rest.), 173 Main St; once home of leader of Whiskey Rebellion, 1794, against Federal taxes.

Pittsburgh Vicinity *(NW, via St. 65).* Approx. 17 mi, near *AMBRIDGE, *Old Economy Village (1825–31), possible architect: Frederick Rapp; fascinating rest. village of members of German communal and religious movement, Pietists, here usually called Harmonists; sometimes called Rappites after their leader George Rapp, whose adopted son, Frederick, is thought to have been architect and builder of some of buildings. Of most interest: *Great House, executive mansion; *Feast Hall, used for offices, library, school, other purposes as well as for "feasts" and other gatherings; *Church of the Harmony Society (St. John's). This is third and last settlement of Harmonists; first is approx. 25 mi NE, via St. 65 & 68: HARMONY. Number of rest. buildings (1804–14). For second Harmonist village, see Indiana—Evansville Vicinity (NW, via St. 66): NEW HARMONY.

Fallingwater—Modern
(Joseph W. Molitor)

Southeastern
States

Alabama

Early inhabitants, ancestors of later Indians, lived here eighty centuries ago or earlier; remains of cliff dwellers have been found in NE part of state. Later Indian tribes included Cherokee, Creek, Choctaw, Chickasaw. First explorer believed to have been Spaniard Alonso Alvarez de Piñeda, 1519, followed by Spaniards Pánfilo de Narváez, 1528, Hernando de Soto, 1540, and Tristán de Luna, 1559. French-Canadian brothers, Pierre le Moyne, Sieur d'Iberville, and Jean Baptiste le Moyne, Sieur d'Bienville, founded Ft. Louis, 1702, on Mobile River; Ft. Louis became first permanent French settlement in state, 1711, when moved to present location of Mobile; name changed to Ft. Condé de Mobile, 1720; ceded to British at end of French and Indian Wars, 1763; renamed Ft. Charlotte. Mobile captured by Spanish allies of Americans, led by Gen. Bernardo de Gálvez, 1780; ceded to Spain, 1783; remainder of region ceded to United States, 1795; Mobile taken from Spain by United States, 1813. Some 500 settlers massacred by Creek Indians at Ft. Mims, 1813. Gen. Andrew Jackson defeated Creeks at Battle of Horseshoe Bend, 1814, forcing them to surrender their land. Became Alabama Territory, 1817; became twenty-second state, Dec. 14, 1819. Seceded from Union, 1861; Republic of Alabama for month; joined Confederacy, Montgomery becoming its capital for about four months; most important action Battle of Mobile Bay, 1864. Readmitted to Union, 1868. Today: Major industries manufacturing, especially metals and textiles; agriculture; forest products also important.

Land Regions: S to N, East Gulf Coastal Plain; Black Belt; Piedmont; Appalachian Ridge and Valley; Cumberland Plateau, also known as Appalachian Plateau; Interior Low Plateau.

Climate: Mild, cooler in N than S; precipitation heavy along coast, moderate elsewhere; snowfall light in N, almost none in S.

Major Building Materials: Timber; iron, limestone; marble; sand and gravel; clay.

Architecture: Number of important buildings, especially in Florence: Huntsville Vicinity (W, via US 72); Mobile; Montgomery; Tuscaloosa.

BIRMINGHAM

Interesting buildings include: *Birmingham-Jefferson County Civic Center (1976), bet. 9th & 11th aves, N & 19th & 21st sts;

architects: Geddes, Brecher & Qualls; modern complex with concert hall, theater, exhibition hall, sports coliseum, all connected. *Arlington (1842; rest.), 331 Cotton Ave; Greek Revival plantation house. Also of interest: *Vulcan,* Red Mountain; sculptor: Giusseppi Moretti; iron sculpture, 53 feet tall on 125-foot base.

HUNTSVILLE

Interesting buildings include: Greek Revival *First Alabama Bank of Huntsville, formerly State Bank of Alabama (1836; later alt.), Civic Square, architect: George W. Steele. Pope-Walter House (about 1815; later alt. & addit.), Adams Ave & McClung St; once home of confederate Secretary of War Leroy Pope Walker; Bibb-Newman House (1837; later alt. & addit.), once home of Gov. Thomas Bibb. Also of interest: *Walker Space Flight Center; *Alabama Space and Rocket Center.

Huntsville Vicinity *(W, via US 72).* Approx. 20 mi: ATHENS. Interesting old buildings include: at *Athens College, Greek Revival *Founders Hall (1842; later alt. & addit.). Approx. 45 mi farther: FLORENCE. Interesting buildings include: at *Florence State University, Greek Revival *Courtview, now called Rogers Hall (1855; later alt.), Court St. Federal *Oscar Kennedy House (about 1820; later alt. & addit.), 303 N. Pine St. *Pope's Tavern (1811; later alt. & addit.), 203 Hermitage Dr; originally stagecoach station, tavern, later residence. Also of interest: *W. C. Handy House about 1870; rest.), Marengo & College sts; log cabin of famous composer of *St. Louis Blues* and other songs. Also of interest in city: large ceremonial *Indian Mound. Approx. 5 mi NW of city, Greek Revival Forks of Cypress (1820; later alt. & addit.) Approx. 6 mi S of city, via US 43: TUSCUMBIA. *Ivy Green, the Helen Keller Birthplace (1820; later alt. & addit.), 300 W. North Common; two frame houses—one birthplace of famous blind and deaf author and lecturer.

MOBILE

Number of fine, interesting old buildings include: *Ft. Condé de la Mobile (1735; reconst. 1976), 104 Theater St; originally built by French, taken by British, 1780, and renamed Ft. Charlotte; captured by Spanish 1780, taken by Americans, 1813. Nearby, *Charlotte House (about 1824; later alt. & addit.; rest.), originally first courthouse and jail in city, later residence. Not far; *Oakleigh (1832; later alt. & addit.; rest.), 350 Oakleigh Pl; fine raised cottage designed by its first owner, James W. Roper. City has number of fine Greek Revival buildings including:
●●**Government Street Presbyterian Church** (1837; later alt. & addit.; rest.), 300 Government St; architects: James Gallier; James and Charles Dakin; handsome example by famous architects.

●*Barton Academy, now Public Schools Office (1836; later alt. & addit.; rest.), 504 Government St; architects: Gallier, Dakin & Dakin; another handsome example, considered one of best of its era. Not far away: ●*Old City Hospital, now Co. Depart. of Pensions and Security Offices (1836; later alt. & addit.; rest.), Broad & St. Anthony sts; architect: William George; architects, rest.: Grider & Laraway; George M. Leake. At 802 Government St, *Adm. Raphael Semmes House (about 1856; rest.), given to Confederate naval hero by citizens of city. *Charles Richards House (1860; rest.), 256 Joachim St. Also of interest, in harbor, battleship *U.S.S. *Alabama*. Approx. 12 mi S, via US I-10 or 90: THEODORE. Approx. 8 mi S via St. 59. *Bellingrath Gardens.

MONTGOMERY

Interesting buildings include: ●*State Capitol (1851; later alt. & addit.), Dexter Ave; architect: George Nichols; Greek Revival; first capitol of Confederacy. At 425 Washington St, *First White House of Confederacy (about 1825; rest.), once residence of Jefferson Davis. Other interesting old houses here: Greek Revival *Teague House, now Chamber of Commerce Offices (1848; rest.), 468 S. Perry St; *Murphy House (1851; rest.), 22 Bibbs St. At 230 N. Hull St, *Shaw House Complex, three quite different houses: Italianate *Ordeman-Shaw House (1851; rest.); Gothic Revival *Dewolf-Cooper House (about 1855; rest.); Greek Revival *Campbell-Holtzclaw House (1852; rest.).

Montgomery Vicinity *(E, via US I-85)*. Approx. 40 mi: TUSKEGEE. *Tuskegee Institute. Interesting buildings include: fine modern *Tuskegee Chapel (1969), architect: Paul Rudolph; assoc. architects: Fry & Welch. Also: *The Oaks (1899; later alt.), once home of founder of institute, Booker T. Washington. Approx. 85 mi SE of Tuskegee, via US 82: EUFAULA. Interesting old buildings include: *Dr. Edmund Sheppard Cottage, now Chamber of Commerce Building, (1837; later alt.), E. Barbour St; simple cottage. Greek Revival *Tavern (1836; rest.), 105 Riverside Dr.

Montgomery Vicinity *(W, via US 60)*. Approx. 50 mi: SELMA. Interesting old buildings include: *Sturdivant Hall, also known as Watts-Parkman-Gillman House (1853; rest.), 713 Mabry St; architect: Thomas H. Lee. Late Greek Revival Mabry House (1850; later alt.), 629 Tremont St. Approx. 40 mi SE of Selma, via St. 41: CAMDEN. Greek Revival *White Columns (1859; rest.).

TUSCALOOSA

Interesting old buildings include: at *University of Alabama, Federal *Gorgas House (1829; later alt. & addit.), architect: William Nichols; university's first building, originally dining hall, later home of Confederate Gen. Josiah Gorgas, who became university president, and of his son, Gen. William C. Gorgas, conqueror of yellow fever in Cuba, Panama Canal and other places. Also: Greek Revival President's House (1840; later alt. & addit.), architect: William Nichols. Other interesting buildings include: Greek Revival *Friedman House (1835; rest.), 1010 Greensboro Ave. Eclectic Italianate *Robert Jemison Home, now Friedman Library (1862; later alt.), 1305 Greensboro Ave. Greek Revival *Swaim House (1836; rest.), 2111 14th St. *Old French Tavern, also known as Wilson House (1827; rest.), Capitol Park; originally stagecoach station, inn, later residence; moved here.

Tuscaloosa Vicinity *(S, via St. 69)*. Approx. 17 mi S, then approx. 1 mi W: *MOUNDVILLE (c. 1200–1400), number of interesting large Indian ceremonial mounds; reprod. of temple and museum. Approx. 21 mi farther: GREENSBORO. Interesting buildings include: Greek Revival *Magnolia Grove, also known as Hobson Memorial (1838; later alt. & addit.), Main St; once home of Rear Adm. Richmond Pearson Hobson of Spanish-American War fame. Approx. 25 mi SW of Greensboro, via St. 69 & US 80: DEMOPOLIS. Interesting buildings include. ●*Gaineswood (1842–60; rest.), 805 S. Cedar St; fine Greek Revival with traces of Italianate, Adam and other Eclectic styles; designed and built by original owner, Gen. Nathan B. Whitfield; *Bluff Hall (1832; rest.), 405 Commissioner St. Approx. 20 mi NW of Demopolis, via US 43 & St. 19: BOLIGEE. Nearby, two fine Greek Revival plantation houses: *Rosemount (1835; later alt. & addit.; rest.), designed and built by original owner, Allen Glover; *Thornhill (1833; rest.), interesting small schoolhouse on grounds.

Arkansas

Early inhabitants Indians of Caddo, Osage, Quapaw tribes. First explored by Spaniard Hernando de Soto, 1514. Explored by French Father Jacques Marquette and fur trader Louis Joliet, 1673; claimed for France by Robert Cavelier, Sieur de La Salle, 1682. First permanent French settlement by Henri de Tonti, 1686: Arkansas Post. Chartered, as part of Louisiana Territory, to Western Company, 1717. Ceded to Spain, 1763; ceded back to France, 1800; sold to United States in Louisiana Purchase, 1803. Became Arkansas Territory, 1819. Became twenty-fifth state, June 15, 1836. Seceded from Union, 1861; readmitted, 1868. Today: Important manufacturing, especially food processing, and agricultural state; oil and natural gas also important.

Land Regions: E, Mississippi Alluvial Plain; in W, from S to N, West Gulf Coastal Plain; Ouachita Mountains; Arkansas Valley; Ozark Plateau.

Climate: Warm summers, cool winters; precipitation moderate, heavier in W and central portions; snowfall light.

Major Building Materials: Timber; bauxite; sand and gravel.

Architecture: Interesting examples in several locations.

FAYETTEVILLE

Interesting old houses include: *Headquarters House (about 1850), 118 E. Dickson St; used as headquarters by Federal troops, 1863.

Fayetteville Vicinity *(NE, via US 62)*. Approx. 60 mi: EUREKA SPRINGS. *Hatchet Hall (1883), 31 Steel St; last home of Carry Nation, noted crusader against alcohol. Few miles E:
••*Thorncrown Chapel (1980), architect: E. Fay Jones; marvelous, inspirational modern wood and glass chapel set in countryside.

Fayetteville Vicinity *(SW, via US 62)*. Approx. 12 mi: PRAIRIE GROVE. *Vineyard Village, collection of Ozark Mountain log houses and other buildings, including *F. F. Latta House (1834; rest.).

LITTLE ROCK

••*State Capitol (1917), Capitol Ave; architect: Cass Gilbert; fine Eclectic Classic Revival by noted architect. Not far: *Arkansas Territorial Restoration, Scott & 3rd sts; number of interesting buildings here include: log *Hinderliter House (1828; rest.). Also: *Trapnall House (1843; rest.), 423 E. Capitol Ave; Greek Revival. *Old State House (1842; later alt.; rest.), now Arkansas History Museum, 300 W. Markham St; architect: Gideon Shryock; very fine Greek Revival by architect noted for that style. *Capital Hotel (1872; later alt.; rest.), W. Markham St; architects, rest.: Cromwell, Neyland, Truemper, Levy & Gatchell; interesting building with cast-iron front. *Villa Angelo Marre (1881; rest.), 1321 Scott St; Victorian Italianate mansion built for wealthy saloonkeeper. Approx. 100 mi SW, via I-30 & St. 4: WASHINGTON. Interesting early buildings include: *Old Hempstead Co. Courthouse & State Capitol (1833; rest.), state capitol, 1863–65. Approx. 25 mi NW, via US I-40: CONWAY. At *Hendrix College, *Bailey Library (1967), Washington Ave & Independence St; architect: Philip C. Johnson; assoc. architects: Wittenberg, Delong & Davidson; interesting modern underground building by famous architect.

Florida

Early inhabitants Indians of Apalachee tribe. Seminoles separated from their tribe, Creeks, and moved here from Georgia, early 18th century. First explored by Spaniard Juan Ponce de León, 1513; later by Spaniards Pánfilo de Narváez and Hernando de Soto. Spaniard Tristán de Luna founded colony, which failed, near Pensacola, 1559. Frenchmen Jean Ribaut explored, 1562, and René de Laudonnière established Ft. Caroline near present-day Jacksonville, 1564. Spaniard Pedro Menéndez de Avilés founded St. Augustine, oldest permanent city in United States, 1565; then sent troops to massacre French at Ft. Caroline. Englishman Sir Francis Drake burned St. Augustine, 1586; rebuilt by Spanish. English colonists from Georgia, led by Gen. James Oglethorpe, defeated Spanish in Battle of Bloody Marsh, on St. Simon's Island, 1742. After end of French and Indian Wars, territory ceded to British, 1763; divided into East Florida with capital at St. Augustine and West Florida with capital at Pensacola. Reconquered by Spanish Gen. Bernardo Gálvez and returned to Spain, 1783. Ceded to United States, 1820. Wars with Seminole Indians began; after actions against them by troops of Gen. Andrew Jackson, Indians agreed to leave state by 1832. Most Seminoles, led by Osceola, refused to go, leading to Second Seminole War, beginning 1835; Osceola captured and died in prison, 1838, but most costly Indian war did not end until 1842. Some Seminoles escaped to Everglades, where their descendants live today. Became twenty-seventh state, Mar. 3, 1845. Seceded from Union, 1861; Federal troops captured major cities, except Tallahassee, only Confederate state capital never captured; readmiited to Union, 1868. Today: Important manufacturing, agricultural and tourist industries.

Land Regions: E, Atlantic Coastal Plain; W, Gulf Coastal Plain.

Climate: N subtropical; S tropical; warm to hot summers, mild winters, cooler in N and W; precipitation moderate; snow rare. Tropical storms and hurricanes threat.

Major Building Materials: Stone; sand and gravel.

Architecture: Important buildings in many locations; vary from simple Spanish Colonial examples of St. Augustine, to large estates in Palm Beach, to early Art Deco and later sumptuous modern hotels in Miami Beach, to fine modern examples in many locations.

JACKSONVILLE

Interesting modern buildings include: *Gulf Life Center, Main St, dominated by exposed concrete structure *Gulf Life Tower (1967), architect: Welton Becket. *Police Memorial Building (1977), E. Bay St; *Florida Regional Service Center (1978), Coast Line Dr; architect of both: William Morgan. Approx. 20 mi NE of Jacksonville, via St. 105, *Kingsley Plantation (about 1810; rest.), State Park, on Ft. George Island. Also of interest, N & NW of Jacksonville, *Okefenokee Swamp.

Jacksonville Vicinity *(S, via US I-95).* Approx. 40 mi: ST. AUGUSTINE. Oldest permanent city in U.S., founded 1565. Interesting buildings include: on St. Francis St, at no. 14, *Oldest House (about 1705; later alt. & addit.; rest.), walls of coquina shells; at no. 31, *Fernandez-Llambias House (about 1760; later alt.; rest.), coquina and oyster shell concrete (tabby) construction. In San Agustin Antiguo Hist. Dist., on St. George St, interesting examples include: *Arrivas House (about 1720; later alt. & addit.; rest.), coquina. At no. 143 St. George St, *Old Spanish Treasurer's House, also known as Dr. Silas Peck House (about 1705; later alt. & addit.; rest.). Nearby, on Matanzas River,
•**Castillo de San Marcos** (1672–95; later alt. & addit.), Castillo Dr; well-preserved old fort; now Nat. Mon. Also: *Ponce de León Hotel, now main building of *Flagler College (1888; later alt.), King & Cordova sts; architects: Carrère & Hastings; interesting Eclectic Spanish Revival by noted architects; built for Henry Morrison Flagler, noted entrepreneur and railroad builder. Across park, in same style and by same architects, *Alcazar Hotel, now City Hall & Lightner Museum (1889; later alt. & addit.); *Cordova Hotel, now St. John's County Courthouse (1885; later alt. & adit.), architect: Franklin Smith. Approx. 15 mi S of St. Augustine, via US A1A, *Ft. Matanzas Nat. Mon. (1742; rest.). Approx. 110 mi S of St. Augustine, via US I-95 or 1: CAPE CANAVERAL. *John F. Kennedy Space Center, modern space-age buildings, including: Vehicle Assembly and Launch Control Facility (1967), architects: Maximilian O. Urbahn & others.

Jacksonville Vicinity *(SW, via US I-10 & 301 & St. 24).* Approx. 70 mi: GAINESVILLE. At *University of Florida, *Florida State Museum (1971), architect: William Morgan; interesting modern. Approx. 30 mi SE, via St. 20 & 319: CROSS CREEK. Nearby, *Marjorie Kinnan Rawlings House (about 1890), simple farmhouse, once home of noted author of *The Yearling.*

MIAMI

*Vizcaya (1916), 3251 S. Miami Ave, by Biscayne Bay; architects: Pauk Chalfin & F. Burral Hoffman, Jr.; extravagant 72-

room Eclectic Italian Renaissance Revival mansion; beautiful grounds, beautiful site. In MIAMI BEACH, large, luxurious modern resort hotels, as well as smaller and earlier hotels and other buildings in Art Deco Hist. Dist. Number of fine, modern houses, all private, in area. Also of interest, W of Miami, via US I-75 or 41: *The Everglades.

Miami Vicinity *(N, via US I-95 or 1)*. Approx. 25 mi: FORT LAUDERDALE. *U.S. Courthouse & Federal Office Building (1979), 299 E. Broward Blvd; architects: William Morgan & H. J. Ross; interesting modern building; fine use of planting and water. Approx. 40 mi farther: PALM BEACH. Sumptuous private mansions along Ocean Blvd. Other interesting buildings here include: *Whitehall (1902), Whiteway Way; architects: Carrère & Hastings; Eclectic Spanish Revival; once home of Henry Morrison Flagler. Also: number of interesting Eclectic Mediterranean buildings by eccentric architect-entrepreneur Addison Mizner, in several locations including *Via Mizner and *Via Parigi.

Miami Vicinity *(SW, via US 1)*. Approx. 50 mi: beginning of Florida Keys; approx. 110 mi farther: KEY WEST. Interesting buildings include: *John James Audubon House (about 1830; rest.), 205 Whitehead St; famous naturalist-painter once lived here. *Ernest Hemingway House (1851; rest.), 907 Whitehead St; famous novelist lived here for about ten years. Approx. 70 mi W of Key West, via boat or seaplane, *Ft. Jefferson Nat. Mon. (begun 1846), Garden Key, Dry Tortugas; interesting fort in which Dr. Samuel Mudd was imprisoned for setting leg bone of John Wilkes Booth.

PENSACOLA

Originally settled 1559; abandoned two years later; permanent settlement 1698. Interesting 19th-century buildings include: Gothic Revival *Old Christ Church, now museum (1834; rest.), S. Adams & E. Zarragossa sts. Only surviving Spanish building: ruins of *Ft. San Carlos (about 1787); nearby, *Ft. Barrancas (1844). On Santa Rosa Island: *Ft. Pickens (1834), Gulf Islands Nat. Seashore.

TALLAHASSEE

Interesting buildings include: *State Capitol (1978), Capitol Center; architects: Edward Durell Stone; Reynolds, Smith & Hills; modern 22-story building. Nearby, *Old State Capitol (1824–45; later alt. & addit.; rest.), architect, alt. & addit.: 1902, Frank P. Milburn; 1923, Henry J. Klutho; architect, rest.: Herschel E. Shepard. Also: *Big Bend Pioneer Farm, late 19th-century farm buildings. Approx. 35 mi NW of Tallahassee, via US 90: CHATTA-

HOOCHEE. Approx. 7 mi S, *Gregory House (1834; rest.), Torreya State Park.

TAMPA

Interesting buildings include: ●*Tampa International Airport (1971). off US I-75; architects: Reynolds, Smith & Hill; fine modern airport, conveniently located W of city. Also of interest: restaurants and other buildings of *Ybor City, Spanish quarter of Tampa.

Tampa Vicinity *(NE, via US I-4).* Approx. 25 mi: LAKELAND. *Florida Southern University (1940–59), master planner & architect: Frank Lloyd Wright; interesting modern complex; largest group of buildings by famous architect but not considered among his finest designs; later buildings by other architects. Approx. 35 mi SE of Lakeland, via US 17 & St. 60: LAKE WALES. *Bok Singing Tower (1929), Mountain Lake; architect: Milton B. Medary; built for Edward William Bok, noted editor of *Ladies' Home Journal.* Approx. 55 mi NE, via US 27 & 17: ORLANDO. *Orlando Public Library (1966), 10 N. Rosalind Ave; architect: John M. Johansen; interesting modern building by noted architect.

Tampa Vicinity *(S, via US 41).* Approx. 35 mi, via US 41 & 301: ELLENTON. *Gamble Plantation (1845; later alt. & addit.; rest.), 3708 Patten Ave; interesting Greek Revival, State Hist. Site. Approx. 15 mi farther: SARASOTA. Interesting modern schools, houses and other buildings by noted architects include: *Van Wezel Performing Arts Hall (1969), 10th St; architect: William Wesley Peters, once student and associate of Frank Lloyd Wright. *St. Paul's Lutheran Church (1959; later addit.), 2256 Bahia Vista St; architect: Victor Lundy. Also: Eclectic Venetian Gothic Revival *Ca d' Zan, the John Ringling House (1926), 5401 Bay Shore Rd; architect: Dwight James Baum. Approx. 4 mi N of city, via US 41, Eclectic Italian Renaissance Revival *John and Mabel Ringling Museum of Art (1930), architect: J. H. Phillips; fine collections, *Circus Museum, *Ringling School of Art. Approx. 75 mi farther: FORT MYERS. *Thomas A. Edison Home (1886; rest.), 2341 McGregor Blvd; famous inventor spent winters here for some 45 years. Also of interest: few miles SW of Fort Myers, *Sanibel and *Captiva Islands, noted for abundance, variety of sea shells; SE of Fort Myers, *the Everglades.

Georgia

First inhabitants Mound Builders, pre-Columbian ancestors of later Indians; some of their structures have survived. Later Indian tribes included Cherokee, Creek. First explored by Spaniards Hernando de Soto, 1540, and Pedro Menéndez de Avilés, 1564, who built fort on St. Catherine's Island near Savannah. British built fort on Altamaha River, 1721; abandoned 1727. Englishman Gen. James Oglethorpe founded chartered colony at Yamacraw Bluff, near Savannah, 1733. His troops defeated Spanish in Battle of Bloody Marsh, St. Simon's Island, 1742, establishing British control of Georgia. Became royal colony, 1754. During Revolutionary War, British occupied almost entire state by 1779; Americans drove them out, 1782. Became fourth state, Jan. 2, 1788. Seceded from Union, 1861; Federal troops of Gen. William Tecumseh Sherman burned Atlanta and burned and pillaged 60-mile-wide path from there to sea at Savannah, 1864; readmitted to Union, 1868; expelled, 1869, for not ratifying Constitution; again readmitted, 1869. Today: Important manufacturing and agricultural state.

Land Regions: S to N, Atlantic Coastal Plain, East Gulf Coastal Plain; Piedmont; Appalachian Ridge and Valley; Blue Ridge; Appalachian Plateau.

Climate: Mild, mostly long, warm, humid summers, short mild winters; cooler in mountains; little snow.

Major Building Materials: Granite; marble; sand and gravel; timber; clay.

Architecture: Rich and varied, not only in major cities, especially Savannah, but in smaller cities and towns, including, in Athens vicinity: Lexington, Washington, and Madison, and in Macon vicinity: Milledgeville.

ATHENS

Large number of interesting old buildings, houses in particular, mostly Greek Revival here, including number on Prince Ave: at no. 194, Brig. Gen. Thomas R. R. Cobb House (about 1830; later alt. & addit.), once home of author of Confederate Constitution, killed in Battle of Fredericksburg, Va. At no. 248, *Joseph Henry Lumpkin House (about 1843; later alt.), once home of first chief justice of state. At no. 570, *John Thomas Grant House, now

University President's House (1858; later alt.). At no. 634, *Taylor-Grady House (about 1845; later alt. & addit.), once home of noted newspaper editor Henry W. Grady. At no. 973, *Edwin King Lumpkin House (about 1859; rest.), ironwork contrasts mightily with columns of other houses. At *University of Georgia, number of interesting buildings, of several styles, include: Colonial *Old College (1805; later alt.); Federal *Demosthenian Hall (1824; later alt.); Greek Revival *Chapel (1832; later alt.) and *Phi Kappa Hall (1836; later alt.).

Athens Vicinity *(N, via US 441 & 23).* Approx. 60 mi: TOCCOA. Approx. 6 mi E, via US 123, *Traveler's Restaurant, the Jesse Walton House, also known as Jarrett Manor (about 1815; later alt. & addit.; rest.), built by Walton, who, with his family, was killed by Indians; served as stagecoach station, inn, post office. Also of interest, just NW of Toccoa, via St. 17, *Toccoa Falls. Approx. 15 mi NW, via St. 17 & US 23, spectacular *Tallulah Gorge and Falls.

Athens Vicinity *(SE, via US 78).* Approx. 20 mi: LEXINGTON. Interesting old buildings include: Classic Revival George Young House (1827; later alt.). Approx. 23 mi farther: WASHINGTON. Surprising number of fine and interesting old houses in small town include: on Robert Toombs Ave, Greek Revival *Barnett-Slaton House, now Washington-Wilkes Hist. Museum (about 1835; later alt. & addit.); Robert Toombs House (1797; later alt. & addit.); William H. Pope House, also known as Tupper-Barnett House (about 1835; later alt. & addit.). Also: Campbell-Jordan House (1786; later alt. & addit.), E. Liberty St; *The Cedars (1793; later alt. & addit.), 201 Sims St.

Athens Vicinity *(S, via US 129).* Approx. 30 mi: MADISON. Another small town with number of old and interesting buildings, including: *Presbyterian Church (1810; later alt. & addit.); *Morgan Co. Courthouse (1906; later alt.), architect: J. W. Golucke. Greek Revival buildings include such small-sized examples as: Nathan Massey House (about 1859; later alt.); Joel Abbott Billups Cottage (1853; later alt.); Georgia Female College (1849; later alt.). E of Madison, via US I-20, interesting old buildings in: GREENSBORO (approx. 22 mi), CRAWFORDVILLE (approx. 20 mi farther), PENFIELD (approx. 7 mi N of Greensboro).

ATLANTA

Interesting buildings include: *State Capitol (1889), Capitol Ave; architects: Willoughby J. Edbrooke & Franklin P. Burnham; limestone, with gilded dome; modeled to extent after U.S. Capitol.

Not far: fine modern *Atlanta Central Library (1980), Margaret Mitchell Pl; architects: Marcel Breuer & Hamilton Smith; assoc. architects: Carl Stein; Frank Richlan; Stevens & Wilkinson. Also: ••*Hyatt Regency Hotel (1969), 265 Peachtree St NE; architect: John Portman; first, and some think best, of modern hotels with full-height atria designed by this architect. Another interesting building by Portman: *Peachtree Plaza Hotel (1976), Peachtree St & International Blvd. Also: *Omni, Techwood Dr & Marietta St; architects: Thompson, Ventulett & Stainback; unusual modern center with facilities for sports, conventions, recreation, dining, other activities; includes: *Omni Sports Coliseum (1972); *Omni International (1976); *George L. Smith II Georgia World Congress Center (1980). At Peachtree & Broad sts, *Flat Iron Building (1897; later alt.), architect: Bradford Gilbert; unusual office building on odd-shaped site. *Wren's Nest (about 1885; rest.), 1051 Gordon St; Victorian; once home of Joel Chandler Harris, author of *Uncle Remus and Brer Rabbit,* other books. At 3099 Andrews Dr NW, *Swan House (1928; rest.), architect: Philip T. Shutze; interesting Eclectic Italian Renaissance Revival; on grounds: *Tullie Smith House, also known as Robert Hiram Smith House (about 1840; rest.), simple, wood-frame; moved here; interesting old outbuildings. Also of interest: *Cyclorama of Battle of Atlanta, Grant Park.

Atlanta Vicinity *(N, via US 19).* Approx. 20 mi: ROSWELL. Number of fine, interesting old buildings here, for many of which Willis Ball was architect, including: Greek Revival *Barrington Hall, the Barrington King House (1840; later alt.); *Presbyterian Church (1840; later alt.); Mimosa Hall (about 1840; later alt.); Bulloch Hall, the James Stephens Bulloch House (1842).

Atlanta Vicinity *(E, via US 78).* Approx. 10 mi: STONE MOUNTAIN. *Antebellum Plantation, Stone Mountain Park; collection of early 19th-century buildings moved here to re-create cotton plantation. Also of interest: huge sculpture on granite *Stone Mountain of Confederate leaders Robert E. Lee, Stonewall Jackson, Jefferson Davis, others; sculptors: Gutzon Borglum, Henry Augustus Lukeman, Walter Kirkland Hancock.

Atlanta Vicinity *(NW, via US I-75).* Approx. 45 mi: CARTERSVILLE. *Etowah Indian Mounds, second largest in U.S. Approx. 30 mi farther: CALHOUN. Approx. 3 mi E, via St. 225, *New Echota, reconst. buildings of capital of Cherokee Nation. Approx. 15 mi NE of New Echota, via St. 225: SPRING PLACE. Federal *Vann House (1805; rest.), once home of Indian Chief James Vann, son of Scottish trader and Cherokee. Approx. 35 mi NW, via US 76, I-75 & St. 2, *Chickamauga and Chattanooga Nat. Mil. Park; several interesting mid-19th-century log cabins.

AUGUSTA

Fine, interesting old buildings include: on Telfair St, at no. 432, *Old Government House, originally Richmond Co. Courthouse (1801; later alt.; rest.); at no. 506, picturesque *Ware's Folly, the Ware-Sibley House (1818; later alt.); at no. 540, *Richmond Academy (1802; remod. 1857; later alt.), remod. into Gothic Revival by architect: William Henry Goodrich; at no. 598, Greek Revival *Old Medical College (1835; later alt.), architect: Charles B. Cluskey; at no. 642, Classic Revival *First Presbyterian Church (1812; later alt.), architect: Robert Mills. Also: late Victorian *Sacred Heart Church (1900; later alt.), Greene & 13th sts; architect: Cornelius Otten. *Harris-Pearson-Walker House, also known as Mackay House and White House (about 1800; later alt. & addit.; rest.), site of Revolutionary battle, 1780, after which several American patriots were reportedly hanged from stairway.

Augusta Vicinity *(NW, via US I-20 & 78 and W, via US I-20).* Interesting buildings in WASHINGTON, LEXINGTON (See Athens Vicinity, SE, via US 78) and in CRAWFORDVILLE, PENFIELD, GREENSBORO, MADISON (See Athens Vicinity, S, via US 129).

COLUMBUS

Interesting buildings, mostly in Hist. Dist., include: James A. Rankin House (1859; later alt.; rest.), 1440 2nd Ave; interesting cast-iron grillwork. Victorian *Springer Opera House (1871; later alt. & addit.; rest.), 1st Ave & 10th St. *Bank of Columbus (1867), 1044 Broadway; cast-iron building prefabricated in Pittsburgh. Federal *Walker-Peters-Langdon House (1828; later alt.; rest.), 716 Broadway. Unusual double octagonal The Folly, the Leander May House (1862; later alt. & addit.), 527 1st Ave. Large Classic Revival Dr. Samuel A. Billings House (1857; later alt. & adit.), 303 12th St. St. Elmo. The Col. Seaborn Jones House, formerly called Eldorado (1832; later alt. & addit.), unusual Federal with Classic Revival columns. Approx. 30 mi NE, via US 80: TALBOTTON. *Zion Episcopal Church (1848), fine wood-frame Gothic Revival. Approx. 30 mi S, via US 27: LUMPKIN. At Town Square: *Beddingfield Inn (1836; rest.), once stagecoach station, inn, residence. Approx. 1 mi S, *Westville Hist. Dist., reconst. mid-19th century farm village; large number of homes and other buildings.

Columbus Vicinity *(N, via US 27 or I-185).* Approx. 50 mi: LA GRANGE. Small town with many fine, imposing Greek Revival houses, including: *Bellevue, the Benjamin Hill House (1855; later alt. & addit.), 204 Ben Hill St; once home of noted Georgia statesman. The Oaks, the Philip Hunter Greene House (1845; later alt.), 1103 Vernon St. James F. Culberson House (1840;

later alt.), Club Rd; moved here. Nuwood, the Joel D. Newsome House (1833; later alt.), Big Springs Rd; architect: Collin Rodgers. Also of interest, off US 27 on way to LaGrange, approx. 30 mi from Columbus, *Callaway Gardens. Approx. 35 mi SE of LaGrange, via US 27 & St. 190, *Warm Springs Foundation and *Franklin D. Roosevelt Memorial, where president vacationed for many years and where he died, 1945.

MACON

Interesting buildings include: Eclectic Italian Renaissance Revival *P. L. Hay House, also known as Johnston-Hay House (1860), 934 Georgia Ave; architect: T. Thomas; ornate materials, fixtures imported from Italy as were workmen. *Old Cannon Ball House, the Judge Asa Holt House (1853; later alt.; rest.), 856 Mulberry St; said to have been struck by cannon ball, 1864. *Sidney Lanier Cottage (about 1835), 213 High St; birthplace of noted poet. On E outskirts of Macon: *Ocmulgee Nat. Mon. (about 900), remains of early Mound Builder Indian culture; *Great Temple Mound, several smaller mounds, reconst. earthen *Council Chamber.

Macon Vicinity *(NE, via St. 49).* Approx. 30 mi: MILLEDGE-VILLE. Number of fine, interesting buildings, mostly Greek Revival, include: ●*Old Governor's Mansion,** now President's House, Georgia College (1838; later alt.; rest.), 120 S. Clark St; architect: Charles B. Cluskey; very fine. *Stetson-Sanford House, also known as George T. Brown House (about 1825; later alt.; rest.), W. Hancock St; moved here. The Cedars, the Charles W. Howard House (1830; later alt.), 131 N. Columbia St. John Williams House (1822; later alt.), 251 S. Liberty St; possible architect: Daniel Pratt. Samuel Rockwell House (1834; later alt.), 19 Allen Memorial Dr; architect: Joseph Lane. Also: Gothic Revival *Old State Capitol (1807; later alt. & addit.), 201 E. Green St; now museum of *Georgia Military College.

SAVANNAH

Marvelous architectural effect of Savannah is not so much in individual buildings, although many are interesting and important, but in overall effect of downtown area, bounded by Bay, E. Broad, Gwinnett & W. Broad sts. Superb plan of city by its founder, Gen. James Oglethorpe, with assistance of engineer Col. William Bull and probably of Robert Castell. Original plan, with its logical and beautiful streets and squares, has been quite well preserved.

Walking tours reveal large number of interesting buildings, including: *Factors' Row (1840–90), Bay St; Eclectic Victorian *Cotton Exchange (1887), architect: William Gibbons Preston; merchants' offices on top of bluff overlooking Savannah River;

number of warehouses at bottom on River St have been rehabilitated into shops, bars, restaurants facing riverfront Esplanade (1978), architects: Gunn & Meyerhoff. Nearby, on Bay St, Greek Revival *U.S. Customs House (1850); architect: J. S. Norris. Across from Johnson Square, Greek Revival *Christ Episcopal Church (1838; rest.), Bull St. Across from Wright Square, *Lutheran Church of the Ascension (1879), Bull St. Across from Oglethorpe Square, ••*Owens-Thomas House (1819; rest.), 124 Abercorn St; architect: William Jay; fine house by English architect who lived in city for time and designed other fine buildings here and in Charleston, S.C. Across from Columbia Square, ••*Davenport House (1820; rest.), 324 E. State St; fine Georgian; architect: Isaiah Davenport. *Colonial Park Cemetery (1750–1853), Abercorn St bet. Oglethorpe Ave & Perry St. Roman Catholic *Cathedral of St. John the Baptist (1900), Abercorn & Harris sts. *Andrew Low House (about 1848; rest.), 329 Abercorn St; architect: John S. Norris; Girl Scouts organized here by Juliette Gordon Low; carriage house, given to Mrs. Low by Girl Scouts, now GSA headquarters. Also: Eclectic Abraham Minis House (1859; later alt.), 204 E. Jones St; architect: Stephen Decatur Button. Eclectic Gen. Hugh Mercer House (1869), 429 Bull St. *Independent Presbyterian Church (1819; burned 1889; reconst. 1890), 207 Bull St; architect: John Holden Greene; interesting reconst. of original church. *Wayne-Gordon House, also known as Juliette Gordon Low Birthplace (1820; later alt. & addit.), 142 Bull St; possible architect: William Jay; Eclectic house, now owned by Girl Scouts. ••*Telfair Mansion, now Telfair Mansion and Art Museum (1818; later alt. & addit.), 121 Barnard St; architect: William Jay, another fine house by noted English architect. Still another fine Jay design: *William Scarbrough House (1818; rest.), 41 W. Broad St. Also see: South Carolina—Charleston Vicinity (SW, via US 17 & 21).

Savannah Vicinity *(E, via US 80)*. Approx. 15 mi: *Ft. Pulaski Nat. Mon. (1829–47), well-restored fort, for which then Lt. Robert E. Lee designed and built dikes and drainage system; French Gen. Simon Bernard designed fort; seized by Confederate troops, 1861; recaptured by Federal troops early next year after bombardment with new experimental rifle cannon; named for Polish Count Casimir Pulaski, who served with American army in Revolution and was killed, 1779, during siege of Savannah.

Savannah Vicinity *(S, via US 17)*. Approx. 30 mi: MIDWAY. *Congregational Church (1792; later alt. & addit.), unusual, in Deep South, New England meetinghouse built by Massachusetts Puritans; fathers of Oliver Wendell Holmes and of Samuel F. B. Morse were once pastors; behind church: *Museum. Also of interest, approx. 80 mi S of Savannah, via US 17 or I-95, near BRUNSWICK, resorts of *Golden Isles, Sea, St. Simon and Jekyll. Approx. 50 mi SW of Brunswick: *Okefenokee Swamp.

Kentucky

First inhabitants prehistoric ancestors of present-day Indians who lived here 150 centuries ago or earlier. Later Indian tribes included Cherokee, Delaware, Iroquois, Shawnee. First explored, late 17th century, by Englishmen Gabriel Arthur, Col. Abram Wood and John Peter Salley and Frenchmen Father Jacques Marquette, Louis Joliet and Robert Cavelier, Sieur de La Salle. Thoroughly explored by pioneer American scouts Thomas Walker, 1750, and Daniel Boone, 1767 and 1769. Boone attempted settlement without success. First permanent English settlement, 1774: Harrodsburg by people from Pennsylvania led by James Harrod. Boone founded Boonesborough, 1775. Became county of Virginia, 1776. Indian attacks during Revolutionary War successfully defended against by forces of Daniel Boone and George Rogers Clark. Became fifteenth state, June 1, 1792. Did not secede from Union during Civil War although many people favored Confederacy and about one-third of Kentucky soldiers fought for South; several battles and many skirmishes in state. Today: Important manufacturing, agricultural and mining industries. Also noted for Bluegrass country and thoroughbred race horse breeding and racing.

Land Regions: From E to W, Appalachian Plateau; Bluegrass; Pennyroyal Region; Western Coal Field; East Gulf Coastal Plain.

Climate: Warm summers, cool winters; precipitation moderate, heaviest in S; snowfall light in W, somewhat heavier in E.

Major Building Materials: Timber; stone; sand and gravel; clay.

Architecture: Important buildings in number of places, including: Frankfort; Lexington; Louisville.

FRANKFORT

Interesting buildings include: *State Capitol (1910), Capitol Ave; architect: Frank Mills Andrews; on grounds: *Governor's Mansion (1914), Eclectic Beaux Arts French Renaissance Revival; architect: Frank Mills Andrews. ●*Old Statehouse (1830; rest.), St. Clair St & Broadway; architect: Gideon Shryock; fine Greek Revival by noted architect. At 202 Wilkinson St, another Shryock design, *Orlando Brown House (1835; rest.), with hints of Georgian, unusual for this Greek Revival architect. Nearby, *Liberty Hall (1800; rest.), 218 Wilkinson St; late Georgian or Federal; once home of John Brown, one of first two Kentucky U.S. senators. At 420 High St, another Georgian example, *Old Governor's Mansion (1797; rest.), residence of governors, 1798–1914; now residence of lieutenant governor.

LEXINGTON

Fine, interesting buildings include: ••**Morrison College** (1834; rest.), *Transylvania University, 3rd St; architect: Gideon Shryock; fine Greek Revival. *Hopemont (about 1814; rest.), 201 Mill St; fine Georgian; built by John Wesley Hunt; once home of his grandson, Confederate Gen. John Hunt Morgan, and birthplace of Nobel Prize winner Thomas Hunt Morgan. In SE area of city: *Ashland (1805; demolished; reconst. 1857; rest.), Richmond Rd; Eclectic Italianate house reconst. using original plans of home of famous statesman Henry Clay. Just S of city, off US 27, on Higbee Mill Rd, *Waveland (1847; rest.), fine Greek Revival mansion, with interesting outbuildings. Approx. 20 mi S of Lexington, via US 25: RICHMOND. Nearby, *White Hall (1864; rest.), architect: Maj. Thomas Lewinski; interesting Eclectic Italian Villa Revival, once home of Cassius Marcellus Clay, famous abolitionist and statesman. Also of interest near Lexington: Bluegrass country and thoroughbred horse farms.

Lexington Vicinity *(NE, via US 68)*. Approx. 17 mi: PARIS. Interesting buildings include: Georgian *Duncan Tavern (1788; rest.), 323 High St; adjoining, *Ann Duncan House (1800; rest.). Approx. 43 mi farther: WASHINGTON. Interesting buildings in Hist. Dist. include: *Albert Sidney Johnston birthplace (about 1797; rest.), once home of Confederate general.

Lexington Vicinity *(SW, via US 68)*. Approx. 25 mi: SHAKERTOWN. Shaker community, *Pleasant Hill; architect: Micajah Burnett; architect, rest.: Washington Reed, Jr. Interesting buildings include: *Farm Manager's House (1809; rest.); *Meeting House (1820; rest.); *East Family House (1819; rest.); *Center Family House (1834; rest.); *Trustees Office (1839; rest.), beautiful stairs. Approx. 7 mi farther: HARRODSBURG. *Old Fort Harrod (1776; later alt. & addit.; rest.), State Park, first English-speaking settlement W of Allegheny Mountains; log blockhouses, cabins. Approx. 7 mi SE of Harrodsburg, via US 150: DANVILLE. Interesting buildings include: *Dr. Ephraim McDowell House and Apothecary Shop (about 1800; rest.), 125–27 2nd St; once home of famous pioneer surgeon. Approx. 20 mi SE of Danville, via US 150: CRAB ORCHARD. Approx. 3 mi NW, *Col. William Whitley House (1792; rest.), simple Georgian; diamond-pattern brick with initials of original owner, noted pioneer leader and Indian fighter, and of his wife, worked into front and back walls.

LOUISVILLE

Interesting buildings, number of them in Old Main Street reha-
bilitation area, include: ●*Old Bank of Louisville,** now Actors Theater, (1837; rest.), 320 W. Main St; architect: James H. Dakin;
architect, rest.: Harry Weese; fine small Greek Revival example
converted into theater. Also on W. Main St, converted cast-iron
examples include: at no. 727–31, *Carter Dry Goods Building and
two adjoining buildings, now Louisville Museum of Natural History (1878; remod.), architect: C. J. Clarke; architects, remod.:
Louis & Henry. At no. 730, *Hart Block, now American Saddle
Horse Museum (1884; remod.), architect: Charles D. Meyer; architect, remod.: Lawrence P. Melillo. At Main & 5th sts, *Riverfront Plaza and Belvedere (1974), planner: Victor Gruen; architects: Constantin Doxiades, Lawrence Melillo & Jasper Ward;
landscape architects: Simonds & Simonds; fine elevated park with
beautiful view of Ohio River; constructed over US I-64 and parking garages. Also of interest, nearby, paddle-wheeler *Belle of Louisville.* Not far: Greek Revival *Jefferson Co. Courthouse (1835–
60; later alt. & addit.), Jefferson St bet. 5th & 6th sts; architect:
Gideon Shryock, replaced by Albert Fink; architects, alt. & addit.:
1912, Brinton B. Davis; 1979, Bickel-Gibson. In NE area of city:
*Locust Grove (1791; rest.), Blankenbaker Lane; interesting
Georgian farm house, outbuildings. Not far:
●*Louisville Water Pumping Station** (1860; rest.), 3005 Upper
River Rd; architect: Theodore R. Scowden; fantastic Classic Revival temple with 135-foot tower belies its utilitarian functions;
considered one of finest designs of its era; now Art Center Assoc.
In SE section of city: *Farmington (1810; rest.), 3033 Bardstown
Rd; interesting example believed to have been derived from design
by Thomas Jefferson; interesting garden and blacksmith shop. In
NW section: *Lincoln Income Life Insurance Building (1965),
6100 Dutchman's Lane; architects: Taliesin Associated Archi-
tects; fanciful modern offices designed by inheritors of practice of
Frank Lloyd Wright. Also of interest, SW section: *Churchill
Downs, scene of Kentucky Derby. Also see: Indiana—New
Albany.

Louisville Vicinity *(SE, via US 31E/150).* Approx. 45 mi: BARDS-
TOWN. Interesting buildings include: approx. 1 mi E, *Federal
Hill, also known as My Old Kentucky Home (1795–1812; rest.),
State Park; fine Georgian; believed to have inspired song by Ste-
phen Foster; once home of Judge & U.S. Senator John Rowan.
Approx. 1 mi NE, on US 62, another fine Georgian example,
*Wickland (1817; rest.), architects: John Marshall Brown & John
Rogers; once home of three governors: of Kentucky, Charles A.
Wickliffe, 1839–40, and his grandson, John Cripps Wickliffe
Beckham, 1900–1907, and of Louisiana, Robert Charles Wick-
liffe, 1856–60, son of first Charles. Also of interest: *Barton Mu-

seum of Whiskey History. Approx. 20 mi SW of Bardstown, via US 31E: HODGENVILLE. Just S, via US 31E & St. 61, *Abraham Lincoln Birthplace Nat. Hist. Site. Just NE of town, via US 31E, *Lincoln's Boyhood Home. Also of interest, approx. 50 mi SE of Hodgenville, via St. 84 & US I-65, *Mammoth Cave Nat. Park.

Louisiana

Early inhabitants Indians of some thirty tribes, including Caddo and Tunica. First explored by Spanish, 1541, led by Hernando de Soto, who died in region, 1542; later by French led by Robert Cavelier, Sieur de La Salle, 1682; claimed for France and named Louisiana. Became royal colony, 1699. French Canadian Pierre Le Moyne, Sieur d'Iberville, named royal governor. Became proprietary colony, 1712, with exclusive trading rights given to Antoine Crozat. Louis Juchereau de St. Denis founded first permanent French settlement, 1714; Natchitoches. Trading rights transferred from Crozat to Scotsman John Law, who started ill-fated land speculation for colonization. New Orleans founded by French-Canadian Jean Baptiste Le Moyne, Sieur d'Bienville, brother of Iberville, 1718; became capital of territory, 1722. Became royal colony again, 1731; New Orleans and other parts of territory secretly ceded to Spain by French, 1762; discovered by French inhabitants, 1764, who succeeded in driving out Spanish governor, 1768; Spanish regained control, 1769. Several thousand French people came to territory in second half of 18th century after having been driven from Acadia, Canada; these Acadians, or Cajuns, settled mostly along Bayous Teche and LaFourche, W of New Orleans. Spain ceded territory back to France, 1800; United States bought territory from France in Louisiana Purchase, 1803. Became eighteenth state, April 30, 1812. In 1815, troops of Gen. Andrew Jackson soundly defeated British in Battle of New Orleans, neither army having received word that peace treaty had been signed two weeks earlier. Seceded from Union, 1861; New Orleans captured by Federal troops, 1862, and held until end of Civil War; readmitted to Union, 1868. Reconstruction after war particularly harsh in state, last in South from which Federal troops removed, 1877. Today: Major industrial state, especially oil and natural gas production; manufacturing and agriculture also very important.

Land Regions: From E to W, East Gulf Coastal Plain; Mississippi Alluvial Plain; West Gulf Coastal Plain.

Climate: S, subtropical, with hot humid summers, warm, humid winters; N, less humidity, cooler; precipitation heavy; snowfall rare; hurricanes and other dangerous storms fairly frequent.

Major Building Materials: Timber; clay.

Architecture: Rich and varied from Colonial era to present in many locations, including Baton Rouge and vicinity; Natchitoches; New Orleans and vicinity.

BATON ROUGE

Interesting buildings include: *State Capitol (1932), N. 3rd St; architects: Weiss, Dreyfous & Seiferth; modern high-rise (approx. 450 ft.) built during administration of Gov. Huey P. Long and scene of his assassination, 1935, while U.S. senator. Not far: ●●**Old State Capitol** (1849; interior burned 1862; rest. 1882; remod. 1969), N. Boulevard & St. Philip St; architect: James H. Dakin; architect, 1882 rest.: William A. Freret; architect, 1969 remod.: George M. Leake; very fine Gothic Revival by noted architect; spectacular interior, especially entrance hall, stair, colored-glass dome. Not far: *Pentagon Barracks (1823; later alt.; rest.), Riverside Mall; architect: Capt. James Gadsden; four identical, not five as in pentagon, Classic Revival buildings. Also: *Magnolia Mound Plantation House (about 1785; rest.), 2161 Nicholson Dr. *Rural Life Museum, SE section of city, off US I-10; 19th-century original and reconst. buildings moved here. Also see: New Orleans Vicinity (W, via St. 44, Old River Rd, E bank of Mississippi), (W, via St. 18, Old River Rd, W bank). On W bank, approx. 20 mi NW, via US 190 & 1: NEW ROADS. Approx. 8 mi S, ●●**Parlange** (about 1750; later alt. & addit.; rest.), very fine French Colonial "raised cottage" plantation house.

Parlange—French Colonial (Louisiana Office of Tourism)

Baton Rouge Vicinity *(NW, via US 61)*. On way to St. Francisville, interesting plantation houses include: approx. 25 mi, via US 61 & St. 68, Greek Revival *Asphodel (1835; rest.). Approx. 8 mi from Asphodel on St. 965, *Oakley (about 1799; rest.), Audubon State Commemorative Area; interesting outbuildings; John James Audubon, famous naturalist–bird painter lived here for time while tutoring daughter of owners. Approx. 32 mi from Baton Rouge, via US 61: St. Francisville. Interesting buildings include: Gothic Revival *Grace Church, Episcopal (1860; alter alt.). Approx. 1 mi N, via St. 10, •*Rosedown (1835; later alt.; rest.), architect, rest.: George M. Leake; fine house; fine gardens, sculpture. Approx. 2 mi farther, via US 61, *The Myrtles (1796; later alt. & addit.; rest.). Approx. 8 mi farther, via US 61 & St. 124, Rosebank (about 1790; later alt.), originally Spanish inn. Approx. 1 mi W, via St. 66, fine Greek Revival Ellerslie (1835; rest.), architect: James Hammond Coulter. Approx. 3 mi farther, •*Greenwood (1830; rest.), very fine Classic Revival. After returning to US 61, short distance N from junction with St. 124, Waverley (1821; later alt.; rest.), unusual, for Louisiana; Georgian. Approx. 1 mi farther, *Catalpa (about 1810; later alt.; rest.), small cottage; fine garden. Short distance: *The Cottage (about 1795; later alt. & addit.; rest.), low, rambling house; many outbuildings; once home of "Fighting Butlers," so-called for exploits of family members during Revolution and War of 1812. Approx. 25 mi E of St. Francisville, via St. 35: Clinton. Interesting old buildings include: Greek Revival *Courthouse (1841; rest.), Courthouse Sq; architect: J. S. Savage. *Lawyers' Row (about 1830; rest.), group of five small buildings around square.

NATCHITOCHES (pronounced Nak-i-tosh)

Oldest permanent settlement, founded 1714, in entire Louisiana Territory. Interesting old buildings here, many of them built by members of Prudhomme family, include: on Jefferson St, at no. 531, St. Amant House (about 1835; later alt.), architect: Triscini; at no. 436, interesting *Prudhomme-Rouquier House (about 1803; later alt.); at no. 424, *Tante Huppe House (about 1850; later alt.; rest.); at no. 308, *Lemee House (about 1830; rest.), architect: Triscini. Also: *Touzin-Wells House (1766; rest.), 607 Williams St; cypress structure with mud and Spanish moss infilling. Of similar construction: *Roque House (1790; rest.), moved here.

Natchitoches Vicinity *(SE along Cane River Rd, St. 20)*. Nearby interesting homes include: *Beaufort (1830; rest.); houses of various Prudhommes, including Bermuda Plantation (1821; later alt.). Approx. 15 mi from Natchitoches, •*Melrose, originally called Yucca (1833; later alt. & addit.), reputed to have been built by wealthy black, "free man of color" Louis Metoyer; interesting outbuildings include: *Yucca House (about 1796); *African House (about 1800), unusual structure of undetermined purpose. Approx. 8 mi from Melrose: CLOUTIERVILLE. *Bayou Folk Museum (about 1810; rest.), once home of Kate Chopin, author of *Bayou Folk*.

NEW IBERIA

Interesting buildings here and in Evangeline country, named for heroine of Henry Wadsworth Longfellow's poem, include: •*Shadows on the Teche, the David Weeks House (1834; later alt.; rest.), 217 E. Main St; fine plantation house beside bayou, once home of noted painter Weeks Hall. Also of interest, few miles S of New Iberia: *Avery Island salt mine, hot pepper farm and factory, bird sanctuary and Jungle Gardens; *Jefferson Island.

New Iberia Vicinity *(N, via St. 31)*. Approx. 8 mi, ST. MARTINVILLE, town to which French exiles, Acadians (Cajuns), came from Canada; now inseparably associated with Longfellow's *Evangeline*. *Acadian House (1765; later alt. & addit.; rest.), Longfellow-Evangeline State Commemorative Area, now museum with Acadian artifacts; on grounds: small *Acadian Craft House, or Cajun House. Nearby, *St. Martinsville Church, Roman Catholic (1832; later alt.), with cemetery in which Emmeline Labiche, traditionally real-life Evangeline, is buried near Evangeline sculpture. Also of interest: Evangeline Live Oak, under which it is believed Emmeline was reunited with Louis Arceneaux, the "Gabriel" of poem. Approx. 11 mi NW, via St. 96 & US 167: LAFAYETTE. *Acadian Village, collection of early Acadian, or Cajun, buildings moved here. Also: *Les Jardins de Mouton. Approx. 13 mi N of Lafayette, via US 167, Classic Revival Chretien Point Plantation House (1831; later alt. & addit.).

NEW ORLEANS

Treasure house of interesting buildings, especially in *Vieux Carré, or French Quarter, original French city, Nat. Hist. Dist. since 1936, bounded by Iberville and N. Rampart sts, Esplanade Ave & Mississippi River; planner: LeBlond de la Tour; director of layout: Adrien de Pauger. Walking tour of the Quarter, beginning at *Jackson Square, originally Place d'Armes: •*Cabildo (1799; later alt. & addit.; rest.), Chartres St, across from Jackson Sq; architect: Gilberto Guillemard; fine Spanish Colonial; originally seat of Spanish government, later used for city hall, other purposes; now part of Louisiana State Museum. Next door, *St. Louis Cathedral, Roman Catholic (1724; burned 1788; rebuilt 1794; part. demolished 1850; rebuilt 1851), architect: Adrien de Pauger; architect, 1st rebuilding: Gilberto Guillemard; architect, 2nd rebuilding: J. N. B. Depouilly. On other side of Cathedral: *Presbytere (1791; later alt. & addit.), architect: Gilberto Guillemard; architect, 1840–47 addit.: Benjamin Buisson; similar to Cabildo in design; built as rectory for cathedral, but first used as courthouse; now part of Louisiana State Museum. On St. Ann and St. Peter sts. sides of square: *Pontalba Buildings (1850; remod. about 1935), architects: James Gallier, Sr., & Henry Howard; twin blocks of row houses, later converted into apartments. Nearby, *French Market (1823; remod. about 1935; later alt. & addit.), Decatur St. from Jackson Sq corner of St. Ann St to Barracks St; architect: Jacques Tanesse, city surveyor. Not far away: ••**Ursuline Convent** (1753; later alt. & addit.), 1114 Chartres St; architect: Ignace François Broutin; only building in city known to have survived from early French Colonial era; served number of functions; now rectory of nearby *St. Mary's Italian Church (1846). Across street: *LeCarpentier-Beauregard House (1826; later alt. & addit.; rest.), 1113 Chartres St; architect: François Correjolles; architects, rest.: Richard Koch & Samuel Wilson, Jr.; once home of Confederate Gen. P. G. T. Beauregard, later home of author Francis Parkinson Keyes. Not far: ••**U.S. Mint** (1835; later alt. & addit.; rest.), 400 Esplanade Ave; architect: William Strickland; architects, rest.: E. Eean McNaughton; Biery & Toups; Bernard S. Lemann; fine Greek Revival by famous architect; now part of Louisiana State Museum. Not far: *Gallier House (1857; rest.), 1132 Royal St; architect: James Gallier, Jr.; architects, rest.: Koch & Wilson; interesting house designed by noted architect for himself. Not far: *Lafitte's Blacksmith Shop (about 1790; later alt.), 941 Bourbon St; not actually associated with pirate Jean Lafitte; interesting *briquette-entre-poteaux,* or brick between posts, construction. Approx. 20 mi S of city, via St. 45, interesting Barataria country, where Lafitte actually lived. At 632 Dumaine St, ••**Madame John's Legacy** (about 1790; rest.), architect, rest.: F. Monroe Labouisse, Jr.; fine French Colonial house, although erected during Spanish era; raised cottage with brick basement and *briquette-entre-poteaux* construction above; name of house from short story by noted author George Washington Cable. At 527 Royal St, *Merieult House (1762; later alt.; rest.), architects, rest.: Koch & Wilson; one of few buildings to survive fire of 1794. At 500 Chartres St, *Girod House, also known as Napoleon House (1814; later alt.), example of continuation of French architecture during Spanish era. At 820 St. Louis St, *Grima House (1831; later alt.; rest.), unusual, for French Quarter; house in style suggestive of Georgian. Not far: *Louisiana State Bank (1820; later alt.), 509 Royal St; architect: Benjamin Henry Latrobe; last building by famous architect. Nearby, *Bank of Louisiana (1826; later alt. & addit.), 334 Royal St; architect, alt. & addit.: James Gallier, Sr. Confusing things further: *Bank of the United States (about 1800; later alt.), 339 Royal St; *Banque de la Louisiane* (about 1800; later alt.), 417 Royal St, now restaurant. Nearby, although not in French Quarter, ●*U.S. Custom House (1848–80; rest.), 423 Canal St; architect: A. T. Wood; superintendent, construction: P. G. T. Beauregard; Eclectic; Egyptian columns and magnificent Greek Revival main business room, Marble Hall.

NE of French Quarter. In Marigny Hist. Dist.: interesting old buildings. NW, in Treme Hist. Dist.: interesting old buildings, old *St. Louis cemeteries nos. 1 and 2 and new *Louis Armstrong Park. In Bywater area, extreme SE area of city, via St. Claude Ave, St. 46: two fascinating "Steamboat Gothic" Doullut Houses (1905), at nos. 400 & 503 Egania St, built by steamboat captain. Not far: *Jackson Barracks (1835; later alt. & addit.), Delery St. at Mississippi River; architect: Lt. Frederick Wilkinson; buildings resemble Louisiana plantation houses. Few miles farther E: ARABI. Approx. 1 mi S, Three Oaks Plantation House (1840; later alt. & addit.). Approx. 2 mi E of Arabi, *Bueno Retiro, the René Beauregard House (1832; remod. 1856, 1865, 1958), Chalmette Nat. Hist. Park; architects, remod.: 1856 & 1865, James Gallier, Jr.; 1958, Samuel Wilson, Jr.; interesting plantation house at site of Battle of New Orleans, 1815, won by troops of Gen. Andrew Jackson over British under Gen. Edward Michael Pakenham. Approx. 12 mi farther, Kenilworth Plantation House (about 1759; later alt. & addit.).

Business District. Interesting buildings include: ●*Old City Hall, now Gallier Hall (1850; rest.), 545 St. Charles Ave, facing Lafayette Square; architect: James Gallier, Sr.; architects, rest.: Cimini & Meric; fine Greek Revival; named for its famous architect. Few blocks away: *St. Patrick's Church, Roman Catholic (1840; later alt.), 724 Camp St; architects: James & Charles Dakin; replaced by James Gallier, Sr.; interesting Gothic Revival. Few blocks farther: *Howard Memorial Library, now office building (1888; later alt.), 615 Howard Ave; architect: Henry Hobson Richardson; interesting Romanesque Revival; only building in South by famous native Louisiana architect; completed after his death by successor architects: Shepley, Rutan & Coolidge. In Garden District (bet. Louisiana, St. Charles & Jackson aves & Camp St), interesting mid-19th-century houses in section of city settled by Americans after Louisiana Purchase. Walking tour interesting although almost all houses are private. In Lower Garden District, closer to downtown, along St. Charles Ave and in uptown area: interesting houses and other buildings. At 719 Carrollton Ave, fine Greek Revival *Carrollton Courthouse, now Benjamin Franklin School (1855; later alt.), architect: Henry Howard; architect, alt.: Murvan M. Maxwell. Along Bayou St. John, interesting small French Colonial plantation houses with West Indies overtones include: on Moss St, at no. 924, Louis Blanc House (about 1798); at no. 1300, Spanish Custom House (about 1784); at no. 1342, Evariste Blanc House, now Holy Rosary Rectory (about 1834; later alt.), Colonial with some Greek Revival details;

at no. 1440, *Pitot House (about 1800; later alt.; rest.), architects, rest.: Koch & Wilson; moved from block away. Greek Revival examples: Morel Wisner House (about 1855), 1347 Moss St; Musgrove-Wilkinson House (about 1855), 1454 Moss St. Also of interest: *Longvue Gardens, 11 Garden Lane, in Metairie section of city.

New Orleans Vicinity *(W, via St. 44, Old River Rd, E bank of Mississippi).* Along this road were once large number of plantation houses; those surviving include: approx. 15 mi from New Orleans: DESTREHAN. Nearby, Destrehan Plantation (about 1790; addit. 1820; remod, 1840; rest.), raised cottage type, remod. in Greek Revival, 1840. Approx. 2 mi farther, Ormond (about 1799; later alt.; rest.), probable architect, addit.: Henry S. Latrobe; fine Spanish Colonial plantation house. Approx. 15 mi farther: RE-SERVE. Nearby, ●*San Francisco (about 1850; later alt.; rest.), fascinating plantation house; unlike others in state, in style sometimes called "Steamboat Gothic." Approx. 4 mi farther, Mount Airey (about 1850; later alt.). Approx. 11 mi farther: CONVENT. *Jefferson College, now Manresa Retreat House (1831; later alt.; rest.), fine Greek Revival building, now operated by Roman Catholic Jesuit Order; also other interesting buildings here. Approx. 14 mi farther: BURNSIDE. Nearby, via St. 942, ●*Houmas House (1800; later alt. & addit.; rest.), fine Greek Revival plantation house; beautiful gardens. Few miles farther: Bocage (1801; later alt. & addit.; rest.) The Hermitage (about 1812; later alt.), possible architect: James Gallier, Sr. Approx. 8 mi farther, *Ashland,

Evergreen—Greek Revival (Louisiana Office of Tourism)

Oak Alley—Greek Revival (Louisiana Office of Tourism)

or Belle Hélène (1840; later alt.; rest.), architect: James Gallier, Sr.; fine plantation house by noted architect.

New Orleans Vicinity *(W, via St. 18, Old River Rd, W bank of Mississippi).* Number of plantation houses survive, including: approx. 22 mi from New Orleans in HAHNVILLE, Home Place (about 1820; later alt. & addit.). Approx. 17 mi farther: WALLACE. •**Evergreen** (about 1830; later alt. & addit.; rest.), architects, rest.: Koch & Wilson; Douglas Freret; magnificent Greek Revival plantation house on very large estate; many rest. original outbuildings, including *garçonnières, pigeonniers,* slave quarters, kitchen and even Greek Revival privy. Approx. 1 mi farther, Whitney (about 1800; later alt. & addit.). Approx. 6 mi farther: VACHERIE. Nearby, ••**Oak Alley,** or *Bon Sejour* (1839; later alt. & addit.), architect: Joseph Pilie; architects, rest.: Koch & Wilson; magnificent Greek Revival plantation house; beautiful avenue of live oaks from which its name. Approx. 30 mi farther, via St. 18, 70, and 1, *Nottaway (1857; later alt. & addit.), architect: Henry Howard; unusual 64-room mansion. SE of Nottaway, approx. 35 mi, via St. 18 & 1: NAPOLEONVILLE. Gothic Revival *Christ Church, Episcopal (1853; later alt.; rest.), architect: Frank Wills. Approx. 2 mi S, via St. 308, ••**Madewood** (1848; later alt.; rest.), architect: Henry Howard; very fine Greek Revival plantation house. Approx. 13 mi S of Napoleonville, via St. 1, *Edward Douglass White House (about 1830; rest.), State Park; raised cottage, birthplace of chief justice of U.S. Supreme Court. Approx. 5 mi S: THIBODEAUX. Rienzi (1796; later alt. & addit.), built, according to legend, as refuge from Napoleonic Wars for Spanish Queen Maria Luisa.

Mississippi

Early inhabitants Indians of three major tribes, Chickasaw, Choctaw, Natchez; other tribes included Biloxi, Pascagoula, Yazoo. First explored by Spanish led by Hernando de Soto, 1540; later by French led by Robert Cavelier, Sieur de La Salle; claimed for France as part of Louisiana Territory. First permanent French settlement, 1699: Ocean Springs, originally named Old Biloxi, by French-Canadian Pierre Le Moyne, Sieur d'Iberville; second settlement by his brother, Jean Baptiste Le Moyne, Sieur d'Bienville, at Natchez, originally Ft. Rosalie, 1716. Scotsman John Law granted trading rights, 1717; his speculative scheme to develop region failed. In early 18th century, Old Biloxi, New Biloxi (now Biloxi) and Ft. Louis de la Mobile (now Mobile, Ala.) served as capitals at various times; in 1722, New Orleans made capital. French and British battled each other and Indians for possession until 1763 when area E of Mississippi River was ceded to British after end of French and Indian Wars; S portion made part of West Florida, N portion of Georgia, both British colonies. Spanish seized West Florida, 1781; ceded to Spain by British, 1783. N Mississippi became part of United States after Revolution; part of S portion taken by United States, 1795; present states of Alabama and Mississippi became Mississippi Territory, 1798; capital Natchez. Part of West Florida Republic, formed by Americans, 1810, taken into territory, 1812. During War of 1812, Choctaw Indians joined forces of Gen. Andrew Jackson in Battle of New Orleans, 1815. Territory divided into states of Alabama and Mississippi. Became twentieth state, Dec. 10, 1817. In addition to Natchez, Columbia and Washington served as capitals; Jackson named, 1822. Seceded from Union, 1861, second state, after S. C., to do so; Mississippian Jefferson Davis, who had been U.S. senator and secretary of war, became president of Confederacy; many important Civil War battles fought in state, including Gen. Ulysses S. Grant's victory in Battle of Vicksburg, 1863. Readmitted to Union, 1870. State suffered from war for many years afterward. Today: Major manufacturing and agricultural industries; also of great importance, oil and natural gas production.

Land Regions: Most of state, East Gulf Coastal Plain; NE, Black Belt; W, Mississippi Alluvial Plain.

Climate: Long, hot, moist summers; short, mild winters; precipitation heavy; snowfall minimal; hurricanes and other tropical storms often threaten.

Major Building Materials: Timber; stone; sand and gravel; clay.

Architecture: Rich and varied from Colonial era to present; important buildings in several places, especially Columbus; Natchez.

BILOXI

Interesting buildings include: *Beauvoir (1852; rest.), US 90, toward Gulfport; raised cottage, last home of Confederate President Jefferson Davis. Modern *Biloxi Public Library and Cultural Center (1977), architects: MLTW/Turnbill; 217 Lameuse St. Across street: *U.S. Courthouse and Custom House, now City Hall (1904; rest.), architect: Stuart Evans. Approx. 90 mi NW, via US I-10 & St. 43 & 35: SANDY HOOK. *John Ford House (about 1800; rest.), interesting pioneer raised cottage.

Biloxi Vicinity (*E, via US 90*). Approx. 5 mi OCEAN SPRINGS. Louis Sullivan Summer House (1890; later alt. & addit.); James Charnley Summer House and Guesthouse (1890; later alt. & addit.), architect: Frank Lloyd Wright; interesting early modern examples which some experts believe were designed by Sullivan himself. Approx. 6 mi farther: GAUTIER. *Old Place, the Fernando Gautier House (1860; rest.), interesting plantation house. Approx. 4 mi farther: PASCAGOULA. *Old Spanish Fort (about 1720; rest.), 4602 Fort St; interesting example, actually house, built by French naval officer Joseph Simon de la Pointe. Also see: Alabama—Mobile.

COLUMBUS

Number of interesting buildings here, some usually open, others only during April Pilgrimage, include: *Amzi Love House (1848; later alt.), 305 7th St S; Italianate. On 7th St N, at no. 316, another Italianate example, *Blewett-Harrison-Lee House (1847; later alt.), once home of Gen. Stephen D. Lee; at no. 416, *Camellia Place (about 1845; later alt.), Greek Revival with Victorian details; at no. 510, Gothic Revival *Thermerlaine (1844; later alt.); at no. 1206, *Hickory Sticks (about 1820; later alt. & addit.), log house covered with wood siding. Also: Greek Revival *Temple Heights (1837; later alt. & addit.), 515 9th St N. *Wisteria Place (1854; later alt.) 524 8th St N. *Franklin Square (1835; later alt. & addit.), 423 3rd Ave N. At 216 3rd Ave S, *Errolton (1848; rest.), Greek Revival with Victorian elements. At 318 2nd St, Victorian Episcopal Rectory (1880), boyhood home of famous playwright Tennessee Williams. At 514 2nd St S, *Riverview (1847), imposing brick mansion. At 122 7th Ave S, *White Arches (1857; rest.), Gothic Revival with Greek Revival elements, 3-story tower. Not far from city, several fine plantation houses including, approx. 6 mi NW, via St. 50: ●*Waverley (1852; rest.), fascinating Greek Revival; unusual large octagonal cupola.

Also: *Commercial Hist. Dist. Approx. 25 mi S, via US 45, MA-CON, location of interesting old houses.

Columbus Vicinity *(NW, via US 45 & 78)*. Approx. 25 mi, ABER-DEEN, location of interesting old buildings. Approx. 100 mi farther: HOLLY SPRINGS. In town of only about 6,000 population, surprising number of fine old buildings, few of which are open to public except during April Spring Pilgrimage. On Salem St, at no. 222, Greek Revival *Montrose (1858; later alt.); across street, at no. 221, Oakleigh, the Clapp-Fant House (about 1845; later alt. & addit.), also Greek Revival; at no. 330, Airliewood (1859; later alt. & addit.), Gothic Revival in Swiss Chalet manner; at no. 411, Gothic Revival Cedarhurst, the Belk-Bonner House (1858; later alt.). At 331 W. Chulahoma St, Walter Place (1845; later alt.; rest.), architect, rest.: Theodore C. Link; large, imposing Greek Revival mansion; Gothic Revival towers and other details. Approx. 30 mi S, via St. 7: OXFORD. Interesting old buildings include: at *University of Mississippi, *Lyceum Building (1848; later alt. & addit.), architect: William Nichols; fine Greek Revival; first university building. Near campus, at 900 Garfield St, Rowan Oak, the William Faulkner House (1848; later addit.), Greek Revival; once home of famous novelist; interesting gardens and outbuildings. On Murray Ave, Greek Revival *Cedar Oaks (1859; later alt.; rest.), threatened by demolition, large house was cut in half, moved here and reassembled. On Lamar Ave, Amma-delle (1848; later alt.), architect: Calvert Vaux; fine Eclectic Italianate villa by noted architect who, with Frederick Law Olmsted, designed New York City's Central Park. Approx. 65 mi NW of Oxford, via St. 6 & US I-55, just S of Memphis, Tenn.: HORN LAKE. Mon Amour (about 1860; later alt. & addit.; rest.), interesting octagonal house, its design based on theories of noted phrenologist and author Orson Squires Fowler. Also see: Tennessee–Memphis.

Columbus Vicinity *(W, via US 82)*. Approx. 80 mi: CARROLL-TON. Interesting old houses, mostly open only during Spring Pilgrimage, include: Cotesworth (about 1840; later alt. & addit.; rest.), Colonial; separate hexagonal *Library (1860; rest.).

JACKSON

Interesting buildings include: *State Capitol (1903; later alt.), Mississippi & Congress sts; architect: Theodore C. Link; reputedly modeled after U.S. Capitol. *Old Capitol, now museum (1839; later alt.), State St; architect: William Nichols; fine Greek Revival example. Not far: *Governor's Mansion (1842; later alt. & addit.), 316 E. Capitol St; architect: William Nichols; fine Greek Revival. At Pascagoula & S. President sts, another interesting Greek Revival public building: *City Hall (about 1850; later alt.), probable architect: William Gibbon. Two small Greek Revival houses of interest: *The Oaks (1846; rest.), 823 N. Jefferson St; Charles H. Manship House (1857; later alt.), N. West St. Just N of Jackson: TOUGALOO. At *Tougaloo College, interesting modern *Dormitories (1973); *L. Zenobia Coleman Library (1973); architect: Gunnar Birkerts; first units of planned new complex. Approx. 14 mi farther, via US 5: CANTON. Interesting buildings include: *Madison Co. Courthouse (1852; later alt.), Courthouse Sq; fine Greek Revival with dome. Approx. 7 mi N of Jackson, via US 49, *Sub Rosa Plantation House (about 1855; later alt.).

NATCHEZ

Relatively small city, of approx. 22,000 population, located high on bluffs overlooking Mississippi River; founded by French, taken by British, then by Spanish, finally, by Americans. Remarkable number of fine 18th- and 19th-century houses and other buildings here; some open only during Natchez Pilgrimages (March-April and October).

Walking tour: ●*Rosalie (1823; rest.), 100 Orleans St; architect: James S. Griffin; very fine late Georgian, Greek Revival details. At 107 S. Broadway, *Evansview, originally Bontura (1790; later alt. & addit.; rest.), Spanish Colonial, iron grillework. Not far: Spanish Colonial *Connelly's Tavern (about 1795; later alt.; rest.), Ellicott's Hill, Jefferson & Canal sts. At Jefferson and N. Rankin sts, *King's Tavern (about 1770; later alt.; rest.), believed to be oldest building in city, now restaurant. At High & N. Wall sts, Greek Revival *Cherokee (1794; later alt. & addit.); also here: *Choctaw, now American Legion Hall (1836; rest.), architect: James Hardie; once home of philanthropist Alvarez Fisk. At 401 High St, ●*Stanton Hall (1857; rest.), architect: Thomas Rose;

Stanton Hall—Greek Revival (Natchez Pilgrimage Tours)

magnificent Greek Revival mansion, now Natchez Pilgrimage Information Center; beautiful gardens and carriage house restaurant. Greek Revival *Green Leaves (about 1812), Washington & S. Rankin sts. Spanish Colonial *The Elms (about 1783; later alt. & addit.), Washington & S. Pine sts. At E end of Main St, Greek Revival *Arlington (1816; later alt.), architect: James H. White. At S end of Arlington St, ••**Dunleith** (1857; later alt. & addit.), very fine Greek Revival; surrounded by two-story columns; some Eclectic details. At Homochitto St & Auburn Rd, *Hope Farm (1775; about 1789; later alt. & addit.), one section English Colonial, other Spanish Colonial built by Spanish Gov. Carlos de Grand Pre. Not far: ••**Auburn** (about 1812; later alt. & addit.), Duncan Park, Auburn Rd & Park Ave; architect: Levi Weeks; very fine Greek Revival by noted architect of other buildings in area. On Melrose Ave, ••**Melrose** (1845), very fine Greek Revival; no structural changes since built; furnishings, gardens almost as in 19th century. On Pine Ridge Rd N, Greek Revival *Lansdowwne (1853; later alt.).

Natchez Vicinity *(NE, via US 61).* Approx. 2 mi: ••**D' Evereux** (1840; later alt.; rest.), architect: James Hardie; magnificent Greek Revival, considered one of finest U.S. buildings. Approx. 4 mi farther: WASHINGTON. Interesting buildings include: *Jefferson Military College, now Museum (1817–38; rest.), Main St; architect: Levi Weeks; Jefferson Davis was student here, John James Audubon teacher; 1807, preliminary treason trial of Aaron Burr held on campus. Approx. 16 mi NE of Natchez on Natchez Trace, old Indian trail from Natchez to Nashville, Tenn.: *Mount Locust (1779; rest.), Colonial house, later inn. Approx. 30 mi NE of Washington, via US 61: PORT GIBSON. Interesting old buildings include: Gothic Revival *First Presbyterian Church (1859; later alt.), Church & Walnut sts; spire has hand with index finger pointing heavenward; chandeliers from old riverboat *Robert E. Lee.*

D'Evereux—Greek Revival (Natchez Pilgrimage Tours)

Longwood—Eclectic (Natchez Pilgrimage Tours)

Natchez Vicinity *(S, via Lower Woodville Rd & US 61)*. Few miles from city: ••**Longwood,** also known as "Nutt's Folly" (begun 1860; never completed), architect: Samuel Sloan; fantastic octagonal Eclectic house said to be partially "Moorish," "Byzantine," "Steamboat Gothic," other styles; design based on theories of Orson Squires Fowler; owner, Haller Nutt, invented number of devices for natural cooling and solar heating. Few miles farther: Gloucester (about 1800; addit. 1808; later alt.), architect, addit.: Levi Weeks; very fine Greek Revival; interesting outbuildings; once home of Winthrop Sargent, first territorial governor. Approx. 30 mi farther: WOODVILLE. Interesting buildings include: *Rosemont (1814; later alt. & addit.; rest.), boyhood home of Jefferson Davis. Approx. 20 mi farther, FORT ADAMS, now almost ghost town; few surviving old houses.

VICKSBURG

Interesting buildings include: *Old Courthouse, now Museum (1861; damaged Civil War; later alt.), Cherry St bet. Grove & Jackson sts; Greek Revival; interesting cupola and four water cisterns converted to offices. *Gov. Alexander McNutt House (about 1828; later alt.; rest.), Monroe & First East sts. Duff Green Mansion (about 1845; later alt.), Locust & First East sts; interesting grillework. Greek Revival *Cedar Grove, the Klein House (1840; later alt.), 2200 Oak St. *McRaven (1797; addit. 1836; addit. 1849; rest.), Harrison East & Gates East sts; built in three stages in Pioneer, French Colonial and Greek Revival styles. Also of interest: *Vicksburg Nat. Mil. Park, in which small farmhouse that survived Civil War siege: *Candon Hearth (about 1845; later alt.), 2530 Confederate Ave.

North Carolina

Early inhabitants Indians of some thirty tribes, including Catawba, Cherokee, Hatteras, Tuscarora. First explored by Italian Giovanni da Verrazano, for France, 1524. Spaniard Lukas Vásquez de Ayllón founded short-lived colony near Cape Fear, about 1526. Spaniard Hernando de Soto explored, 1540. Sir Walter Raleigh sent party to establish colony on Roanoke Island, 1586; after hardships, colonists returned to England, 1587. In same year Raleigh sent second group of colonists led by Gov. John White, who returned to England; when he returned to Roanoke Island, 1590, first English colony in America had completely vanished, along with more than a hundred colonists, including Virginia Dare, first English child born in America. First permanent English settlement near Albermarle Sound, about 1650, by colonists from Virginia. Carolina Colony granted to eight lords proprietors, 1663; North Carolina separated from South Carolina, 1712; made royal colony, 1729. Colony was first to make decision to vote for independence, 1776. Became twelfth state, Nov. 21, 1789. Seceded from Union, 1861; most of E portion captured by Federal troops early in Civil War; in most important action, Federal troops of Gen. William Tecumseh Sherman defeated those of Confederate Gen. Joseph E. Johnston at Battle of Bentonville, 1865. Readmitted to Union, 1868. Today: Major manufacturing, primarily cloth and furniture, and agricultural, primarily tobacco, industries.

Land Regions: From E to W, Atlantic Coastal Plain; Piedmont; Blue Ridge.

Climate: Mild, colder in Blue Ridge than elsewhere; precipitation fairly heavy, more in mountains; snowfall moderate in Blue Ridge, almost none near coast.

Major Building Materials: Stone, especially granite; timber, especially softwoods; sand and gravel; clay.

Architecture: Rich and varied, from Colonial era to present; in addition to examples in large cities such as Raleigh and Winston-Salem, large number of fine examples in smaller places, such as in Elizabeth City Vicinity (SW, via US 17).

ASHEVILLE

Interesting buildings include: •*Biltmore (1895), off US 25 S; architect: Richard Morris Hunt; magnificent Eclectic French Renaissance Revival mansion designed for George Washington Van-

Biltmore—Eclectic French Renaissance Revival (Wayne Andrews)

derbilt by famous architect; many rooms have fine original furnishings; beautiful grounds designed by famous landscape architect Frederick Law Olmsted. Also: *Thomas Wolfe House (about 1890; later alt.; rest.), 48 Spruce St; boyhood home of famous novelist was model for rooming house in his book *Look Homeward Angel.* Approx. 8 mi N of Asheville, via US I-26, near WEAVERVILLE, *Zebulon Baird Vance House (1795; rest.); log cabin birthplace of state governor. Approx. 40 mi E of Asheville, via US I-40 and 70: MARION. Log and clapboard *Col. John Carson House (about 1810; rest.). Also of interest: nearby, *Blue Ridge Pkwy runs both N & S of city: approx. 30 mi W of Asheville, via US I-40: *Great Smoky Mountain Nat. Park.

CHARLOTTE

Interesting buildings include: *Mint Museum, originally U.S. Mint (1840; part. burned 1844; rebuilt 1846; rest.), 501 Hempstead Pl; architect: William Strickland; fine Greek Revival by famous architect. At 3420 Shamrock Dr, *Hezekiah Alexander House (1774; rest.), once home of signer of Mecklenburg Declaration of Independence, 1774, two years before U.S. Declaration. Approx. 60 mi E of Charlotte, via St. 49 & 73: MOUNT GILEAD. *Town Creek Indian Mound (about 1600).

Charlotte Vicinity *(NE, via US I-85).* Approx. 40 mi: SALISBURY. Number of interesting old buildings including: *Maxwell Chambers House, now Rowan Museum (1819; later alt.), 114 S. Jackson St. Approx. 3 mi S of Salisbury, via US 52: GRANITE

QUARRY. *Michael Braun House, also known as Old Stone House (1766; later alt.; rest.), fine German Colonial.

ELIZABETH CITY

Interesting old buildings include: in Hist. Dist., Gothic Revival *Christ Church, Episcopal (1856; later alt.), Church & McMorine sts. W of Elizabeth City, approx. 50 mi, via US 158, MURFREESBORO, interesting old buildings. Approx. 40 mi farther, US 158 & 301, HALIFAX, scene of "Halifax Resolves," April 12, 1776, calling for independence.

Elizabeth City Vicinity *(SE, via US 158)*. Approx. 60 mi, on Roanoke Island, near MANTEO, *Ft. Raleigh Nat. Hist. Site, first attempted English colony; first English child born in America: Virginia Dare; reprod. of early fort, other buildings; theater in which play, *Lost Colony,* by Paul Green is performed each summer. Also of interest, nearby, beautiful *Elizabethan Gardens. Also of interest, approx. 20 mi NE of Manteo, KILL DEVIL HILLS, *Wright Brothers Nat. Memorial. Approx. 50 mi SE of Manteo, via St. 12, *Cape Hatteras Lighthouse (1870; later alt.), *Cape Hatteras Nat. Seashore.

Elizabeth City Vicinity *(SW, via US 17)*. Approx. 17 mi: HERTFORD. Nearby, *Newbold-White House (about 1685; rest.), oldest house in state. Approx. 13 mi farther, EDENTON, founded 1658. Interesting buildings include: *Thomas Barker House (about 1782; later alt. & addit.), S. Broad St, beside Albermarle Sound; Visitors' Center; moved here. Nearby, *Cupola House (about 1725; later alt. & addit.; rest.), 408 S. Broad St; unusual wood-frame Jacobean. Nearby, The Homestead (about 1773; later alt. & addit.), E. Water St; *Chowan Co. Courthouse (1767), E. King St; fine Georgian; in continuous use since construction. Not far: *James Iredell House (about 1760; later alt. & addit.), E. Church St; once home of one of first justices of U.S. Supreme Court. Few blocks: Georgian *St. Paul's Episcopal Church (1736–60; later alt.; rest.), S. Broad & W. Church sts. Not far from Edenton, on Sound, Hayes Plantation (about 1800; later alt. & addit.), fine Classic Revival. Approx. 38 mi SE of Edenton, via St. 32 & US 64, near CRESWELL, *Somerset Place, the Josiah Collins Plantation (about 1830; later alt. & addit.; rest.), Pettigrew State Park, interesting cypress-framed house; old outbuildings. Approx. 20 mi SW of Edenton, via US 17: WINDSOR. Approx. 5 mi W, via St. 308, *Hope Plantation (about 1800; rest.), birthplace of Gov. David Stone. Approx. 35 mi past Windsor, via US 17: WASHINGTON. Interesting old buildings include: *Beaufort Co. Courthouse, now Regional Library (about 1786; later alt. & addit.), Market & 2nd sts; interesting clock tower. Approx. 18 mi E of Washington, via

St. 92: BATH. Whole small town is Hist. Dist. retaining 18th-century character. Interesting buildings include: *St. Thomas Episcopal Church (about 1734; rest.), Craven St. Next door, *Glebe House, now Library (about 1830; later alt.). Not far: *Palmer-Marsh House (about 1744; rest.), once home of Col. Robert Palmer, state surveyor-general; *Bonner House (about 1825; rest.). Approx. 35 mi S of Washington, via US 17: NEW BERN. Interesting buildings include: ●*Tryon Place (1770; burned 1798; reconst. 1959), George & Pollock sts; architect: John Hawks; architects, reconst.: Perry, Shaw & Hepburn; very fine reconst. mansion built for Colonial Gov. William Tryon; very fine outbuildings, gardens; originally both capitol of government and residence of governors. At no. 611 Pollock, Federal *Dixon-Stevenson House (about 1825; rest.), used as Federal hospital during Civil War; small wood-framed *Crispin Jones House (about 1806; rest.) at 231 Eden St.; John Wright Stanly House (about 1780; rest.), 307 George St; probable architect: John Hawks; fine Georgian; fine gardens; moved here. On Pollock St, at no. 216, Federal *Hatch-Washington House (1818; later alt. & addit.). At Pollock & Middle sts, *Christ Church, Episcopal (1873), Gothic Revival on site of two earlier churches; beautiful grounds. Some blocks away: *First Presbyterian Church (1822; later alt. & addit.), New St, bet. Hancock & Middle sts; probable architect: Uriah Sandy; very fine Federal or Early Greek Revival; very much like early churches in New England. Approx. 40 mi SE of New Bern, via US 70: BEAUFORT (pronounced Bo-fort). Interesting old houses here, many of them on Front St; also: *Josiah Bell House (about 1825; rest.), 138 Turner St. Across street: *Joseph Bell House (about 1767; rest.); number of others nearby. Also of interest, approx. 10 mi from Beaufort, via US 70, Morehead Ave & St. 68, near *Atlantic Beach: brick *Ft. Macon (1834), State Park, Bogue Island.

FAYETTEVILLE

Interesting buildings include: Eclectic *Old Market House, now Public Library (1838; later alt.; rest.), Market Square. At *Heritage Square, *Halliday-Williams House (about 1800; later alt. & addit.), interesting oval ballroom added, 1830; *Baker-Haigh-Nimocks House (about 1804; later alt.; rest.); *Sanford House (about 1800; later alt.; rest.). Approx. 25 mi SE of Fayetteville, via St. 53: WHITE OAK. *Harmony Hall, the Col. James Richardson House (about 1765; rest.).

RALEIGH

Interesting buildings include: ●*State Capitol (1840; rest.), Capitol Square; architects: William Nichols, Jr.; Town & Davis; David

North Carolina State Capital—Greek Revival (Wayne Andrews)

Paton; very fine Greek Revival example. Block away: modern
*State Legislative Building (1963), Halifax St, architect: Edward
Durell Stone. Not far: Victorian *Governor's Mansion (1891;
rest.), 200 N. Blount St; architect: Gustavus A. Bauer. Also:
*Christ Church, Episcopal (1848; later alt.), Edenton & Wilming-
ton sts; architect: Richard Upjohn; imposing Gothic Revival by
famous architect. *Joel Lane House (about 1760; later alt. &
addit.), 729 Hargett St; oldest house in city. *Andrew Johnson
Birthplace (about 1800; rest.), Pullen Park; moved here. Also:
*North Carolina State University; ●*J. S. Dorton Arena (1953),
1025 Blue Ridge Blvd, State Fair Grounds; architect: Matthew
Nowicki; assoc. architect: William Deitrick; structural engineer:
Fred N. Severud; fine modern arena, with spectacular roof. Approx. 50 mi NW, via US 401: WARRENTON. Interesting old houses
include: Greek Revival Elgin (1832; later alt. & addit.); Whit-
some, the Coleman-White-Jones House (about 1825; later alt. &
addit.). Approx. 60 mi SE of Raleigh, via US 70 and 117: FRE-
MONT. *Charles B. Aycock House (1840; rest.); birthplace of
state governor; also several original farm outbuildings, old school
(1870; rest.).

Raleigh Vicinity *(E, via US 64).* Approx. 50 mi: ROCKY MOUNT.
Interesting buildings include: Dortch House (about 1803; later alt.
& addit.), unusual Palladian triple windows. Approx. 30 mi N of
Rocky Mount, via US 301: HALIFAX. Interesting old houses include: in Hist. Dist., *Constitution House (about 1770; rest.), first
state constitution drafted here; moved here. *George W. Owen
House (about 1760; rest.).

Raleigh Vicinity *(NW, via US I-40)*. Approx. 20 mi: DURHAM. Interesting buildings include: *Washington Duke Homestead (1852; rest.), Duke Homestead Rd. Near Durham, on Cornwallis Rd, *Research Triangle Park; location of number of interesting modern research laboratories and other buildings, including: •*Burroughs-Wellcome Co. Headquarters** (1972), architect: Paul Rudolph. Approx. 5 mi W of Durham, off US I-85, *Bennett Place (about 1850; rest.); site of surrender of armies of Confederate Gen. Joseph E. Johnston to Federal Gen. William T. Sherman, 1865. Approx. 13 mi W of Durham, via US I-85: HILLSBOROUGH. Interesting buildings include, on S. Churton St: Gothic Revival *St. Matthew's Episcopal Church (1815; later alt.), architect: Francis L. Hawks; Greek Revival *Old Courthouse, now Hist. Museum (1845; later alt.), architect: John Berry. Approx. 12 mi S of Durham, via US 15/501: CHAPEL HILL. Interesting buildings at *University of North Carolina include: Greek Revival *Old Library, now Theater (1850; later alt.), probable architect: Alexander Jackson Davis; Gothic Revival *Chapel of the Cross, Episcopal (1846; later alt.), Franklin St; architect: Francis L. Hawks, built by slave labor. Approx. 2 mi NE of city, via US 15/501, unusually shaped modern glass *Blue Cross/Blue Shield Building (1973), architect: Arthur Gould Odell.

WILMINGTON

Interesting buildings include: *Burgwin-Wright House, also known as Cornwallis House (1771; rest.), 224 Market St; headquarters of Lord Cornwallis during Revolution; opp. Cornwallis House, Gothic Revival *St. James Episcopal Church (1839; later alt. & addit.), architect: Thomas U. Walter. Late flamboyant Classic Revival *Bellamy House (1859; rest.), Market & 5th sts; architect: Rufus F. Bunnell. Italianate *Zebulon Latimer House (1852; rest.), 126 S. 3rd St. Approx. 15 mi S of Wilmington, via US 17 & St. 133, Orton Plantation (about 1725; later alt. & addit.), on Cape Fear River; fine Greek Revival; fine gardens open to public. Approx. 15 mi S of Orton, via St. 133, near SOUTHPORT, interesting buildings of *Brunswick Hist. Dist. Also see: Elizabeth City Vicinity (SW, via US 17); South Carolina—Charleston Vicinity (NE, via US 17).

WINSTON-SALEM

*Old Salem, Main St. Number of fine buildings, many beautifully rest., built by Moravians, German Protestant sect, in German styles, include: on Main St, *Single Brothers House (1769; later alt. & addit.; rest.); *John Vogler House (1819; rest.); *Tavern (1784; rest.); *Boys School, now Wachovia Hist. Museum (1794; rest.). Nearby, at *Salem College, other interesting Moravian buildings include: *Home Moravian Church (1800), 529 S.

Church St; architect: Frederick William Marshall. By same architect, off Reynolda Rd at BETHABARA, *Moravian Church (1788). Not far: *Reynolda House (1917; later alt.), architect: Charles B. Keen; model village, farm established by Mr. & Mrs. R. J. Reynolds. Approx. 13 mi SE, via US 311: HIGH POINT. *John Haley House (1786; later alt.; rest.), 1805 E. Lexington Ave; built by early Quaker settlers. Also see: Charlotte Vicinity (NE, via US I-85).

Winston-Salem Vicinity *(E, via US I-40)*. Approx. 10 mi: KERNERSVILLE. *Korner's Folly (1880; later alt. & addit.), S. Main St; unusual Victorian; no two rooms same size; no doors or ceiling heights same. Approx. 15 mi E of Kernersville: GREENSBORO. *Governmental Center (1973), Green & Sycamore sts; architect: Eduardo Catalano; assoc. architects: Peter C. Sugar and McMinn, Norfleet & Wicker; interesting group of modern buildings includes: *Municipal Office Building; *Guilford Co. Courthouse, by noted Argentine-American architect. Also here: *Old Courthouse (1918), architect: Harry Barton. Also: *Francis McNairy House (1762; rest.), 130 Summit Ave; log cabin. *Blandwood, the John M. Morehead House (1825; later alt. & addit.), 411 W. Washington St; architect: Alexander Jackson Davis; unusual Eclectic Tuscan Revival; once home of state governor. Approx. 18 mi E, via US I-40, another log cabin, *John Allen House (about 1782; later alt.; rest.), moved to *Alamance Battleground.

South Carolina

Early inhabitants Indians of some thirty tribes, including Catawba, Cherokee, Yamasee. First explored by Spanish led by Francisco Gordillo, 1521. Spaniard Vásquez de Ayllón attempted to found colony near Winyah Bay, 1526; French tried, 1562–65, to establish colony at Port Royal; both failed. England claimed North and South Carolina, then called Province of Carolina; granted area to Robert Heath, 1629, then to eight lords proprietors, 1663. First permanent English settlement made by them at Albemarle Point, near Charleston, 1670; moved to present-day Charleston, then called Charles Town, 1680. Withstood attacks by French, Spanish, Indians, pirates, 1702–18; became royal colony, 1719. Region divided into North Carolina and South Carolina, 1730; S portion of South Carolina became part of Georgia, 1732. During Revolutionary War, some 140 important battles and skirmishes took place in state; importantly, American victories at

King's Mountain, 1780, and Cowpens, 1781. Became eighth state, May 23, 1788. State threatened secession from Union as early as 1832; seceded Dec. 20, 1860, first state to do so. Civil War began April 12, 1861, when Confederate troops fired on Ft. Sumter in Charleston harbor. Federal troops later blockaded harbor; troops of Gen. William Tecumseh Sherman pillaged countryside, burning many of finest plantation houses in process, 1865. Readmitted to Union, 1868. Today: Important manufacturing and agricultural industries; tourism also important.

Land Regions: E to W, Atlantic Coastal Plain; Piedmont; in NW, small Blue Ridge.

Climate: Warm; warmer in S than N; precipitation moderate; snowfall light in mountains, rare in remainder of state.

Major Building Materials: Timber; stone; sand and gravel.

Architecture: Rich and varied from early Colonial era to present, particularly in Charleston and vicinity, especially Beaufort.

CHARLESTON

Literally hundreds of interesting buildings here, in Hist. Dist. and elsewhere. Walking tour: beginning near *White Point Gardens (Battery Park), Gibbes House (about 1789; later alt. & addit.), 64 S. Battery; Gen. William Washington House (about 1768; later alt. & addit.), 8 S. Battery. N on E. Battery & E. Bay sts, *Edmonston-Alston House (1829; later alt. & addit.), 21 E. Battery. Vanderhorst Row (1800; later alt. & addit.), 78 E. Bay St; Georgian; considered one of first U.S. apartment buildings. Classic Revival *First National Bank, formerly Planters and Mechanics Bank (about 1845; later alt. & addit.), 139 E. Bay St; contrasts mightily with neighbor: Eclectic Moorish Old Farmers and Exchange Bank (1859), 141 E. Bay St, architect: Francis D. Lee. *Old Exchange and Custom House (1772; later alt. & addit.), 122 E. Bay St; architects: Peter & John Horlbeck. Classic Revival *U.S. Custom House (1855), architects: Ammi B. Young & Edward Blake White, 200 E. Bay St. On E. Bay St at Market St, rear end of *Market Hall (1841; later alt. & addit.), address: 188 Meeting St; architect: Edward Blake White. Classic Revival *St. Johannes Lutheran Church (1842; later alt. & addit.), 48 Hasell St. Col. William Rhett House (about 1712; later alt. & addit.), 54 Hasell St; considered oldest house in city. *Old Powder Magazine (1713; later alt. & addit.), 23 Cumberland St. Next few blocks S on Meeting St, remarkable collection of fine and important buildings includes: ●*Fireproof Building, also known as Records Building (1826; later alt.), 100 Meeting St; architect: Robert Mills; Classic Revival by famous architect of many other fine buildings; believed to be first U.S. building designed to be fireproof. Across

**St. Michael's Church—
Colonial** (Wayne Andrews)

street: Greek Revival Hibernian Hall (1840; later alt.), 105 Meeting St; architect: Thomas U. Walter; by famous architect. Nearby, ●*St. Michael's Church, Episcopal (1761; later alt.), 80 Meeting St; probable architect: Samuel Cardy; one of finest Colonial churches; considered one of finest U.S. buildings. Diagonally across street: Classic Revival *Charleston Co. Courthouse (1792; later alt.), 87 Meeting St. Across from there: Federal *Charleston City Hall, originally First Bank of U.S. (1801; later alt.), 80 Broad St; architect: Gabriel Manigault; Greek Revival by noted lawyer, planter and amateur architect; Council Chamber has famous portrait of George Washington by John Trumbull and other fine portraits. Another of Manigault's designs: South Carolina Society Hall (1804; later alt. & addit.), 72 Meeting St. Not far, at 50 Broad St, *Citizen's and Southern National Bank, originally Bank of South Carolina (about 1798; later alt. & addit.). Not far ●*Nathaniel Russell House (about 1811), 51 Meeting St; very fine Adam mansion. Nearby, *First Scotch Presbyterian Church (1814; later alt.), 53 Meeting St. Not far: Col. John Stuart House (about 1772; later alt. & addit.), 106 Tradd St. Continuing down Meeting St, at no. 34, Daniel Elliott Huger House (about 1760 later alt. & addit.), once home of Lord Campbell, last English royal governor. Not far: ●*Miles Brewton House (about 1769; later alt. & addit.; rest.), 27 King St; architect Ezra Waite; very fine Georgian; fine wood carvings by architect. N on Church St, number of fine and important buildings include: Classic Revival *First Baptist Church (1822; later alt.), 61 Church St; architect: Robert Mills; at no. 69, Jacobe Motte House (1745; later alt.); at no. 71 Col. Robert Brewton House (about 1730; later alt.). Nearby,

●***Heyward-Washington House** (about 1770; later alt. & addit.; rest.), 87 Church St; very fine Georgian; once home of Thomas Heyward, signer of Declaration of Independence. Next door, at 89 & 91 Church St, Cabbage Row (about 1800) famous as model for "Catfish Row" in DuBose Heyward's novel *Porgy* and opera, *Porgy and Bess,* written by Heyward in collaboration with George and Ira Gershwin. Up street, at no. 135, *Dock Street Theater (reconst. 1937) from ruins of old Planters' Hotel (1810). Across street, at no. 136, *Huguenot Church (1845), architect: Edward Blake White; believed to be only church in U.S. still using old French Protestant liturgy. Nearby,

●***St. Philip's Episcopal Church** (1838; tower 1850; later alt.), 146 Church St; architect: Joseph Hyde; architect, tower: Edward Blake White; fine example; replaced Colonial church of similar design which burned, 1835.

In other parts of the city, notable buildings include: *Ashley Hall School (about 1820; later alt.), 172 Rutledge Ave; possible architect: William Jay; reminiscent of houses in Savannah by this noted English architect. *Charleston College, 66 George St, Classic Revival *Main Building, now Harrison Randolph Hall (1829; addit. 1851; later alt. & addit.), architect: William Strickland; architect, 1851 addit.: Edward Blake White. *Lodge (1850; later alt.), architect: Edward Blake White; Library (1856; later alt.), architect: George Edward Walker. Also: *Charleston Orphan House (1794; later alt.), 160 Calhoun St. *Chapel (1802; later alt.), 13 Vanderhorst St; architect: Gabriel Manigault. Few blocks E: ●●***Joseph Manigault House** (about 1803; rest.), 350 Meeting St; architect: Gabriel Manigault; very fine Adam house; interesting Gate House (about 1803). Also of interest: approx. 10 mi NW, via

Miles Brewton House—Georgian (Wayne Andrews)

St. 61 & 171, *Charles Towne Landing, 1500 Old Towne Rd
exhibits on site of first permanent English settlement, 1670. Near
city by ferry, *Ft. Sumter (begun 1827), first shots of Civil War
fired here.

Charleston Vicinity *(N, via US 52)*. Approx. 15 mi: GOOSE
CREEK. Approx 2 mi N, *St. James Episcopal Church (about
1711; later alt.; rest.), unusual stuccoed Colonial church with no
steeple; unusually dominant pulpit, for Anglican church. Approx
10 mi farther, via US 52 & St. 520, *Mulberry Plantation (1714)
on Cooper River, sometimes called "Mulberry Castle" because of
Jacobean flamboyance. Approx. 40 mi farther: ST. STEPHEN'S
*St. Stephen's Episcopal Church (1769; rest.), Church St; unusual
Jacobean example.

Charleston Vicinity *(NE, via US 17)*. Approx. 45 mi, off US 17
*Hampton Plantation (about 1735; later alt. & addit.; rest.), on
Santee River, State Park; once home of noted poet Archibald Rutledge. Approx. 3 mi farther, *Hopsewee Plantation (about 1740)
birthplace of Thomas Lynch, signer of Declaration of Independence. Approx. 12 mi farther: GEORGETOWN. Interesting old
buildings include: *Pyatt-Doyle House (about 1790), 630 Highmarket St; *Prince George Winyan Episcopal Church (about
1740; later alt. & addit.), Highmarket & Broad sts; *Wicklow
Hall (about 1850; rest.), Cat Island Rd. Also of interest, approx
25 mi farther, at MURRELL'S INLET, *Brookgreen Gardens, beautifully landscaped grounds with large number of sculptures.

Charleston Vicinity *(SW, via US 17 & 21)*. Approx. 70 mi: BEAU-
FORT (pronounced Bu-fort). Interesting old buildings in Hist. Dist.
include: *John Mark Verdier House (about 1790; rest.), 801 Bay

Drayton Hall—Georgian (Charleston Convention and Visitors Bureau)

St, also known as Lafayette Building since famous French marquis is believed to have addressed town citizens from gallery; *Tabby Manse (about 1780), Bay & Harrington sts, fine example constructed of tabby (primitive concrete made with oyster shells); *George Elliott House, also known as Holmes-Hall House (about 1840; rest.), 1001 Bay St. Also of interest, near Beaufort: *Fripp Island resort. Approx. 45 mi from Beaufort, via St. 170 & US 278: HILTON HEAD. *Sea Pines Plantation (begun 1959), planner: Hideo Sasaki; well-planned development; almost natural landscaping; interesting modern houses, other buildings. Approx. 10 mi W of Hilton Head, via US 278 & St. 46: BLUFFTON. Gothic Revival *Episcopal Church of the Cross (1854), survivor of shelling by Federal gunboat during Civil War.

Charleston Vicinity *(NW, via St. 61).* Approx. 9 mi: **Drayton Hall** (1742), on Ashley River; Georgian, in Palladian phase; considered one of finest houses in U.S. Approx. 3 mi farther, *St. Andrew's Parish Church (1706; later alt. & addit.; burned, rebuilt 1764); *Magnolia Gardens (begun about 1830), extensive collection of plants and trees; original fine plantation house burned by Federal troops during Civil War. Approx. 4 mi farther, *Middleton Place Gardens (begun 1741), magnificent oldest gardens in U.S.; interesting outbuildings; original fine plantation house, also burned by Federal troops, was built by Henry Middleton, president of Continental Congress.

CLEMSON

At *Clemson University, interesting buildings on campus include: *Tillman Hall (1891), Romanesque Revival; *Fort Hill (1802; later alt. & addit.), once home of John C. Calhoun, famous statesman who was U.S. secretary of war, vice-president (twice), secretary of state; *Hanover House (1716; rest.), moved here.

Clemson Vicinity *(SE, via US 76).* Approx. 8 mi: PENDLETON. Interesting old buildings in Hist. Dist. Not far, via St. 88, *Ashtabula (about 1828; later alt. & addit.; rest.), plantation house. Approx. 50 mi farther, via US 76; COKESBURY. Interesting buildings include: in Hist. Dist., *Cokesbury College, formerly Masonic Female College (about 1854; later alt. & addit.; rest.). Approx. 20 mi SW of Cokesbury, via US 76 & St. 72: ABBEVILLE. Interesting buildings include: Gothic Revival *Trinity Episcopal Church (1860; later alt.), architect: George E. Walker.

COLUMBIA

*State House (1855–1907), Main & Gervais sts; architect: J. R. Niernsee; very fine example; small dome. Across from State House, *Trinity Episcopal Cathedral (1846; later alt. & addit.), 1100 Sumter St; Gothic Revival. At 800 Richland St, *Governor's

Mansion (1856; later alt. & addit.), formerly officers' quarters of military school; across street, at 803 Richland, *Lace House (1854; later alt.; rest.), interesting iron work. Not far:
•**Robert Mills Historic House,** originally Ainsley Hall House, (1825; later alt. & addit.; rest.), 1616 Blanding St; fine Classic Revival by most famous South Carolina architect. Across street: *Hampton-Preston House (about 1820; rest.), 1615 Blanding St; once home of Wade Hampton, noted Civil War general and statesman. At 1705 Hampton St, *Woodrow Wilson's boyhood home (1875; rest.). At *University of South Carolina, interesting buildings of several eras, including modern *Undergraduate Library (1959; later addit.), architect: Edward Durell Stone. Approx. 65 mi N, via US 21 & St. 9: LANCASTER. *Lancaster Co. Courthouse & Jail (1823), architect: Robert Mills, at time South Carolina state architect & engineer.

Columbia Vicinity *(N, via US 321).* Approx. 25 mi: WINNSBORO. Interesting old buildings include: *Fairfield District Courthouse (1822; later alt. & addit.), Classic Revival; built under direction of Robert Mills, who may have designed original portion; *Old Brick Church (1788; later alt.). Approx. 28 mi farther: CHESTER. Gothic Revival *Purity Presbyterian Church (1854; later alt. & addit.). Approx. 20 mi farther: YORK. Interesting buildings include: Latta-Cody House (about 1820; later alt.); Gothic Revival *Episcopal Church of the Good Shepherd (1855; later alt.). Also of interest: approx. 15 mi NW, via St. 161, *King's Mountain Nat. Mil. Park, scene of great American victory, 1780, during Revolution. Approx. 25 mi farther, via St. 161 & US I-85, *Cowpens Nat. Battlefield, scene of another great victory, 1781, by troops of Gen. Daniel Morgan.

Bethesda Presbyterian Church—Greek Revival (Wayne Andrews)

Columbia Vicinity *(NE, via US I-20).* Approx. 30 mi: CAMDEN. Interesting old buildings include: ••**Bethesda Presbyterian Church** (1822; rest.), 502 De Kalb St; architect: Robert Mills; small, elegant Greek Revival; on grounds: *Maj. Gen. Johann DeKalb Monument (1825), architect: Robert Mills; in memory of German in American Revolutionary army, killed here, 1780. Not far: Mills-designed *Old Courthouse (1826; later alt. & addit.), Broad & King sts.

Columbia Vicinity *(SW, via US I-20).* Approx. 42 mi: AIKEN. *St. Thaddeus's Church, Episcopal (1844; later alt. & addit.), architect: F. Wisner; fine Greek Revival. Approx. 15 mi NE, via St. 19: EDGEFIELD. Interesting buildings include: *Trinity Episcopal Church (about 1836; later alt. & addit.); *Magnolia Dale, the Alfred J. Norris House (about 1830; later alt. & addit.; rest.); *Oakley Park, also known as Red Shirt Shrine (1835; later alt.; rest.), named for "Red Shirts" who helped elect Wade Hampton governor, 1876.

Columbia Vicinity *(NW, via US 176).* Approx. 65 mi: UNION. Interesting buildings include: Gothic Revival *Episcopal Church of the Nativity (1852; later alt.). Approx. 9 mi S, off US 176, *Rose Hill, the Gov. William Henry Gist Mansion (about 1828; later alt. & addit.; rest.), State Park; once home of secessionist governor.

Tennessee

Early inhabitants Mound Builders, ancestors of later Indians; believed to have settled here c. 900. Later Indian tribes included Cherokee, Chickamauga, Chickasaw. First explored by Spanish, led by Hernando de Soto, 1540; discovered Mississippi River near Memphis, 1541. Next explored by Englishmen James Needham and Gabriel Arthur and by Frenchman Father Jacques Marquette and Louis Joliet, 1673. Frenchman Robert Cavelier, Sieur de La Salle explored and claimed region for France, 1682; built Ft. Prud'homme on Chickasaw Bluffs, later abandoned; French, led by Charles Charleville established trading post at French Lick, near Nashville, 1716. France, Great Britain and Spain all claimed region but Spanish soon withdrew, leaving others to fight French and Indian Wars; British ceded territory by French, 1763, at end of wars. Settlers moved into area in 1760s and later from Virginia and North Carolina, of which region was part. Daniel Boone opened area for further settlement, beginning 1775; other pioneers, including James Robertson and John Donelson, founded

Nashville, originally Ft. Nashborough, 1779. Forces under John Sevier joined troops in winning Battle of King's Mountain in South Carolina, 1780, during Revolution. Three E counties seceded from North Carolina, 1784, naming new state Franklin and Sevier governor. North Carolina regained control, 1788; gave region to United States, 1789; renamed Tennessee Territory; William Blount first and only territorial governor. Became sixteenth state, Feb. 6, 1796; first governor: John Sevier. Gen. Andrew Jackson of Tennessee defeated Creeks during War of 1812. Chickasaw Indians gave up claims, 1818. People of state were divided about issue of secession; state was last to secede, June 8, 1861. Number of Civil War battles in state, including bloody Battle of Shiloh. President Andrew Johnson, of Tennessee, remained loyal to Union; became president after assassination of President Abraham Lincoln and declared state rebellion ended, 1865; blocked by Congress; first state to be readmitted to Union, 1866. Today: Important manufacturing industry, especially chemicals, metals and metal products, textiles, food products; also important agricultural industry.

Land Regions: E to W, Blue Ridge; Appalachian Ridge and Valley; Appalachian Plateau; Highland Rim; Nashville Basin; Gulf Coastal Plain.

Climate: Temperate, humid; W portion warmer than mountains; precipitation fairly heavy; snowfall moderate in mountains, less elsewhere.

Major Building Materials: Timber; marble and other stone; sand and gravel.

Architecture: Important buildings, including some of finest in United States, in many locations, especially Nashville and Vicinity.

CHATTANOOGA

*Chattanooga Choo Choo, originally Railroad Station (1908; remod. 1973), S Market St; architect: Don Barber; unusual transformation of old station into inn, restaurants, shops. Also of interest, nearby *Chickamauga and Chattanooga Nat. Mil. Park, actually several sites around city and in N Georgia, includes *Lookout Mountain, *Cravens House (1866; rest.), Cravens Terrace; simple wood-frame survivor of great battle here. Also see: Georgia—Atlanta Vicinity (NW, via US I-75).

KNOXVILLE

Interesting buildings include: *William Blount Mansion (1794; later alt. & addit.; rest.), 200 W. Hill Ave; simple wood-frame example, once home of only territorial governor. Nearby, *Craig-head-Jackson House (1818; rest.). In SW part of city: Eclectic Classic Revival *Dulin House, now Dulin Gallery of Art (1915; later alt.), 3100 Kingston Pike; architect: John Russell Pope. Not far: *Bleak House, now Confederate Memorial Hall (1858; rest.), 3148 Kingston Pike. Few miles SE of city, via Boyd Bridge Dr, *Ramsey House (1797; rest.), architect: Thomas Hope; Georgian; marble and bluestone. Approx. 35 mi SW, via St. 73: TOWNSEND. Approx. 10 mi: *Cades Cove (early 19th century), in Hist. Dist., *Great Smoky Mountains Nat. Park; farm community with houses and outbuildings, some rest.; limited farming operations. Also of interest: NW of city, *TVA Norris Dam; W of city, *Oak Ridge.

Knoxville Vicinity *(NE, via US 11E)*. Approx. 25 mi: NEW MAR-KET. Brazelton Place (1832; later alt. & addit.). Approx. 5 mi farther: JEFFERSON CITY. Fairview (about 1850; later alt. & ad-dit.), architect: William Strickland. Approx. 40 mi farther: GREENVILLE. *Andrew Johnson House (1851; rest.), Nat. Hist. Site, Depot & College sts; once home of president; also here, his *Tailor Shop (1830; rest.); grave. Approx. 7 mi farther: JONES-BORO. Interesting houses in Hist. Dist. Approx. 7 mi farther: JOHNSON CITY. Nearby, *Cobb-Massengill House, Rocky Mount Hist. Site (1772; rest.). Approx. 5 mi farther, interesting log house with "dogtrot," opening in center like breezeway, *Tipton-Hayes House (about 1782; later alt.; rest.), on US 23; interesting out-buildings.

MEMPHIS

Interesting buildings include: number in rehabilitated Cotton Row, River Row, Beale Street Hist. Dist., famous for blues and jazz, and in and around Victorian Village Hist. Dist. On Adams St, at no. 707, Greek Revival *Pillow-McIntyre House, now an-tiques shop (about 1852; later alt.). Fine Victorian examples in-clude: at no. 690,*James Lee House (1843; later alt. & addit.; rest.); at no. 680, *Noland Fontaine House (1873; later alt. & addit.; rest.), architects: M. H. Baldwin & E. C. Jones; at no 652, *Mallory-Neely House (1852; later alt. & addit.). Interesting modern buildings include: *First National Bank (1962), 165 Mad-ison Ave; architects: Jones, Mah & Jones; *Commercial & Indus-trial Bank (1972), 200 Madison Ave; architects: Gassner, Nathan & Brown.

NASHVILLE

Interesting buildings include: ●*State Capitol (1845–59; rest.), Capitol Hill; architect: William Strickland; very fine, imposing

Tennessee State Capitol—
Greek Revival (Wayne Andrews)

Greek Revival example on highest hill in city; by famous architect who died 1854, and is buried in wall of building; considered one of finest state capitols and its architect's masterpiece. On grounds: *Tomb of President James Knox Polk; architect: Strickland. Famous for Classic Revival designs, Strickland also employed other styles, including fantastic Egyptian Revival: *Downtown Presbyterian Church, formerly First Presbyterian Church (1851; later alt. & addit.), Church St & 5th Ave. Very fine Greek Revival houses by Strickland include: ●*Belmont (1850; later alt. & addit.), 1900 Belmont Rd; now main building of Belmont College; ●*Belle Meade (1854; later alt.), 5025 Harding Rd; original outbuildings include: log cabin (1807; rest.), birthplace of first owner, Gen. William Giles Harding. Approx. 7 mi SW of city, via Farrell Pkwy, *Traveller's Rest (1799; later alt. & addit.; rest.), simple wood-frame building; first part Federal, second Greek Revival, third Victorian. Also of interest: *The Parthenon (1897; rebuilt 1920–31), Centennial Park; near replica of original building in Athens, Greece; built of plaster for Tennessee Centennial, 1897; rebuilt in concrete.

Nashville Vicinity *(NE, via US 31E).* Approx. 10 mi: HENDERSONVILLE. Interesting houses include: Hazel Path (1857; later alt.), architect: William Strickland; *Rock Castle (about 1800; later alt. & addit.), once home of Gen. Daniel Smith. Approx. 10 mi farther: GALLATIN. Interesting houses include: Fairview (1832; later alt. & addit.; rest.) and Oakley (1852; later alt. & addit.), architect of both: William Strickland. Approx. 8 mi E, via St. 25,

*Castalian Springs, also known as Wynnewood (1828; later alt. & addit.; rest.), interesting large log house, originally tavern. Nearby, *Cragfont (1802; later alt. & addit.; rest.), once home of Gen. James Winchester.

Nashville Vicinity *(E, via US 70N)*. Approx. 12 mi: DONELSON. *The Hermitage (1819; later alt. & addit.; interior burned, 1834; rebuilt 1836), fine Classic Revival home of Andrew Jackson, War of 1812 hero and U.S. president; his wife, Rachel, planned and planted garden in which both are buried. Interesting buildings nearby include: *Log Cabin (about 1795; rest.), in which Jacksons first lived; Greek Revival *Tulip Grove (1836; rest.). Not far: Greek Revival example, Belair (1832; later alt. & addit.).

Nashville Vicinity *(SE, via US I-24)*. Approx. 15 mi: SMYRNA. *Sam Davis House (1810; rest.), once home of noted Confederate scout. Approx. 12 mi farther: MURFREESBORO. Interesting houses include: *Oaklands (about 1815; addit. 1830; addit. about 1855; rest.), N. Maney Ave; actually three houses joined together; first portion small pioneer cabin, second somewhat Romanesque Revival, third vaguely Eclectic Italianate.

Nashville Vicinity *(SW, via US 41)*. Approx. 18 mi: FRANKLIN. *Fountain Branch Carter House (1830; later alt.; rest.), 1140 Columbia Ave; interesting small example. Approx. 25 mi farther: COLUMBIA. Interesting houses, all Greek Revival, include: Clifton Palace (about 1840; later alt.), built by Gen. Gideon Pillow for himself; Pillow-Bethel House (about 1840; later alt.) and Pillow-Haliday House (about 1845; later alt.), built by general for his two sons. The Polk family also built number of houses, including: *James K. Polk House (1861; rest.), once home of president. Approx. 7 mi SW of Columbia, via US 43: ●***Rattle and Snap** (1845; later alt.; rest.), very fine mansion built by George W. Polk; name of house from winning of property in gambling game by his father, Col. William Polk. Nearby, fine Hamilton Place (1832; later alt.), built by Lucius Polk. Approx. 3 mi S, via US 31, Beechlawn (1853; later alt.), architect: William Strickland.

Nashville Vicinity *(NW, via US I-24)*. Approx. 40 mi: CLARKSVILLE. Interesting buildings include: *Old Post Office, now Federal Building (1898; later alt.), architect: William Martin Aiken; fascinating flamboyant Eclectic Victorian; fanciful ornament includes four large eagles perched on roof.

Virginia

Early inhabitants Indians of several tribes, including Cherokee, Powhatan, Susquehanna. First explorers believed to have been Spanish, 16th century. Virginia Company of London, usually called Virginia Company, established first permanent English settlement in America at Jamestown, 1607; first representative government there, 1619; became royal colony, 1624. Nathaniel Bacon led ill-fated first rebellion against royal government, 1676. Williamsburg became capital of colony, 1693. Indian attacks continued to harass colonists until 1774. Last royal governor, James Murray, Lord Dunmore, driven from Virginia, 1776; colony submitted resolution calling for independence to Continental Congress. Lord Cornwallis surrendered British army to Gen. George Washington at Yorktown, 1781, ending Revolutionary War. Became tenth state, June 25, 1788. Three W counties became state of Kentucky, 1792. Seceded from Union, 1861; Richmond Confederate Capital, 1861–65. Number of important Civil War battles fought in state. West Virginia formed from NW counties, 1863. Readmitted to Union, 1870. Today: Major manufacturing, agricultural, mining, especially coal, industries. Also important shipbuilding, fishing and tourist industries.

Land Regions: E to W, Atlantic Coastal Plain; Piedmont; Blue Ridge; Appalachian Ridge and Valley; Appalachian Plateau.

Climate: Mild; precipitation moderate; snowfall moderate; colder, with less precipitation but more snowfall in W than in E.

Major Building Materials: Timber; limestone and other stone; clay; sand and gravel.

Architecture: Rich and varied, from earliest Colonial era to present. Large number of important buildings, many among finest U.S. examples, in many places, especially Alexandria; Charlottesville; Fredericksburg; Richmond and vicinity; Williamsburg and vicinity.

ALEXANDRIA

Tremendous architectural impact of city mostly in total effect of many interesting surviving 18th- and 19th-century buildings in Hist. Dist. and in their setting, rather than in individual examples. Walking tour: *Christ Church, Episcopal (1773; later alt. & addit.), Cameron & N. Washington sts; architect: James Wren; fine Georgian; George Washington and Robert E. Lee worshipped here. Federal *Lloyd House (1796; later alt.), 220 N. Washington St; wood-frame Georgian; home of long line of Lees. Georgian *Robert E. Lee House, also known as Potts-Fitzhugh House, 607 Oronoco St; once home of famous Henry "Light Horse Harry" Lee and his even more famous son. Several interesting houses along Queen St, E of Washington St. Georgian *Gadsby's Tavern (1752; later alt. & addit.; rest.), 134 N. Royal St; known variously at times as Mason's Ordinary, City Hotel, City Tavern; still operated as restaurant. *Bank of Alexandria (about 1805; later alt. & addit.), 133 N. Fairfax St; first bank in state. *Carlyle House (1752; later alt. & addit.; rest.), 121 N. Fairfax St; large mansion. *William Ramsay House (1724; later alt. & addit.; rest.), 221 King St; wood-frame, gambrel-roof; now Visitors' Center. *Stabler-Leadbeater Apothecary Shop (1792; later alt. & addit.; rest.), 107 S. Fairfax St. *Atheneum, formerly Old Dominion Bank and Free Methodist Church (about 1850; later alt. & remod.), 201 Prince St; Greek Revival. Across street in 200 block: number of fine houses in *Gentry Row, named for early leaders who once lived here; in 100 block, *Captains' Row, named for early seafarers who once lived here. Georgian *Old Presbyterian Meeting House (1790; later alt. & addit.), 321 S. Fairfax St. Gothic Revival *St. Paul's Episcopal Church (about 1820; later alt. & addit.), 417 Duke St; architect: Benjamin Henry Latrobe. Later Gothic Revival *Downtown Baptist Church (about 1830; later alt. & addit.), 212 S. Washington St. Greek Revival *Lyceum, formerly McGuire House (1840; later alt. & addit.), 220 N. Washington St. *Friendship Fire Company (1855; later alt. & addit.; rest.), 107 S. Alfred St; organized, 1774. Also of interest: Alexandria waterfront buildings; *Ft. Ward Park, 4301 W. Braddock Rd. Also see: District of Columbia—Washington.

Alexandria Vicinity (NW). Adjoining: ARLINGTON.

●*Arlington House, also known as Custis-Lee Mansion (1802–18; rest.), Arlington Nat. Cemetery; architect: George Hadfield; very fine Greek Revival built for step-grandson of George Washington, George Washington Parke Custis, whose daughter Mary married Robert E. Lee; Lees lived here immediately before beginning of Civil War. Adjoining Arlington, via US 29/211: FALLS CHURCH. *Falls Church (1769; later alt. & addit.), E. Fairfax & N. Washington sts; architect: James Wren; another church attended by George Washington. Few miles W of Falls Church, via US 29, *National Memorial Park Cemetery, beautiful *Fountain of Faith; designer and sculptor of its magnificent figures: Carl Milles. Approx. 6 mi NW of Falls Church, via St. 7 & 502: VIENNA. Not far: *Wolf Trap Farm Park, location of *Filene Center (1971; burned 1982; reconst. 1984), architects: MacFayden & Knowles; assoc. architect: Alfredo deVido; delightful open-air theater. Approx. 8 mi farther, via St. 7 & 606, interesting new town of *RESTON (begun 1965), architect-planners: Conklin & Rossant. Approx. 35 mi from Alexandria, via US I-395 and Dulles

Dulles International Airport—Modern (Joseph W. Molitor)

Airport Access Rd: CHANTILLY. ●∗**Dulles International Airport** (1962; addit. 1982), architect: Eero Saarinen; architects, addit.: Hellmuth, Obata & Kassabaum; magnificent modern building with great soaring roof; considered one of finest U.S. buildings and masterpiece of its famous architect. Approx. 15 mi W of airport, via US 50: MIDDLEBURG. ∗Red Fox Tavern, originally Joseph Chinn's Ordinary (inn), successively Beveridge House and Middleburg Inn (about 1728; later alt. & addit.), still in operation as inn, restaurant. Approx. 18 mi NW of airport, via St. 28 & 7: LEESBURG. Approx. 6 mi S, via St. 15, in Hist. Dist., ∗Oatlands (1803; later alt. & addit.; rest.), unusual example; fine gardens, outbuildings. Just NW of Leesburg, via St. 15 & Old Waterford Rd, Greek Revival ∗Morven Hall (1881; later alt. & addit.) in 1,200-acre Morven Park; interesting gardens, outbuildings. Approx. 6 mi NW of Leesburg, via St. 7 & 662, WATERFORD, relatively unspoiled 18th- and 19th-century village; interesting buildings in Hist. Dist. Approx. 25 mi NW of Leesburg, via St. 7: WINCHESTER. ∗Handley Library (1913), Braddock & Picadilly sts; architects: J. Stewart Barney & Henry Otis Chapman; exuberant Eclectic Beaux Arts. ∗Abrams Delight, the Hollingsworth House (1754; rest.), 610 Tennyson Ave; interesting stone Quaker House. Approx. 15 mi SE of Winchester, via US 50/17 & 340 & St. 628, 626 & 622, near White Post: Long Branch (1812; later alt. & addit.; rest.), architect: Benjamin Henry Latrobe; very fine Classic Revival, Roman on one side, Greek on other; one of few surviving houses by famous architect. Approx. 8 mi S of Winchester, via US 11: MIDDLETOWN. ∗Belle Grove (about 1794; rest.), ∗Cedar Creek Battlefield; Classic Revival. Not far NE of Winchester, via St. 7 & US 340, historic Charles Town, Harpers Ferry, other towns (see: West Virginia—Charles Town). Also of interest, beginning at Front Royal, approx. 15 mi S of Winchester, via US 522, ∗Shenandoah Nat. Park and ∗Skyline Drive.

Alexandria Vicinity *(S, via Mount Vernon Memorial Pkwy).* Approx. 10 mi: MOUNT VERNON. ●∗**Mount Vernon** (about 1740; later alt. & addit.; rest.), architect, alt. & addit.: George Washington; architect, rest.: Walter Macomber; very fine plantation house one of most historic U.S. buildings; original small house built by Augustine Washington, father of president. Nearby, ●*Woodlawn Plantation** (1805), jct. US 1 & St. 235; architect: William Thornton; very fine, elegant Georgian by medical doctor and amateur first architect of U.S. Capitol; built for Lawrence Lewis, nephew of George Washington, and his wife Nelly Custis, granddaughter of Martha Washington. On grounds: *Pope-Leighey House (1941), architect: Frank Lloyd Wright; modern, in style its architect called Usonian; moved here. Approx. 5 mi farther S, via US 1, *Pohick Church (1774; later alt. & addit.; rest.), very fine Georgian; George Washington and George Mason, author of Virginia Declaration of Rights, were members; Washington is believed partially responsible for design, as is William Buckland. Few miles farther S, via US 1 and St. 242, ●*Gunston Hall** (1758; rest.), architect of interiors: William Buckland; simple Georgian exterior; beautiful interiors, especially woodwork, by famous joiner-woodcarver-architect.

CHARLOTTESVILLE

Interesting buildings include: ●*University of Virginia** (1817–26; later alt. & addit.; rest.), architect: Thomas Jefferson; magnificent Roman Revival "academical village" as it was called by its architect; considered among finest U.S. buildings; masterpiece helped establish Jefferson as one of greatest American architects; spacious lawn; five ranges of pavilions, each with columns and details in a different Roman Classic order, serve as housing for students and professors, classrooms, dining rooms; gardens enclosed by famous Jefferson serpentine walls (reconst.). At end of lawn: *Rotunda, originally used for large classes, library. Approx. 5 mi SE of city, via St. 53, another masterpiece, ●*Monticello** (1775;

**University of Virginia—
Roman Revival**
(Library of Congress)

Monticello—Roman Revival (Library of Congress)

later alt. & addit.), architect: Thomas Jefferson; designed and built by its architect-owner in Georgian style; later very much altered in Roman Revival style; also considered one of finest U.S. buildings; beautifully situated on hill from which Jefferson, with his telescope, watched his beloved University of Virginia under construction far below. Approx. 3 mi S of Monticello, via St. 795 & 627, *Ash Lawn (1798; later alt. & addit.; rest.), once home of President James Monroe; partially designed by his friend Jefferson. Approx. 2 mi from Monticello, toward city via St. 53, *Michie Tavern (about 1735; rest.). Other interesting old houses in area, all private, include modern example: Frankel House (1952), 2020 Spotswood Rd; architect: Edward Durell Stone. Approx. 40 mi SE, via US I-64 & 15: BREMO BLUFF. Nearby, Bremo (1820; later alt.), grandiose mansion, its design probably influenced by Jefferson. Approx. 40 mi W of Charlottesville, via US I-64: STAUNTON. *The Manse, President Woodrow Wilson Birthplace (1846; rest.), 24 N. Coalter St; fine Greek Revival; fine gardens; family lived here while president's father was minister of Presbyterian Church.

Charlottesville Vicinity *(N, via US 29).* Three interesting courthouses: approx. 22 mi N, via US 29 & 33, STANARDSVILLE, *Greene Co. (1838); approx. 14 mi NE of Stanardsville, via US 29, MADISON, *Madison Co. (1828); both vaguely Jeffersonian. Approx. 12 mi SE of Madison, via St. 230, ORANGE, *Orange Co. (1858: later alt. & addit.), Eclectic Victorian.

Charlottesville Vicinity *(SW, via US 29).* Approx. 60 mi: LYNCHBURG. Approx. 10 mi W, via US 460 & St. 661, near, FOREST, Poplar Forest (1806; later alt. & addit.), possible architect: Thomas Jefferson; original interiors destroyed in 1845 fire. Approx. 25 mi S of Lynchburg, via US 501 & St. 761: LONG ISLAND. Green Hill (about 1800), amazing collection of some 15 surviving plantation buildings, including house, barn, tobacco barn, slave quarters, ice house; also: slave auction block. Approx.

20 mi E of Lynchburg, via US 460: APPOMATTOX. In *Appomattox Court House Nat. Hist. Park, *Wilmer McLean House (1848; later dismantled and reconst.), scene of surrender of Gen. Robert E. Lee to Gen. Ulysses S. Grant, 1865, ending Civil War. Approx. 16 mi SE of Lynchburg, via US 501 & St. 682 & 659: SOUTH BOSTON. Berry Hill (1840), imposing Greek Revival plantation house; detached schoolhouse, office building on either side of forecourt. Approx. 20 mi E of South Boston, via US 58: CLARKSVILLE. Approx. 3 mi N, via St. 15, *Prestwould (1795; rest.), built for Sir Peyton Skipwith on land said to have been won by his father, Sir William, from William Byrd III.

FREDERICKSBURG

Interesting buildings include: *County Courthouse (1852; later alt. & addit.), Princess Anne & George sts; architect: James Renwick, Jr.; Gothic Revival by famous architect. Opposite: Greek Revival *Presbyterian Church (1835); *St. George's Episcopal Church (1849). Nearby, *James Monroe's Law Office (about 1750; later alt.; rest.), 908 Charles St. Federal *National Bank of Fredericksburg, formerly Farmers Bank of Virginia (1820; later alt.), 900 Princess Anne St. *Hugh Mercer Apothecary Shop (18th century; rest.), Caroline & Amelia sts. *Mary Washington House (about 1750; later alt. & addit.; rest.), 1200 Charles St; last home of mother of president. *Rising Sun Tavern (about 1760; later alt. & addit.; rest.), 1306 Caroline St; built by Charles Washington, brother of president. *Kenmore (1752; later alt. & addit.; rest.), 1201 Washington St; rather plain exterior, very fine interiors; built for Col. Fielding Lewis and his wife, Betty Washington Lewis, sister of president. Approx. 15 mi N, via US I-95 or 1 & St. 11, *Aquia Church (1751; burned 1754; rebuilt 1757), fine Colonial; brick and local sandstone; built, according to inscription, by Mourning Richards, Undertaker (Builder).

Fredericksburg Vicinity *(E, via St. 3 & 214)*. Approx. 42 mi: ●*Stratford Hall (1725; later alt. & addit.; rest.), magnificent

**Stratford Hall—
Georgian**
(W. D. Hunt)

Georgian plantation house; home of Lee family; built by Colonial Gov. Thomas Lee; once home of his sons, Richard Henry and Francis Lightfoot, both signers of Declaration of Independence; later home of Revolutionary War Gen. Henry "Lighthorse Harry" Lee; Civil War Gen. Robert E. Lee. Few miles N, via St. 3 & 204, *Popes Creek Plantation, George Washington Birthplace Nat. Mon; interesting, but not original, buildings.

Fredericksburg Vicinity *(SE, via US 17).* Approx. 55 mi: TAPPAHANNOCK. Along US 17, bet. Fredericksburg and Tappahannock, interesting houses, all private, include: near PORT ROYAL, Victorian Camden (1859). Near LORETTO, Brooke's Bank (1731; later addit.) and Elmwood (about 1775; later alt. & addit.). Near CARET, Colonial Blandfield (about 1750; later alt. & addit.). Approx. 15 mi N of Tappahannock, on St. 17, *Vauter's Church (about 1719; later alt.). In Tappahannock, originally called Hobb's His Hole, interesting buildings include: on Prince St, *Courthouse (1848); *Customs House (about 1750); *Debtor's Prison (about 1750; later alt. & addit.); *Clerk's Office (about 1750). Approx. 6 mi E of Tappahannock, via US 360: WARSAW. Nearby, two fine houses, both private: Mount Airy (1748; later alt. & addit.), N of US 360, on St. 624; Sabine Hall (about 1735; later alt. & addit.), S of US 360 on St. 624. Approx. 14 mi NE of Warsaw, via St. 3, 203, 604 & 606; *Yeocomico Church (1706; later alt. & addit.), interesting combination of Gothic and Classic Revival.

NORFOLK

Interesting buildings include: *Norfolk Scope Convention and Cultural Center (1972), bet. Brambleton Ave, St. Paul's Blvd, Bank & Charlotte sts & Monticello Ave; architects: Williams & Tazewell; structural engineer: Pier Luigi Nervi; spectacular modern domed multipurpose building and theater, *Chrysler Hall. *Freemason Street Baptist Church (1850; later alt. & addit.), Bank & Freemason sts; architect: Thomas U. Walter; Gothic Revival by famous architect. *Moses Myers House (1792; later addit.; rest.), Freemason & Bank sts; fine Georgian. *Willoughby-Baylor House (1794; later addit.; rest.), Freemason & Cumberland sts; Georgian. *Old Norfolk Academy Building (1840; later remod.), 420 Bank St; architect: Thomas U. Walter; Greek Revival; now Chamber of Commerce. *St. Paul's Church (1739; later alt. & addit.; rest.), St. Paul's Blvd; only building that survived bombardment by British, 1796. *Old Norfolk Co. Courthouse, now Gen. Douglas MacArthur Memorial (1850; later alt.), E. City Hall Ave & Bank St; architect: William R. Singleton; consulting architect: Thomas U. Walter; Classic Revival; famous general buried here. *Virginia National Bank (1967), Bank & Main sts; architects: Skidmore, Owings & Merrill; assoc. architects:

Williams & Tazewell; notable high-rise modern office building by famous firm. *U.S. Customs House (1852), W. Main St; architect: Ammi B. Young; Classic Revival. Approx. 7 mi E, via US 60 & 13: VIRGINIA BEACH. ••**Adam Thoroughgood House** (about 1640; later alt. & addit.; rest.), off Pleasure House Rd on Thoroughgood Lane; charming little brick Gothic house, perhaps oldest in U.S. Not far N, via US 60, *Old Cape Henry Lighthouse (1792); Jamestown colonists first landed near here; first lighthouse built by Federal government. Also see: North Carolina— Elizabeth City and Vicinity.

Norfolk Vicinity *(N, via US I-64 and Hampton Roads Bridge-Tunnel).* Approx. 10 mi: HAMPTON. Off I-64, at *Hampton Institute, Eclectic Victorian *Virginia Cleveland Hall (1874); *Academic Hall (1882); architect: Richard Morris Hunt. Romanesque Revival *Memorial Church (1886), architect: J. C. Cady. At Kecoughtan & Ivy Home rds, *Little England Chapel (1880), built by Hampton Institute students. Not far from Institute: *Ft. Monroe (1834), Old Point Comfort; architect: Gen. Simon Bernard; interesting fortifications, moat, rest. casemate in which Jefferson Davis was imprisoned after Civil War. Also of interest and not far: at US 60 & J. Clyde Morris Blvd, *Mariners Museum, Newport News.

Norfolk Vicinity *(NE, via US 13 & Chesapeake Bay Bridge-Tunnel).* Approx. 35 mi, in Virginia portion of Delmarva Peninsula: EASTVILLE. Interesting old buildings include: *Old Courthouse (1731), moved here; *New Courthouse (1795); *Old Clerk's Office (1731); *Old Debtor's Prison (1731). Approx. 30 mi farther: ACCOMAC. *Debtor's Prison (1782), other interesting buildings. In nearby ONANCOCK, interesting marine and farm complex, *Hopkins and Brother Store and Steamship Office (about 1840). Approx. 3 mi S of EASTVILLE, off US 13: Eyre Hall, (1735; later alt. & addit.; remod. 1932), architects, remod.: Victorine & Samuel Homsey; gambrel-roofed, wood-framed house; *formal garden. Approx. 10 mi N of Eastville, via US 13 & St. 622 & 619: BRIDGETOWN. *Hungar's Church (1742–51; later alt. & addit.), fine simple Colonial. Also see: Maryland—Annapolis Vicinity (Eastern Shore, SW, via US 301 & 50).

Norfolk Vicinity *(W, via US 58).* Adjoining Norfolk: PORTSMOUTH, *Public Library, formerly U.S. Post Office (1909; later alt. & addit.), 601 Court St; architect: James Knox Taylor; Eclectic. *Portsmouth Courthouse, originally Norfolk Co. Courthouse (1846; later alt. & addit.; remod. 1983), Court & High sts; architect: William R. Singleton; architect, remod.: J. P. C. Hanbury; interesting Classic Revival; now Community Arts Center. *Old Norfolk Naval Hospital (1832; later alt. & addit.), Effingham St at the river; architect, central portion: John Haviland; Classic Revival. Also: 18th- and 19th-century buildings in *Old Town Hist Dist. Approx. 25 mi from Norfolk, via US 17 & St. 10: BENNS

**St. Luke's Church—
Gothic** (Ken Cassell)

CHURCH. •*St. Luke's Church,** also known as Old Brick Church (about 1682; later alt.; rest.), Isle of Wight Co.; may have been built as early as 1632; oldest actual Gothic church in U.S.; may be oldest U.S. church of any style. Approx. 20 mi farther, via US 17, St. 10 & 617, ••**Bacon's Castle** (1665–70; later alt. & addit.; rest.), Surry Co.; very fine Jacobean, one of few surviving examples in U.S.; named for seizure by followers of Nathaniel Bacon, 1676, in ill-fated Bacon's Rebellion against British. Not far: *Smith's Fort Plantation, also known as Rolfe-Warren House (1652; rebuilt 18th century; rest.), bet. Surry and Scotland Wharf where ferries leave for Jamestown and Williamsburg. Not far, via St. 633 & 658, 1,400-acre *Chippokes Plantation, now state park; working plantation since early 17th century. Also see: Richmond Vicinity (S, via US I-95); Williamsburg and Vicinity.

RICHMOND

Interesting buildings include: ••**State Capitol** (1792; later alt. & addit.), Capitol Square; architect: Thomas Jefferson, with Charles-Louis Clérisseau; Classic Revival in Roman phase; considered one of finest and most important American buildings; Jefferson and his collaborator designed only central portion; wings added later; well-landscaped grounds surrounded by fine cast-iron fence; famous sculpture of George Washington by Jean-Antoine Houdon in Rotunda; on grounds: Federal style *Bell Tower (1824); *Governor's Mansion (1813; many later alt. & addit.), architect: Alexander Parris. Also: *Old City Hall (1894), Broad & 10th sts; architect: Elijah E. Meyers; late Victorian Gothic Revival, sharply contrasting with State Capitol and Governor's Mansion. *John Marshall House (1791; later alt. & addit.), 818 E. Marshall St; once home of first chief justice of U.S. Supreme Court. Not far: *Wickham-Valentine House (1812; later alt.; rest.) 1015 E. Clay St; probable architect: Robert Mills; fine Federal; now part of Valentine Museum, as are adjoining Greek Revival *Bransford-Cecil House (1840); Victorian three-dwelling *Gray-Valentine Row Houses (about 1870). Nearby, *Dr. John Brockenbrough House, also known as Confederate Museum and White House of Confederacy (1818; later alt. & addit.), 1201 E. Clay St; possible architect: Robert Mills; imposing house; once official residence of Jefferson Davis. Not far: on campus of Medical College of Virginia, three contrasting buildings, *Old First Baptist Church, now restaurant (1841; later alt. & addit.), Broad & 12th sts; architect: Thomas U. Walter; fine Greek Revival by famous architect; *Monumental Episcopal Church, now conference center (1814; later alt.), 1224 E. Broad St; architect: Robert Mills; fine Classic Revival by famous architect; originally dedicated to 1811 fire dead who are buried under nave; *Egyptian Building (1845; rest.), College & Marshall sts; architect: Thomas S. Stewart; fine Eclectic Egyptian Revival; fascinating fence with cast-iron mummies for posts. Not far: *Main Street Station (1901), 1520 E. Main St; architects: Wilson, Harris & Richards; fine Eclectic French Renaissance Revival. At 1916 E. Main St, *Old Stone House, also known as Edgar Allan Poe Museum (about 1700), believed to be oldest surviving building in city. Not far: rest. area of Church Hill, the St. John's Church Hist. Dist., with number of interesting 19th-century houses and *St. John's Episcopal Church (1741; later alt. & addit.), E. Broad & 24th sts; here Patrick Henry made his famous "Liberty or Death" speech. Not far: *St. Paul's Episcopal Church (1845; later alt.), 815 E. Grace St; architect: Thomas S. Stewart; interesting Greek Revival. *Ellen Glasgow House (1841; later alt. & addit.), 1 W. Main St; Greek Revival; once home of noted author. *Jefferson Hotel (1895; burned; rebuilt 1905; later alt.), 116 W. Main St; architects: Carrère & Hastings; fascinating Eclectic Mediterranean; fanciful exterior and elegant interiors. Also: *Broad Street Station, now Science Museum of Virginia (1919; later alt. & addit.), W. Broad & Robinson sts; architect: John Russell Pope; Eclectic Classic Revival railroad station by noted architect. Not far: another building by same architect, *Branch House (1916; later alt.), 2501 Monument Ave; Eclectic Tudor Revival. Monument Avenue

Bacon's Castle—Jacobean
(Association for Preservation of Virginia Antiquities, Thomas L. Williams)

is wide and lined with handsome houses, trees, shrubbery; named for monuments to Robert E. Lee, Thomas J. "Stonewall" Jackson, J. E. B. Stuart.

Away from downtown: *Wilton (1750; rest.), S. Wilton Rd; fine Georgian; moved here. Not far: Georgian Ampthill (1732; later alt. & addit.), 211 Ampthill Rd. Not far: Gothic Agecroft Hall, 4395 Sulgrave Rd; moved here from, of all places, near Manchester, England, where it was built in 15th century. At 6601 W. Broad St, *Reynolds Metals Building (1958), architects: Skidmore, Owings & Merrill; fine modern corporate headquarters; fine landscaping and interior courtyard by famous firm. Later example of their work: *Philip Morris Factory (1974), Commerce & Bell rds; also here: modern *Philip Morris Operations Center (1964), architect: Ulrich Franzen. Approx. 20 mi W of Richmond, via St. 6: GOOCHLAND. Interesting Roman Revival *Courthouse (1826), reminiscent of Jefferson's designs.

Richmond Vicinity *(NE, via US 360 & St. 30).* Approx. 27 mi: KING WILLIAM. *King William Co. Courthouse (about 1725; later alt. & addit.), fine Colonial; oldest U.S. courthouse in continuous use since built. Few miles away, via St. 632, Elsing Green (about 1719; later alt. & addit.), imposing plantation house. Approx. 8 mi S of King William, via St. 30 & 669, *Old St. John's Church, Episcopal (1734; rest.). Approx. 30 mi W of King William, via St. 30 & US 301, fine *Hanover Co. Courthouse (1735). Approx. 15 mi W of Hanover, via St. 54 & 685, *Scotchtown (1719; later alt. & addit.; rest.), once home of Patrick Henry; later childhood home of Dolley Madison.

Richmond Vicinity *(E, via St. 5).* Approx. 25 mi: *Shirley (about 1725; later alt. & addit.), fine plantation house; always owned by Carter family. Approx. 1 mi farther, *Berkeley (1826; later alt. & addit.), built by Benjamin Harrison; once home of his son William Henry, great-grandson Benjamin, both U.S. presidents; scene of first Thanksgiving, 1619. Approx. 2 mi farther, •*Westover (about 1730; later alt. & addit.; rest.), considered by many finest Georgian plantation house in U.S. and one of finest in U.S. of any era. Other interesting plantation houses on St. 5: approx. 7 mi farther, *Belle Aire (about 1670; later alt. & addit.); approx. 2 mi farther, *Sherwood Forest (about 1780; later alt. & addit.), retirement home of President John Tyler. Not far: Greenway (about 1790; later alt. & addit.), birthplace of President Tyler.

Richmond Vicinity *(S, via US I-95).* Approx. 25 mi via US I-95 & St. 10: HOPEWELL. Nearby, at CITY POINT, *Appomattox Manor (1763; later alt. & addit.; rest.), Cedar Lane; much damaged by British during Revolution and by Federal gunboats during Civil War; headquarters of Gen. Ulysses S. Grant for last ten months of war; on grounds: *Log Cabin (1864; rest.), once home of General & Mrs. Grant; cabin moved to Philadelphia, 1865;

Westover—Georgian (Wayne Andrews)

returned here 1982. Approx. 15 mi farther, via US I-95 & St. 10 & 611: BURROWSVILLE. Brandon (about 1765; later alt. & addit.), fine plantation house; beautiful gardens open to public. Approx. 10 mi from Brandon, via St. 611 & 653, fine Upper Brandon (1820; later alt. & addit.). Also see: Norfolk Vicinity (W, via US 17).

Richmond Vicinity *(S, via US I-95)*. Approx. 25 mi: PETERS-BURG. Interesting buildings include: Battersea (about 1760; later alt. & addit.; rest.), Battersea Lane; possible architect: Thomas Jefferson; fine plantation house. *Trapezium House (1816; rest.), N. Market St; unusual example having no parallel sides and no right angles because of superstitions of first owner, Charles O'Hara. *Centre Hill (about 1823; later alt. & addit.), Center Hill Lane, N of Franklin St; Federal. *Farmers Bank of Virginia (1817; later alt. & addit.; rest.), 19 Bollingbrook St; now Tourism Information Center. *Exchange Building, now Courts Building (1840; later alt. & addit.), 15 W. Bank St; architect: Berrien. *Farmers Market (1879; later alt. & addit.), W. Old & Rock sts; architect: B. J. Black; now restaurant as well as market. *Old Blandford Church (1735; later alt. & addit.; rest.), Crater Rd; magnificent Tiffany stained-glass windows. Also of interest: *Petersburg Nat. Battlefield Park, crater where Federal troops exploded powder charge under Confederate position.

WILLIAMSBURG

Marvelous architectural and historical effect of Williamsburg primarily in total effect of Georgian buildings and their Colonial setting rather than individual examples; however, fine scholarly rest. & reconst. of Governor's Palace, Capitol, other buildings;

Wren Building, College of William and Mary—Georgian (Library of Congress)

architects of initial, restor. & reconst.: Perry, Shaw & Hepburn. Walking tour: on N side of Duke of Gloucester St: *John Blair House (18th century; rest.); *Bruton Parish Church (1715; later alt. & addit.; rest.), architect: Gov. Alexander Spotswood; on Palace Green: *George Wythe House (1754); ••**Governor's Palace** (1720; later addit.; burned 1781; reconst. 1930); *Brush-Everard House (1719; later alt. & addit.; rest.); on Nicholson St: *St. George Tucker House (about 1714; later alt. & addit.; rest.); *Peyton Randolph House (about 1715; later alt. & addit.), two houses joined together; *Public Gaol, or Jail, (1704; rest.); ••**Capitol** (1704; burned 1747; rebuilt 1753; burned 1832; reconst. 1934). On S side of Duke of Gloucester St: *Ludwell-Paradise House (about 1717; rest.); *Wetherburn's Tavern (about 1740; later addit.; rest.). Across street: *Raleigh Tavern (about 1742; reconst. 1932). In Market Square, *Powder Magazine (1715; rest.). Nearby, *Public Hospital (1773; burned 1885; reconst. 1984), Francis & Henry sts; first American mental hospital; just behind: fine modern *DeWitt Wallace Decorative Arts Gallery (1984), architects: Kevin Roche & John Dinkeloo. Across from square: *Courthouse of 1770 (rest.). On *College of William and Mary campus, most important building, ••**Wren Building** (1699; burned, rebuilt three times; rest.), oldest surviving college building in U.S.; Georgian; said to have been built from design of famous English architect Sir Christopher Wren; also: *Brafferton Hall (1723; rest.); President's House (1732; rest.). Approx. 6 mi SE, via US 60, ••**Carter's Grove** (1755; later alt. & addit.), very fine Georgian house; on grounds: archaeological remains of Wolstenholme Towne (about 1620; destroyed in Indian attack, 1622).

Williamsburg Vicinity *(SW, via Colonial Pkwy)*. Approx. 7 mi: JAMESTOWN. First permanent English settlement in America, 1607, *Jamestown Nat. Hist. Site; little remains except excavated foundations; *Church tower (1647). Nearby, *Jamestown Festival Park, reconst. settlement; ships, *Susan Constant, Godspeed, Discovery*, in which settlers arrived. Also see: Norfolk Vicinity (W, via US 17); Richmond Vicinity (E, via St. 5).

Williamsburg Vicinity *(SE, via Colonial Pkwy)*. Approx. 14 mi: YORKTOWN. Interesting buildings include: on Main St, fine Georgian *Nelson House, also known as York Hall (about 1725; rest.); *Customs House (about 1706; rest.). On Church St, *Grace Church, Episcopal (1697; later alt.; burned, rebuilt, 1848; later alt.). Approx. 2 mi, via Washington & Hamilton rds (St. 238 & 676), Colonial *Moore House (about 1750; rest.), terms for British surrender drafted here, 1781. Also of interest: *Colonial Nat. Hist. Park, very fine rest. battlefield; also includes Jamestown and Colonial Pkwy. Just across York River Bridge: Gloucester Co. Interesting buildings include: along US 17, approx. 1 mi from Yorktown, just off hwy at GLOUCESTER POINT, Georgian Little England (1680; 1716; later alt. & addit.). Approx. 5 mi farther, *Seawell's Ordinary (18th century; later alt. & addit.), old inn, now restaurant. Approx. 1 mi farther, *Abingdon Church (1755; later alt. & addit). W of US 17, via St. 614, 632 & 644, ●*Rosewell (1720–50; later alt.; burned 1916), very fine Georgian; largest and possibly most magnificent house in Colonial America; now magnificent ruin. E of US 17, via St. 614, Classic Revival White Marsh (about 1750; later alt. & addit.). W of US 17, via St. 15, Abingdon Glebe (about 1674; later alt.). Approx. 2 mi farther N, via US 17: GLOUCESTER. Interesting buildings include: on Main St, Long Bridge Ordinary (about 1750; later alt. & addit.), formerly inn, now Gloucester Woman's Club. Few blocks farther: *Botetourt Building (about 1770; later alt. & addit.). Nearby, *Court Green, in which, *Courthouse (1766; later alt. & addit.); *Old Clerk's Office (1824; later alt.); *Debtor's Jail (18th century). Approx. 1 mi E of town, via St. 616, Colonial Roaring Springs (about 1800). E of town, via St. 14: approx. 1 mi, *Ware Church (about 1695; later alt. & addit.). Approx. 1 mi farther, S of hwy, Colonial Lowland Cottage (about 1670; later alt. & addit.). Approx. 1 mi farther, S of hwy, Classic Revival Elmington (1850; later alt.). Approx. 1 mi farther, S of hwy, Colonial Toddsbury (1660; later alt. & addit.). Approx. 13 mi farther: MATHEWS. Interesting buildings include: *Courthouse (1792; later alt.), other public buildings. Approx. 10 mi NE, via St. 198 & 3: HARTFIELD. Nearby, *Lower United Methodist Church (1717; later alt.), orig-

**Christ Church—
Georgian** (Foundation
for Historic Christ Church)

inally Episcopal church. Approx. 15 mi farther, via St. 3: IRVING-TON. Nearby, ●*Christ Church, Episcopal (1732; rest.), one of finest Georgian churches in U.S.; original high-back pews, three-tiered pulpit; built by famous Robert "King" Carter, whose tomb and those of his two wives are just outside.

West Virginia

Early inhabitants Mound Builders, ancestors of present-day Indians; many of their structures have survived. Later Indian tribes included Cherokee, Delaware, Shawnee, Susquehanna. First explorer believed to have been German John Lederer. First settler Morgan Morgan who built cabin at Bunker Hill, about 1726; other settlers soon followed, including Germans, Scottish-Irish and others. During French and Indians Wars, troops of then Col. George Washington were defeated, 1754, as were those of Gen. Edward Braddock, 1755. Part of Virginia Colony, settlers petitioned Continental Congress, 1776, for separate government, but nothing came of it. Indians, led by British, invaded, 1777–82, but were driven out. Abolitionist John Brown and his group seized Federal arsenal at Harpers Ferry, 1859, but were captured by troops of then Col. Robert E. Lee; Brown was tried and hanged at Charles Town, later in year. Settlers declared new state, Kanawha, formed, 1861; some battles fought in first year of Civil War but only skirmishes later; under name West Virginia, admitted to Union as thirty-fifth state, June 20, 1863. Today: Major mining state, especially coal, but also oil and natural gas; important manufacturing industry, especially chemicals, iron and steel.

Land Regions: In W, large Appalachian Plateau; in E, smaller Appalachian Ridge and Valley; in extreme NE, very small Blue Ridge.

Climate: Warm summers, moderately cold winters; precipitation heavy in mountains, less elsewhere; snowfall, heavy in mountains, moderate elsewhere.

Major Building Materials: Timber; limestone; sandstone; sand; clay.

Architecture: Interesting buildings in several locations.

CHARLESTON

Interesting buildings include: *State Capitol (1932), E. Kanawha Dr; architect: Cass Gilbert; Eclectic Italian Renaissance by noted architect of several other state capitols. Not far: Eclectic Colonial Revival *Governor's Mansion (1925), 1716 Kanawha Dr; architect: Walter Martens.

CHARLES TOWN

Charming old town, associated with many members of Washington family. Interesting old buildings include: *Jefferson Co. Courthouse (1836; later alt. & addit.), George & Washington sts; scene of John Brown's trial after capture at Harpers Ferry. Nearby, site of gallows upon which Brown was hanged, 1859. Also of interest: old *Charles Town Race Track. Approx. 4 mi N, via St. 51, Harewood (1770), once home of Samuel Washington, brother of president; Dolley Todd and James Madison married here.

Charles Town Vicinity *(NE, via US 340)*. Approx. 8 mi: HARPERS FERRY. Historic town, in spectacular location where Shenandoah and Potomac rivers join in gorge, and West Virginia, Virginia and Maryland come together. In Nat. Hist. Park, number of interesting buildings include: *Stagecoach Inn (1834; rest.); *Blacksmith Shop (1845; rest.); *Harper House (about 1780; rest.); *Master Armorer's House (1859; rest.); *Armory-Fire-Engine House, now called John Brown's Fort, in which Brown made his last stand and was captured; modern *Visitor's Center (1969), architect: Ulrich Franzen. Approx. 12 mi NW, via US 340 & St. 230, interesting buildings in, SHEPERDSTOWN and approx. 10 mi farther, in MARTINSBURG.

WHEELING

*Mansion House (1835), Oglebay Park, Greek Revival. Few miles N, via St. 88, Willow Glen (1920), very large sandstone house. Approx. 15 mi S of Wheeling, MOUNDSVILLE, site of *Grave Creek Mound, 9th St; very large, conical Indian mound.

WHITE SULPHUR SPRINGS

Spa since late 18th century. Interesting old buildings on grounds of luxurious *Greenbrier Hotel include: *Old Spring House (1835); President's Cottage (1816), once occupied by many U. S. presidents. Nearby, *White Sulphur Springs Hotel (1854; later alt. & addit.), known as Old White, and still in operation. Approx. 10 mi W, via US I-64: LEWISBURG. *Old Stone Presbyterian Church (1796; later alt. & addit.). Approx. 20 mi S of Lewisburg, via US 219 & St. 3: UNION. Log *Rehoboth Church (1786; rest.). Approx. 15 mi E of church: SWEETSPRINGS. Another old spa, *A. W. Rowan Home for the Aged (1833; later alt. & addit.), formerly Sweetsprings Hotel; reminiscent of buildings of Thomas Jefferson and some think designed by him.

Midwestern
States

Illinois

Early inhabitants pre-Columbian Mound Builders, ancestors of later Indians. Thousands of their burial and ceremonial mounds have survived including very important Great Cahokia Mound, sometimes called Monk's Mound, near East St. Louis. Later Indian tribes included Cahokia, Kaskaskia, Peoria, others. First explored by Frenchmen Father Jacques Marquette and Louis Joliet, 1673. First permanent French settlement; Cahokia, 1699; Jesuits founded Kaskaskia, 1703. Became part of Louisiana Territory, 1717. Ceded to Great Britain 1763, at end of French and Indian Wars. During Revolution, George Rogers Clark captured Cahokia and Kaskaskia, 1778; made part of Virginia. Ceded to United States, 1783, at end of Revolution; Virginia gave up claim. Became part of Northwest Territory, 1787; of Indiana Territory, 1800; became Illinois Territory, 1809. Indian attacks increased during War of 1812, climaxing in massacre of number of people by Potawatomi Indians at Ft. Dearborn, 1812. Became twenty-first state, Dec. 3, 1818. Today: Major industrial state, with important agricultural, mining and transportation industries.

Land Regions: Central Plains, covering 90 percent of state; smaller areas: Gulf Coastal Plain in S; Shawnee Hills, just N of Plain.

Climate: Generally cold winter, hot summer; quite changeable; S area warmer in winter and summer than N; precipitation moderate, more in S than in N; snowfall fairly heavy in N, light in S.

Major Building Materials: Clay; limestone; sandstone; timber, mainly hardwoods.

Architecture: Very rich architectural heritage, especially early pioneer; early and later modern in many locations, especially Chicago and vicinity; East St. Louis vicinity; Springfield and vicinity.

CHICAGO

Second largest U.S. city; treasury of fine architecture, especially early modern era, beginning after great Chicago fire of 1871.

LOOP AREA
(Named for elevated train tracks that surround it, bounded by Wabash Ave & Van Buren, Wells & Lake sts).
•*Auditorium Building (1889; rest. 1967), Michigan Ave & Congress St; architects: Dankmar Adler and Louis Sullivan; archi-

**Auditorium Building—
Early Modern**
(Hedrich-Blessing)

tects, rest.: Harry Weese with Crombie Taylor; early modern masterpiece, combining hotel, offices and auditorium, now part of
*Roosevelt University. *Manhattan Building (1891), 431 S. Dear-
born St; architect: William LeBaron Jenney; fine example by noted architect considered founder of Chicago School which pioneered modern high-rise or skyscraper design. Nearby *Second Leiter
Building (1891; later alt. & addit.), Van Buren & State sts; now
Sears, Roebuck store; few blocks away: *First Leiter Building
(1879), 208 W. Monroe St; architect of both: William LeBaron
Jenney. *Fisher Building (1897), 343 S. Dearborn St; architects:
D. H. Burnham & Co., early modern high-rise office building
with Eclectic Gothic Revival terra-cotta details by member of
Chicago School. *Federal Government Center (1963–73), Dear-
born & Jackson sts; architects: Ludwig Mies van der Rohe;
Schmidt, Garden & Erickson; A. E. Epstein and Sons; C. F. Mur-
phy; modern complex, composed of high-rise office building, high-
rise courthouse building, one-story post office. Not far:
•*Monadnock Building (1891; remod. 1938), 53 W. Jackson Blvd;

**Monadnock Building—
Early Modern** (Hedrich-Blessing)

**Carson, Pirie, Scott
Store—Early Modern**
(Hedrich-Blessing)

architect: Burnham and Root; architects, remod.: Skidmore, Owings & Merrill; another pioneering early modern high-rise building, last with brick bearing walls (six feet thick at ground floor), rather than skeleton frame of concrete or steel. *Inland Steel Building (1957), 30 W. Monroe St; architects: Skidmore, Owings & Merrill (SOM); modern, curtain-wall office building by famous firm. Not far: ●*Carson, Pirie, Scott Store (1899; addit. 1904), formerly Schlesinger and Mayer Store, State & Madison sts; architects: Dankmar Adler and Louis Sullivan; very fine example of pioneering modern design of Sullivan, engineering of Adler; considered one of finest U.S. buildings. *Gage Buildings, on S. Michigan Ave: at no. 18 (1899; addit. 1902), architect: Louis Sullivan; at nos. 24 and 30 (1898), architects: Holabird & Roche; distinguished early modern buildings by famous architects of Chicago School. ●*Reliance Building (1891; addit. 1895), 32 S. State St; architects: Burnham & Root; masterpiece of early modern high-rise design with steel skeleton frame by famous members of Chicago School. *Mayor Richard J. Daley Center, formerly Chicago Civic Center (1967), bet. Randolph, Dearborn, Washington & Clark sts; architects: C. F. Murphy Assoc.; Skidmore, Owings & Merrill; Loebl, Schlossmann, Bennett & Dart; modern office building with courthouses, plaza with fountain, 50-foot-high sculpture *Woman* by famous artist Pablo Picasso. Nearby, *Chicago Public Library Cultural Center (1897; rest. 1977), Michigan Ave bet. Washington & Randolph sts; architects: Shepley, Rutan & Coolidge; architects, rest.: Holabird & Root; Eclectic Beaux Arts. *Loop Synagogue (1963), 16 S. Clark St; architects: Loebl,

Schlossmann & Bennett; modern with large stained-glass window by noted painter Abraham Rattner. ●*Rookery Building (1886; later alt.), 209 S. LaSalle St; architects: Burnham & Root; significant early modern building, part bearing wall, part skeleton frame; magnificent lobby remod. 1905 by Frank Lloyd Wright. ●●*Sears, Roebuck Tower (1974), Wacker Dr & Jackson Blvd; architects: Skidmore, Owings & Merrill; distinguished modern office building by famous firm; tallest building in world, 110 stories, 1454 feet. Also of interest, near the Loop, bet. Michigan Ave & Lakeshore Dr: *Grant Park, *Field Museum of Natural History; *Buckingham Fountain; *Art Institute of Chicago; *Adler Planetarium; *Shedd Aquarium.

CHICAGO—SOUTH OF THE LOOP

●●*John J. Glessner House (1886), 1800 S. Prairie Ave; architect: Henry Hobson Richardson; Romanesque Revival by famous architect, his last surviving building in city; considered modern forerunner. *University of Illinois, Chicago Circle Campus (1965–79), S. Halsted & W. Harrison sts; architects & master planners: Skidmore, Owings & Merrill; fine modern university. ●●*Illinois Institute of Technology (1940–58), South State & 34th sts; architect & master planner: Ludwig Mies van der Rohe; considered one of best works of famous German-American architect; his masterpiece here: ●*Crown Hall (1956), School of Architec-

Reliance Building—
Early Modern (Hedrich-Blessing)

Crown Hall, Illinois Institute of Technology—Modern (Hedrich-Blessing)

ture, considered one of finest U.S. buildings; noted for clear simplicity of forms, meticulous detailing. Not far: Henry B. Clarke House (1836), 4526 S. Wabash Ave; oldest house in city; survived Great Fire of 1871; moved here. At 5472 S. Kimbark St, *Church of St. Thomas the Apostle (1922), architect: Barry Byrne; modern church in very personal style by noted architect who once worked for Frank Lloyd Wright. At *University of Chicago, noted for progressive education policies and experiments, Woodlawn Ave & Midway, mostly Eclectic "Collegiate Gothic" buildings; most significant example: *Rockefeller Memorial Chapel (1928), 59th St & Woodlawn Ave; architect: Bertram Grosvenor Goodhue; Eclectic Gothic Revival by famous architect. *Laird Bell Law Quadrangle, 1111 E. 60th St; architect: Eero Saarinen; modern glass and stone complex by famous architect. Not far:
●*Frederick C. Robie House (1906), 5757 S. Woodlawn Ave; architect: Frank Lloyd Wright; Prairie style; one of finest of famous

Frederick C. Robie House—Early Modern (Hedrich-Blessing)

architect's buildings and finest of U.S. buildings; now Adlai Stevenson Institute of International Affairs of university. Nearby, *Museum of Science and Industry (1893; rest. 1929–40), 57th St & S. Lake Shore Dr, Jackson Park; architects: D. H. Burnham & Co.; design architect: Charles B. Atwood; architects, rest.: Graham, Anderson, Probst & White; Shaw, Naess & Murphy; imposing Eclectic Classic Revival building; originally Palace of Fine Arts of World's Columbian Exposition, 1893. Also of interest, S near Lake Calumet, *Pullman, model town built, 1881, by George M. Pullman for employees of his railroad car company.

CHICAGO—NORTH OF THE LOOP

•*Lake Point Tower (1968), 505 N. Lake Shore Dr; architects: G. D. Schipporeit & John C. Heinrich; modern high-rise apartments overlooking Lake Michigan; spectacular undulating walls of dark glass and aluminum; by former students and employees of Ludwig Mies van der Rohe; *Tribune Tower (1925), 435 N. Michigan Ave; architects: Hood, Fouilhoux and Howells; Eclectic Gothic Revival skyscraper, commission for which was won in famous international competition; Finnish-American architect Eliel Saarinen gained worldwide recognition for his much more modern second-place design, as did German-American architect Walter Gropius for even more modern design. At 300 N. State St, *Marina City (1962), architect: Bertrand Goldberg; twin apartment towers; individual apartments with balconies arranged radially around central cores; on Chicago River not far from Lake Michigan; also here: shops, bank, recreational, parking, boat-docking facilities. Not far: ••John Hancock Center (1970), 875 N. Michigan Ave; architects: Skidmore, Owings & Merrill; very fine high-

**John Hancock Center—
Modern** (Hedrich-Blessing)

**860-880 Lakeshore
Drive Apartments—
Modern** (Hedrich-Blessing)

rise tower with offices on lower floors, apartments, shops, restaurants, recreational, other facilities on upper floors; walls incline
inward toward top; structure exposed on outside. *Old Water
Tower (1869; rest.), 800 N. Michigan Ave; architect: William W.
Boyington; fanciful Eclectic Gothic Revival; no longer in use but
revered by Chicagoans as survivor of Great Fire of 1871.
•*860–880 Lake Shore Drive Apartments** (1951), architect: Ludwig Mies van der Rohe; assoc. architects: Pace Assoc.; Holsman,
Klekamp & Taylor; twin towers, very fine modern; considered
among best works of famous architect and among finest U.S.
buildings. *Graceland Cemetery, N. Clark St; Getty Tomb (1890)
and Ryerson Tomb (1889); architect of both: Louis Sullivan; fine
examples by famous architect. •*Charnley House** (1891), 1365
Astor St; architects: Adler & Sullivan; designer: Frank Lloyd
Wright; early modern house by Wright while working in office of
Louis Sullivan, whom he called his master. *Carl Schurz High
School (1910; later alt. & addit.), Milwaukee Ave & Addison St;
architect: Dwight H. Perkins; fine early modern school by noted
architect.

Chicago Vicinity *(N & NW, via US I-94 or 41).* Adjoining city
EVANSTON. Interesting buildings include: *First Congregational
Church (1927), Hinman Ave & Lake St; architect: Thomas Tallmadge; Eclectic Georgian Revival by noted architect and historian. *Charles G. Dawes House (1894; later alt. & addit.), 225
Greenwood St; once home of U.S. vice-president under Calvin
Coolidge and winner of Nobel Peace Prize. *Rest Cottage, the

Frances Willard House (1865; later alt. & addit.), 1739 Chicago Ave; once home of noted crusader for women's suffrage and temperance. Approx. 5 mi farther: WILMETTE. *Bahai House of Worship (1920–52), 112 Linden Ave; architect: Louis Bourgeois; highly ornamental, domed building with forms, details from Middle East and other places; world center of Bahai, religion founded in Iran, 19th century, based on oneness of God, religion and mankind. Approx. 3 mi farther: WINNETKA. ●*Crow Island School (1940; later alt. & addit.), Willow Rd & Glendale Ave; architects: Eliel & Eero Saarinen; Perkins, Wheeler & Will; very fine pioneering modern design for improvement in education; by famous architects. Approx. 2 mi farther: GLENCOE. *North Shore Congregation Israel Synagogue (1964), 1185 Sheridan Rd; architect: Minoru Yamasaki; fine modern; molded, curvilinear forms. Approx. 5 mi farther: HIGHLAND PARK. Interesting buildings include: ●*Ward W. Willitts House (1901), 1445 Sheridan Rd; architect: Frank Lloyd Wright; considered first true Prairie style house by architect and one of his finest buildings; also here: Wright-designed Gardener's Cottage, stables. Other Wright examples here include: Mary M. W. Adams House (1905); George Madison Millard House (1906), both on Lake Ave. Approx. 6 mi farther: LAKE FOREST. *Market Square (1916; later alt. & addit.), planner: Edward H. Bennett; architect: Howard Shaw; early urban example with mall and fountain.

Chicago Vicinity *(SW, via US I-57).* Approx. 55 mi: KANKAKEE. Interesting buildings include: Warren Hickox House (1900), 687 S. Harrison Ave; architect: Frank Lloyd Wright; another house claimed to be architect's first in Prairie style. Just down street, at no. 701, another Wright design, B. Harley Bradley House (1900), also stable of same year. Little-known Wright building, approx. 30

Crow Island School—Early Modern (Hedrich-Blessing)

Dr. Edith Farnsworth House—Modern (Hedrich-Blessing)

mi W, via St. 17, in DWIGHT, *First National Bank, formerly Frank L. Smith Bank (1905). Nearby, interesting wood-frame Gothic Revival *Pioneer Church (1857).

Chicago Vicinity *(W, via US 34)*. Approx. 5 mi: RIVERSIDE. Interesting buildings include: ●*Avery Coonley House (1907), 300 Scottswood Rd; architect: Frank Lloyd Wright; considered one of architect's finest Prairie style examples. Also by Wright, on same road, at no. 290, Coonley Gardener's Cottage (1911); at no. 336, Coach House (1911). At 350 Fairbanks Rd, Coonley Playhouse (1912). Also of interest here: *Riverside Landscape Architectural Dist., mid-19th-century village by famous planners Frederick Law Olmsted & Calvert Vaux. Approx. 25 mi farther: AURORA. Interesting buildings include: *Second National Bank (1923), 37 S. River St; architect: George Grant Elmslie; fine early modern example by noted architect who once worked for Louis Sullivan. *William Tanner House (1857; later alt. & addit.), Oak Ave & Cedar St; interesting Victorian; once home of early merchant. Approx. 20 mi farther: PLANO. Nearby,
●*Dr. Edith Farnsworth House (1950), architect: Ludwig Mies van der Rohe; modern house reduced to simplest terms—two planes of floor and roof supported by steel columns and surrounded by glass; considered one of masterpieces of famous German-American architect and one of finest U.S. buildings.

Chicago Vicinity *(W, via US I-290 & St. 38)*. Adjoining city: OAK PARK. Frank Lloyd Wright had his first architectural practice and designed at least 30 buildings in city. Among most notable: *Frank Lloyd Wright House (1889; rest.), 951 Chicago Ave; Shingle style, with some hint of later Prairie style; oldest surviving Wright house; also here: *Playroom Addit. (1895; rest.); Studio (1898; rest.). Other houses by famous architect, in nearby Hist. Dist., include: on Forest Ave, at no. 210, Frank Wright Thomas House (1901); at no. 238, P. A. Beachey House (1906); at no.

313, Edward R. Hills House (1906); at no. 318, Arthur Heurtley House (1902); at no. 333, Nathan G. Moore House (1895). Not far: ●*Unity Temple, more properly called Unity Church (1908), 875 Lake St; architect: Frank Lloyd Wright; early modern reinforced concrete complex consisting of *Unity Temple, *Unity House; considered one of masterpieces of famous architect and one of finest U.S. buildings. Adjoining Oak Park: RIVER FOREST. William H. Winslow House (1893), 515 Auvergne Pl; architect: Frank Lloyd Wright; first building designed by Wright after leaving office of Adler & Sullivan; once home of publisher of *House Beautiful* magazine. Approx. 14 mi farther: Wheaton. *Cantigny Farm, the Col. Robert R. McCormick House (1896; later alt. & addit.), 115 Winfield Rd; once home of editor and publisher of *Chicago Tribune* newspaper; now war mem. with collection of tanks, field artillery pieces, other items.

Chicago Vicinity *(NW, via US I-90).* Approx. 85 mi: ROCKFORD. Interesting buildings include: *Unitarian Church (1966), Dawn Ave & Turner St; architects: Pietro Belluschi & C. Edward Ware; fine modern by famous architect; *Robert Tinker Swiss Cottage (1865; rest.), 411 Kent St; unusual type like Swiss Chalet; once home of mayor of city. *John Erlander House (1871), 404 S. 3rd St.

EAST ST. LOUIS

Just across from St. Louis, Mo., via very fine *Eads Bridge (1874), engineer: James P. Eads. (See: Missouri—St. Louis & Vicinity). Approx. 8 mi NE, via US I-55, *Cahokia Mounds State Park; fine remains of pre-Columbian mounds built by Mound Builders, ancestors of Indians; large number of examples include: ●*Great Cahokia Mound, sometimes called Monk's Mound, largest man-made earthwork in U.S.

East St. Louis Vicinity *(SE, via US I-64 & St. 142).* Approx. 100 mi: McLEANSBORO. *Peoples' National Bank (1881), Washington

Unity Temple—Early Modern (Hedrich-Blessing)

St; architects: Reid Brothers; fanciful Eclectic Victorian. Approx. 20 mi W of McLeansboro, via St. 14: CARMI. *Robinson-Stewart House (about 1814; rest.), log cabin; courthouse for few years; later home of John M. Robinson, general and U.S. senator.

East St. Louis Vicinity *(S & SE, via St. 3)*. Approx. 4 mi, CAHOKIA, oldest European settlement, 1699, in state. Interesting buildings include: *Cahokia Courthouse (1737; rest.), French Colonial; oldest surviving building in Midwest; of *poteaux-sur-sole,* or posts with clay and straw infilling, construction; originally home of Jean Baptiste Saucier; became St. Clair Co. Courthouse and Jail, 1793; moved several times; *Church of the Holy Family (1786–99; later alt. & addit.; rest.), French Colonial; *poteaux-en-terre,* or posts with rubble and lime infilling, construction. Interesting buildings in nearby BELLEVILLE. Approx. 45 mi S, via St. 3 & 155: PRAIRIE DU ROCHER. Interesting buildings in *French Colonial Hist. Dist. Also: *Ft. de Chartres (1756; part. rest.; part. reconst.), State Park, French fort, later occupied by British, who renamed it Ft. Cavendish. Nearby, *Creole House (about 1800; later alt. & addit.). Approx. 15 mi farther, via St. 3: KASKASKIA. Interesting buildings include: *Pierre Menard House (1802; rest.), fine French Colonial of type called raised cottage; living area on second floor, wide porches. Also of interest nearby: remains of *Ft. Kaskaskia. Approx. 95 mi farther: CAIRO. *Magnolia Manor, the Charles A. Galigher House (1872; later alt. & addit.), 2700 Washington Ave; fine Victorian.

East St. Louis Vicinity *(NW, via St. 3)*. Approx. 40 mi: ELASH. *Principia College (1937), architect: Bernard Maybeck; planned like village by famous California architect; *Chapel and four dormitories; *Mistake House, now Maybeck Museum, where architect experimented with building materials and techniques.

John Deere & Co. Administration Building—Modern (Deere and Co.)

MOLINE

Nearby, ••**John Deere & Co. Administration Building** (1964; addit. 1978), John Deere Rd; architect: Eero Saarinen; architects, addit.: Kevin Roche & John Dinkeloo; very fine modern corporate headquarters; oxidizing steel and glass; on beautifully landscaped site; considered one of famous architect's masterpieces; fine addit. by noted architects who once worked in Saarinen's office; also by them, fine modern, ••**John Deere Financial Services Building** (1982).

Moline Vicinity *(N, via St. 84)*. Approx. 85 mi: GALENA. Interesting buildings include: in Hist. Dist., *Orrin Smith House (1852; rest.); *John Dowling House (1826; rest.). Also: *Ulysses S. Grant House (1859), Bouthillier St; Italianate; once home of Civil War general and U.S. president.

Moline Vicinity *(S & SE, via US I-74)*. Approx. 45 mi: GALESBURG. Interesting buildings include: at *Knox College, *Old Main (1856), Eclectic Gothic Revival; fifth Lincoln-Douglas debate was held on grounds; now Nat. Hist. Landmark; *Carl Sandburg Birthplace (about 1875; later alt. & addit.), once home of famous poet; his ashes buried under Remembrance Rock in yard. Approx. 25 mi NE of Galesburg, via US 34, BISHOP HILL, founded, under leadership of Eric Janson, by immigrants who broke with religious establishment in Sweden. Interesting buildings include: in Hist. Dist., *Old Church (1848); *Old Steeple Building (1853). Approx. 6 mi SW of Galesburg, via US I-74: KNOXVILLE. *Old Knox Co. Courthouse (1840) and *Hall of Records (1854), architect of both: John Mandeville; fine Greek Revival. Approx. 43 mi farther: PEORIA. Interesting buildings include: *Morron House (1862; later alt. & addit.), 1212 W. Moss Ave; Victorian *Judge John C. Flanagan House (1837), 942 N.E. Glen Ave. Also of interest, SW of Peoria: *Dickson Mounds.

Moline Vicinity *(SW, via US 67 & 34)*. Approx. 75 mi: OQUAWKA. Greek Revival *Henderson Co. Courthouse (1842). Approx. 45 mi farther, via St. 96, NAUVOO, founded, 1839, by Mormon leader Joseph Smith, whose followers went on to Salt Lake City, Utah, after his murder here in 1844. Interesting buildings include: *Joseph Smith Homestead (1823), log cabin, first home of family here; *Joseph Smith Mansion (1841), their second home; Brigham Young House (1840); Ivins-Babbitt House (1842); now State Hist. Site.

SPRINGFIELD

Interesting buildings include: *State Capitol (1868–88), S. 2nd St; architect: John Crombie Cochrane with Alfred H. Piquenard; Classic Revival; fifth state capitol. Not far: *Old State Capitol

(1840–53; radically alt.; reconst. 1968), Adams & 5th sts; architect: John Francis Rague; architects, reconst.: Ferry & Henderson; Classic Revival, oddly enough, with Roman Revival dome on essentially Greek Revival frame; fourth state capitol now Hist. Museum. First legislature met in rented rooms in Kaskaskia; first three capitol buildings in Vandalia: first burned; second was demolished; third survives. Interesting houses in city include: *Governor's Mansion (1855; later alt. & addit.), Jackson St, Victorian. *Susan Lawrence Dana House (1904), 301 Lawrence Ave, and adjoining *Lawrence Mem. Museum (1905), architect of both: Frank Lloyd Wright. *Benjamin S. Edwards House (1833; later alt. & addit.), 700 N. 4th St; oldest house in city; once home of noted lawyer. *Vachel Lindsay House (about 1830), 603 S. 5th St; once home of noted poet. *Abraham Lincoln Home (1839; later alt. & addit.; rest.), 420 S. 8th St; only house Lincoln ever owned; family lived here 17 years until his election to presidency; now State Mem.; president and members of his family buried in *Oakridge Cemetery, Monument Ave. Many other buildings and sites associated with Lincoln in various places in state. Approx. 40 mi SW, via St. 4: CARLINVILLE. *Macoupin Co. Courthouse (1870), architect: Elijah E. Myers; fine Classic Revival; caused scandal because actual cost was more than million dollars over budget; last bonds not paid off until 40 years after completion.

Springfield Vicinity *(E, via US I-72)*. Approx. 85 mi: CHAMPAIGN-URBANA. Interesting buildings include, at *University of Illinois, examples of various eras: *Altgeld Hall (1896), architects: Nathan C. Ricker & James M. White, both professors in department of architecture; Romanesque Revival; *Assembly Hall (1963), fine modern by noted architects; one of earliest successful reinforced concrete domes for assembly of large groups for sports and other events; *Krannert Center for the Performing Arts (1969), large modern complex with five theaters, other facilities, architects of both: Harrison & Abramovitz. Approx. 60 mi S, via US I-57 or 45 & St. 16: CHARLESTON. Nearby, *Lincoln Log Cabin (early 19th century; reconst.), once home of Thomas and Sarah Bush Johnston Lincoln, president's father and stepmother; nearby, *Shiloh Cemetery, where both are buried; also nearby, *Ruben Moore House, once home of president's stepsister.

Springfield Vicinity *(SE, via St. 29 & US 51)*. Approx. 70 mi: VANDALIA. *Vandalia State House (1839; later alt. & addit.; rest.), 315 W. Gallatin St; architects: John Taylor & William Hodge; Greek Revival; served as capitol for only two years. Approx. 35 mi SE of Vandalia, via US 51 & 50: SALEM. *William Jennings Bryan House (1842; later alt. & addit.), 408 S. Broadway; birthplace of famous lawyer and political figure called "The Great Commoner."

Springfield Vicinity *(NW, via St. 97)*. Approx. 23 mi: PETERS-
BURG. *Edgar Lee Masters House (about 1850; rest.), Jackson &
8th sts; once home of famous author of *Spoon River Anthology* and
other poems and biographies. Just S of town: *New Salem Village
(19th century; reconst. 1933), village reconst. as of 1831–37 era
when Abraham Lincoln lived here; now State Park. Approx. 10 mi
SW, via St. 97 & 123: PLEASANT PLAINS. *Clayville Rural Life
Center; collection of rest. buildings includes: *Clayville Tavern
(about 1825; rest.), originally Broadwell Tavern; gathering place
for Whig party members supporting Henry Clay for presidency.
Approx. 100 mi W of Pleasant Plains, via St. 125 & US 24:
QUINCY. Unusual number of interesting buildings include: *John
Wood House (1835), 425 S. 12th St; Greek Revival; once home of
state governor. *Lorenzo Bull House (about 1850), Main & 16th
sts; Gothic Revival. *U.S. Post Office (1887), Hampshire & 8th
sts; architect: Mifflin E. Bell; Eclectic Renaissance Revival. M. F.
Huffman House (about 1885), 1469 Maine St; Eclectic Second
Empire Revival. *Old State Savings, Loan & Trust Bank (1892),
428 Main St; architect: Ernest Wood; Romanesque Revival.

Indiana

Early inhabitants pre-Columbian Mound Builders, ancestors of
present-day Indians. Many later tribes here, including Mohican,
Delaware, Shawnee, Huron, Kickapoo, Potawatomi. First European explorer Frenchman Robert Cavelier, Sieur de La Salle, 1679.
First permanent French settlement, about 1731: Vincennes. Ceded
to Great Britain, 1763, after end of French and Indian Wars.
Much of area occupied by British during Revolution; Vincennes
taken by troops of George Rogers Clark, 1778; retaken by British
later that year; again taken by Rogers, 1779. Became Indiana
Territory, 1800; Vincennes capital. Troops of William Henry Harrison defeated Shawnee Indians, led by Chief Tecumseh, at Battle
of Tippecanoe, 1811, and again at Battle of Thames, 1813, in
which famous chief was killed; Corydon became capital same
year. Became nineteenth state, Dec. 11, 1816. During Civil War,
Confederate Gen. John Hunt Morgan led his Morgan's Raiders in
raid on Corydon and across state into Ohio. Today: Leading manufacturing state; also important agricultural and mining industries.

Land Regions: From S to N, Southern Hills, Lowlands; Till
Plains; Great Lakes Plains.

Climate: Cool winters, warm summers, humid; cooler in summer and warmer in winter along Lake Michigan; precipitation moderate, more in S than in N; snowfall fairly heavy in N, less in S.

Major Building Materials: Timber, mostly hardwoods; limestone; sand and gravel; clay.

Architecture: Rich and varied in many locations, especially Indianapolis and vicinity; astonishing number of fine modern buildings by noted architects in small city of Columbus.

COLUMBUS

Small (population of about 30,000) city like museum of modern architecture. J. Irwin Miller of Cummins Engine Co. and Foundation financially supported commissioning of architects for many buildings. Interesting examples include: ●*First Christian Church, also known as Tabernacle Church (1942), 531 5th St; architect: Eliel Saarinen; assoc, architect: Eero Saarinen; very fine church by famous architect and his famous architect-son; thought by many to have begun trend toward modern religious architecture. ●*North Christian Church (1964), 850 Tipton Lane; architect: Eero Saarinen; another very fine example. See map and guide available from Visitors' Center for other fine buildings, including schools, banks, factories, commercial buildings, library, courthouse and other types by noted architects such as Edward Larrabee Barnes; Gunnar Birkerts; Caudill, Rowlett & Scott; Victor Gruen; John M. Johansen; Mitchell & Giurgola; Eliot Noyes; I. M. Pei; James Stewart Polshek; Kevin Roche & John Dinkeloo;

**First Christian,
or Tabernacle, Church—
Early Modern** (Hedrich-Blessing)

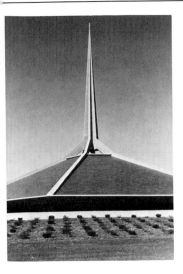

North Christian Church—Modern
(Indiana Department of Commerce)

Skidmore, Owings & Merrill; The Architects Collaborative (TAC); Venturi & Rauch; John Carl Warnecke; Harry Weese.

Columbus Vicinity *(E, via St. 7 & US 50)*. Approx. 65 mi: AURORA. Interesting houses include: *Hillforest, the Thomas Gaff House (1856; rest.), 213 5th St; unusual example with round cupola; overlooks Ohio River; combines elements of Eclectic Italian Renaissance Revival, Victorian and "Steamboat Gothic." Approx. 25 mi N of Aurora, via St. 1 & US 52, near, NEW TRENTON, *Aldianne (about 1810; rest.), Chappelow Rd; *Far Away Acres; log house thought to be oldest in Ohio Valley.

EVANSVILLE

Old Vanderburgh Co. Courthouse (1891; rest.), Court St; architect: Henry Wolters; fine exuberant Eclectic Beaux Arts Second Empire Revival. Approx. 30 mi E, via St. 66: ROCKPORT. Reconst. *Lincoln Pioneer Village, City Park. Approx. 15 mi N of Rockport, via US 231: LINCOLN. *Lincoln Boyhood Nat. Mem.

Evansville Vicinity *(NW, via St. 66)*. Approx. 27 mi: NEW HARMONY. Founded, 1815, by former Lutheran Germans, Harmonist or Rappite (for their leader George Rapp) communal sect; sold, 1825, to John Owen, utopian idealist and theoretician, and William Maclure, geologist and teacher, both Scottish. Interesting buildings include: in Hist. Dist., examples of both Harmonist and Owenite era. Also several modern buildings, including: *Roofless Church (1960), N. Main St; architect: Philip Johnson; fascinating small church; sculpture *Virgin* by famous sculptor Jacques Lipchitz in center. Nearby, *Paul Johannes Tillich Mem. Park

(1966), landscape architects: Zion & Breen; sculptor: James Rosati. *Atheneum (1979), N. Main St. architect: Richard Meier; striking machinelike auditorium.

FORT WAYNE

*Allen Co. Courthouse (1900; later alt.), S. Calhoun St; architect: Brentwood S. Tolan; interesting Eclectic combining number of styles; spectacular rotunda. Also: *Thomas Swinney House (1844; later alt. & addit.), 1424 W. Jefferson St; Greek Revival; Victorian addit. *Concordia Theological Seminary (1958), 6660 N. Clinton St; architect: Eero Saarinen; very fine modern Lutheran college campus with very fine buildings, especially *Kramer Chapel, by famous architect. Approx. 40 mi SE of Fort Wayne, via US 27: GENEVA. *Limberlost Cabin (1895; rest.), Williams & 6th sts; State Mem., once home of Gene Stratton Porter, noted author of *Girl of the Limberlost* and other books. Approx. 25 mi S of Fort Wayne, via St. 1: BLUFFTON. *Wells Co. Courthouse (1891; rest.), S. Main St; architect: George W. Bunting; fine Romanesque Revival; interesting clock tower. Approx. 25 mi W of Fort Wayne, via US 30: COLUMBIA CITY. *Thomas R. Marshall House (about 1875; rest.), 108 W. Jefferson St; once home of state governor and U.S. vice-president under President Wilson.

Fort Wayne Vicinity *(NW, via US 33 & St. 9)*. Approx. 40 mi: ROME CITY. Nearby, *Gene Stratton Porter House (1914; rest.), State Mem., designed and built by author herself. Approx. 55 mi farther, via St. 9, US 6 & 33 (approx. 95 mi NW of Fort Wayne, via US 33): SOUTH BEND. *Century Center (1980), Colfax Ave; at St. Joseph River; architects: Philip Johnson & John Burgee; fine modern arts and convention complex.

INDIANAPOLIS

Interesting buildings include: *State Capitol (1878–88), near Monument Circle; architect: Edwin May; succeeded by Adolf Scherer; Eclectic Classic Revival with dome. Not far:
•*Indianapolis-Marion Co. Public Library (1917; later alt.), 40 E. St. Clair St; architect: Paul Phillipe Cret; assoc. architects: Zantzinger, Borie & Medary; very fine Beaux Arts Eclectic Classic Revival; considered one of the best designs by noted architect. Not far: Eclectic Italianate *James Whitcomb Riley House (1872; rest.), 528 Lockerbie St; famous poet lived here last 23 years of life. Also: *Thomas A. Hendricks House (1830; later alt. & addit.), 1526 S. New Jersey St; once home of state governor, later U.S. vice-president. *Benjamin Harrison House (1875; rest.), 1230 N. Delaware St; once home of U.S. president. *Toll House (about 1855; rest.), 4702 N. Michigan Rd; once store, post office.

Interesting modern buildings include: *Christian Theological Seminary (1966), 1000 W. 42nd St; architect: Edward Larrabee Barnes. At *Butler University, W. 46th St & Sunset Ave. *Clowes Hall (1963), architects: John M. Johansen & Evans Woollen; concert hall-theater. In NW section of city: *College Life Insurance Company of America (1972), 3500 DePauw Blvd; architects: Kevin Roche & John Dinkeloo; modern office complex consisting of three interconnected glass-enclosed pyramids. Also of interest: *Indianapolis Motor Speedway. Approx. 25 mi NE, via US I-70 & St. 37: NOBLESVILLE. *William Conner Prairie settlement (1823; rest. & reconst.), collection of early buildings. Approx. 20 mi E of Noblesville, via St. 32: ANDERSON. *Mounds State Park, with very large pre-Columbian Indian mounds.

Indianapolis Vicinity *(E, via US 40)*. Approx. 20 mi: GREEN-FIELD. *James Whitcomb Riley House (about 1845; rest.), 300 Main St; birthplace of famous poet. Approx. 30 mi farther: CAMBRIDGE CITY. *Huddleston House (1839; rest.), old stagecoach station. Approx. 28 mi NW of Cambridge City, via US 40 & 27: FOUNTAIN CITY. *Levi Fountain House (1827; rest.), 115 N. Main St; once home of leader of underground railroad for runaway slaves.

Indianapolis Vicinity *(NW via US I-65)*. Approx. 65 mi: LA-FAYETTE. *Tippecanoe Co. Courthouse (1884; later alt.), Main St; architects: Elias Max & James F. Alexander; interesting Eclectic Italian Renaissance Revival. Also: Gothic Revival *Moses Fowler House (1852; rest.), 909 South St. Also of interest, nearby, *Tippecanoe Battlefield State Mem. Approx. 85 mi from Lafayette, via US I-65 & 23: CROWN POINT. *Old Lake Co. Courthouse (1879; later alt. & addit.), Courthouse Sq; architect: John C. Cochrane; architects, addit.: 1909, Beers & Beers; 1928, Albert Turner; interesting Eclectic Victorian; clocktower. Also: *Old Homestead (1847; rest.), 227 S. Court St. Also of interest, approx. 25 mi NE of Crown Point, via US I-65 & 12, *Indiana Dunes State Park & Nat. Lakeshore.

NEW ALBANY

*W. S. Culbertson Mansion, now State Mem. (1869; rest.), 914 E. Main St; fine Eclectic Victorian Second Empire Revival; fine interiors. Not far, on E. Main St, *Joel Scribner House (1814; rest.), oldest house in city. Also of interest, approx. 6 mi SE, via St. 62 & US I-65: JEFFERSONVILLE. *Howard Nat. Steamboat Museum. Also see: Kentucky—Louisville.

New Albany Vicinity *(NE, via St. 62)*. Approx. 40 mi: MADISON. Interesting buildings include: in Hist. Dist., on 1st St, Greek Revival *James F. D. Lanier House (1844; rest.), architect: Francis

Costigan; State Mem.; and Charles Shrewsbury House (1849; rest.). At 304 W. 2nd St, Federal *Jeremiah Sullivan House (1818; rest.). At 101 3rd St: Greek Revival *Auditorium (1835; later alt.), architect: E. J. Peck.

New Albany Vicinity *(W, via US I-64).* Approx. 20 mi: CORY-DON. Interesting buildings include: in Hist. Dist., *Old State Capitol (1816; later alt.; rest.), N. Capitol Ave; built as court-house but served as first state capitol, 1816–24.

New Albany Vicinity *(NW, via St. 60).* Approx. 30 mi: SALEM. Interesting buildings include: *John Hay Birthplace (1824; rest.), 106 S. College Ave; once home of noted author, ambassador to Great Britain, U.S. secretary of state. Approx. 25 mi NW of Salem, via St. 60 (55 mi NW of New Albany, via US 150 & St. 37): MITCHELL. Approx. 3 mi E, via St. 60, *Spring Mill Village State Park, part. rest. & reconst. early 19th-century village, gristmill (1817; rest.), houses, shops, other buildings, including distillery and tavern conveniently side by side.

VINCENNES

Interesting buildings include: *First Territorial Capitol (about 1800; rest.), Harrison Park; capitol until 1813. *Grouseland, the William Henry Harrison Mansion (1804; rest.), 3 W. Scott St; home of U.S. president while he was territorial governor. On out-skirts of town: *Sugar Loaf Indian Mound and other mounds. Approx. 55 mi N, via US 41/150: TERRE HAUTE. *Eugene V. Debs House (1885; rest.), 451 N. 8th St; once home of noted labor union leader and five-time Social Democratic Party presidential candidate.

Iowa

Early inhabitants pre-Columbian Mound Builders, ancestors of present-day Indians. Number of their mounds have survived. Lat-er Indian tribes included Illinois, Iowa, Miami, Omaha, Ottawa, Sioux. First exploration by Frenchmen Father Jacques Marquette and Louis Joliet, 1673; later by Frenchmen Michel Aco and Fa-ther Louis Hennepin, 1680, and by Robert Cavelier, Sieur de La Salle, 1682; he named region Louisiana and claimed it for France. Fur traders, missionaries, and others visited region, but no settle-ments attempted for many years. In 1762, France ceded region to

Spain; back to France, 1800; sold to United States, 1803, as part of Louisiana Purchase. Settlement made by French-Canadian Julien Dubuque, 1788, near present-day Dubuque. Made part of Louisiana Territory, 1805. Explored by number of people, including Lewis and Clark, Zebulon M. Pike. Made part of Missouri Territory, 1812; attached to Territory of Michigan, 1834; made part of Wisconsin Territory, 1836; became Iowa Territory, 1838. First capital Burlington; moved to Iowa City, 1841. Became twenty-ninth state, Dec. 28, 1846. Capital moved to Des Moines. Today: Major agricultural and manufacturing industries.

Land Region: S to N, Dissected Till Plains; Young Drift Plains; small Driftless Area in NE.

Climate: Cold winters, hot summers, often with rapid changes in temperatures; precipitation moderate; snowfall heavy in N, moderate in S.

Major Building Materials: Limestone; sand and gravel.

Architecture: Interesting and important buildings in many places, especially Des Moines and vicinity.

CEDAR RAPIDS

Interesting buildings include: *Peoples Savings Bank (1911), 3rd Ave & 1st St; architect: Louis Sullivan; early modern; not considered one of architect's best. *St. Paul's United Methodist Church (1914; later alt. & addit.), 1340 3rd Ave SE; architects: Louis Sullivan and Purcell & Elmslie; early modern; rather uninteresting ornament not designed by famous architect.

Cedar Rapids Vicinity *(N, via St. 150).* Approx. 90 mi, via St. 150 & US 18: CLERMONT. *Montauk, the Gov. William Larrabee House (1874), Victorian Italianate; once home of state governor; interesting farm outbuildings. Approx. 30 mi NW, via US 18 & 52 & St. 124, *Ft. Atkinson (1840). Approx. 30 mi N of Ft. Atkinson, via St. 24 & US 52: *DECORAH. Nearby, *Norwegian Museum. Approx. 40 mi SE of Decorah, via St. 9 & 76: MARQUETTE. Nearby, *Effigy Mounds Nat. Mon. remains of pre-Columbian Indian mounds, forts, villages, cave dwellings.

Cedar Rapids Vicinity *(NE, via US 151).* Approx 70 mi: DUBUQUE. Interesting buildings include: *Dubuque Co. Jail (1858; later alt. & addit.), 36 E. 8th st; architect: John Francis Rague; unusual Eclectic Egyptian Revival. Adjacent: *Dubuque Co. Courthouse (1893), architect: Fridolin Heer; Eclectic Beaux Arts. *Shot Tower (1856; rest.), Commercial St; used for manufacture of lead gun shot. *Mathias Ham House (1840–57; later alt. &

addit.), 2241 Lincoln Ave; fine Gothic Revival; on grounds: interesting buildings including school, log cabin.

Cedar Rapids Vicinity *(E, via US 30)*. Approx. 90 mi: CLINTON. *Peterson Harned Von Mauer, formerly John D. Van Allen, Store (1915; later alt. & addit.), 5th Ave S & S. 2nd St; architect: Louis Sullivan; early modern; typical of late designs by famous architect; terra-cotta ornament. Also of interest: *Showboat Museum.

Cedar Rapids Vicinity *(SE, via US I-380 & I-80)*. Approx. 28 mi: IOWA CITY. *Old State Capitol (1842; later alt. & addit.; rest.), Iowa Ave & Clinton St; architect: John Francis Rague; fine Greek Revival; third territorial and first state capitol; now museum. *Plum Grove, the Gov. Robert Lucas House (1844; rest.), 727 S. Switzer Ave; once home of first territorial governor. Approx. 8 mi farther: WEST BRANCH. *Jesse Hoover House (1871; rest.), Herbert Hoover Nat. Hist. Site, birthplace of president; *Friends Meeting House (1857; rest.). Approx. 55 mi farther: DAVENPORT. Nearby, via US 61, *Cody-McCausland House (1851; later alt. & addit.; rest.), boyhood home of William "Buffalo Bill" Cody. Approx. 25 mi SW of Davenport, via US 61: MUSCATINE. *Laura Musser Art Gallery and Museum (1908; later alt. & addit.), 1314 Mulberry St; 22-room mansion with 731-pipe organ still in operation. Approx. 58 mi SW of Muscatine, via US 61, St. 92 & US 218: MT. PLEASANT. *James A. Harlan House (about 1865; later alt. & addit.; rest.), 122 N. Jefferson St; once home of U.S. senator and secretary of interior under President Lincoln; president's son, Robert Todd, married Mary Harlan; their family spent many summers here. Also of interest: *Old Settlers and Threshers Heritage Museum. Approx. 40 mi SW of Mt. Pleasant, via US 218 & St. 2, BENTONSPORT, part. rest. steamboat town, now almost ghost town.

Cedar Rapids Vicinity *(SW, via St. 149)*. Approx. 20 mi, AMANA, oldest of seven very successful communal villages in area; founded by German Pietist immigrants, mid-19th century; plain, unadorned buildings influenced by German architecture of era. Nearby, other villages include Homestead, East Amana, Middle Amana, West Amana, South Amana, Lower South Amana.

Cedar Rapids Vicinity *(NW, via US 218)*. Approx. 70 mi: WATERLOO. *Rensselaer Russell House (1861; later alt. & addit.; rest.), 520 3rd St; fine Victorian. Approx. 80 mi NW, via US 218 & 18: MASON CITY. Interesting buildings include: *Van Duyn's Clothing Store, formerly City National Bank (1910; later alt. & addit.), S. Federal Ave & State St; adjoining: *Park Inn Hotel (1910; later alt. & addit.), architect of both: Frank Lloyd Wright; both modern Prairie style by famous architect. Other Prairie style buildings here: Joshua G. Melson House (1913), 56 River Heights Rd and Arthur L. Rule House (1913), 11 S. Rock Glen; architect of both: Walter Burley Griffin, who once worked for Wright.

COUNCIL BLUFFS

Interesting buildings include: *Gen. Grenville˘ M. Dodge House (1870; later alt. & addit.; rest.), 605 3rd St; Eclectic Second Empire; once home of famous engineer and builder of railroads. Approx. 35 mi S, via US 275: TABOR. *Rev. John Todd House (1853; rest.), once station of underground railroad by means of which runaway slaves escaped; once headquarters of John Brown and his group.

Council Bluffs Vicinity *(NW, via US I-29)*. Approx. 100 mi: SIOUX CITY. Interesting buildings include: *Woodbury Co. Courthouse (1918), Douglas & 7th sts; architects: Purcell & Elmslie and William L. Steele; fine Prairie style by noted architects, all of whom once worked for Louis Sullivan; interesting murals, sculpture, terra-cotta ornament. *John Pierce Mansion (1890; later alt. & addit.), 2901 Jackson St; now museum.

DES MOINES

Interesting buildings include: *State Capitol (1873–86), E. Locust & E. 12th sts; architects: Cochrane & Piquenard; M. E. Bell & W. F. Hackney; Eclectic Classic Revival. *Home Federal Savings & Loan Assoc. (1963), Grand Ave & 6th St; architect: Ludwig Mies van der Rohe; assoc. architects: Smith, Voorhees & Jensen; fine modern office building by famous architect. Also by Mies: modern *Meredith Hall (1965), *Drake University. *American Republic Insurance Co. (1965), 601 6th Ave; architects: Skidmore, Owings & Merrill; notable modern offices by famous firm. *Des Moines Art Center (1948; addit. 1968), Grand Ave & 45th St; architect: Eliel Saarinen; architect, addit.: I. M. Pei; fine modern by famous Finnish-American architect, with contrasting modern addit. by famous Chinese-American architect. *Terrace Hill, the Allen-Hubbell House (1869; later alt. & addit.; rest.), 2200 Grand Ave; architect: W. W. Boyington; Eclectic Second Empire. Also: *Salisbury House (1928), 4025 Tonawanda Dr; replica of house in Salisbury, England; elements of number of 13th- through 17th-century styles. W of city, via US 6, *Living History Farms. Approx. 40 mi SW of city, via US I-80 & 169: WINTERSET. *Madison Co. Courthouse (1877; later remod.), architect: A. H. Piquenard; Eclectic Renaissance Revival. Approx. 100 mi NW of Des Moines, via US I-35 & 20, *FT. DODGE, interesting replica of 1850 fort.

Des Moines Vicinity *(E, via US I-80).* Approx. 50 mi: GRIN-NELL. ●∗**Poweshiek Co.,** formerly Merchants, National Bank (1914; later alt. & addit.; rest.), Broad St & 4th Ave; architect: Louis Sullivan; early modern gem by famous architect; masterful ornament. Approx. 35 mi S of Grinnell, via St. 146: OSKALOOSA. ∗Nelson Homestead Pioneer Farm (1852). Approx. 18 mi NW of Oskaloosa, via St. 163: PELLA. ∗Wyatt Earp Boyhood Home (1849).

Kansas

Number of Indian tribes lived here, including Pawnee, Wichita, Arapaho, Cheyenne and Comanche. First European explorer Spaniard Francisco Vásquez de Coronado, 1541. Claimed, but not settled, by French, 17th century. Bought by United States from France as part of Louisiana Purchase, 1803; small portion in SW claimed by Spain, then by Mexico, then Texas. Many Eastern Indian tribes resettled here first half of 19th century; other settlers came about same time. Santa Fe Trail established by William Becknell, 1821, making entry to area easier. First permanent American settlement by Col. Henry Leavenworth, 1827: Ft. Leavenworth. Fighting and killing broke out between proslavery and antislavery settlers, including raid on Potawatomie Creek, 1856, by forces of abolitionist John Brown. Became thirty-fourth state, Jan. 29, 1861. Violence continued in state during Civil War, including raids by guerrillas of William C. Quantrill. Today: Leading agricultural and manufacturing state; mining also important.

Land Regions: E to W, Southeastern Plains, Dissected Till Plains; Great Plains.

Climate: Cold winters, warm summers; precipitation moderate in SE, light in W; snowfall moderate; violent changes may cause blizzards, thunderstorms, hail, tornadoes.

Major Building Materials: Clay; gypsum; sand and gravel; stone.

Architecture: Interesting and important buildings, but not numerous.

KANSAS CITY

Interesting buildings include: Jess Hoel House (1916), 2108 Washington Blvd; architect: Louis S. Curtiss; early modern Prairie style by noted architect. Just SW of city, via US I-35, *Shawnee Mission (1839–45; rest.), Mission Rd & W. 53rd St; three surviving early buildings of Methodist mission; twice territorial capital of Kansas. Approx. 60 mi S of Kansas City, via US 169: OSAWATOMIE. *John Brown Log Cabin (1855), in Mem. Park. Also see: Missouri—Kansas City.

TOPEKA

*State Capitol (1866–73; 1879–1903), Topeka Ave; architect, first stages: E. Townsend Mix; architects, later stages: John G. Haskell & L. M. Wood; construction required almost 40 years; unusual combination of Eclectic French Renaissance, Egyptian, other styles; huge mural by noted Kansas painter, John Steuart Curry. Not far: at 110 E. 8th St, another Haskell design, Romanesque Revival *Thacker Building (1888).

Topeka Vicinity *(SW, via US I-35 & 56).* Approx. 55 mi: COUNCIL GROVE. Interesting buildings include: in Hist. Dist., *Old Kaw Indian Mission (1851). Approx. 20 mi S, via St. 177: COTTONWOOD FALLS. Interesting Eclectic *Chase Co. Courthouse (1873), architect: John G. Haskell.

Topeka Vicinity *(W, via US I-70).* Approx. 35 mi, via US I-70 & St. 79: WABAUNSEE. *Beecher Bible & Rifle Church (1862), strange little building; abolitionist minister Henry Ward Beecher sent money here for purchase of rifles and Bibles for congregation. Approx. 25 mi farther, via St. 79 & US 24: MANHATTAN. *Anderson Hall (1884; later remod.), *Kansas State University; architect: E. T. Carr; Eclectic Victorian. At 2301 Claflin Rd, *Isaac T. Goodnow House (1857; later addit.), home of first state superintendent of education and a founder of KSU. Approx. 30 mi W of Manhattan, via US I-70: ABILENE. Reconst. *Old Abilene Town, number of interesting 19th-century buildings. Also: *Dwight D. Eisenhower Home (1870), 201 S.E. 4th St; boyhood home of president; his library and grave here. Approx. 80 mi N of Abilene, via US 24, 77 & 36: HANOVER. *Pony Express Station (1857), formerly G. H. Hollenburg Ranch House; simple cabin; believed to be last surviving unaltered Pony Express station.

WICHITA

*Hist. Wichita Cow Town, 1717 Sim Park Dr; rest. 19th-century buildings include: *Munger House (1870), oldest in city.

Wichita Vicinity *(W, via US 54 & 154).* Approx. 155 mi, DODGE CITY, famous frontier town, site of *Ft. Dodge; interesting 1968 reconst. notorious *Front St. Also of interest: authentic *Boot Hill. Approx. 60 mi NE of Dodge City, via US 56 & 156, *Ft.

Larned (1868; rest.), now Nat. Hist. Site. Approx. 45 mi SW of Dodge City, via US 283 & 54: MEADE. *Hideout of infamous Dalton Gang of outlaws; now museum.

Michigan

Early inhabitants number of Indian tribes, including Chippewa, Miami, Ottawa. Fist explored by Frenchman Etienne Brulé, 1620; then by Frenchman Jean Nicolet. First permanent settlement by Father Jacques Marquette, 1668: Sault Ste. Marie. Later explored by Frenchmen Marquette and Louis Joliet; Robert Cavelier, Sieur de La Salle. Frenchman Antoine de la Mothe Cadillac founded Detroit, originally Ft. Pontchartrain, 1701. Many British massacred by Indians at Ft. Michilimackinac, 1763, during French and Indian Wars; ceded to British, 1763, at end of wars. During Revolution, number of raids in area by British and Indians; ceded to United States, 1783, after end of Revolution. Made part of Northwest Territory, 1787; of Indiana Territory, 1800; became Michigan Territory, 1805. During War of 1812, British captured Detroit and Ft. Mackinac; returned to United States at end of war, 1814. Became twenty-sixth state, Jan. 26, 1837. Today: Major industrial state, with important mining, agricultural and tourist industries.

Land Regions: Divided into two land masses, upper and lower peninsulas, by Straits of Mackinac. W, upper peninsula Superior Uplands, E, Great Lakes Plains; entire lower peninsula Great Lakes Plains.

Climate: Cold winters, warm summers; moist; precipitation moderate; temperatures lower and precipitation greater on upper peninsula than on lower.

Major Building Materials: Iron ore; timber, particularly hardwoods.

Architecture: Rich and varied after becoming state, in many locations, especially Detroit and vicinity; including some of finest U.S. buildings; little has survived from earliest times.

DETROIT

Interesting buildings include: *Michigan Consolidated Gas Co. (1962), 1 Woodward Ave; architect: Minoru Yamasaki; assoc. ar-

chitects: Smith, Hinchman & Grylls; modern high-rise corporate headquarters; also of interest nearby, several other early 20th-century high-rise buildings. *Renaissance Center (1977), Renaissance Dr; architect: John Portman; large modern urban complex, with hotel, offices, shopping, other facilities. *Detroit Public Library (1921; addit. 1965), 5201 Woodward Ave; architect: Cass Gilbert; architects, addit.: Cass Gilbert, Jr., Francis J. Keally & W. B. Ford; Eclectic Italian Renaissance Revival. Across avenue: *Detroit Institute of Fine Arts (1927; addit. 1966), 5200 Woodward Ave; architects: Paul Cret; Zantziger, Borie & Medary; architects, addit.: Harley, Ellington & Stirton; Gunnar Birkerts; Eclectic Italian Renaissance Revival in Beaux Arts manner. Just behind Institute: *Center for Creative Studies (1975), John R St; architect: William J. Kessler; interesting modern. At: *Wayne State University, interesting buildings include:
●*McGregor Memorial Community Conference Center (1958), Ferry & 2nd aves; architect: Minoru Yamasaki; fine modern in ornamental manner. On Lafayette Ave, *Lafayette Park (1963); architect: Ludwig Mies van der Rohe; large modern high-rise apartments, two-story townhouses, other facilities by famous German-American architect. At 2760 W. 7 Mile Rd, Dorothy H. Turkel House (1955), architect: Frank Lloyd Wright; modern, in style its architect called Usonian. At 71 E. Ferry Ave, *Charles Lang Freer House (about 1887; later alt. & addit.), architect: Wilson Eyre, Jr.; Shingle style; once home of famous industrialist and art collector; now school. At Michigan & Wyoming aves, ●*Chrysler Corp. Press Shop (1936; later alt. & addit.), architect: Albert Kahn; fine modern industrial building by famous architect who pioneered type. Also of interest: *Indian Village Hist. Dist.

Detroit Vicinity *(N, via St. 53).* Approx. 12 mi: WARREN. Interesting buildings include: ●*Dodge Half-ton Truck Plant (1938; later alt. & addit.), 21,500 Mound Rd; architect: Albert Kahn; another pioneering modern example. Not far:

Dodge Half-ton Truck Plant—Early Modern (Hedrich-Blessing)

●*General Motors Technical Center** (1956), Mound & 12 Mile rds; architect: Eero Saarinen; assoc. architects: Smith, Hinchman & Grylls; very fine, expansive complex by famous architect; well-landscaped site with fountain by famous sculptor Alexander Calder, sculpture by famous sculptor Antoine Pevsner, other amenities. Approx. 12 mi farther: WASHINGTON. *Andrus House (1860), architect: David Stewart; interesting octagonal example. Approx. 6 mi farther: ROMEO. In Hist. Dist., interesting early 19th-century houses built by New Englanders.

Detroit Vicinity *(NE, via Jefferson Ave)*. Adjoining city, GROSSE POINTE, actually name of five different towns. In GROSSE POINTE PARK, Stratton House (1927), 938 3 Mile Dr; architect: William Buck Stratton; early modern; reminiscent of work of famous California architect Bernard Maybeck. In GROSSE POINTE FARMS, *The Moorings, the Russell A. Alger, Jr. House (1910), 32 Lake Shore Dr; architect: Charles A. Platt; Eclectic Italian Villa Revival; now War Mem. *Grosse Point Public Library (1953), 10 Kercheval Rd; architect: Marcel Breuer; modern by famous architect; contrasts mightily with Eclectic mansions of area. In GROSSE POINTE SHORES, Edsel B. Ford House (1929), architect: Albert Kahn; Eclectic Gothic Revival by famous architect more noted for factories; beautiful grounds by landscape architect Jens Jensen.

Detroit Vicinity *(W, via US I-94)*. Adjoining city: DEARBORN. *Greenfield Village, Village Rd & Oakwood Blvd; hist. buildings Henry Ford had dismantled and re-erected here include birthplaces of Stephen Foster, Luther Burbank and Ford himself, mills, shops, inn, cottages, other types. Also: *Old Detroit Arsenal, 915 Brady St, *Commandant's Quarters (1833; rest.); *McFadden-

General Motors Technical Center—Modern (General Motors Corp.)

Cranbrook—Early Modern (Hedrich-Blessing)

Ross House, originally Powder Magazine (1839; rest.). Approx. 35 mi farther: ANN ARBOR. Interesting buildings include: Wilson-Wahr House (about 1840), 126 N. Division St; Greek Revival. Mack-Ryan House (1850; later alt. & addit.), Division & Ann sts; architect: Gordon W. Lloyd; Gothic Revival by architect noted for this style. Modern William Palmer House (1950), 227 Orchard Hills Dr; architect: Frank Lloyd Wright.

*University of Michigan. Interesting buildings include: oldest building, Greek Revival President's House (1841; later alt. & addit.). *William L. Clements Library of American History (1953), architect: Albert Kahn; Eclectic Italian Renaissance Revival. *Music Building (1965), architect: Eero Saarinen; modern, completed after death of its famous architect. Approx. 25 mi farther: GRASS LAKE. Interesting buildings include: fine Greek Revival Sidney T. Smith House (1840), Michigan Ave; Village Farm (about 1840), 971 Michigan Ave.

Detroit Vicinity *(NW, via St. 1).* Adjoining city: SOUTHFIELD. Interesting buildings include: *Shaarey Zedak Synagogue (1962), Northwestern Hwy; architects: Albert Kahn, Inc. & Percival Goodman; dramatic modern. *Northland Regional Shopping Center (1954), Northwestern Hwy & 8 Mile Rd; architect: Victor Gruen; early modern center of type pioneered by its architect. ●*Reynolds Metal Co. (1959), 16,000 Northland Dr; architect: Minoru Yamasaki; modern; intricate metal screen. Just N of Southfield: FRANKLIN. Interesting Greek Revival, Gothic Revival and Victorian buildings in *Village of Franklin Hist. Dist. Approx. 5 mi N of Southfield, via US 10/24: BLOOMFIELD HILLS. ●*Cranbrook, famous early modern educational complex, considered one of finest examples of U.S. architecture. Interesting buildings include: *Cranbrook School for Boys (1927); *Kingswood School for Girls (1933); *Cranbrook Institute of Science (1933); *Cranbrook Academy of Art (1943); architect of all: Eliel Saarinen; assoc. architect for some, his son, Eero; designer of tapestries,

rugs, other furnishings: his wife, Loja; also of interest: very fine
*Orpheus Fountain (1936) by famous Swedish-American sculptor
Carl Milles. Also: two private modern houses by Frank Lloyd
Wright, Usonian Melvin Maxwell Smith House (1946; later alt.
& addit.), 5045 Pon Valley Rd; Gregory Affleck House (1940),
1925 Woodward Ave. Approx. 4 mi farther: PONTIAC. *Gov. Mo-
ses Wisner House (1844; later alt. & addit.; rest.), 405 Oakland
Ave; Greek Revival; once home of state governor.

LANSING

Interesting buildings include: *State Capitol (1879), Capitol Ave;
architect: Elijah E. Meyers; Eclectic Second Empire Revival.

Lansing Vicinity *(NE, via US I-69 & I-75)*. Approx. 70 mi: SAGI-
NAW. *Henry Passalt House, now Hist. Museum (1868; later alt.
& addit.), 1105 S. Jefferson St. Approx 25 mi farther: MIDLAND.
Interesting buildings include number of fine modern buildings by
noted architect Alden B. Dow, once student of Frank Lloyd
Wright: *First United Methodist Church (1954), Jerome & Main
sts; Alden B. Dow House and Studio (1935), 315 Post St.

Lansing Vicinity *(S, via US 127)*. Approx. 30 mi: JACKSON. *Ella
Sharp Museum (about 1845; later alt. & addit.), 3225 4th St;
Victorian. Approx. 20 mi NE of Jackson, via St. 106: STOCK-
BRIDGE. Nearby, *Waterloo Farm (about 1840; later alt. & ad-
dit.; rest.). Approx. 35 mi SE of Jackson, via US 223: ADRIAN.
*Gov. Charles M. Crosswell House (about 1840; later alt. & ad-
dit.; rest.), 228 N. Broad St; once home of state governor. Approx.
15 mi SW of Jackson, via St. 60: CONCORD. *Daniel Sears Mann
House (about 1885), 205 Hanover St; Victorian. Also see: Detroit
Vicinity (W, via US I-94).

Lansing Vicinity *(SW, via I-69 & I-94)*. Approx. 40 mi: MAR-
SHALL. Interesting buildings include: Dr. Andrew L. Hayes
House (about 1838; rest.), Prospect & Kalamazoo sts; architect,
rest.: Howard P. Young; fine Greek Revival. At same intersection,
across street: fine Greek Revival Jabez Fitch House (about 1840);
on still another corner, Gothic Revival Benedict House (1844; later alt. & addit.). At 107 N. Kalamazoo St, *Honolulu House
(1860), fascinating example built by Abner Pratt to resemble his
house in Sandwich Islands (Hawaii), where he served as U.S. consul. Approx. 25 mi W, via US I-94: GALESBURG. Several 1948
private houses by Frank Lloyd Wright, all on one street, at nos.
294–97 Hawthorne Dr: David J. Weisblat House (1948; addit.
1960); Eric Pratt House; Samuel Epstein House; Curtis Meyer
House. Approx. 10 mi farther: KALAMAZOO. *Parkwyn Village,
planned community with four Frank Lloyd Wright houses, all
quite different from each other, at nos. 298–301 Taliesin St,

named after architect's home in Wisconsin: Robert Levin House (1948); Ward McCartney House (1949; later alt. & addit.); Eric V. Brown House (1949); Robert D. Winn House (1950). Also of interest: *Fountain of the Pioneers (1937), Bronson Sq; sculptor: Alfonso Iannelli, who worked with Wright on famous Chicago Midway Gardens (1913; demolished). Just SE of city: *Upjohn Co. (1961), Portage Rd; architects: Skidmore, Owings & Merrill; fine modern headquarters by famous firm. Approx. 40 mi farther: St. Joseph. Interesting private modern houses by Wright, on fine sites: Carl E. Schultz House (1959), 2704 Highland Ct, overlooking St. Joseph River; Ina Moriss Harper House (1950), 207 Sunnybank St, overlooking Lake Michigan. Approx. 18 mi N of St. Joseph, via US I-196: South Haven. *Liberty Hyde Bailey House (about 1855; later alt. & addit.), 903 Bailey Ave; once home of famous botanist.

Lansing Vicinity *(NW, Via US I-96)*. Approx. 65 mi: Grand Rapids. Interesting buildings include fine modern private houses by Frank Lloyd Wright; Meyer S. May House (1909), 450 Madison Ave, important early example; David B. Amberg House (1909), 505 College Ave, claimed by Wright but attributed by some authorities to Hermann Von Holst & Marion Mahony who once worked in his office. Also: Classic Revival *Abram W. Pike House (1845; later alt. & addit.), 230 Fulton St. Approx. 40 mi farther: Muskegon. Interesting buildings include: *Charles H. Hackley House (1889; later alt. & addit.), 484 W. Webster St; ●*St. Francis de Sales Church,** Roman Catholic (1966), 2929 McCracken Ave; architects: Marcel Breuer & Herbert Beckhard; very fine modern by famous architect; interesting warped, rusticated concrete structure.

SAULT STE. MARIE

Interesting buildings include: *John Johnston House (1795), 415 Park Pl; once home of fur trader. *Bishop Baraga House (about 1860), 305 E. Portage Ave; once home of first Roman Catholic bishop here. Also of interest: *Tower of History (1968), 326 E. Portage Ave; architects: Rafferty, Rafferty & Mikutowski; modern monument.

Sault Ste. Marie Vicinity *(SW, via US I-75)*. Approx. 60 mi: Mackinaw City. *Ft. Michilimackinac (1729; rest.). Via ferry: *Mackinac Island. Interesting buildings include: *Grand Hotel (1887; later alt.), architects: Mason & Rice; one of few surviving examples of very fine, sumptuous 19th-century summer hotels. Nearby, *Ft. Holmes (1812); *Ft. Mackinac (1781; reconst.); *John Jacob Astor's American Fur Co. Trading Post and Agent's House, also known as Stuart House (about 1817; rest.); *Edward Biddle House (about 1800; rest.); *Indian Dormitory (1838; rest.).

Minnesota

Early inhabitants Indians, including Sioux; Chippewa came into area in mid-18th century. First Europeans to arrive believed to have been French fur traders Pierre Esprit Radisson and Médart Chouart, Sieur de Groseilliers, about 1660. First explored by Frenchman Daniel Greysolon, Sieur Duluth, about 1679; claimed region for France. Belgian Father Louis Hennepin explored, 1680; with two companions, captured by Indians; Duluth gained their release. France ceded W portion to Spain, 1762; at end of French and Indian Wars, 1763, France ceded E portion to Great Britain; at end of Revolution, British ceded to United States, which only gained full control after end of War of 1812; W portion returned to France by Spain, 1800; sold to United States in Louisiana Purchase, 1803. American Col. Josiah Snelling founded Ft. St. Anthony, 1819, at S edge of present-day Minneapolis; renamed Ft. Snelling, 1825. After having been part of Illinois, Indiana, Iowa, Louisiana, Michigan, Missouri, and Wisconsin territories, region became Minnesota Territory, 1849. Became thirty-second state, May 11, 1858. During Civil War, uprising of Sioux Indians led to loss of lives of many citizens and great property damage; Federal and state troops put end to uprising. Today: Important manufacturing, agricultural and mining, especially iron, industries; tourism also important.

Land Regions: N to S, large Superior Upland; Young Drift Plain; in SW, small Dissected Drift Plains; in SE, small Driftless Area.

Climate: Long, very cold winters, short mild summers; precipitation moderate in SE, light elsewhere; snowfall varies from moderate in SW to very heavy in NE.

Major Building Materials: Timber; iron; granite; limestone; sandstone.

Architecture: Rich and varied with important buildings in number of locations, especially Minneapolis and vicinity; St. Paul and vicinity.

MINNEAPOLIS

Interesting buildings include:
•*IDS (Investors Diversified Services) Center (1973), bet. Nicollet Mall, Marquette Ave, 7th & 8th sts; architects: Philip Johnson & John Burgee; assoc, architect: Edward F. Baker; 57-story modern

building; tallest in city; 8-story atrium center of downtown life in city; offices, shops, restaurants, parking, other facilities; located on *Nicollet Ave Mall (1968), landscape architect: Lawrence Halprin; tied to elevated second-story pedestrian walks, *Skyway (begun 1962), original architect: Edward F. Baker; connecting downtown office buildings, shopping, other buildings. Nearby, via Skyway, *Foshay Tower (1929), 821 Marquette Ave, architects: Magney & Tusler; fanciful high-rise office building shaped like Egyptian obelisk; was tallest in city, 447 feet, before IDS. Nearby, via Skyway, Art Deco *Dain, formerly Rand, Tower (1929), 527 Marquette Ave; architects: Holabird & Root. At 250 Marquette Ave, *Federal Reserve Bank (1972), architect: Gunnar Birkerts; dramatic modern building; glass walls reveal curves of unusual catenary structure. *Federal Office Building (1912; addit. 1927), 200 Washington Ave S; architect: James Knox Taylor; Beaux Arts. *First National Bank (1981) and *Pillsbury Center Building (1981), bet. 5th & 6th sts, 2nd & 3rd aves; architects of both: Skidmore, Owings & Merrill; high-rise office towers of similar design by famous firm; tied together with glass-covered atrium. Bet. 3rd & 4th aves S, 5th & 7th sts, *Hennepin Co. Government Center (1975), architect: John Carl Warnecke; two interesting high-rise units, one courts, other offices; full-height atrium with bridges connecting floors of two units. Across plaza: Romanesque Revival *Municipal Building, formerly City Hall and Hennepin Co. Courthouse (1905), architects: Long & Kees; interesting courtyard. Not far: *Lutheran Brotherhood Building (1981), 4th Ave S; architects: Skidmore, Owings & Merrill; dramatic modern offices; glass walls slant inward in sections toward top. *Lutheran Brotherhood Life Insurance Building (1955), 701 2nd Ave S; architects: Perkins & Will; earlier modern office building; glass walls rounded at corners. Few blocks away: *Butler Square, formerly Butler Brothers Warehouse (1906; remod. 1974), 100 6th St N; architect: Harry Jones; architects, remod.: Miller, Hanson, Westerbeck & Bell; interesting old building converted to shops, restaurants, other uses; 8-story interior court with original wood timbers and skylight. Nearby, *Hennepin Center for the Arts, formerly Masonic Temple (1889; remod. 1979), 528 Hennepin Ave; architects: Long & Kees; architects, remod: Svedberg & Wermeland. Approx. 7 blocks away, *Orchestra Hall (1974), 1111 Nicollet Ave; architects: Hardy, Holzman & Pfeiffer and Hammel, Green & Abrahamson; interesting modern; almost like two buildings, one brick, other metal and glass; faces *Peavey Plaza Park (1977), landscape architect: M. Paul Friedberg.

Near *Loring Park: *Tyrone Guthrie Theater (1963; later alt. & addit.), 725 Vineland Pl; architect: Ralph Rapson; fine modern by noted architect and educator; original metal fins later removed to detriment of design. Next door and connected by wing,
•*Walker Art Center (1971), Vineland & Lyndale aves; architect: Edward Larrabee Barnes; fine modern gallery of modern art and

architecture by noted architect. Not far: *Basilica of St. Mary (1907–25), Lyndale & Hennepin aves; architect: Emmanuel Masqueray; imposing Eclectic Baroque Revival. Some blocks away: *Minneapolis Institute of Arts (1914; addit. 1974), 2400 3rd Ave S; architects: McKim, Mead & White; architects, addit.: Kenzo Tange, with Parker & Klein; strange combination of small Beaux Arts original building by famous firm, with very large, modern addition by famous Japanese architect. Several blocks away: *Swan J. Turnblad House, now American Swedish Institute (1907), 2600 Park Ave; architects: Christopher A. Boehme & Victor Cordella; Eclectic mixture of Romanesque, Gothic, Renaissance and other revival styles; like castle in fairy tale. Also: on *University of Minnesota Minneapolis campus, 19th- and 20th-century buildings; also see West Bank and St. Paul campuses. On Cedar Ave, bet 4th & 6th sts S, near West Bank campus: *Cedar Square West (1973), architect: Ralph Rapson; five fine modern apartment towers; part of new town: *Cedar Riverside.

In W area of city: Henry J. Neils House (1951), 2801 Burnham Ave; architect: Frank Lloyd Wright; fine modern example overlooking Cedar Lake. Not far: William G. Purcell House (1913), 2328 Lake Pl; architects: Purcell & Elmslie; fine early modern Prairie style example by noted architects who, with Wright, once worked for Louis Sullivan. Some distance S. *Stewart Memorial Church (1909; later alt. & addit.), 116 32nd St E; architects: Purcell & Feick; early modern; reminiscent of designs of era by Wright. Some blocks S, 5000 block of Nicollet Ave and 4000 block of Cedar Ave: private examples of Lustron homes, 1948 prefabricated porcelain enamel on steel houses. Some 30 blocks W of Nicollet Ave, in 4000 block of Upton Ave S: speculative houses of earlier era, 1927–32; architects: Purcell & Strauel. Not far, in suburb EDINA, *Southdale Shopping Center (1956), W. 66th St & France Ave S; architect: Victor Gruen; pioneering modern regional example, first to be built around enclosed court or mall; by noted Austrian-American architect who designed many others, including *Rosedale (1969), in ROSEVILLE, just N of St. Paul, and *Ridgedale, in MINNETONKA, NW of Edina.

In SE area of city: *Milwaukee Ave Hist. Dist., bet. Franklin Ave & 24th St; interesting small late 19th-century houses for immigrant workers. Approx. 20 blocks away: ●*Christ Church, Lutheran (1950), 3244 34th Ave S; architect: Eliel Saarinen; assoc. architects: Eero Saarinen; Hills, Glibertson & Hayes; very fine modern example by famous Finnish-American architect; considered one of best of U.S. buildings of its time.

ST. PAUL

Interesting buildings include: ●*State Capitol (1893–1904), Aurora Ave & Park St; architect: Cass Gilbert; impressive, fine Beaux Arts building by famous architect; great dome; interesting murals and sculpture. Not far from *University of Minneapolis–St. Paul

Campus: Malcolm E. Willey House (1934), 255 Bedford St SE; architect: Frank Lloyd Wright; modern by famous architect; considered link between his Prairie and Usonian styles; *University Grove (begun 1929), planned community of houses for university faculty members; residential styles from late 1920s to present. Not far: *Gibbs Farm (1854; later alt. & addit.; rest.), 2097 Larpenteur Ave W; interesting operating farm complex with buildings, animals, crop fields. Some blocks away: *St. Columba Church (1951), 1305 LaFond Ave; architect: Barry Byrne; interesting modern example in highly personal style by noted architect who once worked for Frank Lloyd Wright. At 90 4th St W, *St. Paul Public and Hill Reference Libraries Building, formerly Central Library (1916); architect: Electus D. Litchfield; interesting Eclectic Beaux Arts Classic Revival. Nearby, *Landmark Center, formerly Old Federal Courts Building (1894–1904; rest. 1981), 75 W. 5th St; architect: Willoughby J. Edbrooke; architects, rest.: Stahl & Bennett; impressive Romanesque Revival; now used by civic organizations; faces small *Hamm Park on one side; on other, larger *Rice Park (1849; remod. 1949), architects, remod.: Hammell, Green & Abrahamson. Not far: on Kellogg Ave, Adult Detention Center (1980), architects: Wold Assoc.; Gruzen Assoc.; unusually fine example for this building type. *City Hall and Ramsey Co. Courthouse (1932), 15 Kellogg Ave; architects: Holabird & Root; assoc. architects: Ellerbe Co.; high-rise Art Deco; interesting murals and sculpture, some of latter by famous Swedish sculptor Carl Milles. Nearby, Art Deco *Minnesota Museum of Art, formerly Women's City Club (1931), 305 St. Peter St; architect: Magnus Jemne. Few blocks away: *Pioneer Building (1889; later alt. & addit.), Robert & 4th sts E; architect: Solon S. Beman; Romanesque Revival; reminiscent of early pioneer modern work in Chicago; interesting atrium; top three stories added later. At Summit & Dayton aves, on St. Anthony Hill, *Cathedral of St. Paul (1906–15; some later work), architect: Emmanuel L. Masqueray; assoc. architects: Whitney Warren; Maginnis & Walsh; very fine Eclectic Beaux Arts Baroque Revival; fine dome. Not far, on Summit & Grand aves & nearby streets, interesting Eclectic houses in various styles include: Cass Gilbert House (about 1890), 1 Heather Pl; *James C. Burbank House, also known as Burbank–Livingston Griggs House (1865; later alt. & addit.), 432 Summit Ave; architect: Otis E. Wheelock; impressive Eclectic Italian Villa Revival; several complete rooms of antiques, including Jacobean, 18th-century Venetian, Louis XV, Louis XVI, imported from Europe by later owner, Livingston Griggs. At Summit & Hamline aves, *Mount Zion Temple (1954), architect: Eric Mendelsohn; assoc. architects: Bergstedt & Hirsch; fine modern synagogue by German architect more famous for his work in Europe. In SE area of city: *Alexander Ramsey House (1872), 265 S. Exchange St; architect: Monroe Sheire; fine Victorian; once home of first territorial governor, later second state governor, U.S. senator and secretary of war under President Rutherford B.

Hayes. Not far, suburb MENDOTA, first permanent American settlement in state, founded about 1820. Interesting buildings include: in Hist. Dist., on 1st St, *Gov. Henry H. Sibley House (1835; rest.), once home of first state governor; *Jean Baptiste Faribault House (1837; rest.), once home of pioneer fur trader. Also, across river from town: *Ft. Snelling, originally Ft. St. Anthony (begun 1820; rest.), on cliff above Mississippi and Minnesota rivers. Approx. 8 mi E of St. Paul, via St. 36: STILLWATER. Number of interesting mid-19th to early 20th-century houses and other buildings, in diverse styles.

Minneapolis–St. Paul Vicinity *(NE, via US 61).* Approx. 35 mi: TAYLORS FALLS. *William H. C. Folsom House (1855), Government Rd; once home of pioneer lumberman. Also of interest N of town: *St. Croix Nat. Waterway; *Voyageurs Nat. Park; in extreme N part of state, just below Canadian border, *Grand Portage Nat. Mon.

Minneapolis–St. Paul Vicinity *(SE, via US 61).* Approx. 15 mi: HASTINGS. Interesting buildings include: *Fasbender Medical Clinic (1959), Pine St; architect: Frank Lloyd Wright; low modern building on well-landscaped site. *Gen. William G. LeDuc House (about 1863), 1629 Vermilion St; Gothic Revival; once home of pioneer agriculture and railroad entrepreneur. Italianate *Octagon House (1859), Spring & 2nd St W; remains of *Old Ramsey Mill (1857), Old Mill Park. Approx. 25 mi farther: RED WING. Interesting buildings include: Hoyt House (1913), 300 Hill St; architects: Purcell, Feick & Elmslie; fine modern Prairie style by architects who once worked for Louis Sullivan. Approx. 56 mi farther, WINONA, picturesquely situated between Lake Winona, Mississippi River. Interesting buildings include:
•*Merchants National Bank** (1912; addit. 1970), 102 3rd St E; architects: Purcell & Elmslie; architects, addit.: Dykins & Handford; very fine Prairie style example by noted architects; considered finest of their designs; beautiful ornament. Nearby, *Winona National Savings Bank (1914), Main St; architect: George W. Maher; strange combination of early modern, Eclectic Classic Revival, Egyptian, other styles. Near town: *Willard Bunnell House (about 1855), interesting wood-frame with unusual trim; built on land given first owner by Chief Wapasha of Dakota Indians. Also of interest: *Steamboat Museum.

Minneapolis–St. Paul Vicinity *(SE, via US 52).* Approx. 100 mi ROCHESTER. Interesting buildings include several private modern houses by Frank Lloyd Wright; on Skyline Dr SW, at no. 36 Thomas E. Keys House (1950), in style architect called Usonian at no. 22 A. H. Bulbulian House (1950); at 1500 Woodland Dr SW, prefabricated James B. McBean House (1957). On Mayowood Dr, *Mayowood, the Dr. Charles H. Mayo House (1912), impressive 38-room mansion of concrete, on well-landscaped site; fine antiques and other furnishings; once home of famous founder of Mayo Clinic. At junction of US 52 & 37th St NW, *International Business Machines Corp. Building (1958), architects: Eliel & Eero Saarinen; fine modern offices on well-landscaped site by famous father-son team of architects. Approx. 35 mi SW of city, via US I-90 & St. 7: ADAMS. *Municipal Liquor Store, originally First National Bank (1920; later alt. & addit.), Main & 4th sts; architects: Purcell & Elmslie; fine design badly altered. Approx. 10 mi SE of Adams, via St. 56: LE ROY. *First State Bank (1914), Main St; architects: Purcell & Elmslie. Approx. 15 mi W of Rochester, via US 14 & St. 57: MANTORVILLE. Interesting buildings here in Greek, Gothic Revival, other revival styles, from mid-19th century on.

Minneapolis–St. Paul Vicinity *(S, via US I-35).* Approx. 45 mi: FARIBAULT. *Alexander Faribault House (1853; rest.), 12 N.E. 1st Ave; once home of fur trader. Approx. 15 mi farther: OWATONNA. ••**Northwestern National Bank,** formerly National Farmers' Bank, Security National Bank (1908; addit. & alt., 1957), 101 Cedar St N; architects: Louis Sullivan; George Grant Elmslie; architect, addit. & alt.: Harwell Hamilton Harris; very fine early modern by famous architect; noted for ornamentation, much of which was designed by Elmslie; considered one of finest U.S. buildings; alt. & addit. sensitively handled by noted architect. Not far: fine early modern Buxton Bungalow (1912), 424 Main St E; architects: Purcell, Feick & Elmslie.

Minneapolis–St. Paul Vicinity *(SW, via US 169).* Approx. 10 mi: EDEN PRAIRIE. *Gelco Corp. Building (1979), architect:

Northwestern National Bank—Early Modern (Hedrich-Blessing)

Leonard Parker; interesting modern headquarters with glass walls.
Few miles farther, via US 212, *JONATHAN, new town planned in
1960s; planner: Benjamin H. Cunningham; landscape architects:
Masao Kinoshita; Sasaki, Dawson & DeMay; Bailey Assoc., interesting modern buildings. Approx. 70 mi farther, via US 169:
MANKATO. *Hubbard House (1871; rest.), 606 S. Broad St; large
Victorian; interesting furnishings; log cabin in basement. Approx.
75 mi SW of Mankato, via St. 60: WINDOM. *Monson Log Cabin
(1869; later alt. & addit.), Island Park; built by Mons O. Monson,
Thomas Chester on line between homestead claims, thus satisfy-
ing legal requirements for dwelling on both; later moved to Monson claim.

Minneapolis–St. Paul Vicinity *(W, via US 12)*. Just W of Minneapolis: GOLDEN VALLEY. *General Mills Headquarters (1957–
66), 9200 Wayzata Rd; architects: Skidmore, Owings & Merrill;
fine modern complex with several buildings by famous firm; also
here: *Betty Crocker Kitchens by famous industrial designer Walter Dorwin Teague. Approx. 6 mi farther: WAYZATA. Two mi W,
via St. 101 & Co. Rt. 6, *Spring Hill Conference Center, originally John Cowles, Jr. House (1963; later alt. & addit.), architect:
Edward Larrabee Barnes; fine modern complex of buildings with
simple materials and forms by noted architect. Approx. 45 mi
farther: LITCHFIELD. *Trinity Episcopal Church (1872; later alt.
& addit.), Sibley Ave N & 4th St E; probable architect: Richard
Upjohn; fine wood-frame Gothic Revival. Approx. 27 mi farther:
WILLMAR. *Lars Endreson Log Cabin (1870), once home of Norwegian immigrant. Approx. 52 mi SW of Willmar, via St. 23 &
US 212; MONTEVIDEO. Nearby, via St. 7, *Chippewa City Pioneer Village; late 19th-century pioneer buildings include farmhouse, trading post, other types. Approx. 5 mi S, via St. 7, *Olof

St. John's University Church—Modern (Hedrich-Blessing)

Swensson Farmhouse (1901), once home of pioneer farmer, lay preacher. Approx. 100 mi NW of Montevideo, via US 59 & St. 7: Brown's Valley. *Sam Brown Log House (about 1863), Mem. Park; once home of boy who rode 120 mi to warn settlers of Sioux attack.

Minneapolis–St. Paul Vicinity *(NW, Via US I-94 or 10)*. Approx. 20 mi: Elk River. *Oliver H. Kelley Farmhouse (about 1865; rest.), once home of founder of National Grange, farm organization. Approx. 45 mi farther: St. Cloud. Interesting buildings include: *Rosenberger Log House (about 1855), Munsinger Park; one of oldest log buildings in state. Approx. 10 mi farther: Collegeville. At *St. John's University, Roman Catholic Benedictine campus planned by famous Hungarian-American architect Marcel Breuer; fine modern buildings, all by Breuer, with assoc. architect Hamilton P. Smith, include: *Alcuin College Library (1967); *Science Hall (1968); *Dormitories (1959 & 1968); *Ecumenical Center (1968); and very finest of all,
•*St. John's University Church** (1961), large, sculptural concrete building with imposing free-standing Bell Banner Tower; considered one of finest U.S. buildings. Nearby, fine modern *St. John's Preparatory School (1963), architects: Hanson & Michelson. Approx. 30 mi farther: Sauk Centre. *Sinclair Lewis Boyhood Home (about 1882), 812 Sinclair Lewis Ave; once home of famous novelist, first American to win Nobel Prize in literature. Approx. 30 mi NW of St. Cloud, via US 10: Little Falls. *Charles A. Lindbergh House (1907; rest.), Mem. Park; boyhood home of famous airplane pilot, explorer; built by his father, noted pioneer lawyer, member of U.S. Congress. Approx. 30 mi farther, via US 10: Brainerd. Nearby, *Lumbertown, USA, reconst. and rest. 19th-century lumbering community.

Missouri

Early inhabitants pre-Columbian ancestors of Indians, known as Mound Builders; later Indian tribes included Fox, Missouri, Osage, Sauk. First explorers Frenchmen Father Jacques Marquette and Louis Joliet, 1673; Frenchman Robert Cavelier, Sieur de La Salle followed, 1682; claimed for France as part of region he named Louisiana. In years following, French fur trappers and traders, missionaries active in region. First permanent French settlement made by settlers from nearby Illinois, 1735: Ste. Genevieve; Frenchmen Pierre Laclède Liguest and René Auguste Chouteau founded St. Louis, 1764. Region ceded by France to

Spain, 1762; returned to France, 1800; sold to United States in Louisiana Purchase, 1803. Famous frontiersman Daniel Boone settled here, 1800. Became Missouri Territory, 1812. Became twenty-fourth state, Aug. 10, 1821. Frequent Indian attacks, especially during War of 1812, ended 1815. As border state, sympathies of people divided at beginning of Civil War. Although State Convention called for remaining in Union, pro-South Gov. Claiborne F. Jackson led Missouri state troops against Federal troops in several battles. Other battles fought in state and both Confederate and Federal guerilla warfare took heavy toll in citizens killed and property damage. Today: Major manufacturing and agricultural industries.

Land Regions: In SE corner, small Mississippi Alluvial Plain; S to N, Ozark Plateau; Osage Plains; Dissected Till Plains.

Climate: Moderate; winters and summers milder in mountains than in plains; precipitation fairly heavy; snowfall light in S, heavier in N.

Major Building Materials: Timber, mostly hardwoods; marble; granite; limestone; sandstone; lead.

Architecture: Rich and varied, including some of finest U.S. examples, in many locations, especially Kansas City, St. Louis; Ste. Genevieve.

JEFFERSON CITY

Interesting buildings include: *State Capitol (1918), N. High St; architects: Egerton Swartwout & Evarts Tracy; Eclectic Italian Renaissance Revival. *Gov. B. Gratz Brown House (1871; rest.), 109 Madison St; Greek Revival. *Central Motor Bank (1962), 500 Madison St, architects: Skidmore, Owings & Merrill; assoc. architects: Wedemeyer & Hecker; fine modern by famous firm. Approx. 25 mi NE of Jefferson City, via US 54: FULTON. *Westminster College, *St. Mary Aldermanbury Church, now known as Winston Churchill Memorial (1670–86; badly damaged World War II; dismantled and re-erected here 1969), architect: Sir Christopher Wren; moved here from London, England, to honor famous statesman and his "Iron Curtain" speech here, 1946; also nearby, *Winston Churchill Library. Approx. 45 mi E of Jefferson City, via St. 94: HERMANN. Interesting buildings include: *Carl P. Strehly House (about 1845), 131 W. 2nd St; G. Henry Gentner House (about 1850), 108 Market St. Approx. 72 mi NW of Jefferson City, via US 63 & I-70 & St. 41: ARROW ROCK. Interesting buildings include: *George Caleb Bingham House (about 1837), High & 1st sts, once home of famous painter.

*Matthew Hall House (1847), Main St; once home of original settler. *Old Tavern (about 1834; later addit.; rest.), Main St.

KANSAS CITY

Interesting buildings include: *Boley Clothing Co. (1909), 1124 Walnut St; architect: Louis S. Curtiss; fine early modern by noted architect; early ornamental glass curtain wall; other buildings designed by him here include: *Curtiss Studio (1909), 1118 McGee St; with less ornamental glass curtain wall; earlier Eclectic Beaux Arts Classic Revival *Standard, originally Folly, Theater (1900), 300 W. 12th St. Not far: *Crown Center (1978), Grand Ave & 25th St; master planner: Edward Larrabee Barnes, who also was architect of office buildings, shopping center; other buildings here include: *Crown Center Hotel (1973), architect: Harry Weese; Crown Center Apartments (1976), architects: The Architects Collaborative (TAC); very successful modern downtown multi-use complex; assoc. architects, all buildings: Marshall & Brown. Nearby, *Twenty West Ninth Building, originally New York State Life Co. (1890; later alt. & addit.; rest.), architects: McKim, Mead & White; Eclectic by famous firm. *Union Railroad Station (1914), 2400 Main St; architect: Jarvis Hunt; fine Eclectic Beaux Arts Classic Revival. Across plaza: *Liberty Memorial (1926), 100 W. 26th St; architect: H. Van Buren Magonigle; fine Moderne, or Art Deco, memorial to dead of World War I. Not far: *Kemper Arena (1975), Genesee & 17th sts; architect: C. F. Murphy; interesting modern space-frame structure. At Wyandotte & 13th sts, *Municipal Auditorium (1936), architects: Alonzo H. Gentry; Voscamp & Neville; Hoit, Price & Barnes; interesting Moderne, or Art Deco. Also: *Business Men's Assurance Co. (1963), 700 W. 31st St; architects: Skidmore, Owings & Merrill; fine modern offices by famous firm. S of business district: *Country Club Plaza (1925; later alt. & addit.), architect: Edward B. Delk; architect, alt. & addit.: Edward W. Tanner, Eclectic Spanish Revival; one of first U.S. suburban shopping centers. *St. Francis Xavier Church (1950), 1001 E. 52nd St; architects: Barry Byrne & Joseph Shaughnessy, Sr.; interesting modern church in shape of fish by noted architect who once worked for Frank Lloyd Wright. Number of houses by Wright, all private, in city. At 146 W. 61st St, *Wornall House (1858; later alt. & addit.; rest.), Greek Revival; used as headquarters and hospital at times by both Confederate and Federal troops. Approx. 18 mi NW of city, via US I-29, *Kansas City International Airport (1972), architects: Kivett & Meyers; considered one of best U.S. airports. Also see: Kansas—Kansas City.

Kansas City Vicinity *(N, via US I-29)*. Approx. 55 mi: ST. JOSEPH. *Wyeth-Tootle House (1879; later alt. & addit.), Charles

Gateway Arch—Modern (Missouri Tourism—Walker)

& 11th sts; 43-room Gothic Revival; octagonal tower with battlements; *Jesse James House (1879), where outlaw, posing as "Mr. Howard," was killed by Bob Ford, for reward. Also of interest: *Pony Express Museum.

Kansas City Vicinity *(E, via US I-70).* Adjoining Kansas City, via Truman Ave: INDEPENDENCE. Interesting buildings include: *Old Jackson Co. Courthouse (1827), 107 Kansas St; log cabin. *Marshal's House (1859), 217 Main St; on grounds: *Old Jail (1859). *Harry S Truman House (1867; later alt. & addit.), 219 N. Delaware St; once home of president; now Nat. Hist. Site; also here, *Truman Library and Museum. Approx. 40 mi farther, via US I-70 & St. 13: LEXINGTON. *Col. Oliver Anderson House (1853; later alt. & addit.), Battle of Lexington State Park; Greek Revival survivor of Civil War battle.

ST. LOUIS

Mississippi Riverfront dominated by towering modern
••**Gateway Arch** (1968), Jefferson National Expansion Memorial, Memorial Dr; architect: Eero Saarinen; magnificent stainless steel structure by famous architect; considered one of finest U.S. architectural achievements of any era. Nearby, *Basilica of St. Louis, King of France, also known as Old Cathedral (1834; rest.), Walnut St & Memorial Dr; architects: Joseph C. Laveille & George Morton; architects, rest.: Murphy & Mackey; fine Greek Revival; oldest cathedral W of Mississippi River. Nearby, very fine *Eads Bridge, originally Great Illinois & St. Louis Bridge (1867–74), Washington Ave & Riverfront; engineer: James B. Eads. Across

bridge: see Illinois—East St. Louis. At 727 N. 1st St, *Raeder Place, originally Christian Peper Tobacco Co. (1874; remod. 1978); architect: Frederick W. Raeder; architect, remod.: Kimble A. Cohn; interesting cast-iron-front building remod. into restaurant, office, shops; in hist. Laclède's Landing area where city was founded. At 11 N. 4th St, *Old St. Louis Courthouse (1845; later alt. & addit.; rest.), architects: Henry Singleton, Robert S. Mitchell & William Rumbold; architects, rest.: Charles E. Peterson & Ralph Emerson; fine Greek Revival. Not far, at 634 S. Broadway, *Eugene Field House (1845), once home of famous author. Few blocks away: ●*Wainwright Building (1891; rest. & addit. 1981), 709 Chestnut St; architects: Adler & Sullivan; architects, rest. & addit.: Mitchell & Giurgola; assoc. architects: Hastings & Chivetta; magnificent early modern office building designed by famous architect Louis H. Sullivan; considered one of its architect's masterpieces and one of finest U.S. buildings; also by same architect, Wainwright Tomb (1892), *Bellefontaine Cemetery, 4947 Florissant Ave, where original owner of building, Ellis Wainwright, and his wife are buried. On Olive bet. 8th & 9th sts, ●*Old St. Louis Post Office & Custom House (1884; remod. 1984), architect: Alfred B. Mullett; architects, remod.: Harry Weese; Patty, Berkebile & Nelson; exuberant Eclectic French Second Empire Revival; sculpture by famous sculptor Daniel Chester French; now government offices. Not far away: *Christ Church Cathedral, Episcopal (1867; later alt. & addit.; rest.), Locust & 13th sts; architect: Leopold Eidlitz; architects, alt. & addit.: J. B. Legg; Kivas B. Tully & W. A. Caldwell; Jamieson & Spearl; architects, rest.: Frederick Dunn & Nolan Stinson, Jr.;

**Wainwright Building—
Early Modern**
(Missouri Historical Society)

fine Gothic Revival. At Market St & 12th Blvd, *City Hall (1896; later alt. & addit.), architects: Eckel & Mann; exuberant Eclectic French Renaissance Revival. Few blocks: *John Hall–Robert Campbell House (1851; later alt. & addit.; rest.), 1508 Locust St, probable architect: William Fulton. Few blocks: ●*Union Station (1894), Market bet. 18th & 20th sts; architect: Theodore C. Link; fine Romanesque Revival; clock tower. Across Market St: *Aloe Plaza, beautiful fountain and fine sculptures by famous Swedish sculptor Carl Milles. Not far: *Powell Symphony Hall (1925; remod. 1968), 718 N. Grand Blvd; architects: Rapp & Rapp; architects, remod.: Wedemeyer, Cernik & Corrubia; fantastic old moving-picture theater remod. for use of St. Louis Symphony. In N part of city: *Grand Ave Water Tower (1870), E. Grand Ave & 20th St; architect: George I. Barnett; fascinating 154-foot-high Corinthian column for storing water. Few miles N, via Florissant St, at 10225 Bellefontaine Rd, *Gen. Daniel Bissell House (about 1812; later alt. & addit.; rest.), once home of general in Revolution and War of 1812. In NW part of city, via US I-70, very fine modern ●*Lambert–St. Louis Airport (1957; addit. 1965), architects: Hellmuth, Yamasaki & Leinweber; architects, addit.: Hellmuth, Obata & Kassabaum; interesting vaulted roof.

In S part of city: *Chatillon-DeMenil House (1848; later alt. & addit.; rest.), 3352 S. 13th St; architect: Henry Pitcher; simple farmhouse converted to fine Greek Revival. Not far: *Missouri Botanical Garden, 2315 Tower Grove Ave; familiarly called Shaw's Garden, for Henry Shaw, noted botanist who founded it. Interesting buildings here include: *Tower Grove, the Shaw Country House (1849), architects: Barnett & Peck; Eclectic Italian

Climatron—Modern
(Hedrich-Blessing)

Renaissance Revival; in same style and by same architects: *Shaw Town House (1851); moved here. Number of other buildings built for Shaw here, including fine modern, •*Climatron (1960), architects: Murphy & Mackey; architect, geodesic dome: R. Buckminster Fuller; very interesting building with interior climate controlled to reproduce tropical, subtropical, other zones for growing of various plants. In W part of city: *Forest Park, location of 1904 World's Fair, Louisiana Purchase Exposition, *City Art Museum, originally Art Building of Louisiana Purchase Exposition (1904; addit. 1959), architect: Cass Gilbert; architects, addit.: Murphy & Mackey; Eclectic Classic Revival. *McDonnell Planetarium (1963), Forest Park; architects: Hellmuth, Obata & Kassabaum; fine modern concrete hyperbolic structure by noted firm. Approx. 10 mi farther W, via US 40/61 & 67: CREVE COUER. By same architects, •*Priory of St. Mary and St. Louis (1962), Mason & Conway rds; very fine modern thin-shell concrete structure. Approx. 25 mi SW, via US 40/61 & St. 94 & 7, near DEFIANCE, *Daniel Boone House (1810), last home of famous frontiersman; he died here and is buried nearby.

St. Louis Vicinity *(NW, via US 61).* Approx. 95 mi, via US 61 & 54: LOUISIANA. *James Stark House (about 1830; later alt. & addit.; rest.), log cabin built by founder of nursery here. Approx. 50 mi farther, via US 54 & 61: HANNIBAL. Interesting buildings include: *Rockcliffe Mansion (1900; rest.), 1000 Bird St; Eclectic Victorian; many innovations usually thought of as modern. On Hill St, at no 206, *Mark Twain Boyhood Home (1844; rest.); at no. 211, *Becky Thatcher House (1840; rest.), once home of Laura Hawkins, thought to have been model for Twain's heroine in *Tom Sawyer* and *Huckleberry Finn.* Approx. 55 mi SW, via US 61 & St. 19 & 154, near FLORIDA, *Mark Twain Birthplace (about 1830; rest.), Mark Twain State Park.

St. Louis Vicinity *(S, via US I-55).* Approx. 60 mi, via US I-55 & 61, STE. GENEVIEVE, oldest town in state. Interesting buildings include: in Hist. Dist., *Ste. Genevieve Church, Roman Catholic (1880), DuBourg Pl; Gothic Revival. Interesting French Colonial houses include, on S. Main St, at no. 20, *Beauvais House (about 1775; later alt. & addit.; rest.); moved here; also interesting smokehouse; at Market St, Valle House (1782; later alt. & addit.), dungeon below; at no. 123, *Bolduc House (about 1787; later alt. & addit.; rest.), *poteaux sur sole,* or posts with clay, straw and hair infilling, construction; interesting garden and outbuildings. S of town, via St. Mary's Rd (US 61): *Green Tree Tavern, also known as Janis-Ziegler House (1790; later alt. & addit.; rest.), also *poteaux sur sole;* *Amoreaux House (about 1770; later alt. & addit.), now antiques shop. Approx. 65 mi SW, via St. 32, US 67 & St. 72: IRONTON. *St. Paul's Episcopal Church (1871), E. Reynolds St; fine wood-frame Victorian Gothic Revival.

SPRINGFIELD

John Polk Campbell House (1851; later alt. & addit.), 975 Mary
Ave; oldest house in city; built by city founder. Approx. 50 mi E,
via US 60: MANSFIELD. *Rocky Ridge Farm (1895; later alt. &
addit.), once home of noted author of children's books Laura Ingalls Wilder. Approx. 70 mi NW of Springfield, via US 160: LA-
MAR. *Harry S Truman Birthplace (about 1881; later alt. &
addit.), 1009 Truman Ave.

Nebraska

First inhabitants believed to have been prehistoric people who may
have lived here 250 centuries ago or even earlier; stone age tools
and weapons have been found here. Early Indian tribes included
Missouri, Omaha, Pawnee; later arrivals included Fox, Iowa,
Sauk, Winnebago. First explorer Spaniard Francisco Vásquez de
Coronado, 1514; later, Frenchman Robert Cavelier, Sieur de La
Salle, 1682, named region Louisiana and claimed it for France.
French trappers and traders moved in. Frenchman Etienne Ven-
iard de Bourgmont explored, 1714; followed by Spaniard Pedro de
Villasur, 1729, and French brothers Paul and Pierre Mallet, 1739.
Ceded by France to Spain, 1762; back to France, 1800; sold to
United States in Louisiana Purchase, 1803. Explored by Ameri-
cans Meriwether Lewis and William Clark, 1804, Zebulon M.
Pike, 1806, later by others. Made part of Nebraska Territory,
1854. Became thirty-seventh state, Mar. 1, 1867. Population in-
creased rapidly after passage of Homestead Act, 1862. Today:
Major agricultural and manufacturing industries.

Land Regions: E to W, small Dissected Till Plains; very large
Great Plains.

Climate: Cold winters, hot summers; often rapid, sometimes violent changes; precipitation moderate in E, somewhat low in W;
snowfall moderate, more in E than in W. Subject to blizzards,
tornadoes, thunderstorms, hail.

Major Building Materials: Small amounts of limestone; clay;
sand and gravel.

Architecture: Interesting and important buildings, relatively few
in number, in several locations, especially Lincoln.

GRAND ISLAND

Interesting buildings include: *Stuhr Museum of the Prairie Pioneer; rest. and reconst. houses, barns, church, other types moved here: *Milisen House (1880; rest); *Fonda House (about 1887; rest.), birthplace of actor Henry Fonda; *Railroad Station (1895; rest.), with operating steam train. Also: modern *Museum Building (1967), architect: Edward Durell Stone. Approx. 50 mi SW of Grand Island, via US 34, near MINDEN, *Harold Warp Pioneer Village, rest. or reconst. houses and other type, include: log *Elm Creek Fort (1869; rest.); replica of *Sod House, or Soddy, as settlers called this type. Approx. 40 mi S of Grand Island, via US 34 & 281: RED CLOUD. *Willa Cather House (1878; later alt. & addit.; rest.), 3rd & Cedar sts; childhood home of famous novelist who wrote *Death Comes to the Archbishop* and other books. Approx. 80 mi NW of Grand Island, via St. 2, near BROKEN BOW, original soddy *Isadore Haumont House (1884).

LINCOLN

Interesting buildings include: ●*State Capitol (1922–32), bet. 14th, 16th, H & K sts; architect: Bertram Grosvenor Goodhue; magnificent example over 400 feet high, dominating Nebraska prairie setting; Eclectic Gothic Revival with modern aspects; completed eight years after death of its famous architect; fine ornament and sculpture, including *Sower* by Lee Lawrie on top of dome, and *Lincoln* by Daniel Chester French; considered one of

Nebraska State Capitol—Eclectic Gothic Revival (Library of Congress)

finest U.S. buildings. Block away *Thomas P. Kennard House, also known as Nebraska Statehood Memorial (1868; rest.), 1627 H St; fine Eclectic Victorian Italianate mansion; architect: John Keyes Winchell. Not far: *The Citibank, originally Rock Island Railroad Station (1893; rest. & remod. 1969), 20th & O sts; architect, rest. & remod.: Clark Enersen; fine recycling of old station to bank. *U.S. Post Office and Courthouse (1879; remod.), 930 O St; architects: Alfred B. Mullett & William A. Potter; once city hall, now city office building. At *University of Nebraska: **Sheldon Memorial Art Gallery (1963), N. 12th & R sts; architect: Philip Johnson; superv. architects: Hazen & Robinson; fine modern building with fine sunken garden. At 4900 Sumner St, *Fairview (1902; rest.), once home of "The Great Commoner," William Jennings Bryan. Approx. 90 mi N of Lincoln, via US 77: BANCROFT. *John G. Neihardt Center (about 1898; rest.), Washington & Groves sts; once home of noted prairie poet. Approx. 60 mi NE of Lincoln, via US I-80 & 75, near Omaha: BELLEVUE. *Log Cabin (1835; rest.), 1805 Hancock St; moved here.

Lincoln Vicinity *(E, via St. 2)*. Approx. 50 mi: NEBRASKA CITY. In *Arbor Lodge State Hist. Park, *J. Sterling Morton House (1855; later alt. & addit.), once home of noted journalist who initiated Arbor Day. Nearby, *Garden (about 1903), landscape architect: Frederick Law Olmsted. Also of interest: *John Brown's Cave, in which abolitionist hid runaway slaves. Approx. 30 mi SE of Nebraska City, via US 75 & 136: BROWNVILLE. Interesting buildings here, some rest. in Hist. Dist. Approx. 60 mi W of Brownville, via US 136 (approx. 40 mi S of Lincoln, via US 77): BEATRICE (pronounced be-at′-ris). Approx. 4 mi NW, via St. 4, *Homestead Nat. Mon., location of one of first claims under Homestead Act, 1862; original home of homesteader gone, but still surviving *Palmer-Epard Log Cabin (1867; rest.), very small, 14-by-16-foot cabin, moved here from nearby site; once home, incredibly, of Mr. & Mrs. Palmer and their ten children.

NORTH PLATTE

Approx. 3 mi W, via Buffalo Bill Ave, in *Scouts Rest. State Park, *Buffalo Bill Home (1886; rest.), once home of Col. William F. Cody, famous frontiersman and showman known as "Buffalo Bill"; interesting outbuildings include barn and log cabin. Approx. 70 mi S of North Platte, via US 83: McCOOK. *Sen. George W. Norris Home (about 1896; rest.), 706 Norris Ave; once home of initiator of Tennessee Valley Authority, who served 10 years in U.S. House of Representatives and another 30 years in Senate.

Northwest Nebraska. Interesting buildings include: in CHADRON, *James Bordeaux Trading Post, also known as Museum of the Fur Trade (about 1850; reconst.), log house with trade room and separate storehouse. Approx. 25 mi W of Chadron, via US 20, *Ft. Robinson (begun 1874; rest.), now State Park.

North Dakota

Early inhabitants Indian tribes, including Cheyenne, Chippewa, Mandan, Sioux. Claimed by France, 1682. NE portion ceded to Great Britain by France, 1713. First explorer French-Canadian Pierre Gaultier de Varennes, Sieur de la Vérendrye, 1738. Remainder ceded to Spain by France, 1762; back to France, 1800; sold to United States in Louisiana Purchase, 1803. Americans Meriwether Lewis and William Clark explored, 1804, on way to West Coast. NE portion ceded to United States by British, 1818. Made part of Dakota Territory, 1861. In 1863, territory opened to homesteading but settlement proceeded slowly. Frequent battles between Indians and Federal troops ended 1881. Became thirty-ninth state, Nov. 2, 1889. Today: Major agricultural and mining, especially oil and coal, industries.

Land Regions: E to W, small Red River Valley; large Young Drift Plains; Great Plains.

Climate: Cold winters, mild pleasant summers; precipitation fairly light, more in E than W; snowfall fairly heavy.

Major Building Materials: Clay; sand and gravel.

Architecture: Interesting buildings, relatively few in number, in several places.

BISMARCK

*State Capitol (1934; later alt. & addit.), Capitol Park; architects: Joseph B. de Remer & William F. Kurke; assoc. architects: Holabird & Root; unusual, early modern high-rise (18 stories). S of town: ●*Annunciation Priory (1963), St. 1804; architect: Marcel Breuer; assoc. architect: Hamilton P. Smith; fine modern complex by famous architect. Nearby, *Mary College (1968), another fine modern complex by same architect; assoc. architects: Hamilton P. Smith and Tician Papachristou. Approx. 12 mi E, via US I-94, *Menoken Village. Approx. 16 mi farther, *Chaska Hist. Site.

Bismarck Vicinity *(N. via US 83).* Approx. 40 mi: WASHBURN. *Joseph Henry Taylor Cabin (about 1869), one-room log example moved to park. Few miles W, via St. 200, *Ft. Mandan, *Ft. Clark and *Knife River Indian Village Hist. sites. Also of interest, approx. 20 mi NW, via US 83 & St. 200: *Garrison Dam.

Bismarck Vicinity *(W, via US I-94).* Approx. 4 mi: MANDAN. *Slant Indian Village (about 1650–1785; later reconst.), Ft. Lincoln State Park. Approx. 5 mi S, reconst. lodges of Mandan tribe; also reconst. blockhouses of *Ft. McKeen and site of *Ft. Abraham Lincoln. Approx. 135 mi farther, via US I-94: MEDORA. Interesting buildings include: *Chateau de Mores (1883), though called "chateau," actually large, simple wood-frame house built for Marquis de Mores, who established town and huge meat-packing operation; *Baron Von Hoffman House (1884; rest.), now called Medora Doll House for its collection; *Athenais Chapel (1884; rest.); *Rough Riders Hotel (1884; rest.), where Teddy Roosevelt spent considerable time. Nearby, in Theodore Roosevelt Nat. Mem. Park, *Maltese Cross Ranch Cabin (1883), built for future president.

FARGO

*Forsberg House (1905), 815 Third Ave S; interesting Victorian; members of Forsberg family still live here. Adjoining Fargo, WEST FARGO, *Bonanzaville, collection of early buildings. Approx. 45 mi NW, via US I-29 & St. 18: BLANCHARD. KTHI Television Tower (1963), amazing 2,063 feet tall. Approx. 95 mi W of Fargo, via US I-94: JAMESTOWN. *Frontier Village, collection of early buildings. Approx. 90 mi N of Jamestown, via US 281 & St. 57, *Ft. Totten (1871), well-preserved buildings of era of wars with Indians.

Ohio

Early inhabitants believed to have been prehistoric ancestors of Mound Builders. Many structures of Mound Builders have survived in numerous places in state. Later Indian tribes included Delaware, Miami, Shawnee, Wyandot. First explorers believed to have been French, led by Robert Cavelier, Sieur de La Salle, about 1670; area claimed by French, also by British. Englishman Christopher Gist, of Ohio Co. of Virginia explored, 1750. French gave up claims to British at end of French and Indian Wars, 1763. During Revolution, Gen. George Rogers Clark defeated Shawnee Indian allies of British in Battle of Piqua, 1780, freeing region from British rule. Made part of Northwest Territory, 1787. First permanent American settlement, 1788: Marietta. Indian uprisings lasted until 1794 when troops of Gen. "Mad" Anthony Wayne defeated them in Battle of Fallen Timbers. Became seventeenth state, Mar. 1, 1803. During War of 1812, Commodore Oliver Perry gained important victory over British fleet in Battle of Lake Erie, 1813. In years before outbreak of Civil War, many people in state aided runaway slaves to escape through "Underground Railroad." Although no great battles took place in Ohio, farthest incursion into North by regular Confederate troops was accomplished by Morgan's Raiders, led by Gen. John Hunt Morgan, 1863; captured in Columbiana County, Morgan was imprisoned in Ohio State Prison; he escaped and returned to South to fight again. Today: Major manufacturing industry; agriculture also important.

Land Regions: Appalachian Plateau in E; Till Plains in W; smaller Great Lakes Plains along Lake Erie; very small Bluegrass in S.

Climate: Cold winters, cool, humid summers; precipitation moderate; snowfall moderate, heavier in W and N, less in E and S.

Major Building Materials: Sandstone; limestone; clay.

Architecture: Rich and varied, especially 19th and 20th century, in many locations in state, especially in large cities and vicinities.

CINCINNATI

Interesting buildings include modern examples around what natives consider heart of city: *Fountain Square (1870; remod. 1970), architects, remod.: Rogers, Taliaferro, Kostritsky & Lamb. *Taft Museum, originally Martin Baum House (about 1820; later alt.), 316 Pike St; possible architect: Benjamin Henry Latrobe or James Hoban; Federal; once home of President William Howard Taft; now museum with fine gardens, collections of art and Duncan Phyfe furniture. *Isaac M. Wise Temple, also known as Plum Street Temple (1866; later renov.), 8th & Plum sts; architect: James K. Wilson; fascinating, probably unique in U.S.; Eclectic Gothic-Byzantine synagogue. Across street, highly contrasting *Cathedral of St. Peter in Chains, Roman Catholic (1845; later alt. & addit.; rest.), 8th & Plum sts; architect: Henry Walter. On other corner: *City Hall (1893; later alt.), 801 Plum St; architect: Samuel Hannaford; Romanesque Revival. Not far: *Music Hall (1878; rest. 1972), Elm & 4th sts; architects: Hannaford & Proctor; Victorian Gothic Revival with elements of Romanesque Revival. Not far: ••*Cincinnati Union Terminal (1933; remod. 1980), Ezzard Charles Dr; architects: Fellheimer & Wagner; fanciful

Moderne or Art Deco railroad station converted to shops, offices, restaurant, other uses; considered one of finest examples of its style in U.S. Interesting houses include: at 2038 Auburn Ave, William Howard Taft Birthplace; at 812 Dayton St, *John Hauck House (1870; rest.), High Victorian Italianate; at *Cincinnati Zoological Gardens, *James Kemper Log Cabin (1804; rest.), moved here. Also of interest: old riverboat *Delta Queen.

Cincinnati Vicinity *(NE, via US 42)*. Approx. 27 mi: LEBANON. Nearby, *Glendower (1836; later alt. & addit.; rest.), fine Greek Revival, now State Mem. Approx. 8 mi. E of Lebanon, via St. 350, *Ft. Ancient, pre-Columbian mounds, ruins, museum.

Cincinnati Vicinity *(SE, via US 52)*. Approx. 30 mi: POINT PLEASANT. *Ulysses S. Grant Birthplace (1817; rest.). Approx. 25 mi farther, via US 52 & St. 221: GEORGETOWN. *U.S. Grant Boyhood Home (1823; later alt.; rest.), 219 Grant Ave.

Cincinnati Vicinity *(NW, via US 27)*. Approx. 35 mi: OXFORD. Interesting buildings include: at *Miami University, Greek Revival Lewis Place, now President's House (about 1837; later remod.), 321 E. High St. At Spring & Oak sts, *William H. McGuffey House (about 1833; rest.), once home of noted author of McGuffey readers. Nearby, on Doty Rd, *Pioneer Farm and House (about 1835; later renov.).

CLEVELAND

Interesting buildings include: *Cleveland Arcade (1890; later renov.), 401 Euclid Ave; architects: John M. Eisenmann & George H. Smith; early multilevel shopping arcade with fascinating skylighted interior. *Dunham Tavern (early 19th century; later alt. & addit.), 6709 Euclid Ave; originally stagecoach station, now museum with antiques. *Cleveland Art Museum (1916; addit. 1970), 11150 East Blvd; architects: Hubbell & Benes; architects, addit.: Marcel Breuer & Hamilton P. Smith; interesting Eclectic Greek Revival with modern addit.; among finest collections in U.S.

Cleveland Vicinity *(NE, via US I-90)*. Approx. 20 mi: MENTOR. *Lawnfield, the James A. Garfield Home (1831; later alt. & addit.; rest.), 8095 Mentor Ave; Victorian; once home of president. Approx. 6 mi S of Mentor, via St. 306: KIRTLAND. *Kirtland Temple (1836), interesting Eclectic Mormon temple of separatist Reorganized Church of Jesus Christ of Latter-day Saints; only Mormon temple open to general public. Approx. 9 mi NE of Mentor, via US I-90 & St. 44: PAINESVILLE. Interesting modern *James F. Lincoln Library, *Lake Erie College; architect: Victor F. Christ-Janer; also on campus: Matthews House (1829; later alt.), architect: Jonathan Goldsmith. Approx. 20 mi NE of Paines-ville, via US 20: UNIONVILLE. *Shandy Hall (1815; rest.).

Cleveland Vicinity *(SE, via US 422)*. Approx. 32 mi, via US 422 & St. 700: BURTON. Mid-19th-century *Pioneer Village, 14653 E. Park St; rest. & reconst. houses, church, barn, school, shops, other buildings. Approx. 25 mi farther, via St. 700 & US 422: WARREN. Early frame *John Stark Edwards House (1807; rest.), 309 South St SE. Greek Revival *Frederick Kinsman House (1832; later alt. & addit.), Mahoning Ave.

Cleveland Vicinity *(SE, via St. 14)*. Approx. 40 mi: RAVENNA. *Charlotte Strickland House (1829; rest.), 337 Main St, origi-nally tavern. Approx. 40 mi from Ravenna, via St. 14 & 45: LIS-BON. *Old Stone House (1805; rest.), 100 E. Washington St; once tavern, stagecoach station, courthouse, bank, church, private house; now museum. Approx. 15 mi from Lisbon, via St. 45: WELLSVILLE. *Henry Aten Mansion (1811; later alt.), 1607 Buck-eye Ave.

Cleveland Vicinity *(S, via US I-77)*. Approx. 14 mi: BRECKS-VILLE. Federal *Squire Rich House (1845; rest.), 9367 Brecks-ville Rd. Approx. 13 mi SE of Brecksville, via St. 21 & US I-80: HUDSON. Interesting buildings include: Greek Revival *Baldwin-Babcock House (about 1833; rest.), 49 Main St. At *Western Reserve Academy, *Chapel (1836; later alt. & addit.), architect: Simeon Porter; fine Greek Revival; David Hudson House (1806; later alt.). Approx. 12 mi S of Hudson, via St. 8: CUYAHOGA FALLS. *Blossom Music Center (1968), W. Steels Corners Rd; architects: Schafer, Flynn & van Dijk; assoc. architect: R. M. Gensert; interesting modern steel-framed building. Approx. 8 mi farther: AKRON. Interesting buildings include: modern *Edwin J. Thomas Performing Arts Hall (1973), Center & Hill sts; archi-tects: Dalton, van Dijk & Johnson and Caudill, Rowlett & Scott. Interesting houses include: *Col. Simon Perkins House (1835), 550 Copley Rd; Greek Revival mansion built by founder of Akron, also named Simon Perkins, for his son; now museum. At 514 Di-agonal & Copley rds, *John Brown House (about 1840), once home of abolitionist hanged for raid on Harpers Ferry, W. Va. *Stan Hywet Hall (1915), 714 Portage Path; architect: Charles Schneider; Eclectic Jacobean 65-room mansion, built for Frank A. Seiberling, founder of tire companies; mansions of other rubber magnates here are private. Just E of Akron: TALLMADGE. ●*First Congregational Church (1825; later alt.; rest.), 115 Tall-madge Circle; architect: Lemuel Porter; unlikely as it may seem, fine New England Colonial Revival by noted architect; other buildings in same style nearby. Approx. 25 mi S of Akron, via US I-77 & 30: MASSILLON. Interesting buildings include: *James Duncan House, now Massillon Museum (1835; later alt.), 212

Lincoln Way E. *Five Oaks, the J. M. McClymonds House (1893), 210 4th St; architect: Charles F. Schweinfurth; imposing Romanesque Revival; fine interiors; stained-glass window, chandeliers, other light fixtures by Louis Comfort Tiffany. Approx. 10 mi SE of Massillon, via US 62 & St. 212: ZOAR. Interesting buildings and gardens in Hist. Dist., now State Mem.; settled, 1817, by German religious sect known as Separatists under leadership of Joseph Baumler: brick and stone *Number One House (1835; rest.), originally home for aged, now museum; half-timbered *Tinsmith Shop (early 19th-century; rest.); log *Bimeler Cabin (1817; rest.). Approx. 10 mi S of Zoar, via St. 212 & 800, near NEW PHILADELPHIA, interesting reconst. town built by another German religious sect, Moravians, for Indians: *Schoenbrunn Village (about 1772; abandoned 1777; reconst. 1920s). Approx. 25 mi E of New Philadelphia, via St. 39; CARROLLTON. Federal *McCook House (about 1837; rest.), Public Square, once home of Maj. Daniel McCook who with nine sons and five nephews were known as "Fighting McCooks" for service in several wars, including Civil.

Cleveland Vicinity *(W, via US 20).* Adjoining city: LAKEWOOD. *Oldest Stone House (1838; rest.), 14710 Lake Ave; moved here. Approx. 25 mi farther, via US 20 & St. 58: OBERLIN. Interesting buildings at *Oberlin College include: *Allen Art Museum (1917; later alt. & addit.), architect: Cass Gilbert, architects, alt. & addit.: Venturi, Rauch & Scott-Brown; Eclectic Renaissance Revival; modern addit.; modern *Bibbins Hall (1968) and *King Mem. Hall (1966); architect of both: Minoru Yamasaki; *Sophronia Brooks Hall Auditorium (1953), architect: Wallace K. Harrison. Approx. 20 mi farther, via US 20: NORWALK. Interesting buildings include: on W. Main St, Wooster-Boalt House (1848; later alt.), originally girls' seminary; Sturgis-Fulstow House (1834; later alt.), architect: William Gale Meade. Also: *Preston-Wickham House (1835; later alt.), 5 Case St. Approx. 4 mi N of Norwalk, via US 250 & St. 113; MILAN. Interesting buildings include: Federal *Thomas Alva Edison Birthplace (1846; later alt.), 9 Edison Dr; *Dr. Lehman Galpin House (1846; later alt.), once home of doctor who assisted at birth of Edison.

COLUMBUS

Interesting buildings include: •*State Capitol (1839–61), bet. Broad, State, 3rd & High sts; architects: Henry Walter, W. R. West, Nathan B. Kelly, Isaiah Rogers; consult. architects: Alexander Jackson Davis, Thomas U. Walter, Richard Upjohn; Greek Revival, considered one of finest state capitols, amazingly since it required seven architects and 22 years to design and build. Not far: *Wyandotte Building (1898; later renov.), 21 W. Broad St; architects: D. H. Burnham & Co.; fine early modern office building by famous architect who helped pioneer such designs in Chicago. Also: *German Village (mid-19th century; rest. & renov. mid-20th).

Columbus Vicinity *(N, via US 23)*. Adjoining city: WORTHINGTON. Interesting buildings include: Federal *Orange Johnson House (1816; rest.), 956 High St; *St. John's Episcopal Church (about 1831; rest.), believed to be first Gothic Revival example in state. Approx. 40 mi farther: MARION. *Warren G. Harding House (1891; rest.), 380 Mt. Vernon Ave.

Columbus Vicinity *(NE, via St. 3 & 229)*. Approx. 55 mi: GAMBIER, *Kenyon College. Interesting buildings include: Gothic Revival *Old Kenyon Hall (1836; burned 1949; reconst.), architect: Rev. Norman Nash; *Bexley Hall (1843; later alt.), architect: Henry Roberts; *Church of the Holy Spirit (1871), architect: Gordon M. Lloyd. Also: ornate Gothic Revival Peter Neff House (about 1860; later alt. & addit.), Wiggin St.

Columbus Vicinity *(E, via US I-70)*. Approx. 30 mi via US I-70 & St. 79: NEWARK. Just W, famous *Hopewell Indian Mounds, *Mound Builders State Mem., *Octagon Mounds State Mem. Approx. 25 mi farther: ZANESVILLE, state capital, 1810–12. Interesting buildings include: *Bailey House, now Art Institute (1893; later alt.), Maple & Adair sts. Approx. 35 mi N of Zanesville, via St. 60: COSHOCTON. *Roscoe Village (early 19th century; rest.), on Ohio & Erie Canal; interesting old warehouse (1833; rest.), now restaurant, other buildings. Approx. 40 mi SW of Zanesville, via US 22 (approx. 30 mi SE of Columbus, via US 33): LANCASTER. Interesting buildings include: *Sherman House (1811; later alt. & addit.; rest.), 137 E. Main St; Eclectic Victorian Italianate birthplace of Civil War Gen. William Tecumseh Sherman and his brother U.S. Sen. John Sherman. Next door, at no. 145 E. Main St, Federal Reese-Peters House (1835; later alt.), once home of William J. Reese and his wife, Mary Elizabeth, sister of general and senator; at no. 162, *Mumaugh House (1805; later alt.; rest.). Approx. 80 mi SE of Lancaster, via US 33 & St. 550, MARIETTA, oldest permanent American settlement in state, founded 1788. Interesting buildings include: *Rufus Putnam House (1788; later addit.; rest.), Campus Martius Museum, Washington & 2nd sts.

Columbus Vicinity *(S, via US 23)*. Approx. 45 mi: CHILLICOTHE, first state capital, 1803–10; also 1812–16. Interesting buildings include remarkable group of Greek Revival houses on S. Paint St: at no. 52, Reeves-Woodrow-Butler House (about 1840; later alt.); at no. 94, McLairdburg-Fullerton House (mid-19th century); at no. 122, Atwood-Wilson House (1845; later alt.); at no. 134, Bartlett-Cunningham-Gerber House (about 1855). At 45 W. 5th St,

*Sen. Allen G. Thurman House (1838; rest.). Also of interest: replica of Georgian *Old State Capitol built in 1940 to resemble 1800 building; now newspaper offices. NW of town, via St. 104, ●●**Adena, the Thomas Worthington House** (1807; rest.), architect: Benjamin Henry Latrobe; very fine late Georgian or early Federal mansion by famous architect; beautiful gardens and hilltop location; once home of one of first two Ohio U.S. senators; now State Mem.; on site of Adena Mound, which was excavated. Few miles NW, via St. 104, *Mound City Group Nat. Mon., almost 70 acres of pre-Columbian Indian Mounds, some part. rest. Not far, off US 23: another mound group, *Hopetown Works. Other interesting mounds SW of Chillicothe, via US 50 & St. 41 include: at approx. 5 mi, *Hopewell Mounds; at approx. 17 mi, *Seip Mound State Mem.; at approx. 33 mi, via St. 41, *Ft. Hill State Mem., interesting pre-Columbian fort; at approx. 46 mi, via St. 41 & 73, *Great Serpent Mound, largest and finest effigy mound in U.S.

DAYTON

Interesting buildings include: *Old Courthouse (1850; later alt.), 3rd & Main sts, across from plaza; architect: Howard Daniels; fine Greek Revival. In Deeds Park: *Newcom Tavern (1796; rest.), log cabin, moved here; once post office, church, courthouse. At 219 N. Summit St, *Paul Laurence Dunbar House (about 1890; rest.), once home of noted Negro writer; now State Mem. At 1815 Brown St: Federal *Rubicon, the Col. Robert Patterson House (1816; rest.). At Park & Harmon sts, Eclectic Georgian Revival Hawthorne Hill (1914; later alt.), architects: Schenck & Williams; once home of famous airplane inventor Orville Wright.

Dayton Vicinity *(N, via US I-75)*. Approx. 25 mi: TROY. *Miami Co. Courthouse (1888; later alt.), W. Main St; architect: John Warren Yost; amazing example in Eclectic Renaissance and miscellaneous styles. Approx. 10 mi N of Troy, via US I-75 & 36: PIQUA. Interesting buildings include: in Hist. Dist. nearby on St. 66, *John Johnston House (1811; rest.), once home of noted Indian agent; also springhouse. Approx. 10 mi farther: SIDNEY. Interesting buildings include:
●●**People's Federal Savings & Loan Association** (1918), Ohio & Court sts; architect: Louis Sullivan; very fine early modern by famous architect; fine ornament.

Dayton Vicinity *(NE, via US I-675 & I-70)*. Approx. 30 mi: SPRINGFIELD. Interesting Romanesque Revival *Warder Free Library (1890; later alt.), E. High & Spring sts; architects: Shepley, Rutan & Coolidge, successors to Henry Hobson Richardson who initiated style. At 838 E. High St, another example by same architects: Asa Bushnell House (1887; later alt.). At 1311 W. Main St,

*Pennsylvania House (about 1839; rest.), once inn, tavern. Approx. 25 mi N of Springfield, via US 68: WEST LIBERTY. Nearby, on St. 245, fantastic *Castle Piatt Mac-A-Cheek (1864) and Mac-O-Chee Castle (1879), the first Eclectic Norman Revival built by Gen. Abram Saunders Piatt; other Eclectic Flemish built by general's brother, Col. Donn Piatt. Approx. 18 mi SE of Dayton, via US 35: XENIA. *Warren K. Moorehead House (about 1865; rest.), once home of noted archaeologist and author; nearby, *James Gallaway House (1799; rest.), log cabin; moved here.

TOLEDO

Many Eclectic buildings of almost every imaginable style; old residential avenues such as Scottwood, Collingwood and Robinwood abound in late 19th- and 20th-century revival examples, including French, Victorian, Queen Anne, Romanesque, Italianate, Chateau, Renaissance, Georgian, others. Approx. 30 mi SE of Toledo, via US 20: FREMONT. *Spiegel Grove (1863; later alt. & addit.), 1337 Hayes Ave; the Rutherford B. Hayes State Mem.; beautiful wooded grounds, library and President Hayes tomb.

Toledo Vicinity *(S & SW, via US I-75).* Approx. 25 mi: BOWLING GREEN. Romanesque Revival *Wood Co. Courthouse (1896; later alt.), E. Court St; architects: Joseph W. Yost & Frank L. Packard. Approx. 55 mi farther: LIMA. Eclectic Second Empire Revival *Allen Co. Courthouse (1882; later alt.), architect: G. Maetzel. Victorian Shingle style *Banta-McDonell House (1890), 632 Market St. ●*Ohio Steel Foundry Co. Machine Shop** (1938; later alt.), architect: Albert Kahn; very fine early modern by noted architect who pioneered such industrial buildings. Approx. 30 mi SW of Lima, via US 30: VAN WERT. Eclectic Second Empire Revival *Van Wert Co. Courthouse (1876; later alt.), 121 E. Main St, architects: Thomas J. Tolan & Brentwood Tolan.

Toledo Vicinity *(SW, via US 24).* Approx. 10 mi: MAUMEE. Interesting houses include: fine Greek Revival House of Four Pillars (about 1835; rest.); Federal *Judge James Wolcott House (1827; rest.). Approx. 6 mi farther: WATERVILLE. *Columbian House (1818; later alt. & addit.), fine Federal; once trading post, post office, inn; now restaurant.

South Dakota

Early inhabitants Indian tribes, including Arikara, Cheyenne, Sioux. Claimed by France, 1682. First explorers believed to have been French-Canadian brothers, François and Louis-Joseph Vérendrye, 1743; lead plate buried by them near present-day Ft. Pierre was found, 1913. France ceded region to Spain, 1762; took back, 1800; sold to United States in Louisiana Purchase, 1803. Americans Meriwether Lewis and William Clark passed through region on way to West Coast, 1804. First permanent settlement founded by French fur trader Joseph La Framboise, 1817: Ft. Pierre. Wars with Indians began 1823 and continued, sporadically, until 1890, when Federal troops massacred some 200 Indians, including women and children, at Battle of Wounded Knee. Became Dakota Territory, 1861. Gold discovered, 1874, and even richer lodes, 1876; gold rush brought large numbers of people to towns of Lead and Deadwood, along with lawlessness and famous characters including Deadwood Dick, "Wild Bill" Hickock, Calamity Jane. Became fortieth state, Nov. 2, 1889. Today: Major agricultural industry; important manufacturing, mining industries.

Land Regions: E to W, small Dissected Till Plains; Young Drift Plains; large Great Plains; Black Hills.

Climate: Very cold winters, moderate summers in W portion; hot, low humidity in central and E; precipitation light in NW, moderate in SE; snowfall moderate to heavy.

Major Building Materials: Granite; limestone; gypsum.

Architecture: Interesting buildings, though relatively few in number, in several locations, especially Rapid City vicinity.

PIERRE

*State Capitol (1910), E. Capitol Ave; architects: Bell & Detweiler; Eclectic Classic Revival. Approx. 3 mi W, via US 14, *FT. PIERRE, oldest surviving settlement in state.

Pierre Vicinity *(NE, via US 83).* Approx. 20 mi via US 83 & 14: BLUNT. *Mentor Graham House, also known as Lincoln Prairie Shrine (about 1880; rest.), once home of schoolmaster who taught Abraham Lincoln in New Salem, Ill. Approx. 80 mi farther, via

US 83 & 21: FAULKTON. *John H. Pickler House (about 1900; rest.), Pickler Park, home of noted congressman.

RAPID CITY

Noted for proximity to wonderful Black Hills and other attractions, rather than for architecture. In *Black Hills, approx. 12 mi SW, via US 16: ROCKERVILLE, gold mining center, now ghost town. Approx. 9 mi farther, *Mt. Rushmore Nat. Mem., huge sculptured heads of Washington, Jefferson, Teddy Roosevelt, Lincoln, by sculptors Gutzon Borglum and his son, Lincoln. Approx. 8 mi farther, via US 16 & 16A, *Custer State Park, *Gordon Stockade (1875; reconst.). Approx. 3 mi farther, via US 16A: CUSTER. *Log Cabin (1875), built by soldiers. Few miles N of Custer, via US 16: 563-foot-high, 641-foot-long *Crazy Horse Sioux Memorial, Thunderhead Mountain; sculptor: Korczak Ziolkowski, who worked on uncompleted sculpture 45 years, until his death, 1982; his five sons carry on work. Also of interest, approx. 70 mi E of Rapid City, via US I-90: *Badlands.

Rapid City Vicinity *(NW, via US I-90 & 85).* Approx. 40 mi: DEADWOOD, legendary for gold rush of 1876 and for its characters such as Deadwood Dick, "Wild Bill" Hickock, Calamity Jane. Interesting buildings include: *No. 10 Saloon, in which Wild Bill, while holding so-called dead man's hand, pairs of aces and eights, in poker game, was shot dead from behind by Jack McCall. In *Mt. Moriah Cemetery, or Boot Hill, Wild Bill, Calamity Jane, Preacher Smith, other famous characters, are buried. Approx. 3 mi W, via US 85: LEAD. *Homestake Mine, largest U.S. gold mine. On Sunrise Mountain: *Richard W. Clarke House (about 1890), home of Deadwood Dick.

SIOUX FALLS

*Minnehaha Co. Courthouse, now Old Courthouse Museum (1890; later alt.), Main Ave & 6th St; architect: Wallace L. Dow; interesting Romanesque Revival. *Sen. Richard F. Pettigrew House (1875), 131 N. Duluth Ave; Victorian; once home of South Dakota's first U.S. senator. Also of interest: *Pettigrew Museum of Natural Arts and History. Approx. 70 mi W of Sioux Falls, via US I-90: MITCHELL. Fantastic *Corn Palace (1892; later rebuilding & remod.), 604 N. Main St; each fall, front decorated with tons of corn, wheat, other grains, grasses.

Sioux Falls Vicinity *(N, via US I-29).* Approx. 45 mi via US I-29 & St. 34: MADISON. Nearby, at junction of US 81 & St. 34, *Prairie Village, rest. & reconst. early houses, other buildings.

Approx. 55 mi farther: WATERTOWN. *Arthur C. Mellette House (about 1883; rest.), 421 5th Ave NW; Victorian; once home of first governor of state. Near town, via US 81, *Oliver Chateau (about 1883); interesting Victorian.

Wisconsin

Early inhabitants Indian tribes, including Dakota, Menominee, Winnebago; other tribes moved here, including Chippewa, Kickapoo, Ottawa, Sauk. First explored by Frenchman Jean Nicolet, 1634; later French explorers included Pierre Esprit Radisson and Médart Chouart, Sieur de Groseilliers, about 1654. French missionaries followed, including Father René Ménard, about 1660, and Father Claude Jean Allouez, about 1665. Frenchmen Father Jacques Marquette and Louis Joliet explored, 1673, as did Robert Cavelier, Sieur de La Salle about same time. French fought Indians in long war, 1712–40. Region ceded to Great Britain at end of French and Indian Wars, 1763; made part of Province of Quebec, 1774. Ceded by Great Britain to United States after end of Revolution, 1783. Battles with Indians ended with defeat of Sauk Chief Black Hawk, 1832. Became Wisconsin Territory, 1836; Madison became capital. Became thirtieth state, May 29, 1848. Today: Major manufacturing and agricultural industries.

Land Regions: S to N, Western Upland and Great Lakes Plains; Central Plain; Superior Upland; very small NW Lake Superior Lowlands.

Climate: Long, cold winters, short, warm summers; somewhat warmer in winter and cooler in summer along shores of Lake Michigan and Lake Superior; precipitation moderate; snowfall very heavy in N, moderate in S.

Major Building Materials: Timber, primarily hardwoods; limestone; granite; sandstone; sand and gravel; lead; zinc.

Architecture: Rich and varied in number of places, especially Madison and vicinity and Milwaukee and vicinity. Some of finest U.S. buildings here, including number by Frank Lloyd Wright.

GREEN BAY

Oldest settlement, 1669, in state. Interesting buildings include examples moved to *Heritage Hill State Park, 2640 S. Webster Ave;

*Roi-Porlier-Tank House (1776; addit. 1850), original portion oldest in state; interesting *poteaux-et-pièces-en-couillisant* construction, vertical logs with interwoven twigs and mud plaster; fine Greek Revival *Cotton House (about 1840; rest.); *Henry S. Baird Law Office (about 1835; rest.). At 1008 S. Monroe St, *Hazelwood, the Morgan L. Martin House (1837; rest.), once home of president of state constitutional convention.

Green Bay Vicinity *(SW, via US 41)*. Approx. 20 mi: KAU-KAUNA. Mansion in the Woods, the Charles R. Grignon House (1839; rest.), Augustine St; Classic Revival; interesting interiors. Approx. 20 mi farther: NEENAH. *Grand Loggery (1847; rest.), Doty Park, once home of James Duane Doty, territorial governor. Nearby, MENASHA, *Indian Effigy Mounds.

MADISON

Interesting buildings include: *State Capitol (1906–17; later alt.), Capitol Park; architect: George Browne Post; interesting Eclectic Renaissance Revival by noted architect; granite dome with sculpture *Forward* by Daniel Chester French on top. At 130 E. Gilman St, Executive Mansion (1854; later alt.). Near *University of Wisconsin campus, in Shorewood Hills, at 900 University Bay Dr: ●*First Unitarian Meeting House (1951), architect: Frank Lloyd Wright; very fine modern church by famous architect; considered one of his finest designs. At 501 Walnut St, *U.S. Forest Products Laboratory (1932; later alt.), architects: Holabird & Root; interesting Moderne or Art Deco; interesting exhibits. Approx. 37 mi N, via US 51: PORTAGE. *Old Indian Agency House (1832; rest.). Approx. 20 mi NE of Madison via US 151: COLUMBUS. ●*Farmers' and Merchants' Union Bank (1919), architect: Louis Sullivan; fine early modern by famous modern pioneer; fine ornament. Approx. 20 mi SW of Madison, via US 18 & St. 69: NEW GLARUS. Interesting rest. & reconst. buildings of *Swiss Hist. Village founded by Swiss settlers, 1845.

Madison Vicinity *(E, via US 18)*. Approx. 30 mi: JEFFERSON. *Aztalan Museum; *Baptist Church (1852; rest.); *Pettey Cabin (1843; rest.); *Loom House (1849; rest.), with spinning and weaving implements; *Zickert House (about 1867; rest.). Few miles NW: *Aztalan Mound Park. Approx. 6 mi SW of Jefferson, via St. 26: FT. ATKINSON. *Hoard House, now Museum (1865; later alt. & addit.), 407 Merchants Ave. Nearby, *Dwight Foster House (1841). Approx. 15 mi NE of Ft. Atkinson, via St. 26: WATERTOWN. Interesting *Octagon House (1854), 919 Charles St; on grounds: building (about 1850) in which Margarethe Meyer Schurz, wife of Civil War Gen. Carl Schurz, established first U.S. kindergarten.

Taliesin III—
Early Modern
(Hedrich-Blessing)

Madison Vicinity *(SE, via US I-90)*. Approx. 35 mi: MILTON.
*Milton House (1844; rest.), originally stagecoach station; con-
nected: *Goodrich Log Cabin (1837; rest.). Approx. 5 mi SW of
Milton, via St. 26: JANESVILLE. *William Morrison Tallman
House (1857; rest.), 440 N. Jackson St, fine Eclectic Italianate;
once home of land speculator and abolitionist; on grounds: Greek
Revival *Stone House (1842; rest.), moved here; interesting Carriage House. Approx. 15 mi S of Janesville, via US I-90: BELOIT.
*Bartlett Mem. Hist. Museum (1851; later alt.), 2149 St. Law-
rence Ave; architect: James J. Hanchett. *Rasey House (1850;
later alt.), 517 Prospect Ave.

Madison Vicinity *(W, via US 18)*. Approx. 25 mi: BLUE MOUNDS.
Nearby, *Little Norway (1856; rest.), built by Norwegian settlers.
Approx. 17 mi farther: DODGEVILLE. Greek Revival *Iowa Co.
Courthouse (1859; later alt. & addit.; rest.), Iowa St; architect:
Ernest Wiesen. Approx. 12 mi N of Dodgeville, via St. 23: SPRING
GREEN. Just S: Taliesin East, home, studios, other buildings designed and built by famous architect Frank Lloyd Wright for his
family, students, employees. Nearby, *Hillside (1903; part.
burned & rebuilt 1952; later remod.), offices and drafting rooms
of Taliesin Fellowship; N of Hillside, interesting farm buildings
designed by Wright include Romeo and Juliet Windmill (1896;
later alt.). Not far: •Taliesin III (begun 1925), early modern magnificent private home, considered one of finest U.S. buildings; replaced Taliesin I & II, both part. destroyed by fires. Nearby,

earlier private Tanyderi (1907), house designed by Wright for his sister Jane and her husband, Andrew Porter. Not far: Wright-designed restaurant *The Spring Green (1957–69); *Unity Chapel (1886), architect: James L. Silsbee, in whose office Wright first worked; Frank Lloyd Wright buried here. Approx. 25 mi NW of Spring Green, via US 14: RICHLAND CENTER, where Wright was born and location of his Maya-like *A. D. German Warehouse, now Richland Museum (1915; later alt.). Approx. 20 mi S of Spring Green, via St. 23 & US 151 (approx. 10 mi S of Dodgeville), MINERAL POINT, once called Shake Rag, because dishcloths were waved to call miners home. Houses built by miners from Cornwall, England, include: *Pendarvis House (about 1828; rest.), Shake Rag St; *Joseph Gundry House (1867; rest.), Pine & Davis sts. Approx. 60 mi W of Dodgeville, via US 18: PRAIRIE DU CHIEN. *Villa Louis (1843; remod. 1872; rest.), architect, remod.: Edward Townsend Mix; large imposing mansion; once home of Hercules Louis Dousman, influential and wealthy agent for John Jacob Astor's American Fur Co.; interesting rest. outbuildings. Approx. 35 mi SE of Prairie du Chien, via St. 133: CASSVILLE. *Nelson Dewey State Park, *Nelsen Dewey House (about 1850; burned; rebuilt 1873; rest.), once home of first state governor; interesting outbuildings; *Stonefield Village (about 1890; rest.), store, stables, cheese factory.

Madison Vicinity *(NW, via US 12)*. Approx. 20 mi: SAUK CITY. *Hahn House (about 1865; later alt.), 626 Water St; built into riverbank. Approx. 15 mi farther: *BARABOO. *Van Orden House, now Sauk Co. Hist. Museum (1906), 531 4th Ave; displays include circus mementos; nearby, original *Ringling Brothers Circus buildings. Also of interest, not far away: *Wisconsin Dells, fantastic sandstone formations along Wisconsin River.

MILWAUKEE

Interesting buildings include: *First Wisconsin Center (1974), E. Wisconsin Ave & Van Buren St; architects: Skidmore, Owings & Merrill; fine modern high-rise office tower by famous firm. Not far: *Federal Building (1899; later alt. & addit.), 515 E. Wisconsin St; probable architect: Willoughby J. Edbrooke; fine Romanesque Revival. Side by side, at nos. 207 & 225 E. Michigan St, Eclectic Victorian *Mitchell Building (1878); *Mackie Building (1880), architect of both: Edward Townsend Mix. Not far: *Center for Performing Arts (1969), N. Water St bet. E. Kilbourn Ave & E. State St; architect: Harry Weese; fine modern complex, with Uihlein, Todd Wehr, Charles P. Vogel halls. At 1630 E. Royall Pl, Eclectic Tudor *Charles Allis House, now Art Library (1908; later alt.). In NE part of city: in *Estabrook Park, Greek Revival *Benjamin Church House, also known as Kilbourntown House

S. C. Johnson Company Administration Building and Research Tower—Modern (Johnson Wax)

(1844; part. dest. by fire; reconst.). At 2420 N. Terrace Ave, early modern F. C. Bogk House (1916), architect: Frank Lloyd Wright. In suburb WAUWATOSA, just W of city, another famous modern building: *Annunciation Greek Orthodox Church (1961), N. 92nd & W. Congress sts; architect: Frank Lloyd Wright. Approx. 25 mi W of Milwaukee via US I-94: DELAFIELD.
••*St. John Chrysostum Church, Episcopal (1853; rest.), architect: Richard Upjohn; delightful little wooden Gothic Revival church by architect famous for style; fine detached bell tower.

Milwaukee Vicinity *(N, via US I-43)*. Approx. 25 mi: WAUBEKA. *Pioneer Village (1840–60; rest.), number of houses, other buildings. Approx. 30 mi farther: *SHEBOYGAN. *Judge David Taylor House (1852; later alt.), 3110 Erie Ave. Approx. 12 mi W of Sheboygan, via St. 23: PLYMOUTH. *John G. Voight Log House (1850; rest.). Just W of Plymouth, via St. 23: GREENBUSH. *Old Wade House (1851; rest.), State Park, formerly inn; rest. outbuildings include smokehouse, blacksmith shop.

Milwaukee Vicinity *(S, via St. 32)*. Approx. 25 mi: RACINE, very fine modern buildings by Frank Lloyd Wright include
••*S. C. Johnson Co. Administration Building (1939) and
••*Research Tower (1950), Franklin, bet. 15th & 16th sts, magnificent modern complex; considered among finest of U.S. buildings

and among its famous architect's masterpieces. Other very fine buildings by Wright: NE of city at Wind Point, Wingspread, the H. F. Johnson House, now Johnson Foundation Conference Center (1937; later alt.), 33 E. Mile Rd. At 1319 S. Main St, Thomas P. Hardy House (1905). At 1425 Valley View Dr, Willard H. Keland House (1954). Approx. 10 mi W of Racine, via St. 11: BURLINGTON. *Pioneer Log Cabin (about 1864; rest.), Echo Park. Approx. 7 mi N of Burlington, via St. 36: WATERFORD. *Heg Mem. Museum (1837; rest.), Heg Park, S. Loomis Rd.

Milwaukee Vicinity *(NW, via US 41)*. Approx. 15 mi: MENOMO-NEE FALLS. *Miller-Davidson House (1858; rest.), County Line Rd. Approx. 45 mi farther: FOND DU LAC. *Galloway Village, 336 Old Pioneer Rd; 19th-century buildings include Victorian *Galloway House (about 1847; rest.).

SUPERIOR

Interesting buildings include: *Martin Pattison Mansion (1890; later alt.), 906 E. 2nd St; Eclectic French Chateau style. Approx. 85 mi NE of Superior, via St. 13 & ferry: LAPOINTE. *Madeline Island Hist. Museum, early log cabins.

Rocky Mountain States

Colorado

Early inhabitants pre-Columbian ancestors of Indians, including Anasazi who built wonderful cliff dwellings of Mesa Verde in SW corner of state. Later Indian tribes included Arapaho, Cheyenne, Comanche, Utes. First explored by Spanish, 16th century; claimed for France by Robert Cavelier, Sieur de La Salle, 1682; claimed for Spain by Juan de Ulibarri, 1706. Eastern and central portions included in Louisiana Purchase, 1803; explored by Americans Zebulon M. Pike, 1806; Stephen H. Long, 1820. First permanent American settlement, 1833: Bent's Fort. Mexico took W Colorado from Spain, 1821; United States took from Mexico, 1848, during Mexican War. Gold rush began, 1858. Made Colorado Territory, 1861. Battles between white settlers and Indians, including killing of hundreds of Cheyenne by Colorado militiamen at Sand Creek Massacre, 1864; continued until killing of Indian agent Nathan C. Meeker and troops by Ute Indians in Meeker Massacre, 1879. Became thirty-eighth state, August 1, 1876. Today: Major manufacturing, mining, agricultural, tourist industries.

Land Regions: From E to W, Great Plains; Rocky Mountains; Colorado Plateau; Intermediate Basin.

Climate: Generally dry and sunny; great differences in temperatures caused by great differences in altitude; mountains almost always cooler than plains; precipitation light; more on W slopes of mountains than E slopes; snowfall heavy on W slopes, light on E.

Major Building Materials: Sand and gravel; stone; timber, mostly softwoods.

Architecture: Rich and varied, in later eras as well as in pre-Columbian times, especially in Denver and vicinity and Mesa Verde Nat. Mon.

COLORADO SPRINGS

Interesting buildings include: *McAllister House (1873; rest.) 423 N. Cascade Ave. Not far: *Broadmoor Hotel (1922; later alt & addit.), S of Colorado Springs, off US 85; architects: Warren & Wetmore; architects, 1962 addit.: Francis & Guy; elegant Eclectic Italian Renaissance Revival; beautifully landscaped grounds.

Colorado Springs Vicinity *(N, via US I-25).* Approx. 10 mi **•*U.S. Air Force Academy** (1963; later alt. & addit.), architects

Skidmore, Owings & Merrill; very fine modern campus by famous architects; in beautiful setting near mountains; considered one of finest 20th-century achievements; chapel especially fine.

Colorado Springs Vicinity *(W, via US 24 & St. 67)*. Approx. 45 mi, CRIPPLE CREEK, ghost town; number of interesting buildings here; also of interest: *Blue Bird Gold Mine. Approx. 4 mi S, VICTOR, another ghost mining town. Interesting buildings include: *Masonic Hall (about 1890); *Lowell Thomas Boyhood Home (1897), once home of famous traveler, writer, radio commentator. Also of interest nearby: *Pike's Peak; *Garden of the Gods.

Colorado Springs Vicinity *(NW, via US 24 & 285)*. Approx. 100 mi, via US 24 & 285, FAIRPLAY, another old mining town. Interesting buildings include: in Hist. Dist., small Gothic Revival *Sheldon Jackson Memorial Chapel (1874), Hathaway & 6th sts; named for noted Presbyterian missionary; *South Park City, reconst. mining village. Approx. 70 mi from Fairplay, via US 285 & 24 (approx. 130 mi from Colorado Springs, via US 24), LEADVILLE, another old mining town: highest town above sea level, 10,152 feet, in U.S. Interesting buildings include: in Hist. Dist., *Tabor Opera House (1879; rest.), 308 Harrison Ave; architects: Brooke & Brooke. Victorian *Healy House (1878); log *Dexter Cabin (1879), both at 912 Harrison Ave. *Tabor House (1877; rest.), 116 E. 5th St. Strange *House with Eye (1879), 127 W. 4th St, with stained-glass window representing all-seeing eye of God. Also of interest: *Matchless Mine, still in operation.

Colorado Springs Vicinity *(S, via US I-25)*. Approx. 45 mi: PUEBLO. *Gov. Adams House (1891; later alt. & addit.), Colorado & E. Orman aves; architect: William W. Stickney; Romanesque

U.S. Air Force Academy—Modern (Colorado Department of Public Relations)

Revival; now offices. *Rosemount (1891), 37-room Victorian mansion. Also of interest nearby: *Royal Gorge. Approx. 85 mi S of Pueblo, via US I-25: TRINIDAD. Interesting buildings include: *Don Felipe Baca House (1869), Main St; adobe; building behind: *Frank G. Bloom House (1882), Victorian; fine garden.

DENVER

Interesting buildings include: *State Capitol (1908), Broadway & W. Colfax St; architect: Elijah E. Myers & Frank E. Edbrooke; Eclectic Classic Revival. In *Denver Civic Center, Eclectic Classic Revival *Old Denver Library (1910), architect: A. R. Ross; *Denver City and County Building (1932), architects: Denver Architects Assoc.; modern *Denver Art Museum (1971), architects: James Sudler & Gio Ponti; modern *Currigan Exhibition Hall (1969), Curtis & 14th sts; architects: Muchow, Ream & Larson. Not far: *Denver Center for Performing Arts, modern *Boettcher Concert Hall (1978), architects: Hardy, Holzman & Pfeiffer; *Helen G. Bonfils Theater (1980), architects: Kevin Roche & John Dinkeloo. Not far: *Larimer Square (1874; rest. & remod.), 1400 block of Larimer St; architect, rest.: Langdon Morris; Victorian with arcade; remod. into shopping complex. *Daniels and Fisher Tower (1911; later remod.), Arapahoe & 16th sts; architects: Sterner & Williamson; architects, remod.: Gensler Assoc.; offices based on design of Cathedral of San Marco (1085), Venice, Italy. Not far: •*Brown Palace Hotel (1892; later alt. & addit.), Tremont & 17th sts; architect: Frank E. Edbrooke; archi-

Red Rocks Amphitheater—Modern (Hedrich-Blessing)

tect, addit.: William Tabler; fine old hotel; very fine nine-story interior court or atrium. *Trinity United Methodist Church (1888; later alt. & addit.), Broadway & 18th St; architect: Robert S. Roeschlaub; Victorian Gothic Revival. Just S of city, via US 85: LITTLETON. Nearby, fine modern
•*Johns Manville Headquarters (1976), Ken-Caryl Ranch, architects: The Architects Collaborative (TAC).

Denver Vicinity *(SW, via US 285 & St. 26)*. Approx. 15 mi: MORRISON. In spectacular mountain setting, very fine modern, •*Red Rocks Amphitheater (1941), architect: Burnham Hoyt; red sandstone, concrete, wood structure. Ghost towns of FAIRPLAY and LEADVILLE, see Colorado Springs Vicinity (NW, via US 24 & 285).

Denver Vicinity *(W, via US I-70)*. Approx. 32 mi, via US I-70 & St. 119, CENTRAL CITY, old mining town. Interesting buildings include: Victorian *Opera House (1878; rest.), architect: Robert S. Roeschlaub; still in operation. Not far, another old mining town, BLACK HAWK. Approx. 8 mi farther, GEORGETOWN and SILVER PLUME, two other old mining towns. Interesting buildings include: in Georgetown-Silver Plume Hist. Dist., *Hotel de Paris (1875; later alt. & addit.; rest.); *Gen. William A. Hamill House (about 1868; later alt. & addit.); *Frank Maxwell House (about 1890); *Firehouse (1871). Approx. 50 mi N of Georgetown, via US 40, near GRANBY, ruins of oldest known buildings (perhaps 2000 B.C. or earlier) in North America; threatened by Federal reclamation project.

Denver Vicinity *(NW, via US 36)*. Approx. 25 mi: BOULDER. At *University of Colorado, interesting modern buildings include: *Engineering Sciences Complex (1963), architects: Architectural Assoc. of Colorado; eight modern buildings of concrete and red sandstone with red tile roofs, harmonizing with earlier buildings on campus. Just S of city, at Table Mountain.
•*National Center for Atmospheric Research (1966), architect: I. M. Pei; fine modern complex of sandstone aggregate concrete, complementing beautiful mesa and mountain setting. Also of interest near city: *Estes Park; *Rocky Mountain Nat. Park.

MESA VERDE NATIONAL PARK

In extreme SW corner of state, off St. 160, approx. 35 mi W of DURANGO, 12 mi E of CORTEZ: Magnificent remains of pre-Columbian Anasazi Indian cliff dwellings (begun c. 1100 B.C.); among many very fine structures here: •*Spruce Tree House, considered masterpiece, together with •*Cliff Palace and •*Square Tower House. Others include: *Fire Temple; *Far View

Cliff Palace, Mesa Verde National Park—Pre-Columbian
(Colorado Department of Public Relations)

House; *Square Tower House. Nearby, other fine pre-Columbian structures at *Hovenweep Nat. Mon., partially in state, partially in Utah. Also: Arizona—Flagstaff Vicinity (E, via US I-40); New Mexico—Albuquerque Vicinity (NW, via St. 44).

Idaho

Early inhabitants ancestors of present-day Indians believed to have lived here 100 centuries ago or before; rock markings and other remains have survived in many places. Later Indian tribes include Bannock, Coeur d'Alene, Nez Percé, Shoshoni. First explorers Americans Meriwether Lewis and William Clark, 1805, during expedition to West Coast. Canadian David Thompson built fur-trading post at Pend Oreille Lake, 1809; Ft. Boise and Ft. Hall built, 1834. American Presbyterian missionaries Henry H. Spalding and his wife established Lapwai Mission, near Lewiston, 1836; Mormons built Ft. Lemhi, 1855; driven out by Indians; other Mormons founded first permanent American settlement, 1860: Franklin. Gold discovered, 1860, at Orofino Creek and later at other locations; along with would-be prospectors came settlers who were farmers and cattlemen. Made part of Idaho Territory, 1863; capital: Lewiston; in 1864, Boise became capital. Nez Percé, led by Chief Joseph, forced to move from Oregon to Idaho, badly defeated U.S. troops in battle at White Bird Canyon, 1877; captured in Montana later in year. Bannock Indians revolted because of loss of hunting grounds, 1877; Chief Buffalo Horn killed, 1878, ending struggle. Became forty-third state, July 3, 1890. Today: Important manufacturing, agricultural industries; mining, especially silver, lead, zinc, also important.

Land Regions: S to N, large Columbia Plateau and small Basin and Range Region; Rocky Mountains; Columbia Plateau.

Climate: Moderate, cooler in mountains than elsewhere; precipitation light; snowfall heavy.

Major Building Materials: Timber, especially softwoods; lead; zinc; copper; sand and gravel.

Architecture: Interesting buildings, though not numerous, in several places, especially Boise and vicinity; Coeur d'Alene and vicinity; Idaho Falls and vicinity.

BOISE

Interesting buildings include: *Statehouse (1905–20), Capitol Blvd & Jefferson St; architects: J. E. Tourtellote & Charles F. Hummel; Eclectic Roman Revival. *Borah Substation (1904; later alt. & addit.), 304 N. 8th St; architect: James Knox Taylor; Eclectic Renaissance Revival; post office, government offices. *Boise-Cascade Building (1971), 1 Jefferson St; architects: Skidmore, Owings & Merrill; modern offices by famous firm. *Old Assay Office (1872; later alt.), 210 Main St; architect: Alfred B. Mullett; Eclectic Italian Renaissance Revival; originally used for assaying gold and silver mined in area; used later for several other purposes. *Christ Chapel, formerly St. Michael's Church, Episcopal (1866), Broadway & Campus Dr; wood-frame Gothic Revival; oldest church in city; moved here. *Union Pacific Depot (1925), 1701 Eastover Terr.; architects: Carrère & Hastings and Shreve & Lamb; Eclectic Spanish Colonial Revival; rare in state. In *Pioneer Village, Julia Davis Park: *I. N. Coston Cabin (1863), built of driftwood; believed to be oldest house in state; *Ira B. Pierce Log Cabin (1863); adobe *Mayor Thomas E. Logan House (1865).

Boise Vicinity *(NE, via St. 21).* Approx. 40 mi, IDAHO CITY, major gold rush center, now almost ghost town. Interesting buildings include: Masonic Temple (1865; later alt.), *Miners' Exchange (1871; rest.); *Boise Basin Museum (1867), formerly post office; *St. Joseph's Roman Catholic Church (1867); *Boise Co. Courthouse (1873; remod.), formerly general store.

Boise Vicinity *(SE, via US I-80N).* Approx. 45 mi: MOUNTAIN HOME. Approx. 9 mi W, *Daniels-Hansen House (about 1871;

later alt. & addit.), Canyon Creek Rd; well-preserved former stagecoach station. Approx. 45 mi farther: BLISS. Archie Boyd Teater House and Studio (1952); architect: Frank Lloyd Wright; high on bluff overlooking Snake River. Approx. 85 mi NE of Bliss, via US 26 & St. 75: KETCHUM. *First Security Bank (1887; rest.), Main St; architect, rest.: Nat J. Adams; formerly general store. Also of interest nearby, resort: SUN VALLEY.

Boise Vicinity *(NW, via US I-80N)*. Approx. 16 mi: NAMPA. Interesting buildings include: *Union Pacific Railroad Station (1925), 1211 1st St N; architect: Gilbert Stanley; fine example reminiscent of Prairie style. Nearby, Eclectic Baroque Revival *Canyon Co. Hist. Museum (1903; later alt. & addit.), 12th Ave S; architect; F. W. Clarke; originally railroad station. *Cleo's Ferry Museum (1862; rest.), 311 14th St; originally home of operator of Snake River ferry. Approx. 32 mi S, via St. 45 & 78, SILVER CITY, another ghost town. Interesting buildings include: *Masonic Temple (1869); Stoddard House (1871); Schoolhouse (1892; later alt. & addit.), now museum. Few miles W, DE LAMAR, another ghost town.

COEUR D'ALENE

Interesting buildings include: *Ft. Sherman (about 1878), now part of *Northern Idaho State College. *Hagedorn Newspapers Building (1973), 1st St; architect: R. G. Nelson; unusual modern example built on pilings over Lake Coeur d'Alene. Approx. 33 mi E, via US I-90: CATALDO.
••*Mission of Sacred Heart to the Coeur d'Alenes** (1853; rest.), architect: Father Anthony Ravalli; architect, rest.: Geoffrey W. Fairfax; oldest, and considered finest, early building in state.

Coeur d'Alene Vicinity *(S, via US I-95)*. Approx. 85 mi: MOSCOW. Interesting buildings include: *Gov. William J. McConnell House (1886; rest.), 110 S. Adams St; Eastlake style, rarity in state; once home of first Idaho U.S. senator and third governor. Nearby, on N. Polk St, at no. 325, Mart Miller House (1911); at no. 403, Charles F. Butterfield House (1902), Eclectic Classic Revival. Approx. 35 mi farther, first territorial capital of state, 1863–64: LEWISTON. Nearby, *Nez Percé Nat. Hist. Park, part of Indian Reservation, some 25 scattered sites of Indians and early settlers at camp headquarters, SPALDING; also at LAPWAI, SLICKPOO, other locations. Also of interest nearby, *Snake River Canyon, including *Hell's Canyon, 7,900 feet deep.

IDAHO FALLS

Interesting buildings include: Mormon Temple (1943; later alt. & addit.), 1000 Memorial Dr; architects: committee of six firms; Art Deco or Moderne; only example in state; open only to Mormons in good standing; open to public: several chapels, tabernacles in other locations. Old Stage Station (about 1868; later alt. & addit.), 208 8th St; now private home. Approx. 5 mi N, via US 26, IONA, interesting 19th-century Mormon village. Also of interest: W of city, *Craters of the Moon Nat. Mon.; NE of city, *Yellowstone Nat. Park; see Wyoming—Yellowstone.

Idaho Falls Vicinity *(S, via US I-15).* Approx. 50 mi: POCATEL-LO. *Judge Drew Standrod House (1902; rest.), 648 N. Garfield St; architect: Marcus Grundfor; Victorian. Approx. 75 mi farther, via US I-15 & 91, FRANKLIN, oldest town in state, founded by Mormons, 1860. Interesting buildings include: *Mormon Tabernacle (1889), architect: Joseph Don Carlos Young, son of Brigham; unusually large Romanesque Revival example for small community. *Bear Lake Co. Courthouse (1885), architect: Truman O. Angell; elegant Eclectic Classic Revival.

Montana

Early inhabitants number of Indian tribes, including Arapaho, Blackfoot, Cheyenne and Crow. French trappers believed to have come here, about 1740. First explored by Americans Meriwether Lewis and William Clark during expedition to West Coast, 1805; American fur traders in area, beginning 1807. First permanent American settlement by American Fur Co., 1847: Ft. Benton. Most of state acquired by United States in Louisiana Purchase, 1803; NW portion ceded by Great Britain, 1846. Gold rush began, 1862, at Grasshopper Creek; other strikes soon followed, bringing with them lawless times. To bring law and order into area, Montana Territory established, 1864; Sidney Edgerton first territorial governor. Cattle ranching became well established. Building of Northern Pacific Railroad, 1883, opened territory to eastern United States. Heavy fighting with Indians continued for many years, including Battle of the Little Bighorn, in which Gen. George A. Custer and his Seventh Cavalry were killed, 1876, by Sioux and Cheyenne Indians led by Sitting Bull and Crazy Horse; last battles led to capture of Chief Joseph and his Nez Percé Indians, 1877. Became forty-first state, Nov. 8, 1889. Today: Important agricultural, especially ranching and wheat, manufacturing, mining industries.

Land Regions: E to W, large Great Plains; smaller Rocky Mountains.

Climate: Varies considerably; W of Continental Divide, moderate winters, cool summers; E, cold winters, somewhat warmer summers; precipitation light in E, heavier in W; snowfall light in E, very heavy in W. Chinook winds warm E slopes of mountains in winter at times.

Major Building Materials: Timber, mostly softwoods; copper; gypsum; limestone; sand and gravel; vermiculite.

Architecture: Interesting buildings in several locations, especially Helena and vicinity.

BUTTE

Interesting buildings include: in Hist. Dist., *Copper King Mansion, the William Andrews Clark House (1888; later alt. & addit.), 219 W. Granite St; fine Victorian; once home of noted copper mining industrialist, U.S. senator; later Roman Catholic convent; now private home. Also of interest: copper mines. Approx. 225 mi E of Butte, near BILLINGS, *Pompey's Pillar; *Custer Battlefield Nat. Mon.

Butte Vicinity *(SE, via St. 41 & 287).* Approx. 75 mi, VIRGINIA CITY, gold rush town; territorial capital, 1865–75. Interesting buildings include: *Madison Co. Courthouse (1876; later alt. & addit.; rest.), Wallace St; fine example; still in use. *Content Corner (1864; later alt. & addit.), Wallace St; once home, tavern. In Hist. Dist., reconst. & rest. early buildings. Also of interest, SE of Virginia City, *Yellowstone Nat. Park; also see: Wyoming—Yellowstone.

Butte Vicinity *(SW, via US I-15, St. 278 & Co. Rd).* Approx. 90 mi, BANNACK, oldest town in state; first territorial capital. Interesting buildings include: in Hist. Dist., *Beaverhead Co. Courthouse (1876; later alt. & addit.), Main St.

Butte Vicinity *(NW, via US 10A).* Approx. 50 mi, GRANITE, originally Silver Queen City; now ghost town. Interesting buildings include: of local granite, *Miners Union Hall (1890), Main St; social center during silver-mining days. *Superintendent's House (about 1885), Magnolia Ave; once home of Granite Mountain Mining Co. superintendent.

HELENA

Interesting buildings include: *State Capitol (1902; later alt. & addit.), 1301 6th Ave; architects: Bell & Kent; architect, 1912 addit.: Frank Andrews; copper dome with reproduction of Statue of Liberty on top. Few blocks: *Governor's Old Mansion (1885; later alt. & addit.; rest.), 304 N. Ewing St; residence of state governors, 1913–58. Nearby, *Lewis and Clark Co. Courthouse (1887; later alt. & addit.), Broadway & Ewing sts; architects: Hodgson & Stem; Romanesque Revival. On city's main street, Last Chance Gulch, named for famous 1864 gold strike, preserved, rest. and reconst. early buildings include: at no. 7–9, *Atlas Block (1888), architects: Shaffer & Stranahan; vaguely Romanesque Revival; at nos. 58, 60 & 62, *Powers Block (1889), architects: Shaffer & Read; Romanesque Revival. Nearby, *Pioneer Cabin (1864; later alt. & addit.), 280 S. Park Ave at Reeder's Alley. At 540 W. Main St, Emil Kluge House (about 1880), rare example of type found almost exclusively in Silesian region of Germany; first story of logs with brick infilling, second half-timbered; built by German immigrant. Nearby, *Diamond Block (1889; remod. 1975), N. Park & 6th aves; architects: Shaffer & Stranahan; architects, remod.: Richard I. Shope & Herbert L. Jacobson; interesting small granite office building. At 415 N. Main St, *Templeton Hotel (1887; later alt. & addit.), architects: T. F. Mathias & Fred Heinlein; interesting cast-iron front. *Civic Center (1920), Neill & Benton aves; architects: Link & Haire; interesting Eclectic Moslem type with minaret; originally Algeria Shrine Temple. Approx. 90 mi NE, via US I-15: GREAT FALLS. Charles M. Russell House and *Studio (about 1900), 12th St & 4th Ave N; once home and studio of famous western painter and sculptor. Nearby, *C. M. Russell Gallery, fine collection of artist's works. Approx. 75 mi E of Helena, via US 12: WHITE SULPHUR SPRINGS. *Stone Castle, the B. R. Sherman House (1890–1902), 310 2nd Ave NE; once home of noted rancher and miner. Approx. 30 mi S of Helena, via US I-15 & St. 281, ELKHORN, interesting gold-, silver-mining ghost town.

Helena Vicinity *(NW, via US 12 & I-90)*. Approx. 120 mi: MISSOULA. *Ft. Missoula, now Hist. Site. Interesting buildings include: log *Noncommissioned Officers' Quarters (1878); stone *Powder Magazine (1878). Approx. 30 mi S of Missoula, via US 93: STEVENSVILLE. Interesting buildings include: *St. Mary's Mission Church (1866; rest.), architect: Father Anthony Ravalli, who also designed and built famous church in Cataldo, Idaho; log mission to Salish (Flathead) Indians; now chapel. Nearby, *St. Mary's Pharmacy (about 1866), architect: Father Ravalli; for dispensing of medicines to Indians, settlers. Approx. 1 mi N, *Ft. Owen (about 1860; rest.), adobe; trading post of John Owen, early trader, Indian agent. Also of interest, N of Missoula, *Waterton-Glacier International Peace Park.

Nevada

Early inhabitants ancestors of present-day Indians who lived here 200 or more centuries ago; some of their picture writing survives in S part of state. Later, Basket Makers and Pueblos lived here and, still later, tribes included Mohave, Paiute, Shoshoni, Washoe. First explorer believed to have been Spaniard Francisco Garcés, about 1775; Spain claimed region. Fur traders and trappers entered region about 1825. Explored by Americans William Wolfskill, 1830, and Joseph Walker, 1833. Walker established California Trail over which wagon trains of settlers travelled. American Lt. John C. Frémont explored, 1843–45. Became part of Mexico after its independence from Spain, 1821; region ceded to United States after end of Mexican War, 1848. Mormon leader Brigham Young petitioned Congress to include region, along with Utah, in State of Deseret, founded by him, 1849; instead, two were made Utah Territory, 1850. Mormons from Utah established, in 1851: Mormon Station, now Genoa; in 1857, Mormons returned to Utah. Discovery of famous Comstock Lode of silver at Virginia City, 1859, led to influx of would-be prospectors and to lawlessness. Became Nevada Territory, 1861. Became thirty-sixth state Oct. 31, 1864. As price of precious metals fell, mining lessened in importance in state, while ranching became much more important. Today: Important manufacturing, mining, especially copper, agricultural industries; tourism, especially in Las Vegas and Reno, also of importance.

Land Regions: Very large Basin and Range Region; very small Sierra Nevada in W; very small Columbia Plateau in NE.

Climate: Varied; mountains and N, long, cold winters, short, hot, summers; winters moderate, summers long and hot in S; temperatures often change radically during day; precipitation very little in SE, moderate in NW and NE; snowfall very heavy in mountains, almost none in SE.

Major Building Materials: Copper and, in lesser degree, other metals; gypsum; sand and gravel.

Architecture: Important buildings, though relatively few in number, in several locations.

CARSON CITY

Interesting buildings include: *State Capitol (1871; later alt. & addit.; rest.), N. Carson St; architect: Joseph Gosling; small Eclectic example of local sandstone. Not far: *U.S. Post Office, now State Library (1891; later alt. & addit.), Carson St; architect: W. E. Bell. *State Printing Office, now State Office Building (1886; later alt. & addit.), S. Fall St; architect: M. J. Curtis. *U.S. Mint, now State Museum (1869; later alt. & addit.), Carson & Robinson sts; architect: Alfred B. Mullett. *Duane Bliss Mansion (1879), 710 W. Robinson St; Victorian with fine woodwork. *Governor's Mansion (1909), 600 Mountain St; architect: George A. Ferris; Eclectic Beaux Arts. Also of interest *Lake Tahoe.

Carson City Vicinity *(NW, via US I-395).* Approx. 10 mi, near GOLD HILL, *Sandy Bowers Mansion (about 1865; later alt. & addit.; rest.), interesting home built for gold prospector who struck it rich in famous Comstock Lode, and his wife Eilley. Nearby, *Bowers Mine. Approx. 20 mi farther, RENO, noted for easy divorces and gambling, not for architecture.

Carson City Vicinity *(NE, via US 50 & St. 17).* Approx. 15 mi, VIRGINIA CITY, famed mining town on Comstock Lode, now ghost town. Interesting buildings include: in Hist. Dist., *Storey Co. Courthouse (1876), B St; *John W. Mackay Mansion (1860; rest.), 129 D St; once home of wealthiest Comstock millionaire; *Savage Mining Co. Office (1862; rest.); also houses, saloons.

LAS VEGAS

Noted for gambling, garish buildings and high living, especially along "The Strip." Approx. 25 mi SW of city, via US 93: BOULDER CITY. Nearby, spectacular *Hoover Dam, originally named Boulder Dam. Approx. 115 mi NW of Las Vegas, via US 95: BEATTY. Approx. 5 mi S, via St. 58, haunting ruins of ghost town: RHYOLITE. Also of interest, few miles S, via St. 58, *Death Valley Nat. Mon.; small portion in state, remainder in California; location of *Scotty's Castle, once home of Death Valley Scotty.

Utah

Early inhabitants ancestors of present-day Indians; later tribes included Paiute, Shoshoni, Ute; Navaho arrived here mid-19th century. First explorers believed to have been Spanish Franciscan fathers Silvestre Velez de Escalante, Francisco Atanasio Domínguez, 1776, long after exploration of other regions of present-day United States; fur traders believed to have first entered region, about 1811; explored by famous frontiersman Jim Bridger, 1824–

25. First permanent American settlement made by members of Church of Jesus Christ of Latter-day Saints, or Mormons, led by Brigham Young, 1847: Salt Lake City. Mormons established State of Deseret and called upon U.S. Congress for recognition. Region ceded to United States by Mexico, at end of Mexican War, 1848. Congress established Utah Territory, 1850. Fighting between Mormons and Indians began with Walker War, 1853; did not end until 1867, after Black Hawk War, led by Ute Chief Black Hawk. Primarily because of Mormon practice of polygamy, numerous petitions for statehood were denied. U.S. government decided to take control of region from Mormons, replaced Brigham Young as governor, 1857, and sent troops into area. Violence ensued, known as Utah, or Mormon, War, resulting in number of people traveling through area being killed by Indians and Mormons at Mountains Meadows Massacre, 1857. Troops arrived, with Jim Bridger as guide; violence subsided; troops withdrawn at beginning of Civil War, 1861. Troops were again sent to region, 1862; U.S. Congress passed law same year forbidding polygamy. Troops, led by Col. Patrick E. Conner, discovered gold and silver, 1863, bringing non-Mormons into area; Central Pacific Railroad joined Union Pacific at Promontory, Utah, 1869. After many court trials and other troubles, Mormons prohibited polygamy, 1890. Became forty-fifth state, Jan. 4, 1896. Today: Important manufacturing, mining, especially copper, oil, coal, and agricultural industries.

Land Regions: E to W, large Colorado Plateau; Basin and Range Region; in NE, small Rocky Mountains.

Climate: Moderate winters, cool summers in NE, warm in SW; precipitation minimal in Great Salt Lake Desert, fairly heavy in NE mountains; snowfall minimal in SW, very heavy in mountains.

Major Building Materials: Copper, lesser amounts of other metals; sand and gravel; gypsum; iron.

Architecture: Number of important buildings, architecturally and historically, especially Mormon examples, and especially in St. George and vicinity and Salt Lake City and vicinity.

ST. GEORGE

Interesting buildings include: ●*St. George Tabernacle** (1863–76), Main & Tabernacle sts; architect: Miles Romney; sandstone; considered finest example in state. St. George Temple (1877), bet. 2nd E, 3rd E, 4th S & 5th S sts; architect: Truman O. Angell; first temple in state; open only to Mormons in good standing. *Brigham Young Winter House (about 1850; later alt. & addit.; rest.), 200 N. 400 W St; architect, 1874 addit.: Miles Romney; architect, rest.: George Cannon Young; stuccoed adobe. Next door, Brigham Young Office (1874). Also of interest, in St. George Vicinity: national parks *Zion, *Bryce Canyon, *Capitol Reef; *Cedar Break Nat. Mon.; pre-Columbian ruins at *KANAB and ZION.

St. George Vicinity *(NE, via US I-15)*. Approx. 12 mi: LEEDS. Two almost identical houses, with "Dixie" dormers, named for 19th-century cotton-growing experiment that failed: William Stirling House (about 1876); Charles Wilkinson House (about 1876). About 2 mi from Leeds, *SILVER REEF, once famous silver-mining center. *Wells Fargo & Co. Express Building (about 1877); *Rice Bank (about 1875), only surviving structures. Approx. 43 mi farther: CEDAR CITY. *George Lamar Cabin (1851), log house; moved here. Approx. 20 mi farther: PAROWAN. Nearby, *Parowan Gap Petroglyphs. Approx. 40 mi farther: BEAVER. *Beaver Co. Courthouse (1882; part. rebuilt after fire, 1889), Center & 1st sts E; cast iron and stamped metal trim; octagonal dome cupola. Approx. 45 mi NE of Beaver, via St. 21, ghost town: FRISCO. *Horn Silver Mine; reputed to have been wildest camp in state. Approx. 25 mi farther: COVE FORT. *Old Cove Fort (1867; rest.), two rows of six interconnected houses each, facing each other across court. Approx. 30 mi farther: FILLMORE. *Territorial Capitol (about 1855; rest.), 50 W. Capitol Ave; architect: Truman O. Angell; architects, rest.: Young & Hansen; only one wing of four completed before Salt Lake City became capital; territorial legislature met here, 1855–56.

St. George Vicinity *(NW, via St. 18)*. Approx. 5 mi: SANTA CLARA. *Jacob Hamblin House (1863; rest.), Dixie State Park; once home of pioneer Mormon scout and missionary. Approx. 20 mi farther: PINE VALLEY. *Pine Valley Ward Chapel (1868), Main & Grass Valley sts; architect: Ebenezer Bryce; notable early Mormon chapel: originally very numerous but few have survived. *Pine Valley Tithing Office (about 1868), Mormon building for receiving, storing tithes paid "in kind," by goods or commodities.

SALT LAKE CITY

Interesting buildings include: *State Capitol (1916), State St; architect: Richard K. A. Kletting; Eclectic Classic Revival with dome. Not far: *City and County Building (1894; later alt. & addit.; rest.), 4th S & State sts; architects: Proudfoot, Bird & Monheim; architect, rest.: Burtch W. Beall, Jr.; impressive Romanesque Revival; part city hall, part county courthouse; first state capitol, 1896–1916. *Temple Square, 10-acre site, surrounded by 15-foot-high wall, with impressive buildings of Church of Jesus Christ of Latter-day Saints (Mormons), including: Salt Lake Temple (1853–93), architect: Truman O. Angell; majestic six-spired structure of somewhat Eclectic Gothic Revival style;

open only to Mormons in good standing; *Assembly Hall (1880), architect: Obed Taylor. Also: ••**Salt Lake Tabernacle** (1868), architects: William H. Folsom & Truman O. Angell; structural engineer: Henry Grow; very fine building; large dome, 150 by 250 feet, with arched trusses supported by sandstone columns; largest enclosed interior space of any building of era; considered great engineering feat; also famous for wonderful 375-member choir, magnificent organ, with almost 11,000 pipes. Also in Square: log *Osmyn Deuel Cabin (1847), moved here.

Other interesting houses in city include: on E. South Temple St, at no. 75, *Beehive House, the Brigham Young House (1855; later alt. & addit.; rest.); architect: Truman O. Angell; architect, rest.: George Cannon Young; adobe; somewhat Greek Revival with Southern Colonial, Victorian touches; named for beehive-shaped cupola. Adjacent: Young Office and Lion House (1856; rest.), architect: Truman O. Angell; named for sculptured lion over entrance; once home of wives and children of Young. At no. 529, *Keith-Brown Mansion (1900; later alt. & addit.; rest.), Eclectic Classic Revival; at no. 603, *Thomas Kearns Mansion (1902; later alt. & addit.), large example with three towers. On W. South Temple St, at no. 334, Devereaux, the Staines-Jennings Mansion (1857; later alt. & addit.), architect: William Paul; fine interior woodwork. Other interesting buildings include: *St. Mark's Episcopal Cathedral (1870–1902), 231 E. 2nd South St; architect: Richard Upjohn; Gothic Revival by architect famous for style; believed to be his last church. *Lester Wire House (1887; later alt. & addit.), 668 E. 3rd South St; unusual, for city; Eclectic Dutch Colonial Revival; *Zion's Cooperative Mercantile Institution (ZCMI) Store (1876; later alt. & addit.), architects: William H. Folsom & Obed Taylor; example of fine cast-iron front; built as department store, first in U.S., for Brigham Young cooperative; replaced by new building, 1976, utilizing cast-iron front; architects: Gruen Assoc. *Forest Farm Home (1863; rest.), 732 Ashton Ave; once part of experimental farm established by Brigham Young. *Pioneer Village Museum, 2998 Connor St; some 25 Mormon buildings moved here and reconst. Also of interest: W of city, *Great Salt Lake and *Bonneville Salt Flats.

Note: In extreme SE corner of state, not near any major town: *Hovenweep Nat. Mon., intriguing pre-Columbian Indian ruins. Also see: Arizona—Flagstaff Vicinity (E, via US I-40); Colorado—Mesa Verde Nat. Park; New Mexico—Albuquerque Vicinity (NW, via St. 44). Also of interest, not far away: *Glen Canyon Nat. Recreation Area; *Canyonlands and *Arches Nat. parks.

Salt Lake City Vicinity *(N, via St I-15).* Approx. 10 mi: BOUNTIFUL. *Bountiful Tabernacle (1863), architect: Augustus A. Farnham, stuccoed adobe; oldest Mormon tabernacle in state. Approx. 15 mi farther: BRIGHAM CITY. *Brigham City Tabernacle (1881; later alt. & addit.), Main St; fine example. Approx. 10 mi farther, near COLLINSVILLE, *Hampton's Ford Stage Station, also known as Bear River Hotel (1868). Approx. 10 mi farther, via US 89/90: LOGAN. Interesting buildings include: *Logan Tabernacle (1865–1915), Main & Center sts; Logan Temple (1884), 1st N & 2nd E sts; architect: Truman O. Angell, Jr.; interesting example on hill; open only to Mormons in good standing. At *Utah State University, *Fine Arts Center (1968), architect: Burtch W. Beall, Jr.; interesting modern complex.

Salt Lake City Vicinity *(E & SE, via US I-80 & 40)*. Approx. 30 mi: ALTA. Just S, via St. 210, *Snowbird Village (begun 1972), architects: Brixen & Christopher; fine modern skiing and recreational complex. Approx. 20 mi farther, via US 40: SILVER CREEK JUNCTION. Nearby, *Kimball Hotel (about 1860; later alt. & addit.), another old stagecoach station. Approx. 185 mi farther: VERNAL. *Little Rock House (1887; rest.), 178 S. 5th St W, first Mormon tithing office; moved here. Also of interest: *Flaming Gorge Nat. Recreational Area; *Dinosaur Nat. Mon.

Salt Lake City Vicinity *(S, via US 80)*. Approx. 95 mi, SPRING CITY, well-preserved Mormon town; late 19th- and early 20th-century buildings include *Bishop's Storehouse, *Tithing Office, *Tithing Barn, others, of adobe, logs, wood frame, stone and brick. Approx. 20 mi farther: MANTI. Manti Temple (1877–88), architect: William H. Folsom; considered finest of Mormon temples; open only to Mormons in good standing.

Salt Lake City Vicinity *(SW, via US I-15 & St. 73)*. Approx. 40 mi: FAIRFIELD. *Stagecoach Inn, originally John Carson House (about 1858; later alt. & addit.; rest.), architect, rest.: Burtch W. Beall, Jr.; adobe; once home of Gen. Albert S. Johnston commander of nearby Camp Floyd, largest mid-19th-century U.S. military camp. Approx. 10 mi farther, via St. 73, ruins of MERCUR, once prosperous mining center, now ghost town.

Wyoming

Early inhabitants ancestors of Indians who lived here 100 centuries ago or before. Later tribes included Arapaho, Bannock, Cheyenne, Crow, Sioux, others. French trappers believed to have come here, mid-18th century. Region sold by France to United States, 1803, as part of Louisiana Purchase. American trappers arrived. First American permanent settlement established 1834: Ft. William; later renamed Ft. John; finally named Ft. Laramie, after U.S. government bought it to protect settlers on way west, 1849.

In 1843, famous frontiersman Jim Bridger established Ft. Bridger. Lt. John C. Frémont, with Kit Carson as guide, explored extensively, 1842–43. Portions of area were once included in several U.S. territories; finally made part of United States when Texas joined Union, 1845. Beginning about mid-19th century, wagon trains passed through state on famous trails. Indians attacked wagon trains and U.S. troops frequently. In 1866, army built Ft. Phil Kearny to aid in protection of settlers; Indians laid siege and killed many troopers, 1868. United States gave up fort in return for Indian pledge not to hinder Union Pacific Railroad construction, 1867. Region made Wyoming Territory, 1868. Uneasy peace lasted until 1874, when gold was discovered in Black Hills, considered sacred by Indians. New fighting began, but ended in 1876. Became forty-fourth state, July 10, 1890. Growing incidence of cattle rustling during latter part of 19th century led to considerable violence; as did troubles between cattlemen and sheepmen in early 20th. Today: Major mining, especially oil and natural gas, and agricultural, especially cattle ranching, industries; manufacturing also important.

Land Regions: E to W, Great Plains and Black Hills; Rocky Mountains; Intermontane Basins; Rocky Mountains.

Climate: Cold winters, warm summers, dry; cooler in mountains; precipitation varied, from very slight in Bighorn Basin to very heavy in Yellowstone Park; snowfall moderate in Bighorn Basin to very heavy in NW mountains; danger of blizzards.

Major Building Materials: Timber; limestone; gypsum; iron; vermiculite.

Architecture: Interesting buildings, though few in number, in several places.

CHEYENNE

Interesting buildings include: *State Capitol (1888; later alt. & addit.), Capitol Ave & 24th St; architect: D. W. Gibbs; Eclectic Classic Revival, with Romanesque Revival. *Union Pacific Railroad Station (1887; later alt. & addit.), Capitol Ave & 15th St; architects: Van Brunt & Howe; Romanesque Revival. *First United Methodist Church (1890; later alt. & addit.), 18th St bet. Central & Warren aves; architect: J. P. Julien; architects, 1967 addit.: Muchow Assoc.

Cheyenne Vicinity *(N, via US I-25).* Approx. 110 mi via US I-25 & US 26, Ft. Laramie, important post during Westward expansion (1834–90). Number of interesting buildings, some rest. or reconst., of several eras. Approx. 65 mi farther, via US 26 & I-25: Douglas. Nearby, *Ft. Fetterman (1867; later alt. & addit.; rest.), major mid-19th-century supply post.

Cheyenne Vicinity *(NW, via US I-80)*. Approx. 45 mi: LARAMIE. Interesting buildings include: at *University of Wyoming, *Old Main (1887; later alt. & addit.), 9th St & Ivinson Ave; architect: Frederick A. Hale. Approx. 20 mi SE of Laramie, via US I-80 & Blair Rd, *Ames Monument (1882), architect: Henry Hobson Richardson; on lonely site; very fine memorial to Oliver and Oakes Ames, builders of Union Pacific Railroad to west, by famous architect.

SHERIDAN

Interesting buildings include: *John B. Kendrick House, now Trail End Museum (1913; later alt. & addit.), 400 Clarendon Ave; once home of state governor, U.S. senator. *Sheridan Inn (1893; later alt. & addit.; rest.), Broadway & 5th St; architect: Thomas R. Kimball; interesting example with long front porch and 69 gables on roof; once managed by Buffalo Bill Cody. Approx. 150 mi W of city, via US 14: CODY. *Buffalo Bill's Boyhood Home (1840; rest.), 720 Sheridan Ave. Few miles S of Sheridan, via US 87: BIG HORN. *Quarter Circle A Ranch, also known as Bradford Brinton Memorial (1892; later alt. & addit.), interesting buildings of western ranch. Also of interest, approx. 150 mi E of Sheridan, via US 14 or I-90 & St. 24, *Devil's Tower. Also see: South Dakota— Rapid City Vicinity.

YELLOWSTONE NATIONAL PARK

Although man-made architecture here is overwhelmed by magnificent natural architecture, interesting buildings include: *Old Faithful Inn (1904; later alt. & addit.), across from famous geyser; architect: Robert C. Reamer; large, fine rustic hotel in beautiful setting. *Norris Soldiers Station (about 1908), Norris Junction, bet. Norris Campground & Gibbon River; log cabin, last survivor of 15 built by U.S. Army for use in keeping order. Approx. 35 mi S of Inn, via US 89, magnificent *Grand Teton Nat. Park, with *Jackson Lake and *Jackson Hole. Interesting buildings include, near MOOSE, *James H. Mangus Log Cabin (1911); *Bill Menor's Homestead (about 1892; rest.) on bank of Snake River, log house, smokehouse, storage building, ferry. Nearby, *Maud Noble Log Cabin (1916; rest.), once home of woman who bought ferry from Menor, 1918. Not far, bet. Snake River & US 89: ELK. *James Pierce Cunningham Cabin (about 1890; rest.), unusual log, sod-roofed house, blacksmith shop; dogtrot, or breezeway, between; scene of shooting, 1893, of two horse thieves by sheriff's posse. Not far: JACKSON. *Robert A. Miller Log Cabin (1898; rest.); on grounds: another log cabin. Approx. 200 mi S of Jackson, via US 189, *FT. BRIDGER, founded, 1843, by Jim Bridger, famous fur trader; interesting buildings, some rest.

Southwestern States

Arizona

Early inhabitants prehistoric ancestors of present-day Indians believed to have lived in region as early as 200 centuries ago or before. Pre-Columbian Anasazi, Hohokam, Mogollon lived here from about 500 B.C. to about A.D. 1300. Later Indian tribes included Papago, Pima, Pueblo; Apache and Navaho tribes moved into region in 16th century. State has many surviving structures built by Anasazi and some of their contemporaries and descendants. First explorers believed to have been Spanish Franciscan priest Marcos de Niza, 1539, and Francisco Vásquez de Coronado, 1640. During late 17th century, number of Spanish priests, including Father Eusebio Kino, 1692, explored region and founded missions. Tucson founded as Spanish fort, 1776. Became part of Empire of Mexico after its independence from Spain, 1821; most of region became part of United States after end of Mexican War, 1846; S portion added, 1853. During Civil War, many favored Southern cause; elected delegate to Confederate Congress; in 1862, Confederate troops occupied region but were driven out by Federal forces; area named Confederate Territory of Arizona, 1863, but only real result was Congress's making it U.S. territory same year. Fighting with Indians continued for many years; Navahos defeated by forces of Kit Carson, 1863; Apaches, led by famous chiefs such as Cochise, continued to fight until surrender of Chief Geronimo, 1886. Became forty-eighth state, Feb. 14, 1912. Today: Important manufacturing, agricultural, mining, especially copper, industries; tourism also important.

Land Regions: S to N, Basin and Range Region; Colorado Plateau.

Climate: Quite varied, winters very cold in mountains, moderate in S, summer moderate in mountains, hot in S; precipitation moderate in mountains, almost none SW deserts; snowfall rare in deserts, moderate, sometimes heavy, in mountains.

Major Building Materials: Copper; clay; gypsum.

Architecture: Rich and varied, from pre-Columbian era to present, including some of finest U.S. examples, in several locations, especially Flagstaff vicinity; Phoenix vicinity; Tucson and vicinity.

FLAGSTAFF

In almost every direction, wonderful pre-Columbian buildings, other structures; natural phenomena. Approx. 55 mi S, via US I-

17: Camp Verde. Nearby, *Montezuma Castle (c. 1300), Nat. Mon., wonderfully preserved cliff dwelling, misnamed for Aztec chief, who never saw it; other fine examples here.

Flagstaff Vicinity *(NE, via US 89 & 160).* Approx. 20 mi: dormant crater and lava beds of *Sunset Crater Nat. Mon. Approx. 15 mi farther, *Wupatki Nat. Mon. (c. 1100–1300), part. excavated ruins of some 800 pueblos. Approx. 20 mi farther, near Cameron, edge of *Painted Desert. Approx. 90 mi NW of Cameron, via US I-89 & 160, *Navajo Nat. Mon. (13th century), preColumbian cliff dwellings, other structures, including *Inscription House; *Betatakin; *Keet Seel. Not far, via US 160 & 163, *Monument Valley, strangely beautiful sandstone formations.

Flagstaff Vicinity *(E, via US I-40).* Approx. 15 mi: *Walnut Canyon Nat. Mon. (c. 1300–1500), several pre-Columbian cliff dwellings. Approx. 30 mi farther, *Meteor Crater, several hundred feet deep, caused by giant meteor some 50 centuries ago. Approx. 75 mi farther, *Petrified Forest. Approx. 50 mi NE of Petrified Forest, via US I-40 & St. 63: Ganado. *Hubbell Trading Post (1915), now Nat. Hist. Site. Approx. 40 mi N of Ganado, via St. 264 & 63: Chinle. •*Canyon de Chelly (begun about 300), Nat. Mon., buildings of pre-Columbian Anasazi, later Hopi Indians and present-day Navajos include cliff dwellings, pueblos, hogans; finest ancient building: •*White House. Also see: Colorado—Mesa Verde Nat. Park; New Mexico—Albuquerque Vicinity (NW, via St. 44); Utah—Hovenweep Nat. Mon.

Flagstaff Vicinity *(SW, via US 89A).* Approx. 25 mi: Sedona. Approx. 4 mi S, via St. 179, •*Chapel of the Holy Cross (1956), architects: Anshen & Allen, very fine modern concrete Roman Catholic chapel; blends into and contrasts with rugged red sandstone bluffs. Approx. 25 mi farther: Clarkdale. Approx. 4 mi S, *Tuzigoot (c. 1100–1400), Nat. Hist. Mon.; impressive ruins of adobe and stone pueblo. Approx. 5 mi farther, Jerome, old mining town; in Hist. Dist., early wood-frame buildings, many rest., on stilts along mountainside; also of interest, rest. old wooden water flume. Approx. 35 mi farther: Prescott. *Old Governor's Mansion (1864; later alt. & addit.), now Sharlott Hall Museum, 400 Gurley St; log; once home of John N. Goodwin, first territorial governor; on grounds: another old log cabin.

Flagstaff Vicinity *(NW, via US 180).* Also of interest, approx. 80 mi, S rim of *Grand Canyon; N Rim, approx. 200 mi NW of Flagstaff, via US 89, 89A & St. 67. Approx. 85 mi NW of N Rim: Fredonia. Nearby, *Pipe Springs Nat. Mon. Approx. 15 mi W of Fredonia, via St. 389: Moccasin. *Winsor Castle (1871; later alt. & addit.; rest.), monument to early Mormon pioneers.

Taliesin West—Modern (Julius Shulman)

PHOENIX

Interesting buildings include: *State Capitol (1900; later alt. & addit.), W. Washington St & 17th Ave; architect: James Reily Gordon; architects, 1980 addit.: Assoc. Capitol Architects; Eclectic. *Arizona Biltmore Hotel and Cottages (1927; later alt. & addit.), E. Sahuaro Dr & Camino Acequia; architect: Frank Lloyd Wright. At Monroe & 6th sts, *Heritage Square, location of original settlement; interesting buildings include: *Dr. Roland L. Rosson House (1894; rest.), architect: Alexander P. Petit; also here: *Lath House (1980), architect: Robert R. Frankeberger; interesting modern open-air pavilion. On E. Washington St, part. excavated ruins of pre-Columbian *Pueblo Grande. Approx. 60 mi S of city, via US I-10 & St. 87, pre-Columbian ruins of *Casa Grande. Approx. 20 mi N of city, via US I-17, *Pioneer Arizona Village, some 25 reconst. 19th-century buildings.

Phoenix Vicinity *(E, via US 60/89).* Adjoining city: SCOTTSDALE. ••*Taliesin West (1938–59), Maricopa Mesa, 11,000 Shea Blvd; architect: Frank Lloyd Wright; magnificent modern complex was famous architect's winter home, studio; considered one of his masterpieces and one of finest U.S. buildings; now headquarters of Frank Lloyd Wright Foundation. *Cosanti Foundation Workshop and House (begun 1962), 6433 Doubletree Rd; architect: Paolo Soleri; fantastic modern by visionary Italian-American architect. Approx. 60 mi N of Phoenix, via Black Canyon Frwy, US I-17, *ARCOSANTI, equally fantastic city, begun 1970, by same architect; being built by amateur workers. Just S of Scottsdale: TEMPE. At *Arizona State University, *Grady Gammage Memorial Auditorium (1959), Apache Blvd & Mill Ave; architect: Frank Lloyd

Wright, one of last nonresidential buildings by famous architect. Approx. 75 mi NE of Phoenix, via US 60/89 & St. 88: cliff dwellings of ＊Tonto Nat. Mon. (c.1100–1400); also of interest nearby: ＊Theodore Roosevelt Dam.

TUCSON

Interesting buildings include: ＊Charles O. Brown House, also known as Old Patio Adobe (1868; later alt. & addit.), 40 W. Broadway. Gustav Anton Hoff House (about 1880), 127 W. Franklin St; well-preserved adobe with stone columns. Kitt House (1899; later alt. & addit.), 319 S. 4th Ave; unusual adobe in modified Greek Revival. ＊Edward Nye Fish House (1868), 208 N. Main St; Victorian. nearby, stuccoed adobe ＊Hiram S. Stevens House (about 1860; later alt. & addit.), two houses joined together. William Bray House (1919), 203 N. Grande Ave; architect: Henry C. Trost; early modern, reminiscent of houses of Frank Lloyd Wright of era, by Tucson architect who once worked for Louis Sullivan; earlier modern house by same architect: ＊Goodrich House (1908; later alt. & addit.), 645 3rd St; now fraternity house. On ＊University of Arizona campus, interesting buildings include: oldest, ＊Old Main (1891; later alt. & addit.), great verandas; ＊Herring Hall (1903; later alt. & addit.), Eclectic Classic Revival.

Tucson Vicinity *(SE via US I-10 & 80)*. Approx. 70 mi, Tombstone, town famous for early history of gunfighters such as Wyatt Earp and Doc Holliday and for their fight with Clanton Gang at O.K. Corral. Interesting buildings include: in Hist. Dist., ＊Cochise Co. Courthouse (1882; later alt. & addit.); ＊Bird Cage Theater (1881); on outskirts of town: ＊Boot Hill Graveyard.

Tucson Vicinity *(S, via US I-19)*. Approx. 10 mi, via US I-19, St. 86 & Mission Rd, ●＊**Mission San Xavier del Bac** (1776–97; rest.), magnificent Spanish Baroque; considered one of finest of U.S.

**Mission San Xavier
del Bac—Spanish Baroque**
(Wayne Andrews)

buildings. Approx. 40 mi farther, *Mission San Jose (about 1815; part. rest.), Tumacacori Nat. Mon.

Tucson Vicinity *(W, via St. 86)*. Approx. 15 mi: *Old Tucson, replica of original town built for motion picture set. Of interest nearby: *Arizona–Sonora Desert Museum; *Saguaro Nat. Mon. Approx. 40 mi, via St. 86 & 386, *McMath Solar Telescope (1966), architects: Skidmore, Owings & Merrill; startling, abstract modern structure by famous firm.

New Mexico

Early inhabitants prehistoric ancestors of Indians believed to have lived here about 200 centuries ago or before; stone age spearheads, or Folsom points, dating back at least 100 centuries have been found in several places. Later pre-Columbian Indians included Anasazi, Mogollon, believed to have inhabited region from about 500 B.C. to A.D. 1300; numerous remains of structures of era have survived. Later Indian tribes included Pueblo, descendants of Anasazi; other tribes, including Apache, Comanche, Navaho, Ute, came here in early 16th century. First explored by Spaniard Núñez Cabeza de Vaca, about 1535; Spanish Father Marcos de Niza explored, 1539; claimed for Spain. In 1540–42, Spaniard Francisco Vásquez de Coronado explored; followed by other Spaniards, including Father Augustín Rodríguez and Capt. Francisco Sánchez Chamuscado, 1581. First Spanish colony, 1598: San Juan de Los Caballeros Pueblo; became capital. In 1610, capital moved to Santa Fe, now oldest governmental center in United States. Spanish established missions and schools for Indians; revolt by Indians, led by Popé, destroyed church, other property at San Juan Pueblo; many Spaniards killed, others driven away, 1680. Spanish Gov. Diego de Vargas regained control, 1692; after some renewed fighting, peace was restored. Region became province of Mexico after its independence from Spain, 1821. Period of turmoil followed, culminating in rebellion of Mexicans and Indians against government, 1837; led by Indian, José Gonzalez, rebels seized Santa Fe Palace of Governors and executed Mexican governor; revolt ended with victory of Mexican Gen. Manuel Armijo, who then became governor. Republic of Texas attempted to capture region, 1841, but defeated by Mexicans. Major portion of region ceded to United States at end of Mexican War, 1848; remainder in Gadsden Purchase, 1853. Made part of New Mexico Territory, 1850. In Civil War, forces from Texas captured much of region, but were driven out by Federal troops, 1862. Famous frontiersman Col. Kit Carson led successful efforts to keep Indians on reservations, 1862–64; unrest in state brought fighting involving various American factions, sometimes led by outlaws such as Billy the Kid. Gen. Lew Wallace, noted for his Civil War record as well as for being author of *Ben Hur,* appointed territorial governor, 1878; restored law and order by use of Federal troops and martial law. Threats from Indians ended with surrender of Apache Chief Geronimo, 1886. Became forty-seventh state, Jan. 6, 1912. Mexican bandit chief Francisco "Pancho" Villa raided various places in state, including Columbus, 1916, killing Americans and destroying property; chased back to Mexico by American troops led by Gen. John J. Pershing. Today: Major mining industry, especially oil and natural gas, potash, uranium, copper; also important agricultural industry, manufacturing, and tourism.

Land Regions: E to W, Great Plains; Rocky Mountains; Basin and Range Region; Colorado Plateau.

Climate: Dry, warm; day and night temperatures vary considerably; precipitation varies from almost none in S to moderate in N; snowfall almost none in S, very heavy in mountains.

Major Building Materials: Timber, mostly softwoods; copper; clay; gypsum; perlite; stone.

Architecture: Rich and varied, from pre-Columbian era to present, including some of finest U.S. examples, in several locations, especially Albuquerque vicinity; Santa Fe and vicinity.

ALBUQUERQUE

Interesting buildings include: *San Felipe de Neri Church (1706; later alt.), Old Town Plaza, adobe. Approx. 3 mi W of city, via St. 448, *La Luz Houses (1974), architect: Antoine Precock; fine modern adapted to SW climate, traditions; almost 100 attached houses of adobe. Approx. 75 mi SE of city, via US I-25 & 60 & St. 10, near MOUNTAINAIR, *Gran Quivira Nat. Mon. (c. 900–1700), interesting ruins of pueblos and churches. In extreme S part of state, approx. 220 mi S of Albuquerque, via US I-25: LAS CRUCES. *Mesilla Plaza (1848), interesting buildings of Mexican era. Approx. 100 mi NW of Las Cruces, via US 180, near SILVER CITY, interesting ruins of *Gila Cliff Dwellings Nat. Mon. (c. 1270–85). Approx. 140 mi NE of Las Cruces, via US 70: LINCOLN. Interesting well-preserved frontier cattle town, in *Lincoln Hist. Dist.

Albuquerque Vicinity *(W, via US I-40).* Approx. 45 mi: LAGUNA. *Mission Church of San José de la Laguna (1706; later alt.

Mission Church of San Estévan del Rey—Spanish Colonial (Wayne Andrews)

& addit.; rest.), small stuccoed example; also pueblo. Approx. 20 mi SW, St. 23: ÁCOMA. *Ácoma Pueblo (begun before 1500); believed to be oldest continuously occupied community in U.S.; spectacularly situated on top of rock mesa or butte. Nearby, ●*Mission Church of San Estévan del Rey** (1629–42; later alt. & addit.; rest.), Spanish Colonial adobe, stone and wood church; considered one of finest U.S. buildings. Other interesting pre-Columbian remains: approx. 70 mi W of Laguna, via US I-40 & St. 53, *El Morro Nat. Mon. Approx. 35 mi farther, via St. 53, *Zuni Pueblo. Approx. 115 mi NW of Laguna, via US I-40 & St. 57: *Chaco Canyon Nat. Mon.; large number of interesting pre-Columbian ruins include: ●**Pueblo Bonito** (c. 800–1200), magnifi-

Pueblo Bonito, Chaco Canyon—Pre-Columbian
(New Mexico Tourism and Travel Division)

cent sandstone complex; considered one of finest in U.S. Nearby, *Casa Rinconada (about 1150; rest.), fine Great Kiva; many other interesting sites here in area of about 15 square mi.

Albuquerque Vicinity *(NW, via St. 44)*. Approx. 165 mi: AZTEC. ●*Aztec Ruins Nat. Mon.,* *Pueblo (c. 1110–1250), ruins of sandstone complex of dwellings, storage rooms, some 30 kivas, or great rooms; reconst. *Great Kiva; believed, falsely, by early Spanish explorers and missionaries to have been constructed by Aztecs. Also see: Albuquerque Vicinity (W, via US I-40); Arizona—Flagstaff Vicinity (NE, via US I-89 & 160); Colorado—Mesa Verde Nat. Park; Utah—Hovenweep Nat. Mon.

SANTA FE

Founded 1610; second oldest, after St. Augustine, Fla., continuously inhabited city in U.S. settled by Europeans. Interesting buildings here include: *State Capitol, actually named Executive-Legislative Building (1966), De Vargas St; architect: W. C. Kruger; locally called "The Roundhouse" for its unusual shape. Not far: *Old State Capitol (1902; major alt. & addit. 1953), Galisteo & Montezuma sts; architect of dome: W. C. Kruger; Eclectic. Nearby, *Mission San Miguel (about 1640; burned by Indians and reconst., about 1680). Across Santa Fe River: *Santa Fe Plaza (1610). N, *Palace of the Governors (1612; later alt. & addit.; rest.), Spanish Colonial; adobe and *Vigas,* or tree trunks; oldest building constructed by Europeans in U.S.; now part of *Museum of New Mexico. Also of interest, adjacent *Hall of Ethnology. Across Plaza: *St. Francis Cathedral (begun 1869; never completed), architect: Archibishop Jean Baptiste Lamy, who was model for main character in famous author Willa Cather's novel *Death Comes for the Archbishop.* Just down Palace Ave, *Fine Arts Museum. Nearby, old buildings of *Barrio de Analco Hist. Dist. At 116 Lincoln Ave, *Hewett House (about 1865; later alt. & addit.), once officers' quarters at Ft. Marcy. On Upper Canyon Rd, *Randall Davey House (1847; later alt. & addit.), stone and adobe; originally U.S. Army sawmill; converted to house and studio, 1920, by artist Davey. Of interest, SE side of city, via Old Santa Fe Trail: *Museum of Navajo Ceremonial Art; *Museum of International Folk Art. SW of city, via Cerrillos Rd, US 85, at Teseuque Dr: *Institute of American Indian Arts, *Outdoor Theater (1970), architect: Paolo Soleri; assoc. architects: Pacheco & Graham; fascinating modern building, reminiscent of ancient structures of Mediterranean area; by Italian-American architect considered talented but controversial designer. Also: NW of city, near LOS ALAMOS, cliff dwellings and ruins of pueblos in *Bandelier Nat. Mon. (c. 1220–1500). Approx. 20 mi SE, via US I-25: PECOS. *Pecos Nat. Mon. (begun about 1300), interesting ruins of pueblos, church, convent and rest. kiva.

Taos Pueblo—Pre-Columbian (New Mexico Tourism and Travel Division)

Santa Fe Vicinity *(N, via US 84/285).* Approx. 5 mi: *Santa Fe Opera House (1967), architects: McHugh & Kidder; fine modern example, partially roofed, partially open to sky. Approx. 20 mi father, via US 84/285 & St. 4W: SAN ILDEFONSO. *San Ildefonso Pueblo (begun about 1300), interesting village of about 200 people. Few miles E, via St. 4E: CHIMAYO. *Plaza de Cerro (about 1730), interesting fortified village, last surviving in state; *El Santuario de Chimayo (1816; later alt. & addit.), small church privately constructed by Spanish settlers to give thanks. Also nearby: other pueblos; *Puye Cliff Dwellings. Approx. 8 mi farther, via US 285 & St. 76: LAS TRAMPAS. *San José de Gracia Church (about 1775; rest.), Village Plaza; small adobe church in small village. Approx. 35 mi farther, via St. 68: TAOS. Interesting buildings include: *Ernest L. Blumenchein House (18th century; later

Mission Church of San Francisco de Asís—Spanish Colonial
(New Mexico Tourism and Travel Division)

alt. & addit.), Ledoux St; once home of one of founders of Taos Art Colony. Also of interest nearby, artists' studios, galleries. On Old Kit Carson Rd, *Kit Carson House (1825; later alt. & addit.), adobe with fine patio; once home of famous scout, trader, trapper. Approx. 3 mi N, via Pueblo Rd, ●●*Taos Pueblo (begun about 1300), famous early village; still inhabited. Approx. 5 mi S of Taos, via St. 3, *Ranchos De Taos, location of: ●●*Mission Church of San Francisco de Asís (about 1813; later alt.), magnificent sculptural adobe church; favorite of painters and photographers for many years; considered one of finest of U.S. buildings.

Oklahoma

Early inhabitants Indians, including Arapaho, Cheyenne, Comanche, Pawnee, Wichita. First explored by Spaniards Franciso Vásquez de Coronado and Hernando de Soto, 1841. Explored by Frenchman Robert Cavelier, Sieur de La Salle, 1682; claimed for France. Ceded to Spain, 1762; back to France, 1800; sold to United States in Louisiana Purchase, 1803. Became part of Louisiana Territory, 1805; of Missouri Territory, 1812. Largest portion became part of Arkansas Territory, 1819, remainder ceded to Spain. Between 1820 and 1842, many Indians were moved from their homelands to territory via route called by Cherokees and Choctaws the "Trail of Tears"; Indians had rights to entire region except Panhandle. During Civil War, some Indians fought for Union, others for South, including Cherokees, one of whom, Stand Watie, became Confederate brig. general. After end of war, Indians forced to give up much of their land to settlers. U.S. government was urged to open land by people who came to be called "boomers"; other people who rushed in early to make claims became known as "sooners." Became Territory of Oklahoma, 1890. Together with small remaining Indian Territory, became forty-sixth state, Nov. 16, 1907. Today: Major mining, especially oil and natural gas, manufacturing, agricultural industries.

Land Regions: In N portion from E to W, Ozark Plateau; Sandstone Hills; Red Beds Plains; Gypsum Hills; High Plains; in S portion, E to W, Ouachita Mountains and Red River Regions; Arbuckle Mountains; Sandstone Hills; Red Beds Plains; Wichita Mountains; Gypsum Hills.

Climate: Warm, dry, NW cooler and drier than SE; precipitation minimal in SE, moderate in NW; snowfall moderate, more in Panhandle.

Major Building Materials: Timber, mostly softwoods; lead; zinc; clay; granite; limestone; sand and gravel.

Architecture: Interesting buildings in several locations, though not in great numbers.

OKLAHOMA CITY

Interesting buildings include: *State Capitol (1917; later alt. & addit.), Lincoln Blvd & 23rd St; architect: Solomon A. Layton; Eclectic Classic Revival by respected native architect; unlike most state capitols, this one has no dome and is surrounded by oil wells; by same architect: *Oklahoma Publishing Co. Building (1909), 500 N. Broadway. At 400 W. Sheriden St, *Oklahoma Theater Center, formerly New Mummers Theater (1970), architect: John M. Johansen; supervising architects: Seminoff, Bowman & Bode; fascinating fine modern complex by noted architect; main and arena theaters and administrative area.

Oklahoma City Vicinity *(N, via US I-35 or 77).* Approx. 14 mi: EDMOND. *Hopewell Baptist Church (1953), architect: Bruce Goff; very fine modern example by extremely talented, but controversial architect. Approx. 16 mi farther, GUTHRIE, first territorial capital, 1890–1907, and first state capital, 1907–10. Interesting buildings include: in Hist. Dist., *Scottish Rite Temple (1922), Oklahoma Ave; architects: Hawk & Parr; imposing Eclectic Greek Revival; believed to be largest fraternal order building in world. Approx. 35 mi E, via US 40: SHAWNEE. *Santa Fe Railroad Station (1903), E. Main St; sandstone Romanesque Revival with tower; resembles castle. Approx. 30 mi W of Oklahoma City , via St. 33: KINGFISHER. *Gov. Abraham Jefferson Seay Mansion (1892; rest.), Overstreet & 11th St; Classic Revival; once home of second territorial governor. Approx. 68 mi NW of Kingfisher, via US 81 & 60: CLEO SPRINGS. Approx. 5 mi N, via St. 8, *Homesteader's Sod House, also known as Marshall McCully House (1894; rest.), only original "soddy" in state; walls 3 feet thick.

Oklahoma City Vicinity *(S, via US I-35).* Approx. 18 mi: NORMAN. ●*Bavinger House (1955), N.E. 60th St; architect: Bruce Goff; spectacular private modern house by controversial architect who taught for many years at University of Oklahoma here and who designed many fine houses in state. Approx. 65 mi SW, via US I-35 & St. 19: LINDSAY. *Erin Springs, also known as Murray-Lindsay Mansion (1880; rest.), once ranch home of Irish immigrant Frank Murray and his Choctaw wife.

Oklahoma City Vicinity *(SW, via US 62).* Approx. 55 mi: ANARDARKO. *Indian City, USA, interesting early Indian shelters, reconst. under supervision of University of Oklahoma Anthropology Dept., include: Pawnee earth house; Plains Indian tepee; Chiri-cahua-Apache wickiup; Wichita grass house; Caddo wattle and daub (log and clay, with straw) house. Approx. 35 mi farther: LAWTON. Interesting buildings include, at *Ft. Sill, famous U.S. Army Artillery base, founded by Gen. Philip H. Sheriden, 1869; *Old Chapel (1870); *Old Corral (1870); *Commandant's Quarters (1871). Approx. 7 mi W, via US 62: CACHE. *Quanah Parker's Star House (1884; rest.), Eagle Park, Wichita Mountains Hwy; named for large stars painted on roof; once home of last chief of Choctaws; moved here with other early buildings.

TULSA

Interesting buildings include: *Boston Avenue United Methodist Church (1929; later alt. & addit.), S. Boston Ave & 13th St; architects: Rush, Endacott & Rush; architects, 1965 addit.: McCune & McCune; fine early modern example, slightly Art Deco, slightly Gothic Revival; believed to have been designed by Bruce Goff with aid of artist Adah Robinson. Also of interest: pedestrian malls (1978), architects: Hudgins, Thompson & Ball. Approx. 45 mi N, via US 75: BARTLESVILLE. **•*H. C. Price Tower** (1955), E. 6th St & S. Dewey Ave; architect: Frank Lloyd Wright; very fine modern skyscraper, only one by famous architect; contains apartments and offices; interesting ornamental exterior. Approx. 40 mi NE of Tulsa, via US 169: OOLOGAH. Nearby, *Will Rogers Birthplace (1875), Will Rogers Park; once home of famous humorist; moved here; also of interest, approx. 15 mi S, CLAREMORE, *Will Rogers Memorial.

Tulsa Vicinity *(SE, via Muskogee Pkwy)*. Approx. 50 mi: MUS-KOGEE. *Foreman House (1898), 1419 W. Okmulgee St; once home of Grant and Carolyn Thomas Foreman, noted historians, writers. Approx. 5 mi farther, via US 62: FT. GIBSON. *Old Ft. Gibson reconst. early stockaded log fort (1824–57); ruins of later stone fort (1866–89). Approx. 20 mi farther, via US 62: TAHLE-QUAH. Nearby, *George Murrell House (1844), once home of noted Cherokee leader; not far: *Tsa-La-Gi, reconst. Cherokee village. Approx. 50 mi SE of Tahlequah, via St. 82 & US I-40: SALLISAW. Nearby, off St. 101, *Sequoyah House (1829), one-room log cabin; home of famous inventor of Cherokee alphabet.

Tulsa Vicinity *(W, via Cimarron Tpk or US 64)*. Approx. 55 mi: PAWNEE. *Pawnee Bill Mansion (1910), Blue Hawk Peak; once home of Gordon W. Lillie who, as Pawnee Bill, led Wild West Circus; on grounds: log cabin built by Lillie. Approx. 18 mi S, via St. 18 & 51: YALE. *Jim Thorpe House (1916; rest.), once home of famous Indian athlete. Approx. 50 mi NW of Pawnee, via US 64 & 177: PONCA CITY. *E. W. Marland House, now Indian Museum (1916), 1000 E. Grand Ave; once home of oil millionaire, tenth governor of state.

Texas

Early inhabitants Indians of many tribes, including Caddo, Apache, Comanche. First explorer believed to have been Spaniard Alonso Alvarez de Pinĕda, 1519; followed by Spaniards Alvar Núñez Cabeza de Vaca, 1528, Francisco Vásquez de Coronado, 1540, members of Hernando de Soto expedition, 1542, after he died. Claimed by Spain. First missions built by Franciscans, near present-day El Paso, 1683. Frenchman Robert Cavelier, Sieur de La Salle explored, 1685; established Ft. St. Louis; killed by his own men, 1687; fort destroyed by Indians; Spanish forces, led by Alonso de León, sent to destroy fort arrived too late; Spanish sent almost 100 expeditions into region and established number of missions and forts, including Ft. San Antonio Bexar and San Antonio de Valero Mission, at present iocation of San Antonio. Freed from Spain, 1821, Empire, and later Republic, of Mexico included Texas. Mexicans allowed Americans, led by Stephen C. Austin, to establish colonies at Washington, Columbus, San Felipe; afterward, many Americans came to Texas. Mexican Gen. Antonio López de Santa Anna overthrew government, 1834; Americans in Texas revolted, 1835; Texans, led by Col. Benjamin Milam, took San Antonio, late same year. For about two weeks, 1836, Americans defended Alamo, but all, including William Travis, Jim Bowie and Davy Crockett, were killed; Declaration of Independence issued, Mar. 2, 1863, creating Republic of Texas; David G. Burnet named provisional president, Sam Houston, commander of army. On Mar. 27, Santa Anna had about 330 prisoners from other battles shot. On April 21, forces of Sam Houston almost destroyed army of Santa Anna in Battle of San Jacinto; Sam Houston elected first president. After ten years of independence, became twenty-eighth state, Dec. 29, 1845. Seceded from Union, 1861; Sam Houston refused Confederate oath of office and was ousted. Federal forces blockaded coast and occupied Galveston for time; last battle of Civil War fought at Palmito Hill, May 13, 1865; word had not arrived of end of war, April 9. Today: Major manufacturing, agricultural and mining, especially oil, industries.

Land Regions: E to W, West Gulf Coastal Plain; North Central Plains; Great Plains; Basin and Range Region.

Climate: Great differences, from subtropical, warm and humid in extreme S to moderate in NW; precipitation ranges from fairly heavy in E to very light in W; snowfall fairly heavy in High Plains to almost none in central and southern areas.

Major Building Materials: Timber; copper; limestone; gypsum; sand and gravel; clay; asphalt.

Architecture: Rich and varied from early Spanish Colonial era to present, especially in Austin and vicinity; Dallas and Fort Worth and vicinity; Galveston; San Antonio and vicinity.

AUSTIN

Interesting buildings include: *State Capitol (1888), Congress St; architect: Elijah E. Myers; very large pink granite Eclectic Classic Revival; very large dome. Not far: *Old Land Office Building (1857; later alt. & addit.), 108 E. 11th St; architect: Conrad C. Stremme; Gothic Revival with Romanesque Revival details; now museum. Not far: *Governor's Mansion (1855), Colorado & 11th sts; architect: Abner Cook; fine Greek Revival. At 802 San Marcos St, *Old French Legation (1841; rest.), French Colonial; only surviving Republic of Texas era embassy; probably oldest building in city. At 409 E. 5th St, *O. Henry Museum (1886), famous author William Sydney Porter, who wrote under name of O. Henry, lived here for year, 1893–94, while working as draftsman in Land Office. At 708 San Antonio St, *North-Evans House (1874), Victorian. At 1511 Colorado St, *L. Davis Carrington House (about 1850; rest.), Victorian; once home of land speculator. At 24th St & Whitis Ave, *Maj. George W. Littlefield House (1894), once home of banker, cattleman. At 2310 San Gabriel St, *Neill-Cochran House (1853; rest.), architect: Abner Cook; fine Greek Revival; fine antique furnishings. Also: *Bremond Block Hist. Dist., six private late 19th-century houses in various Eclectic styles. W of downtown, in Zelker Park, 2220 Barton Springs Rd, *Swedish Pioneer Cabin (about 1840), cedar log example; moved here. Two other early log cabins (about 1855) moved approx. 50 mi NW of city, via US 183 & St. 29 to, BURNET, in rest. *Ft. Croghan.

Austin Vicinity *(NE, via US I-35)*. Approx. 10 mi: ROUND ROCK. Nearby, via US 79, *El Milagro Museum (1859; rest.). Approx. 35 mi farther: SALADO. *Col. Sterling C. Robertson House (about 1856; later alt. & addit.), one of few surviving early ranches still in operation; interesting outbuildings include: slave cabins, stables; on Old Chisholm Trail, over which Texas cattle were driven to Kansas markets. Not far: *Shady Villa, originally stagecoach station, inn on Trail.

Austin Vicinity *(E, via St. 71)*. Approx. 26 mi: BASTROP. Joseph Pugh Wilbarger House (1842), 1403 Main St; originally home of man who lived after scalping by Indians. Approx. 55 mi farther: ROUND TOP. Interesting buildings include number built by 19th-century German immigrants. Approx. 4 mi E, *Winedale Stagecoach Inn (1834; later alt. & addit.; rest.); Hist. Center; on grounds: other interesting rest. buildings. Approx. 15 mi S of Round Top, via St. 237: LA GRANGE. Interesting buildings in

*Monument Hill State Hist. Site: *Nathaniel W. Faison House (about 1845; rest.), 822 S. Jefferson St; once home of participant in 1842 battle against Mexican troops; *Max Aue Stagecoach Inn, with stone *Stagehouse (1878); log former *Stagehouse (about 1855); stone *Aue House (about 1853), all built by German immigrant.

Austin Vicinity *(SW, via US I-35).* Approx. 30 mi: SAN MARCOS. *Texana Village, Aquarena Springs; rest. and reconst. early buildings include: houses, gristmill, jail, others. Approx. 15 mi farther, NEW BRAUNFELS, founded 1845 by German immigrants led by Prince Carl zu Solms-Braunfels. Interesting buildings here include: *fachwerk,* or half-timber construction *Ferdinand Lindheimer House (about 1852; rest.), 491 S. Comal St; fine example; originally home of noted botanist, journalist. *Ervendburg *Waisenhaus,* or orphanage, also known as West Texas Orphan Asylum (1850), Ervendburg St; half-timber, adobe; first orphanage in state; built for children of cholera victims. Approx. 10 mi NW of New Braunfels, via St. 32 & 12: WIMBERLEY. *Pioneer Town, 7-A Ranch Resort; buildings include: *Adolph Schlameus House (1854), two log cabins with dogtrot, or breezeway.

Austin Vicinity *(W, via US 290).* Approx. 50 mi: JOHNSON CITY. *Lyndon B. Johnson Boyhood Home (1896), 9th St & Ave G, once home of president. Approx. 15 mi farther: STONEWALL. Nearby, via Park Rte 49, LBJ Ranch, *Lyndon B. Johnson Birthplace (about 1900; reconst.). Approx. 15 mi farther, FREDERICKSBURG, founded by German immigrants, 1846. Interesting buildings include: in Hist. Dist., *Heinrich Kammler House (1849; later alt. & addit.) and *Country Store (about 1850), now known as Pioneer Museum, 309 W. Main St; *Old St. Mary's Roman Catholic Church (1863), N. Orange & San Antonio sts.

DALLAS

DOWNTOWN

*John F. Kennedy Memorial (1970), bet. Main, Market, Elm & Record sts; architect: Philip Johnson; simple modern memorial to president near where he was fatally shot, 1963. Nearby, *John Neely Bryan Cabin (1843; rest.), log home of founder of city; also served as post office and courthouse; moved here. Not far: *Dallas Co. Courthouse (1892; later alt. & addit.; remod. 1966), architects: Orlopp & Kusener; architect, remod.: Moffatt D. Adams; Romanesque Revival; original tower removed 1919. Not far, at Stemmons Frwy & Reunion Blvd, *Hyatt Regency Hotel and Reunion Tower (1978), architects: Welton Becket Assoc.; fascinating modern glass-sheathed hotel with atrium; 565-foot tower alongside with revolving restaurant, lounge and observation deck on top; connected with complex: *Union Railroad Station (1916; remod.

1978), architect: Jarvis Hunt; now shops, other facilities. Nearby, *Reunion Arena (1980), architect: Harwood K. Smith. At Main & Griffin sts, ●*One Main Place (1968), architects: Skidmore, Owings & Merrill; assoc. architect: Harwood K. Smith; fine high-rise building by famous firm. Not far: *Dallas City Hall (1978), Young bet. Akard & Ervay sts; architect: I. M. Pei; assoc. architects: Harper & Kemp; unusual modern building with front inclined outward toward top; sculpture *The Dallas Piece* by famous sculptor Henry Moore. Not far: *Thanks-Giving Square (1977), Pacific & Ervay sts; architects: Philip Johnson & John Burgee; small modern park; garden; water channels, pool; helical interdenominational chapel. In *City Park, 1717 Gano St, old buildings moved here include: log *Miller Cabin (1847; rest.); Greek Revival *Millermore House (1862; rest.); once homes of prospector William Miller; *Morehead-Gano Log House (about 1847; rest.).

N OF DOWNTOWN AREA

At 3636 Turtle Creek Rd, ●*Kalita Humphreys Theater (1959), Dallas Theater Center; architect: Frank Lloyd Wright; fine modern theater, his first, by famous architect. At Hillcrest Rd & Northwest Hwy, *Temple Emanu-El (1956), architects: Howard E. Meyer & Max M. Sandfield; consult. architect: William W. Wurster; interesting modern synagogue, cylindrical in form with dome. Just NW of downtown business dist., at 2710 Stemmons Frwy, *Stemmons Towers (1967), architect: Harold A. Berry; four interesting modern office buildings. Nearby, at Stemmons Frwy & Mockingbird Lane, *Brookhollow Plaza (1970), architects: Paul Rudolph & Harwood K. Smith; another interesting modern office tower, first of planned four. Approx. 20 mi NW of Dallas (approx. 25 mi NE of Fort Worth), via St. 183, *Dallas-Fort Worth Regional Airport (1973), architects: Hellmuth, Obata & Kassabaum; assoc. architects: Brodsky, Hopf & Adler; gargantuan, almost 4-mile-long airport terminal; considered among finest of very large examples. Also in Dallas: many fine modern houses, all private, by famous architects. Approx. 60 mi N of Dallas, via US 75: DENNISON. *Dwight D. Eisenhower Birthplace (about 1880; rest.), Lamar & Day sts; once home of general, president.

Dallas Vicinity *(SE, via US I-20 or 80).* Approx. 100 mi: TYLER. *Goodman House (1859; later alt. & addit.), 624 N. Broadway; Classic Revival. Approx. 35 mi SE of Tyler, via St. 64: HENDERSON. *Howard-Dickinson House (1855; later alt. & addit.; rest.), S. Main St; of hand-made mud bricks by Howard brothers who later invented brick-making machine. *Michael Kangerga House (1901; later alt. & addit.), N. High St & Webster Walk; architect: George F. Barker; originally home of Croatian merchant. Approx. 55 mi NE of Henderson, via St. 43 & US 59: JEFFERSON. Interesting buildings include, mostly in Hist. Dist.: *The Old Manse, originally Gen. James H. Rogers House (about 1840; rest.), 411 E. Delta St; once home of officer under Sam Houston in war for independence from Mexico. *U.S. Courthouse & Post Office (1890; later alt. & addit.; rest.), 224 Austin St; architect; Will A. Freret; Romanesque Revival; now museum. *Excelsior Hotel (about 1859; later alt. & addit.; rest.), Austin St; wood-frame, brick hotel continuously in operation. House of the Seasons, the Benajmin H. Epperson House (about 1872), 409 S. Alley St; interesting Italianate; cupola. Approx. 25 mi SE of Henderson, via US 259 & 84: MT. ENTERPRISE. *Dr. William MacDonald Ross House (1845; later alt. & addit.), once home of pioneer doctor who was also sheriff, surveyor, member of state legislature. Approx. 25 mi S of Mt. Enterprise, via US 84 & 259: NACOGDO-CHES. *Hoya Mem. Library and Museum, originally Adolphus Sterne House (about 1828; later alt. & addit.), 211 S. La Nana St; once home of *alcalde,* or mayor, of town under Mexican rule, later member of Republic of Texas, state legislatures. Approx. 15 mi E of Nacogdoches, via St. 21: CHIRENO. *Halfway House, the James B. Johnson House (about 1835), built by slaves; once stage-coach inn halfway bet. Nacogdoches and next town on Camino Real, SAN AUGUSTINE. Interesting buildings include: *Ezekiel Cullen House (1839; later alt. & addit.), 205 S. Congress St. Approx. 2 mi W, *William Garrett Plantation (1864; rest.).

Dallas Vicinity *(S, via US I-35E).* Approx. 25 mi: WAXAHAT-CHIE. *Ellis Co. Courthouse (1897), Main St; architect: J. Reily Gordon; interesting Romanesque Revival with tower. Approx. 35 mi farther: HILLSBORO. *Hill Co. Courthouse (1891), Courthouse Sq; architect: W. C. Dodson.

EL PASO

Westernmost city in state; across Rio Grande from Ciudad Juárez, Mexico. At *Ft. Bliss, replica of original adobe fort (1848). SE of city, via US I-10, old Camino Real; oldest missions in state include: *Mission Nuestra Señora del Carmen, originally Mission Corpus Christi de la Ysleta del Sur (1683; part. burned 1906); *Mission de la Purísima Concepción (mid-17th century). Also: *Mission Nuestra del Socorro (1848). Approx. 225 mi SE of El Paso, via US I-10 & St. 17, *FT. DAVIS, Nat. Hist. Site, named for Jefferson Davis, then U.S. secretary of war. Approx. 50 rest. buildings, mostly adobe, include: *Hospital (1875; later alt. & addit.; rest.); *Quarters (1886; rest.); first use of camels by U.S. Army here, shortly before Civil War. Nearby, *Trueheart, the Neill Museum (1899), collection of antique toys and dolls.

FORT WORTH

Interesting buildings include: ●*Amon Carter Museum (1961; addit. 1978), 3501 Camp Bowie Blvd; architect: Philip Johnson; ar-

Kimbell Art Museum—Modern (Kimbell Art Museum, Bob Wharton)

chitects, addit.: Philip Johnson & John Burgee; very fine modern art museum by famous architect; unequalled collections of western art include works of Charles M. Russell and Frederic Remington. Nearby, ••**Kimbell Art Museum** (1972), Will Rogers Rd bet. Camp Bowie Blvd & W. Lancaster Rd; architect: Louis I. Kahn; very fine modern vaulted building by famous architect; fine landscaping, terraces, pool; considered one of finest U.S. buildings and one of its architect's finest designs. Bet. 12th, Commerce, Lancaster & Houston sts, *Water Garden (1974); architects: Philip Johnson & John Burgee; fascinating modern sunken complex of terraces, gardens, water in every form imaginable—quiet pools, fountains, waterfalls, cascades. In *Forest Park, 2121 Colonial Pkwy, *Log Cabin Village, seven rest. examples, oldest built in 1832, latest in 1870. Approx. 15 mi W of city, via US 180: WEATHERFORD. *Parker Co. Courthouse (1886), architects: W. C. Dodson & W. W. Dudley. Approx. 40 mi NW of Fort Worth, via US 81/287: DECATUR. *Wise Co. Courthouse (1895), architect: J. Reily Gordon. Nearby, *Old Stone Prison (about 1859), built by prisoners.

GALVESTON

Wonderful old town on Galveston Island, bet. Galveston Bay & Gulf of Mexico; thought to be first landing place in state of Spanish explorer Cabeza de Vaca, 1728. Interesting buildings include: *Trinity Church (1857; raised with jacks, 1925), 700 Kempner St; architect: John de Young; Gothic Revival; second Episcopal church in state. Next door, *Eaton Memorial Chapel (1882), architects: Clayton & Lynch; named for Rev. Benjamin Eaton, Irish immigrant who organized chapel and was first rector here. Nearby, *U.S. Courthouse & Federal Building, originally U.S. Post Office & Custom House (1861; later alt. & addit.; rest.), 1927 Post Office St; fine Greek Revival. Few blocks away: *Henry A.

Landes House (1887), 1604 Post Office St; architect: George E. Dickey; of pressed brick. Few blocks away: Mrs. John L. Darragh House (1888), 519 15th St; architect: Alfred Muller; assoc. architect: Nicholas J. Clayton; wood-frame; octagonal tower, fine iron fence. Few blocks away: *Ashbel Smith Hall, also known as "Old Red" (1891; later alt. & addit.), *Medical College of University of Texas, 913 The Strand; architect: Nicholas J. Clayton; Romanesque Revival by first professional architect in state; also interesting houses in *The Strand Hist. Dist. Approx. 10 blocks away, at 1402 Broadway, ●*Bishop's Palace, originally the Col. Walter Gresham House (1893), architect: Nicholas J. Clayton; extravagant Eclectic Victorian; considered its architect's masterpiece and finest building in city; once home of noted attorney; later official residence of Roman Catholic Bishop of Diocese of Galveston. Nearby, Sydnor-Heidenheimer House (1855; alt. & addit. 1885), 1604 Sealy St; architect, alt. & addit.: Nicholas J. Clayton; very large house remod. into Gothic Revival. Not far: J. Sonnenthiel House (1887), 1826 Sealy St; Victorian Gothic Revival. Not far: *Ashton Villa, the Col. James Mareau Brown House (1859; later alt. & addit.; rest.), 2328 Broadway; ornamental Italianate most probably designed by first owner. Not far: Open Gates, the George Sealy House (1891), 2424 Broadway; architects: McKim, Mead & White; assoc. architect: Nicholas J. Clayton; imposing house by famous architects; of Roman brick imported from Belgium. On grounds: Stable (1891), architect: Clayton. Not far: *Ursuline Convent (1858; later alt. & addit.), Ave N & 25th St; architect: John de Young; stuccoed brick; hospital during Civil War, survived shellfire; later building (1894) by Nicholas J. Clayton demolished. Few blocks away: *Samuel May Williams House (1840), 3601 Ave. P; vaguely Greek Revival, French Colonial; part. pine prefabricated in Maine; originally home of land agent for Stephen Austin.

HOUSTON

DOWNTOWN

*Church of the Annunciation, Roman Catholic (1871; later alt. & addit.), 1618 Texas Ave, architect, alt. & addit.: Nicholas J. Clayton; Romanesque Revival by noted architect. *Christ Church Cathedral, Episcopal (1893; renov. 1938), 1111 Texas Ave; architect: Silas McBee; assoc. architect: J. A. Tempest; architect, renov.: Carl A. Mulvey; assoc. architect: William Ward Watkin; interesting Gothic Revival. Not far: *Harris Co. Courthouse (1911), 300 San Jacinto St; architects: Lang & Winchell; large Eclectic Classic Revival with dome. Not far: *Houston Cotton Exchange & Board of Trade (1885; later alt. & addit.; rest.), 202 Travis St; architect: Eugene T. Heiner; architect, rest.: Graham B. Luhn; Italianate. Not far: *Kennedy Trading Post (1848), 813 Congress Ave; oldest building in city; built by Indian trader. Few blocks away, in *Oscar Holcombe Civic Center, *Alley Theater (1968), 615 Texas Ave; architect: Ulrich Franzen; assoc. architects: MacKie & Kamrath; fine modern example, actually two interconnected separate theaters. *Jesse H. Jones Hall (1966), 615 Louisiana St; architects: Caudill, Rowlett & Scott; very large fine modern building, home of Houston Symphony; also used for ballet, opera, other performances. Nearby, another large modern building by same architects, *Albert Thomas Convention Exhibition Center (1968), 612 Smith St; includes *National Space Hall of Fame. Also: *Sam Houston Coliseum & Music Hall (1937), 810 Bagby St; architect: Alfred C. Finn. Nearby, bet. Louisiana, Capitol, Milan & Rusk sts, •*Pennzoil Plaza (1976), architects: Philip Johnson & John Burgee; assoc. architect: S. I. Morris; very fine modern glass enclosed twin office towers by famous architect; striking angular walls and roofs. Not far: •*Tenneco Building (1963), 1010 Milam St; architects: Skidmore, Owings & Merrill; very fine modern office tower by famous firm; very fine details include horizontal sun shields. Few blocks away, in *Sam Houston Park, 1100 Bagby St, early buildings; all moved here from original locations in county except *Kellum-Noble House (1847; rest.), fine brick Southern Colonial; galleries reminiscent of Louisiana plantation houses; other buildings include: *Old Place (1824; rest.), one-room cabin; believed to be oldest house in county; *San Felipe Cottage (about 1840; rest.); Greek Revival *Nichols-Rice-Cherry House (about 1850; rest.); Victorian *Pillot House (1868; rest.).

SW OF DOWNTOWN
Interesting buildings include: *Museum of Fine Arts (1924; addit. 1926; 1953; 1958; 1973), 1001 Bissonet Ave; architect, 1924 & 1926: William Ward Atkin; assoc. architects: Cram & Ferguson; architects of addit.: 1953 (Blaffer Wing), Kenneth Franzheim; assoc. architect: Higford Griffith; 1958 (Cullinan Hall), Ludwig Mies van der Rohe; assoc. architects: Staub, Rather & Howze; 1973 (Brown Pavilion): Mies van der Rohe; combination of Eclectic Classic Revival portions, very fine modern later portions by famous German-American architect. Nearby,
•*Contemporary Arts Museum (1972), 5210 Montrose Blvd; architect: Gunnar Birkerts; very fine modern example by noted architect; unusual stainless steel walls. Also of interest in SW: *Astrodome (1965), South Loop W; architects: Wilson, Morris, Crain & Anderson; assoc. architects: Lloyd, Morgan & Jones.

W OF DOWNTOWN, MONTROSE AREA
At Montrose Ave & W. Alabama St, *University of St. Thomas; master planner: Philip Johnson; fine modern buildings by Johnson. Work of other noted architects include: •*Rothko Chapel (1971), architects: Howard Barnstone & Eugene Aubry; very fine, small modern chapel by noted architect; dedicated to famous painter Mark Rothko; contains several large paintings by him; in reflect-

ing pool, sculpture *Broken Obelisk* by famous sculptor Barnett Newman. Farther W, in City Post Oak area, *The Galleria (1969–73), Westheimer & Post Oak rds; architects: Hellmuth, Obata & Kassabaum; assoc. architects: Neuhaus & Taylor; mammoth, still unfinished modern enclosed shopping center with more than 200 stores and 2 large hotels. Nearby, interesting high-rise buildings by these noted architects and others, include Skidmore, Owings & Merrill; I. M. Pei; Philip Johnson & John Burgee. Also of interest, SE of city: *Lyndon B. Johnson Space Center. Approx. 70 mi SW of Houston, via US 59 & Co. Rd, WEST COLUMBIA, capital of Republic of Texas. Approx. 2 mi N, *Varner-Hogg Plantation House (about 1835; later alt. & addit.; rest.), on original land grant of Stephen Austin's first colony; later home of Gov. James Hogg.

Houston Vicinity *(NE, via US 59)*. Approx. 75 mi: LIVINGSTON. Approx. 15 mi E, via US 190, on *Alabama-Coushatta Indian Reservation, *Living Indian Village, 19th-century village replica. Approx. 15 mi farther: WOODVILLE. *Heritage Garden Village, twenty-seven 19th-century buildings; authentic furnishings.

Houston Vicinity *(NW, via US I-45)*. Approx. 75 mi: HUNTSVILLE. At *Sam Houston University, *Wigwam (about 1840; later alt. & addit.), home of Sam Houston, famous Texas patriot, president of Republic of Texas, state governor; on grounds: other buildings, including *Steamboat House (1858), built by Houston to resemble Mississippi riverboat; he died here; grave short distance away. Approx. 50 mi SW of Huntsville, via St. 149, 105 & 6: WASHINGTON. *Barrington, the Dr. Anson Jones House (1844), once home of last president of Republic of Texas; on grounds: replica of blacksmith shop in which Texas Declaration of Independence was signed.

SAN ANTONIO

Fascinating old city retains much of charm of its Spanish and Mexican past. Location of largest military establishment in U.S., including *Ft. Sam Houston; *Kelly Air Force Base; *Lackland Air Force Base; *Randolph Air Force Base; *Brooks Aero Medical Center.

DOWNTOWN

Interesting buildings include: *The Alamo (1744–77; part. rest.), Alamo Plaza; official name Mission San Antonio de Valero; venerated as location of valiant stand against siege of Mexican Gen. Santa Anna, 1836, in which all defenders, including William B. Travis, Jim Bowie, Davy Crockett, were killed. Also of interest nearby, *Alamo Museum and Theater. *Paseo del Rio, or river walk, along San Antonio River, lined with interesting shops, restaurants, other facilities, fine landscaping. Nearby, on Villita St bet. S. Presa & S. Alamo sts, *La Villita, rest. early part of city with interesting adobe shops, art galleries, other buildings including: *Casa Villita, the Col. Jeremiah Y. Dashiell House (about 1850; rest.), 511 Villita St: Not far, on HemisFair Grounds, *Tower of the Americas (1968), architects: Ford, Powell & Carson; soaring 652-foot tower was symbol of fair; on top: revolving restaurant, stationary restaurant, observation deck. At Main Plaza, *San Fernando Cathedral, Roman Catholic (1859–73), architect: Francis Giraud; Gothic Revival; incorporates portions of older church (1734–49). Nearby, *Bexar Co. Courthouse (1896), 20 Dolorosa St; architect: James Reily Gordon; Romanesque Revival with towers. At Military Plaza, *Spanish Governor's Palace (1722–49; rest.), architect, rest.: Harvey P. Smith; impressive ten-room adobe residence of Spanish governors until 1821.

NORTH OF DOWNTOWN

*San Antonio Museum of Art, originally Lone Star Brewery (1904; remod. 1981), 200 W. Jones Ave; architect: E. Jungerfield; assoc. architects: Wahrenberger & Beckman; architects, remod. Cambridge Seven; interesting Romanesque Revival converted to museum. In *Brackenridge Park, *Witte Mem. Museum, 3801 Broadway; *Celso Navarro House (1835; rest.); *John Twohig House (1841; rest.); both limestone; both moved here. Also of interest in park: *Sunken Gardens; *San Antonio Zoo; at *Trinity University, modern *Ruth Taylor Theater (1966); *Lowrie Auditorium and Communications Center (1971); architects: Ford, Powell & Carson; Bartlett Cocke.

SOUTH OF DOWNTOWN

At S. Flores & Arsenal sts, *U.S. Arsenal (begun 1858), oldest military facility in city, now used mostly for offices; on grounds: *Office Building (1860); *Magazine (1868); Commanding Officer's Quarters (1886). Not far: interesting early houses include, at 228 S. Laredo St, in José Antonio Navarro State Hist. Dist., complex of three houses (1850; rest.), once home of patriot who with his uncle Francisco Ruiz were only native Texans to sign Texas Declaration of Independence. At 257 Yellowstone St, *Yturri-Edmunds House (about 1729; rest.); nearby, early mill. In *King William State Hist. Dist., *Edward Steves House (1876), 509 King William St; architect: Alfred Giles; fine Victorian House in grove of pecan trees on bank of San Antonio River; fine formal gardens.

In addition to Alamo, four other fine missions S of city, via Mission Rd: *Mission Concepción (1731–55), 807 Mission Rd; properly named Mission Nuestra de la Purísima Concepción de Acuña; although built of tufa, or soft limestone, best-preserved of city's missions; unrestored but still in use. Not far:
●*Mission San José (about 1739–70; rest.), 6539 San Jose Rd;

**Mission San José y Miguel
de Aguayo—Spanish Colonial**
(Texas Tourist Development Agency)

properly Mission San José y Miguel de Aguayo; very fine example; considered finest in state and one of best U.S buildings of Spanish era; now Nat. Hist. Site; on grounds: remains of early fortifications. Not far: *Mission San Juan Capistrano (1756; reconst. 1909), 9101 Graf Rd. Not far: *Mission Espada (1856; rebuilt 1858; part. rest.), properly Mission San Francisco de la Espada, 10040 Espada Rd; rough stone church; other buildings include barracks. On Espada Rd, Espada Aqueduct over Piedra Creek, built by Franciscan missionaries of this mission. Approx. 40 mi SW of San Antonio, via US I-35 & St. 173: BIGFOOT. *Bigfoot Wallace House (mid-19th century), log cabin; once home of William Alexander "Bigfoot" Wallace, hero of Mexican War; on grounds: early school. Approx. 215 mi NW of San Antonio, via US I-10 & 87: SAN ANGELO. *Ft. Concho (1868–81; part. rest.), 714 Burgess St; interesting fort important during Indian Wars. *Central High School (1958), W. Harris Ave. & Cottonwood St; architects: Caudill, Rowlett & Scott; assoc. architect: Max D. Lovett; fine pioneering modern campus plan school by noted firm.

San Antonio Vicinity *(SE, via US 181 & St. 239)*. Approx. 90 mi: GOLIAD. *La Bahia Presidio Chapel (about 1756), State Hist. Park; stone barrel-vaulted example in reconst. fort. Approx. 25 mi NE of Goliad, via US 59: VICTORIA. *W. J. McNamara House (about 1870; rest.), 502 N. Liberty St. Approx. 100 mi S, via US 77 & I-37. CORPUS CHRISTI. Interesting buildings include: *Centennial House, the Capt. Forbes Britton House (1849; rest.), 411 N. Broadway; during Civil War, served as Confederate hospital;

after war, Federal headquarters. At 1902 N. Shoreline Dr,
•*Art Museum of South Texas (1972), architects: Philip Johnson
& John Burgee; very fine modern white reinforced concrete beside
Corpus Christi Bay.

San Antonio Vicinity *(W, via US 90).* Approx. 30 mi, CASTRO-
VILLE, founded, 1844, by Alsatian immigrants from France led
by Count Henri de Castro; in Hist. Dist., town still has appear-
ance of Alsatian Village beside Rhine River. Interesting buildings,
all of stone and stucco, include: *Landmark Inn, formerly Vance
Hotel (about 1850; later alt. & addit.), Florella & Florence sts;
originally house, later inn, post office; still in use; separate bath-
house, kitchen; behind: John Vance House (about 1855); at Ma-
drid & Angelo sts; *Joseph Carlé House and Store (about 1850);
at Main & Lafayette sts, Andrew Carlé House (1844), built by
Count de Castro. Approx. 50 mi farther: UVALDE. *John Nance
Garner House (1920), once home of vice-president for two terms
under Franklin D. Roosevelt; now Mem. Museum.

WACO

Interesting buildings include: on S. 4th St, at no. 814, *Earle-
Napier-Kinnard House (about 1868; later alt. & addit.; rest.),
Greek Revival; built by John Baylis Earle, who made Confederate
uniforms; at no. 503, *Fort House (about 1868; rest.), Greek Revival. At 100 Mill St, *East Terrace (about 1872; rest.), large
Victorian Italianate. On N. 5th St, at no. 1705, *Nell Pape Garden Center (about 1879); Classic Revival; fine garden; at no.
1901, *Earle-Harrison House (1858; rest.), Greek Revival; once
home of Dr. Baylis Wood Earle, later of Gen. Tom Harrison; at
1020 Sleepy Hollow, *Sims Log Cabin (1859; rest.).

Waco Vicinity *(E, via US 84).* Approx. 65 mi: FAIRFIELD. Greek
Revival *Moody-Bradley House (about 1855), Coleman St. Ap-
prox. 30 mi NW of Fairfield, via US I-45: CORSICANA. *Pioneer
Village, mid-19th-century log cabins; moved here. Approx. 37 mi
E of Fairfield, via US 84: PALESTINE. Interesting buildings in-
clude: *Howard House (about 1853; rest.), 1011 N. Perry St;
*Watford Hall (about 1890; rest.), 107 S. Sycamore St; Victorian.

Waco Vicinity *(SE, via St. 6).* Approx. 25 mi: MARLIN. Nearby,
*Highlands Mansion (1890–1900; rest.), rich ornament. Approx.
30 mi farther, via St. 6 & 14: CALVERT. *Hammond House
(about 1879; later alt. & addit.), Gothic Revival; built as courthouse but used for county offices, jail; converted into house, 1885.

Pacific
States

Alaska

Early inhabitants: Eskimos, in far N and W; Aleuts, in Aleutian Islands and Alaska Peninsula; Indians, in central and S areas. First European explorer Danish Vitus Bering, for Russia, 1728 and 1741; later explorers included French, Spanish and English, led by Capt. James Cook, 1778. Russian traders and hunters entered area; trader Gregory Shelikof founded first permanent Russian settlement, 1784, on Kodiak Island. Russian-American Company established by Russians, with Alexander Baranoff as manager, 1799; governed area entire time of Russian ownership. Natives, treated badly, attacked Russians, leading to massacre of people and destruction of town of Sitka, 1802; rebuilt and made headquarters, 1817. With declining fur trade, Russians lost interest in Alaska and sold it to United States, 1867. No real government provided until 1884. After gold found in Klondike, just across border in Canada, 1896, prospectors increased efforts in Alaska, finding large deposits in Nome, 1899, and Fairbanks, 1903. During World War II, Japanese bombed Dutch Harbor in Aleutian Islands and occupied three of smaller islands far from mainland. Became forty-ninth state, Jan. 3, 1959. Severe earthquake caused great damage, 1964. Today: Important manufacturing, fishing, and mining, especially oil, industries.

Land Regions: S to N, Pacific Mountain System; Central Uplands and Lowlands; Rocky Mountain System; Arctic Coastal Plain.

Climate : Varied; in S coastal areas, moderate winters, cool summers; in central and N areas, colder winter, but cool summers; precipitation very heavy in S, less in central, very light in N; snowfall heavy in N, less along coast in S.

Major Building Materials: Timber; stone; iron; sand and gravel.

Architecture: Few, but interesting, buildings in several places; includes Russian examples unlike other U.S. buildings.

ANCHORAGE

Interesting buildings include: *Hist. and Fine Arts Museum (1968; addit. 1974), 7th Ave & A St; architects: Shultz & Maynard; architect, addit.: Kenneth Maynard; consult. architects: Kirk, Wallace & McKinley; interesting modern building; interesting exhibits.

Anchorage Vicinity (SW). Approx. 65 air mi: KENAI. Interesting buildings include: *Church of the Holy Assumption (about 1894), simple church in Russian tradition. Approx. 235 air mi: KODIAK. *Baranoff-Erskine House (about 1795; later alt. & addit.), Main & Mission sts; believed to be oldest Russian colonial building. Also of interest, approx. 50 air mi NW, *Katmai Nat. Mon.

FAIRBANKS

Interesting buildings include: *Alaskaland, reconst. native Alaskan houses. Approx. 185 mi E, via St. 2 & 5; EAGLE. Interesting buildings in Hist. Dist. Also of interest, SW of Fairbanks, *McKinley Nat. Park, location of *Mt. McKinley, highest mountain, 20,320 feet, in North America.

JUNEAU

Interesting buildings include: *State Capitol, originally Federal and Territorial Building (1911–31), 4th St bet. Main & Seward sts; architect: James A. Wetmore; undistinguished Eclectic. Governor's House (1913), 716 Calhoun Ave; architect: William N. Collier; territorial, state governors lived here in, unlikely though it may seem, Eclectic New England Colonial house. *House of Wickersham (1889), once home of James Wickersham, pioneer judge. *St. Nicholas Orthodox Church (1894), 326 5th St; interesting simple example of Russian design. Also of interest nearby, via boat, *Glacier Bay Nat. Mon.

Juneau Vicinity. Approx. 100 air mi NW: SKAGWAY. Interesting buildings of Gold Rush era include: in Hist. Dist., *Golden North Hotel (1898; later alt. & addit.), Broadway. Also of interest: *Klondike Gold Rush Nat. Hist. Park. Not far: *Mendenhall Glacier and *Glacier Bay Nat. Mon. Approx. 150 air mi SE: WRANGELL. On Shake's Island, interesting Indian buildings include *Tribal House of the Bear (1834; reconst.), community house of Tlingit Indians; also of interest: fine totems. Approx. 90 air mi SE of Wrangell: KETCHIKAN. Nearby, in *Totem Bight State Hist. Site, excellent totems. Approx. 100 air mi SW of Juneau, SITKA, formerly Arcangel; Russian capital until 1867. Interesting buildings include: *Bishop's House (1843; rest.). Also of interest nearby: *Sitka Nat. Hist. Park.

California

Early inhabitants Indians of many tribes, including Hupa, Modoc, Mohave, Yuma. Believed to have been first visited by Portuguese Juan Rodríguez Cabrillo, for Spain, 1543. Englishman Sir Francis Drake sailed along coast, 1579; claimed region for England. Several Spanish expeditions followed, including that of Sebastián Vizcaíno, 1602. After establishment of missions and forts in Baja California, now part of Mexico, beginning 1697, Spanish, led by Gen. Gaspar de Portolá, founded first *presidio,* or fort, in present-day California, and Franciscans, led by Father Junípero Serra, established Mission San Diego de Alcalá, 1769, at San Diego. By 1823, they had established twenty-one missions in all, and four *presidios* along coast from San Diego to Sonoma, N of San Francisco. Before he died, 1784, Father Serra had constructed nine missions. Russians searching for furs established Ft. Ross on N coast, 1812. Area became province of Mexico after its independence from Spain, 1821. American explorers came to area, beginning with expedition of Jedediah Strong Smith, 1826; others, including famous frontiersman Kit Carson, followed. American settlers began to arrive, 1841, when John Bidwell and John Bartleson led pioneers here. American explorer John C. Frémont led military surveying expeditions, 1844–46; Mexicans ordered them out of region. Group, led by frontiersman Ezekiel Merritt, seized Mexican fort at Sonoma, 1846, raised flag with star, grizzly bear, and words "California Republic." When word came that United States was at war with Mexico, Frémont became major of California Battalion, composed of his troops and volunteers. By 1847, Frémont, together with troops of Gen. Stephen Watts Kearny and fleet of Commodore Robert F. Stockton, had won entire region. Became part of United States at end of Mexican War, 1848. About same time, gold was discovered at Sutter's Mill and gold rush was on. Became thirty-first state, Sept. 9, 1850. Population has grown rapidly ever since. Today: Major manufacturing and agricultural industries: mining, especially oil and natural gas, and tourism also important.

Land Regions: From S to N, San Diego Ranges; Los Angeles Ranges; Basin and Range Region; Coast Ranges, Central Valley, Sierra Nevada; Coast Ranges, Cascade Mountains, Basin and Range Region; Klamath Mountains; Cascade Mountains.

Climate: Great variety; quite mild in S along coast, mild along central and N coast, hot and dry in SE, cold in Sierra Nevadas; precipitation very light in summer, heavy other seasons; very heavy along N coast, moderate central and S, almost none in SE;

snowfall very heavy in Sierra Nevadas, very light or none along central and S coast. State subject to dangerous earthquakes.

Major Building Materials: Timber: especially softwoods; sand and gravel; clay; gypsum.

Architecture: Unusually rich and varied from early Spanish Colonial era to present, including many of finest U.S. examples, architecturally as well as historically, in many locations, especially Los Angeles and vicinity; San Diego and vicinity; San Francisco and vicinity.

LOS ANGELES

Of U.S. cities, third largest in population (approx. 3 million; approx. 7.5 million in county); approx. 465 square miles in city, completely surrounding some towns; number of others adjoin city. Buildings listed here in five major sections: Downtown; NE, SE, SW & NW Metropolitan areas. Since distances between buildings are usually so great, walking tours are not feasible except in Downtown area. In others, automobile a necessity.

LOS ANGELES DOWNTOWN

•*Bradbury Building** (1893; rest.), 304 S. Broadway; architect: George H. Wyman; fine office building; beautiful skylighted court interior; highly ornamental iron work. *Biltmore Hotel (1923; later alt. & addit.), Olive & 5th sts; architects: Shultze & Weaver; architects, 1977 alt.: Phyllis Lambert & Gene Summers; Eclectic Beaux Arts. *Los Angeles Public Library (1926), 5th St bet. Flower St & Grand Ave; architect: Bertram Grosvenor Goodhue; assoc. architect: Carleton M. Winslow; Eclectic Beaux Arts by famous architect. *Los Angeles Bonaventure Hotel (1976), Figueroa & 5th Sts; architect: John Portman; group of five modern glass cylinders by noted hotel architect. Not far: *Music Center of Los Angeles Co. (1969), 1st St bet. Hope St & Grand Ave; architect: Welton Becket; fine modern complex for performing arts; includes *Dorothy Chandler Pavilion; *Mark Taper Forum; *Ahmanson Theater; fine fountain and sculpture by famous sculptor Jacques Lipchitz. Not far: *Olvera Street & *El Pueblo de Los Angeles Hist. Park, off Hollywood Frwy, bet. Sunset Blvd & Alameda & Hill sts; interesting Hispanic area with number of early buildings, including: *Francisco Avila Adobe (1818; rest.), 14 Olvera St; oldest house in city; also: other interesting early buildings; shops, restaurants; others; some rest.; now Mexican area of city; also of interest here: *Old Plaza.

Los Angeles NE Metropolitan Area *(via St. 11, Pasadena Frwy).* Interesting buildings include: *El Alisal, the Charles Lummis House (about 1900), 200 E. Ave 43; stone example designed

David B. Gamble House—Stick Style (Stephen C. M. Hunt)

by writer who once lived here. Not far: *Heritage Square, N. Homer St; number of old houses moved here and rest. Approx. 10 mi: SOUTH PASADENA. Miltimore House (1911), 1301 Cheltenham Way; architect: Irving J. Gill, fine modern by famous architect. Just N, PASADENA. Interesting buildings include: *City Hall (1927), 100 N. Garfield St; architects: Bakewell & Brown; Eclectic Spanish Revival; fine gardens. Also: ●*David B. Gamble House (1908), 4 Westmoreland Dr; architects: Charles & Henry Greene; wonderfully preserved Stick style masterpiece by famous architects; original fixtures and furnishings designed by architect-brothers; other fine houses by brothers include whole block on Arroyo Terr, with Charles Sumner Greene House (1901; later alt. & addit.), at no. 368. Also: ●*La Miniatura, the Millard House (1923), 645 Prospect Crescent; architect: Frank Lloyd Wright, early modern masterpiece by famous architect; considered one of finest U.S buildings; on grounds: Studio House (1926), by his son,

La Miniatura, the Millard House— Early Modern
(Julius Shulman)

R. R. Blacker House—Stick Style (Stephen C. M. Hunt)

Lloyd Wright. At 1177 Hillcrest, ●∗**R. R. Blacker House** (1907), architects: Charles & Henry Greene; another Stick style masterpiece; also here: Gatehouse and Gardener's Cottage, both now separate residences. Few blocks away, at 675 S. Madison St, fine modern E. J. Blacker House (1912), architects: Greene & Greene. Just SE of Pasadena: SAN MARINO. ∗Huntington Gallery (1910), Library (1925), 1151 Oxford Rd; architects, Gallery: Myron Hunt & Elmer Grey; architects, Library: Myron Hunt & H. C. Chambers; Eclectic Classic Revival; beautifully landscaped grounds; built for railroad magnate Henry Edwards Huntington; art and literary collections among greatest in world; also: Huntington Mausoleum (1933), architect: John Russell Pope. Just S. of San Marino: SAN GABRIEL. ∗Mission San Gabriel Arcángel (1798–1812; later rest. & rebuilding), 314 Mission Dr; originally adobe, but now mostly fired brick with buttressed walls. Nearby: EAST PASADENA. ∗Stuart Co. Building (1958), E. Foothill Dr & Halsted St; architect: Edward Durell Stone; fine modern office building with grilles characteristic of noted architect; well-landscaped grounds. Adjoining Pasadena, on E, via US I-210: SIERRA MADRE. Lewis Courts (1910), Mountain Trail & Alegria St; architect: Irving J. Gill; interesting early modern housing complex. Just S of Sierra Madre: ARCADIA. E. J. Baldwin Guest House (1885; rest.) and ∗Stables (1897; rest.), 301 N. Baldwin Ave, in Los Angeles Co. Arboretum; architect: A. A. Bennett; charming Queen Anne house, stables built for noted gold-mining, real estate, horse-racing entrepreneur "Lucky" Baldwin; also: ∗Hugo Reid Adobe (about 1840; rest.), in which Baldwin actually lived; ∗Santa Anita Sante Fe Railroad Station (1889), moved here. Also of interest: ∗Botanical Gardens; not far: ∗Santa Anita Race Track.

Los Angeles SE Metropolitan Area *(via US I-5, Santa Ana Frwy)*. Approx. 12 mi: WHITTIER. ∗Casa de Gov. Pio Pico (about 1850; later rebuilding; rest.), 6003 Pioneer Blvd; State Hist. Park;

early adobe of last Mexican governor of California. Approx. 15 mi S of Whittier: GARDEN GROVE. ●*Community Church (1961; later alt. & addit.), 12141 Lewis St; architect: Richard J. Neutra; architect, addit.: Dion Neutra; fine modern drive-in church by famous architect and his son. Nearby, mammoth glass *Crystal Cathedral (1980), architects: Philip Johnson & John Burgee. Adjoining Garden Grove, SW: SANTA ANA, *Orange Co. Civic Center (1960; 1968), by same architects. Approx. 10 mi S of Santa Ana, via St. 55: NEWPORT BEACH. ●*Philip Lovell Beach House (1926; later alt.), 13th St & Beach Walk, Balboa; architect: R. M. Schindler; one of finest examples of modern International style architecture by noted architect; another fine building by this architect, via ferry to Santa Catalina Island, in AVALON, Wolfe Summer House (1929). Approx. 20 mi SE of Newport Beach, via US 1 & I-5, *Mission San Juan Capistrano (1777–1806), romantic ruins of state's best-known mission; home of famous swallows; chapel has been restored.

Los Angeles SW Metropolitan Area *(via US I-110, Harbor Frwy)*. Interesting buildings here include: *St. Vincent De Paul Roman Catholic Church (1925), Figueroa & Adams sts; architect: Albert C. Martin; Eclectic Spanish Colonial Revival. Not far: contrasting *St. John's Episcopal Church (1923), 514 W. Adams St; architects: Pierpont & Walter S. Davis; Eclectic Romanesque Revival. Not far: bet. Jefferson, Exposition, Figueroa & Vermont sts, *University of Southern California; number of interesting buildings on crowded campus. At Bell & Corona aves, *Bell, formerly Corona Avenue Elementary School (1935), architect: Richard J. Neutra; pioneering early modern open-plan school by famous architect. Not far away: at 1765 E. 107th St, *Watts

Wayfarers' Chapel—
Modern (Stephen C. M. Hunt)

Hollyhock House—Early Modern (Stephen C. M. Hunt)

Towers (1921–54), fantastic structure of cast-off steel, concrete, bottle caps, shells, tiles, other items too numerous to mention; life work of its untutored designer and builder, Simon Rodia. SW of city: TORRANCE; planners: Olmsted Brothers. Von Koerber House (1931), 408 Via Monte de Oro; architect: R. M. Schindler; another fine early modern house by noted architect. Also here: fine early modern houses and other buildings by famous architect Irving J. Gill. Not far: PALOS VERDES. ●*Wayfarers' Chapel, also known as Swedenborgian Memorial Chapel (1951), Palos Verdes Dr; architect: Lloyd Wright; marvelous small, modern chapel; redwood and glass; in natural setting of trees and plants; by noted architect-son of Frank Lloyd Wright. Just SE of Torrance: in San Pedro area, *Channel Heights Housing (1943), Ocralmont Dr; architect: Richard Neutra; interesting modern World War II housing development. Approx. 8 mi E of San Pedro, via St. 47: LONG BEACH. *La Casa de Rancho Los Cerritos (1844; later alt.; rest.), 4600 Virginia Rd; fine Spanish Colonial Revival adobe, in phase called Monterey style. *La Casa De Rancho Los Alamitos (1806; rest.), 6400 E. Bixby Rd; adobe; oldest surviving in Southern California. Also of interest here: luxury liner *Queen Mary; *Spruce Goose, huge wood airplane designed by famous airplane pilot, industrialist Howard Hughes.

Los Angeles NW Metropolitan Area. Interesting buildings include: *Bullocks-Wilshire Dept. Store (1928; later alt.), 3050 Wilshire Blvd; architects: John & Donald B. Parkinson; excellent Art Deco or Moderne; with many examples of art in same style. Not far: in area of *MacArthur Park, especially on Bonnie Brae, off Wilshire, number of interesting turn-of-the-century houses, in number of styles, especially Queen Anne. In Hollywood area, interesting buildings include: ●*Hollyhock House, the Aline Barnsdall House (1920; rest.), 4800 Hollywood Blvd, Barnsdall Park; architect: Frank Lloyd Wright; famous early modern masterpiece

Philip Lovell "Health" House—Modern (Julius Shulman)

by famous architect; reminiscent of Mayan architecture; interesting buildings on grounds include: *Studio Residence A, now called Arts and Crafts Center (1920). Not far, another Wright-designed masterpiece, *Ennis House (1924; rest.), 2607 Glendower St; also somewhat Mayan. Just W, via Sunset Blvd, in Silver Lake area, remarkable number of modern houses, all private, by famous architects, including Richard J. Neutra; R. M. Schindler; Gregory Ain; John Lautner; Raphael Soriano; Harwell H. Harris. At 4616 Dundee St, •*Philip Lovell House, also known as "Health House" (1929), architect: Richard J. Neutra; modern masterpiece, in style sometimes called International, by famous architect. On Waverly Pl, at no. 3412, Anthony House, now Roman Catholic Retreat (1927; later alt.), architect: Bernard Maybeck; romantic example by famous architect; at no. 2721, McAlmon House (1936), architect: R. M. Schindler; another fine modern example by noted architect. At 1962 Glencoe Way, •*Freeman House (1924), architect: Frank Lloyd Wright; another very fine early modern example by famous architect. At 6925 Hollywood Blvd, *Grauman's, now Mann's, Chinese Theater (1927), architects: Meyer & Holler; famous "Oriental" extravaganza. At 5128 W. Marathon St, Garden Apartments (1927), Hollywood Hills; architect: Richard J. Neutra; another fine early modern example by famous architect. In West Hollywood, Storer House (1923; rest.), 8161 Hollywood Blvd; architect: Frank Lloyd Wright. At 835 N. Kings Rd, very fine early modern •*Schindler House (1921), architect: R. M. Schindler; designed by noted architect for his own use; considered to be one of his finest designs. At 8687 Melrose Ave, *Pacific Design Center (1975), Melrose Ave & San Vicente Ave; architects: Victor Gruen & Cesar Pelli; large modern steel-frame building with blue and bronze glass; for display of building materials, equipment, furniture; nickname: "The Blue Whale." *Pan-Pacific

Auditorium (1935), 7600 Beverly Blvd; architects: Wurdeman & Becket; Art Deco or Moderne. Also of interest: fine art collections of *Los Angeles Co. Art Museum (1964), architect: William Pereira; *Rancho La Brea prehistoric animal pits, both in *Hancock Park, off Wilshire Blvd. In BEVERLY HILLS, *Anderton Court Building (1954; later alt.), 328 Rodeo St; architect: Frank Lloyd Wright; strange little shop building by famous architect. Beverly Hills best known for houses of movie stars, palatial, but not notable architecturally; number of fine examples here, including Anthony House (1909; rest.), 910 Bedford St; architects: Charles & Henry Greene; example of work of famous architect-brothers; number of fine modern houses, all private, here by noted architects including: Gregory Ain; Harwell H. Harris; Richard J. Neutra; R. M. Schindler. Not far: in Bel Air, fine modern examples include Johnson House (1949), 10280 Chrysanthemum; architect: Harwell H. Harris. Not far: in Westwood, interesting modern houses and apartments include Tishler House (1949), 175 Greenfield St; architect: R. M. Schindler; also several by Neutra. Interesting older and modern examples on campus of *University of California, Los Angeles. In Brentwood Area: very fine modern, ●*Sturgis House (1939), 449 Skyeway, architect: Frank Lloyd Wright; considered one of famous architect's finest houses. In SANTA MONICA, Horatio West Court (1919; rest.), 140 Hillister St; architect: Irving J. Gill; fine early modern apartment building by famous architect. Not far: in Pacific Palisades area, number of fine modern private houses by noted modern architects. Also *Will Rogers Ranch (about 1920; later alt. & addit.), off Sunset Blvd; in State Hist. Park. Approx. 10 mi W, via St. 1, MALIBU, number of other interesting modern houses. Also: *J. Paul Getty Museum (1973), 17985 Pacific Coast Hwy; architects: Langdon & Wilson; matchless collection of classical Greek and Roman art in building and gardens of almost unbelievable complexity modeled after Roman villa more than 2,000 years old.

Los Angeles NW Metropolitan Area *(Via US 101, Hollywood & Ventura Frwys)*. In Studio City area, number of interesting modern houses by famous architects, including Neutra and Schindler. In Encino, *Ranchos de los Encinos, 16756 Moorpark St; State Hist. Mon.; interesting buildings of varied types, materials include: *Reyes Hut (about 1800), of stone; *Osa Adobe (1849); *Garnier House (about 1867), limestone, somewhat Greek Revival. Approx. 4 mi N of Encino, via US 405, modern manufacturing plant, *Torrington Company (1953), 16300 Roscoe Blvd; architect: Marcel Breuer. Approx. 4 mi farther, *Mission San Fernando Rey de España (convent 1822; church 1974), 15151 San Fernando Mission Blvd; reconst. of old church (1806), destroyed in 1971 earthquake. Approx. 8 mi farther N, in Mission Hills area, *Pico Adobe (about 1840), 10940 Sepulveda Blvd; believed to have been part of mission complex.

Los Angeles Vicinity *(E, via US I-10, San Bernardino Frwy)*. Approx. 28 mi: LA PUENTE. *John H. Rowland House (1855; later alt. & addit.), 16021 E. Gale St; once home of one of leaders of first Southern California settlers to arrive by wagon train. Approx. 10 mi farther: POMONA. *Adobe de Palomares (1854; rest.), 491 E. Arrow Hwy, Palomares Park; other interesting buildings, gardens here. *La Casa Primera Adobe, also known as Ygnacio Palomares (1837; rest.), Park Ave & McKinley St. Adjoining Pomona, N: CLAREMONT. *Pitzer House (about 1910), Towne & Baseline sts; architect: Robert H. Orr; unusual rustic stone example; tile roof. Approx. 40 mi farther: SAN BERNARDINO. *San Bernardino City Hall (1973), 300 N. D St, Civic Plaza; architects: Victor Gruen & Cesar Pelli; fine modern by noted architects; nearby, another fine modern building by same architects: *Security Pacific National Bank (1973). Approx. 20 mi SW of San Bernardino, via St. 91: RIVERSIDE. *Glenwood Mission Inn (1902; later alt. & addit.), bet. Main, Orange, 6th & 7th sts; architect: Arthur B. Benton; architect, 1914 addit.: Myron Hunt; architect, 1929 addit.: G. Stanley Wilson; architect, later alt.: Bruce Wendell Beebe; charming Spanish Colonial Revival. *Riverside Co. Courthouse (1904; later alt.), 4050 Main St; architects: Burnham & Bliesner; notable Beaux Arts example. Approx. 5 mi past Riverside, via US I-10: REDLANDS. Morey House (1890), 140 Terrecina; one of best California Victorian examples. Approx. 45 mi farther: PALM SPRINGS. ●**Kaufmann Desert House** (1947), 470 W. Chino Canyon Rd; architect: Richard J. Neutra; modern International style house by famous architect; one of his masterpieces; other interesting buildings in city. Also of interest, W of city: *Joshua Tree Nat. Mon.

Los Angeles Vicinity *(NW, via Hollywood & Ventura Frwys, US 101)*. Approx. 35 mi: THOUSAND OAKS. *Thousand Oaks Civic Center (1973), 401 W. Hillcrest Dr; architect: Robert M. Houvener; interesting modern concrete complex on top of hill. Approx. 25 mi farther: VENTURA. *Mission San Buenaventura (1809; later

Kaufmann Desert House—Modern (Julius Shulman)

alt. & addit.; rest.), Main St; interesting brick, stone example, much damaged by earthquakes. *Olivas Adobe (about 1841; rest.), Olivas Park Dr; early example in so-called Monterey Style. Approx. 12 mi N of Ventura, via St. 33: OJAI. Gould House (1924), 3441 Gale Way; architects: Charles & Henry Greene; fine example by famous architect-brothers; Pratt House (1909), 1330 N. Foothill; architects: Charles & Henry Greene; another fine example; several later houses by other noted architects here. Approx. 27 mi NW of Ventura, via US 101: SANTA BARBARA. Interesting buildings include: *Santa Barbara Co. Courthouse (1929), 1120 Anacapa St; architect: William Mooser; fine Spanish Colonial Revival in city noted for style. Few blocks away, shops of *El Paseo (1923; later alt.), Anacapa & De Guerra sts; architects: James Osborne Craig; Mary Craig; Carleton Winslow. *Fox Arlington Theater (1930), 1317 State St; architects: Edwards & Plunkett; interesting Spanish Colonial Revival. *Jose Maria Covarrubias Adobe (1817; rest.), 715 Santa Barbara St; constructed by Indians. Judge Charles Fernald House (1862), 414 W. Montecito St; Victorian. *Trussell-Winchester House (1854; later alt. & addit.), 412 W. Montecito St; built by Capt. Horatio Gates Trussell, of adobe and timbers from wrecked ship, *Winfield Scott*. On Mission Canyon rd, *Mission Santa Barbara (1820; later alt. & addit.; rest.). Approx. 3 mi NE of Santa Barbara: MONTECITO. Number of fine modern houses, all private, most difficult to view from street, by famous architects including Frank Lloyd Wright, Bernard Maybeck, Richard Neutra. Other interesting missions NW of Santa Barbara: approx. 60 mi farther, via US 101 & St. 1, LOMPOC. *Mission La Purísima (about 1820; later alt. & addit.; rest.). Approx. 40 mi farther: SAN LUIS OBISPO. *Mission San Luis Rey Obispo de Tolosa (1792–1820; later alt. & addit.; rest.). Also here: *Pierre Hyppolite Dallidet Adobe (1853; rest.), Pacific & Touro sts; once home of French wine maker. Also *Sauer Adobe (about 1860), 964 Chorro St. Approx. 40 mi farther, in SAN MIGUEL, *Mission San Miguel Arcángel (about 1820).

Approx. 40 mi NW of San Luis Obispo, via St. 1: SAN SIMEON. *La Cuesta Encantada, the William Randolph Hearst Castle (1919–47), architect: Julia Morgan; almost unbelievable extravaganza of elaborate buildings, elaborate landscaping, art works; home of famous newspaper magnate; designed by noted architect.

Los Angeles Vicinity *(NW, via US I-5)*. Approx. 30 mi: NEWHALL. *La Loma de Los Vientos, the William S. Hart House (1928), Spanish Colonial Revival ranch house of famous early star of western motion pictures; interesting outbuildings, collection of western art. Approx. 70 mi farther: BAKERSFIELD. *Pioneer Village, early buildings representing frontier community. Approx. 70 mi SW of Bakersfield, via St. 58 & 14: ROSAMOND. *Burton's Tropico Gold Camp, late 19th-century buildings moved here. Approx. 70 mi NW of Bakersfield, via US I-5: VISALIA. *Tulare Co. Museum, early buildings, moved here from locations in county.

SACRAMENTO

Interesting buildings include: *State Capitol (1860–74; later alt. & addit.; part. reconst. 1982), Capitol Park, bet. 10th, L, 12th & N sts; architect: Miner F. Butler; architects, reconst.: Welton Becket Assoc.; interesting example, part. reconst. because of earthquake dangers. Not far: *Old Governor's Mansion, originally Albert Gallatin House (1878; later alt. & addit.), 11th & H sts; architect: Nathaniel D. Goodell; fine Victorian; now museum. Few blocks away: another fine Victorian example, *Stanford-Lathrop House (1860; later alt. & addit.), 800 N St; architect: Seth Babson; once home of famous railroad magnate, U.S. Senator Leland Stanford; now Roman Catholic children's home. Few blocks away: *Crocker Art Gallery, 3rd bet. O & P sts; with Italianate Crocker House (1852; later alt. & addit.); Eclectic Renaissance Revival *Art Gallery (1873; rest.); architect of both: Seth Babson; architects, rest.: Rosekrans & Broder; assoc. architects: Anra Hung Buchanan & Tom Jones; modern *R. A. Herold Mem. Wing (1969), architects: Dodd, McCabe, Cox & Liske; fine collections. Not far: in *Old Sacramento Hist. Dist., *The Embarcadero, beside Sacramento River; number of buildings from gold rush days. At 2701 L St, *Sutter's Fort (1844; part. rest.; part. reconst.), built by German immigrant and pioneer John Sutter.

Sacramento Vicinity *(NE, via US 50 & St. 49)*. Approx. 45 mi, PLACERVILLE, important center of 1848 gold rush; most old buildings here have been considerably altered. Semi-ghost towns of gold rush era, with interesting old buildings, along St. 49, in both directions from town: NW of Placerville, approx. 8 mi: COLOMA, where gold rush started. Nearby, *Marshall Gold Discovery State Park. Approx. 30 mi farther: GRASS VALLEY. *Lola Montez House (about 1850), Walsh & Mill sts; once home of famous dancer who became countess of Lansfeld. Approx. 5 mi farther: NEVADA CITY. S. of Placerville, approx. 30 mi: SUTTER CREEK. Approx. 10 mi farther: MOKELUMNE HILL. Approx. 35 mi farther: SONORA. Approx. 5 mi N of Sonora: COLUMBIA, capital of state for brief period; best preserved of all gold rush towns in area; some 40 buildings, some rest., survive here in State Hist. Park. Also of interest: NE of area, *Calaveras Big Trees State Park; *Squaw Valley; *Lake Tahoe; E of area, *Yosemite Nat. Park.

Sacramento Vicinity *(SE, via St. 99)*. Approx. 155 mi: FRESNO. *Martin Theodore Kearney Mansion (1903; later alt. & addit.), Kearney Park; architect: Willis J. Polk; Eclectic; on grounds: *Carriage House. Also *Fulton Street Mall (1964), planners: Victor Gruen Assoc.; landscape architects: Eckbo, Dean, Austin & Williams; early, urban street converted into most successful pedestrian mall. Also of interest: E of city, *King's Canyon Park, *Sequoia Nat. Park; *Death Valley Nat. Mon., *Scotty's Castle, once home of Death Valley Scotty; see Nevada—Las Vegas.

Sacramento Vicinity *(NW, via US I-5).* Approx. 135 mi, via US I-5 & St. 32: CHICO. *Gen. John Bidwell Mansion (1868), *Chico State University, 525 Esplanade; architect: H. W. Cleaveland; Eclectic Tuscan Revival; once home of early pioneer. Approx. 60 mi NW of Chico, via St. 99: RED BLUFF. Nearby, *William B. Ide Adobe (about 1850), Adobe Rd, once home of leader of Bear Flag revolt, 1846, and only California Republic president. Approx. 105 mi E of Red Bluff, via St. 36. SUSANVILLE. *Roop's Fort (1854), 75 N. Weatherlow St; log cabin built by pioneer prospector Isaac N. Roop; used during Nevada-California boundary dispute, 1864, called "Sagebrush War." Approx. 30 mi N of Red Bluff, via US I-5: REDDING. Six mi W, via St. 299, old gold-mining town of SHAS-TA, with interesting buildings of era. Also of interest: N & NE of Redding, *Mt. Shasta, *Lava Beds Nat. Mon.; E of Redding, *Lassen Volcanic Nat. Park.

SAN DIEGO

Interesting buildings include: in *Old Town San Diego Hist. Park, *Casa de Estudillo (1829; rest.), Mason St; early adobe with courtyard; other adobe houses include: *Casa de Machado-Stewart (1829; rest.), Congress St; Casa de Bandini (1829), Calhoun & Mason sts; Casa Machado de Silvas (1832), Wallace & San Diego sts. Nearby, *Adobe Chapel (1858; rest.), 3950 Conde St; *Whaley House (1857; rest.), San Diego & Harney sts; brick Greek Revival. In Balboa Park: *California Building, now Museum of Man (1915), architect: Bertram Grosvenor Goodhue; Eclectic Spanish Baroque building; originally Fine Arts Building of Panama-California Exposition; by chief architect of that World's Fair. Also: *Villa Montezuma, the Jesse Shepherd House (1887; rest.), 1925 K St; architects: Comstock & Trotsche; extravagant Eclectic Victorian. *Mission San Diego de Alcala (1814; part. rebuilt; rest.), off US I-15 & Friars Rd; first California mission. Also of interest, NE of city: *Salton Sea.

San Diego Vicinity *(W, via St. Rte 75).* Approx. 2 mi: CORONA-DO. Interesting buildings include:
•*First Church of Christ, Scientist (1929), C & 8th sts; architect: Irving J. Gill; fine early modern building by famous architect; several Gill-designed houses and other buildings here and in San Diego and other locations, especially La Jolla.
•*Hotel del Coronado (1888), 1500 Orange Ave; architects: Reid & Reid; grand resort hotel in Eclectic Queen Anne-Eastlake style; still in operation.

San Diego Vicinity *(NW, via US I-5).* Approx. 9 mi: LA JOLLA. Number of very fine buildings by famous architect Irving Gill, in very personal modern style, somewhat Eclectic Mission Revival, include: three early modern examples, at *Bishop's School for

Girls (1916; later alt. & addit.), *Bentham Hall (1909); *Scripps Hall (1910); *Gilman Hall (1916). Also by Gill, not far:

●*La Jolla Community Center (1914), 615 Prospect St; very fine modern example; pioneering use of tilt-slab concrete;

●*La Jolla Women's Club (1913), 715 Silverado St; another modern tilt-slab example; ●*Ellen Scripps House, now La Jolla Museum of Contemporary Art (1915; later alt.), 700 Prospect St; considered masterpiece of this architect; drastically altered. At 10010 Torrey Pines Rd, ●*Salk Institute (1966), architect: Louis Kahn; magnificent group of modern buildings by famous architect; considered one of finest U.S. buildings. Approx. 22 mi farther: OCEANSIDE. *Oceanside City Hall and Fire Station (1929), Ditmar & 3rd sts; architect: Irving J. Gill; fine modern; architect also designed other buildings here. Approx. 4 mi NE, via St. 76, *Mission San Luis Rey de Francia (1851; rest.), Mission Rd; one of finest California missions.

SAN FRANCISCO

Picturesque "City by the Bay" has great many attractions, not the least of which is fine architecture. Interesting buildings are to be found in many locations; some considerable distances apart accessible via Bay Area Rapid Transit (BART); examples nearer each other accessible by walking tours or cable cars, when in operation. Tours on foot or by various vehicles all reveal many fascinating sights, including number of fine buildings of several eras.

SAN FRANCISCO DOWNTOWN

Interesting buildings include: *City Hall (1915), in *Civic Center bet. Franklin, McAllister, Market & Hayes sts; architects: Bakewell & Brown; other government buildings here. Few blocks away: *Old U.S. Mint (1870; rest.), Mission & 5th sts; architect: A. B. Mullett; Eclectic Classic Revival; now monetary museum. Few blocks away: ●*140 Maiden Lane Building, originally V. C.

Ellen Scripps House—Early Modern (Wayne Andrews)

Salk Institute—Modern (Salk Institute)

Morris Gift Shop (1949), architect: Frank Lloyd Wright; small modern gem by famous architect; interior spiral ramp forerunner of ramp in architect's famous Guggenheim Museum, New York City. Nearby, *450 Sutter Place Building (1929; later alt. & addit.), architect: Timothy L. Pflueger; fine Art Deco or Moderne; medical and dental offices. ••**Hallidie Building** (1918; later alt. & addit.; rest.), 130 Sutter St; architect: Willis Polk; architects, rest.: Kaplan, McLaughlin & Diaz; very fine pioneering cast-iron and glass building. Not far: *Bank of America (1971), 555 California St; architects: Wurster, Bernardi & Emmons; Skidmore, Owings & Merrill; design consultant: Pietro Belluschi; fine modern skyscraper by distinguished group of architects; fine plaza. Not far: *Old U.S. Subtreasury Building (1877; part. destroyed 1906 fire; rest.), 608 Commercial St. Few blocks away: another fine modern example, *Alcoa Building (1967), 1 Maritime Plaza; architects: Skidmore, Owings & Merrill; interesting exposed structure; elevated plaza with sculpture by several famous sculptors, including Henry Moore. Nearby, other modern buildings in Golden Gate Redevelopment area bet. Embarcadero, Clay & Battery sts & Broadway. Nearby, very large modern *Embarcadero Center, bet. Embarcadero & Sacramento, Battery & Clay sts; architect: John Portman; five high-rise buildings, *Hyatt Regency Hotel (1973), with atrium as in architect's other hotels, four office towers (1971; 1974; 1976; 1982), interesting pedestrian malls, shops, stores, restaurants, other facilities. Few blocks away: *Telegraph Hill, on top of which, interesting *Coit Tower (1934), architect: Arthur Brown, Jr. Also: Kahn House (1939), 66 Calhoun Terr.; architect: Richard J. Neutra; fine modern example by famous architect. Some blocks away, in Nob Hill area, *Fairmont Hotel (1906; later alt. & addit.), California & Mason sts; architects: Reid & Reid; Eclectic Renaissance Revival with newer addit. Nearby, *Mark Hopkins Hotel (1927; later alt. & addit.), architects: Weeks & Day; architect of noted Top of the Mark lounge: Timothy Pflueger. Some blocks W of Nob Hill ••**St. Mary's Cathedral**

(1971), Geary & Gough sts; architects: Pietro Belluschi; McSweeney, Ryan & Lee; structural engineer: Pier Luigi Nervi; imposing large modern church by famous Italian-American architect and famous Italian engineer. Not far: *Chrysler Showroom, originally Earle C. Anthony Packard Showroom (1928; later alt. & addit.), 901 Van Ness Ave; architect: Bernard Maybeck; elaborate and ornamental building by famous architect for dealer who fancied fine architecture and fine motor cars. Number of blocks SW of Cathedral: Phelps House (about 1850), 329 Divisadero St; believed to be oldest surviving house in city; prefabricated in New Orleans and shipped around the Horn. Some blocks farther: *Mission San Francisco de Asis, also known as Mission Dolores (1782; rest. 1920), 1321 16th St; architect, rest.: Willis Polk; oldest building in city. Not far: Valencia Gardens (1943), 15th St bet. Guerrero & Valencia sts; architects: Wurster, Bernardi & Emmons; Harry Thomsen; pioneering modern public housing. N of Cathedral, some fine examples of various Eclectic styles, including: *Haas-Lilienthal House (1886), 2007 Franklin St; Queen Anne, with traces of Stick and Eastlake styles. Not far: *Frank Whittier House (1896; later alt. & addit.), 2090 Jackson St; architects: Edward R. Swain & N. J. Thorp; fine Romanesque Revival. Not far: *Schubert Hall, the John D. Spreckels House (1905), 2209 Pacific Ave; Eclectic Baroque Revival. Few blocks away: *The Octagon, the William G. McElroy House (about 1860; rest.), 2545 Gough St; architect, rest.: Warren Perry; Victorian; moved here; many other houses of Victorian era in this and other sections of city.

Some blocks away, in N Waterfront section of city, number of interesting old buildings remod. for new uses include:
•*Ghirardelli Square (about 1860–1915; remod. 1964), bet. North Point, Polk, Beach & Larkin sts; architect: William Mooser; architects, remod.: Wurster, Bernardi & Emmons; landscape archi-

First Church of Christ, Scientist—Eclectic Beaux Arts (Julius Shulman)

tect: Lawrence Halprin; originally Ghirardelli Chocolate Co., now fascinating, playful complex of shops, restaurants. Not far, another fascinating remod. building: *The Cannery (about 1900; remod. 1969), 2801 Leavenworth St; architect, remod: Joseph Esherick; landscape architect: Thomas Church. Not far, still another: *The Ice House (1914; remod. 1969), Union St & Ice House Alley; architects, remod.: Wurster, Bernardi & Emmons; landscape architect: Lawrence Halprin; two old ice houses remod. into furniture and furnishings showrooms. Also of interest nearby, *Fisherman's Wharf. Some blocks W, in Pacific Heights area, on site of Panama-Pacific International Exposition, 1915:
●*Palace of Fine Arts (1915; reconst. 1967), Baker & Beach sts; architect: Bernard Maybeck; architects, reconst.: Welton Becket; with William G. Merchant & Hans U. Gerson, both former partners of Maybeck; fascinating romantic Eclectic Beaux Arts by famous architect; originally built for World's Fair of plaster of paris on wood frame; reconst. in concrete, other permanent materials. Also of interest, not far away, marvelous *Golden Gate Bridge (1937), chief engineer: Joseph Strauss; consult. engineers: Othmar B. Ammann; Leon S. Moisseiff; Charles Derleth, Jr.; consult. architect: Irving Morrow. Some blocks away, in Richmond area of city, *Golden Gate Park, *Conservatory (1875), John F. Kennedy Dr; fine Victorian iron and glass example, prefabricated and shipped around the Horn.

San Francisco Vicinity *(E, via San Francisco-Oakland Bay Bridge, US I-80).* Approx. 8 mi: OAKLAND. Interesting buildings include: at *Jack London Square, Broadway & waterfront, *Last Chance Saloon made famous by famous writer; also here: *London cabin moved from Klondike. Not far: ●*Oakland Museum (1960), 1000 Oak St; architects: Kevin Roche & John Dinkeloo; landscape architect: Dan Kiley; very fine modern complex, with natural history, history, art sections; beautifully landscaped park on top of building, much of which is underground. Not far: *Paramount Theater (1931; later alt. & renov.), 2025 Broadway; architects: Miller & Pflueger; architects, alt. & renov.: Skidmore, Owings & Merrill; fanciful Art Deco or Moderne building; highly ornamental exterior and interior splendor. On Joaquin Miller Rd, *The Abbey, the Joaquin Miller House (1886), once home of noted western poet. In S part of city: *Oakland-Alameda Co. Coliseum & Stadium (1968), Coliseum Way & 66th Ave; architects: Skidmore, Owings & Merrill; one of most interesting modern sports facilities; exposed structural members. Just NE, adjoining city: BERKELEY. Interesting buildings include: *Thorsen House (1908; later alt. & addit.), 2307 Piedmont Ave; architects: Charles & Henry Greene; fine example by famous architect-brothers. Not far: ●*First Church of Christ, Scientist (1910; addit. 1929), 2619 Dwight Way; architect: Bernard Maybeck; architect, addit.: Henry Gutterson; marvelous ornamental Eclectic Beaux Arts church by famous architect; considered his masterpiece and

one of finest U.S buildings. Not far: another fine Maybeck building, Town and Gown Club (1899), 2401 Dwight Way; some
blocks S, still another: •**Chick House** (1913), 7133 Chabot Rd;
very fine house, very fine woodwork, details. Other fine buildings
by this architect in various parts of city, including campus of
∗University of California, Berkeley, ∗Faculty Club (1902; addit.
1904; 1914; 1925; 1959), architect: Bernard Maybeck; architects,
addit.: 1904, John Galen Howard; 1914 & 1925, Warren Perry;
1959, Downs & Lagorio. ∗Phoebe Apperson Hearst Mem. Gym-
nasium for Women (1925), architects: Bernard Maybeck & Julia
Morgan; also of interest on campus: ∗Northgate Hall (1906), familiarly referred to as "The Ark," former School of Architecture
building; architect: John Galen Howard, who succeeded Maybeck
as its head; school now located in modern ∗Wurster Hall (1965),
architects: DeMars, Esherick & Olsen; named for noted architect
and dean of school William Wilson Wurster. Also by Howard,
∗Hearst Mining Building (1907), Eclectic Renaissance Revival;
very fine atrium; very fine ornament. N of campus, interesting
private homes by Maybeck, other noted architets; also his fine
∗Rose Walk (1913), with interesting retaining walls, landscaping
and houses. Approx. 30 mi NE of Berkeley, via US I-80 & I-680:
BENICIA. ∗Old State Capitol (1854; later alt. & addit.; rest.), 1st
& G sts; architects: Houghton & Ryder; interesting small Greek
Revival example, used for capitol only two years. ∗Benicia Arsenal
and Barracks (begun 1849), E M St; interesting buildings include:
∗Clock Tower (1859; damaged by fire 1912; rebuilt), ∗Comman-
dant's House (1860; later alt. & addit.), ∗Camel Barns (1854),
used for U.S Army experiments with camel cavalry. Approx. 2 mi
farther: MARTINEZ. ∗John Muir House (1883; rest.), 4202 Al-
hambra Ave; Victorian; once home of famous naturalist, writer
who was instrumental in establishing national park system.

San Francisco Vicinity *(S & SE, via US I-280 or 101)*. Approx.
5 mi: PACIFICA. ∗Don Fernando Sanchez Adobe (1846; rest.), Lin-
da Mar Blvd; once home of mayor of San Francisco. Approx. 15
mi farther: BELMONT. On campus of ∗College of Notre Dame.
∗Ralston Hall, originally the Count Aconetto Cipriani House
(1855; enlarged 1865–75), architect, enlargement: John P
Gaynor, enormous 88-room mansion enlarged by owner, financier
William C. Ralston; fantastic rooms include replica of Palm Court
of old San Francisco Palace Hotel and of Hall of Mirrors of palace at Versailles, France. Approx. 5 mi farther: WOODSIDE. ∗Fi-
loli, the William P. Bourn House (1916), off Cañada Rd; architect: Willis Polk; landscape architects: Bruce Porter & Chesley
Bonestell; interesting Eclectic Georgian Revival; large, beautiful
gardens; once home of mining magnate. Approx. 8 mi farther
STANFORD. •**Honeycomb, the Paul R. Hanna House** (1936), 737
Frenchman's Rd; architect: Frank Lloyd Wright; considered one
of finest examples by famous architect. Approx. 5 mi farther: LOS
ALTOS HILLS. ••**Foothill College** (1961), 12345 El Monte Ave

architects: Ernest J. Kump; Marsten & Hurd; landscape architects: Sasaki & Walker; very fine college complex; simple, inviting
buildings and fine landscaping by noted architects. Approx. 15 mi
farther, near San Jose, via Co. Rd. G: NEW ALMADEN. Old wood
and adobe buildings here from early 19th-century mining days
and later. Approx. 30 mi SW of San Jose, via St. 12: SANTA
CRUZ. On campus of *University of California at Santa Cruz
(begun 1963), master planner: John Carl Warnecke; consultants:
Anshen & Allen; Theodore C. Bernardi; Ernest J. Kump; landscape architect: Thomas D. Church; fine modern complex; modern
buildings by noted architects including those already named and
Hugh Stubbins; Marquis & Stoller; Joseph Esherick; Campbell &
Wong; McCue, Boone & Tomsick; Ralph Rapson; Reid & Tarics;
John Funk; MLTW/Turnbull. Approx. 50 mi SE of San Jose, via
US 101: SAN JUAN BAUTISTA. Interesting buildings include: in
*Plaza Hist. Dist., *Mission San Juan Bautista (1812; rest.);
*Gen. Jose Maria Castro Adobe (1841; rest.), fine Spanish Colo-
nial; Monterey style. Next door, *Plaza Hotel (1814; later alt. &
addit.; rest.), pair of adobes joined together; wood second floor
added; *Zanetta House (1868), adobe first floor; wood-frame second. Approx. 35 mi SE of San Juan Bautista, via US 101, St. 156
& 1, MONTEREY, most important city in region until state admitted to union. Interesting buildings include: in *Old Town Hist.
Dist., close together, ●●**Thomas Oliver Larkin House** (1835; rest.),
464 Calle Principal; adobe; wide balconies; considered finest in
Monterey style; originally home of U.S. Consul to Mexico. Not
far: adobe *Casa Gutierrez (1841; rest.), 580 Calle Principal. Not
far away: *Casa Amesti (1825; rest.), very fine Monterey style.
Not far: Stevenson House (1838; rest.), 530 Houston St; adobe;
originally home of Don Rafael Gonzalez, early customs administra-
trator; named for famous author Robert Louis Stevenson, who
lived here for short period. Near waterfront: *Old Custom House
(about 1825; later alt. & addit.; rest.), 115 Alvarado St; interesting adobe and stone; built by Mexicans; oldest public building in
state. At Thomas & Josselyn Canyon rds, *St. John's Episcopal
Church (1891; later alt. & addit.), architect: Ernest Coxhead;
very fine Shingle style church, amazingly cut in two, put back
together with extension between halves. Approx. 5 mi farther,
CARMEL, the village by the sea. *Mission San Carlos Borromeo del
Rio Carmelo (1797; later alt. & addit.; rest.), Lasuen Dr; among
most famous California missions. Also of interest, S of Carmel
along coast: marvelous *Big Sur country. Approx. 5 mi SE of
Carmel, via Carmel Valley Rd: CARMEL VALLEY. *Carmel Valley
Manor (1963), architects: Skidmore, Owings & Merrill; landscape architects: Sasaki & Walker; fine small-scale complex for
elderly; in villagelike groupings; fine landscaping. Approx. 30 mi
SE of Carmel, via Co. rds G16 & G17 (approx. 45 mi SE of San
Juan Bautista, via US 101): SOLEDAD. Nearby, *Los Coches Rancho, the William Brunner Richardson Adobe (1843; rest.), site of
camp, 1846–47, of Maj. John C. Frémont, who captured much of

Marin County Civic Center—Modern (Lucille Dandelet)

state from Mexicans; nearby, ruins of *Mission Nuestra Señora de la Soledad (begun about 1795). Approx. 35 mi S, via US 101 & Co. Rd G14: JOLON. Nearby, *Mission San Antonio de Padua (1813; rest.).

San Francisco Vicinity *(NW, via US 101)*. Approx. 15 mi: SAN RAFAEL. Interesting buildings include: *Ira Cook House (1879), Boyd Park; Victorian; fine grounds. Also:
••*Marin Co. Civic Center (1962; later alt. & addit.), off US 101 on San Pedro Rd; architect: Frank Lloyd Wright; architect, alt. & addit.: William Wesley Peters of Taliesin Assoc.; assoc. architect: Aaron G. Green; very fine modern complex by famous architect; completed after his death; considered one of his many masterpieces. Approx. 20 mi farther: PETALUMA.*Petaluma Adobe, also known as Casa Grande (1836–46; rest.), 3325 Adobe Rd; very large house; once home of Gen. Mariano Guadelupe Vallejo; also of interest, W of city, *Point Reyes Nat. Seashore. Approx, 17 mi farther: SANTA ROSA. *Luther Burbank House (1883), Santa Rosa Ave; once home of famous horticulturist; on grounds: interesting gardens; Burbank buried here under Cedar of Lebanon tree he planted. Approx. 20 mi SE, via St. 12, in heart of wine country: SONOMA. *Lachrymae Montis, the Gen. Mariano Guadelupe Vallejo House (1852), Sonoma State Hist. Park; Victorian; beautiful gardens; on grounds: Swiss chalet. Also of interest: *Sonoma Plaza, planned by General Vallejo; *Mission San Francisco Solano (1823), northernmost mission; only one established by Mexicans. Approx. 25 mi NW of Santa Rosa, via St. 116: JENNER. *Ft. Ross, *Commander's House (1812; rest.), log building constructed by Russians; also other rest. buildings. Approx. 15 mi SE of Santa Rosa: GLEN ELLEN. *Jack London Ranch, also known as Beauty Ranch, (1905), State Hist. Park; once home of famous writer; on grounds: other buildings of significance in his life; his grave on hiking trail. Approx. 50 mi NW of Jenner, via St. 1,
••*Sea Ranch, marvelous residential complex on high meadowland overlooking Pacific Ocean; planner & landscape architect: Law-

rence Halprin; fine modern houses, condominiums, other facilities blending with beautiful natural setting, include: Condominium I (1965), architects: Moore, Turnbull, Lyndon & Whitaker; *Lodge, with restaurant, general store (1965; later alt. & addit.), architect: Joseph Esherick; architects, alt. & addit.: Alfred Boeke & Louis McLane. Approx. 190 mi farther, via St. 1 & US 101: EUREKA. Interesting buildings include: ●*William Carson House, now Ingomar Club (1886; later alt.), M & 2nd sts; architects: Samuel & Joseph C. Newsom; very fine late Victorian with forms and details in variety of styles, including Queen Anne, Italianate, Eastlake; once home of lumber magnate. Across street: *J. Milton Carson House (1887; rest.), 202 M St; architects: Samuel & Joseph C. Newsom; mostly Queen Anne; once home of son of William Carson. Also of interest here: *The Wooden Garden (1972), 1415 Pine St; delightful fantasy figures sawed out and painted by Romano Gabriel. Also of interest: S of city, *Humboldt Redwoods State Park; N of city, *Redwood Nat. Park.

Hawaii

Early inhabitants Polynesians who arrived as long ago as 50 B.C.; others may have arrived about 1200. Explorers from Spain, Holland, or Japan may have arrived here, 16th century. Englishman Capt. James Cook landed here, 1778; named area Sandwich Islands; returned later in year and was killed by Hawaiians. Other Europeans followed. After considerable fighting, King Kamehameha succeeded in uniting most of islands, 1795, as Kingdom of Hawaii; King Kaumaulii of Kauai and Niihau brought those islands under Kamehameha rule, 1810. Liholiho, son of Kamehameha, became King Kamehameha II, after father's death, 1819; abolished Hawaiian religion, including human sacrifice. In 1820, Protestant missionaries, led by Hiram Bingham, arrived; soon converted natives to their religion. In 1827, Roman Catholic missionaries arrived, but most were forced to leave, 1831; French warship *L' Artémise* blockaded Honolulu; Capt. C. P. T. Laplace demanded religious freedom for Roman Catholics; Hawaiians acceded to his request. First constitution of Kingdom of Hawaii, 1840; recognized by United States, 1842; by France and Great Britain, 1843. Many immigrants, 1854–72. Republic of Hawaii formed, 1894; Stanford B. Dole only president. Became U.S. territory, 1900. On Dec. 7, 1941, Japan attacked Hawaii, without warning, destroying many ships, aircraft, other property, and killing many people at Pearl Harbor and other places. Starting early in 20th century, petitions made for statehood. Finally, on Aug. 21, 1959, Hawaii became fiftieth and latest state. Today: Major agricultural, manufacturing, and tourist industries.

Land Regions: Some 122 islands, eight of major size, with smaller islands of rock, coral, sand in W.

Climate: Mild, little difference days and nights; precipitation heavy in mountains, slight in lowlands.

Major Building Materials: Lava, coral.

Architecture: Small number of important, exotic buildings; unlike any others in United States.

ISLAND OF OAHU

HONOLULU
Interesting buildings include: *State Capitol (1969), Beretania & Punchbowl sts; architects: John Carl Warnecke; Belt, Lemmon & Lo; modern. Nearby, ••**Iolani Palace** (1882; rest.), 364 S. King St; architects: Thomas J. Baker, C. S. Wall & Isaac Moore; interesting example; unusual, in U.S., royal palace; verandas and ornamental cast-iron columns, railings, stairs; at same location, *Iolani Barracks (1870; rest.), architect: Theodore C. Heuck; originally quarters for royal guard. Not far: *Honolulu Hale, or City Hall, (1927), King & Punchbowl sts; architects: Dickey & Wood and Rothwell, Kangster & Lester; vaguely Mediterranean style; fine interior court. Not far: *Mission Buildings, S. King & Kawaiahao sts; interesting group, occupied and used by missionaries from Boston, includes: *Oldest Frame House (1821), of precut timbers sent from Boston around The Horn; *Printing House (1841), two-bedroom addit. to house; *Chamberlain House (1831), of coral blocks with timber salvaged from ships and lumber sent from Maine; adobe Schoolhouse (1832), used for classes taught by Mrs. Hiram Bingham. Nearby, *Kawaiahao Church (1842), 957 Punchbowl St, architect: Hiram Bingham; coral rock Eclectic Classic Revival; built by noted missionary; on grounds: *Lunalilo Tomb (1876), architect: Robert Lishman; burial place of King Lunalilo, last king of Kamehameha dynasty. ••**Aliiolani Hale** (1874), now Judiciary Building, S. King & Mililani sts; architect: Thomas Rowe; in English, "House of the Heavenly Chiefs," originally palace; later served other governmental purposes. Few blocks: *Alexander and Baldwin Building (1929), Bishop, Merchant & Queen sts; architects: C. W. Dickey & Hart Wood; noted office building with balconies and fine details. Not far: *Young Women's Christian Assoc. Building (1927), architect: Julia Morgan; office building by pioneer woman architect who once worked for Bernard Maybeck. Not far: *Washington Place (1846), 320 S. Beretania St; architect: Isaac Hart; Classic Revival; originally

home of John Dominis, later of Queen Liliuokalani and her husband, John Owen Dominis; since 1922, residence of state governor. Not far: *St. Andrew's Cathedral, Episcopal (1867–88; later alt. & addit.), S. Beretania & Queen Emma sts; architects: B. F. Ingelow & Carleton Winslow, Jr.; Gothic Revival; plans sent from England for King Kamehameha IV and Queen Emma. At 1230 College Walk, *Toyo Theater (1938), architect: C. W. Dickey; interesting Japanese design by American architect; fine garden. At 215 Kukui St, *Izumu Taishakyo Mission (1923), architect: Hego Fuchino; interesting Japanese design by Japanese architect. E of downtown: *Honolulu Academy of Arts (1927; later alt. & addit.), 900 S. Beretania St; architect: Bertram Grosvenor Goodhue; architects, addit.: 1956 & 1968, Albert Ives; 1977, John Hara; interesting Eclectic building by famous architect; fine Oriental collections. *First Chinese Church of Christ (1929), 1054 S. King St; architect: Hart Wood; Chinese-American style building by noted architect, also acclaimed for his nearby *First Church of Christ, Scientist (1923), 1508 Punahou St. Nearby, *Punahou School, 1601 Punahou St. Interesting buildings include: *Old School Hall (1852), architect: William Harrison Rice; resembles New England meeting house; *Punahou Chapel (1966), architect: Vladimir Ossipoff; fine modern example in delightful setting with lily pool; *Central Union Church (1924), 1660 S. Beretania St; architects: Cram & Ferguson; Eclectic Classic Revival by famous architects.

In Waikiki Beach, interesting buildings include: *Halekulani Hotel (1931), 2199 Kalia Blvd; architect: C. W. Dickey; appealing modest group by noted architect; *Royal Hawaiian Hotel (1927), 2259 Kalakua Ave; architects: Warren & Wetmore; distinctive pink building has long been beloved city landmark; other notable Waikiki hotels include: *Moana (1901), 2365 Kalakua Blvd; architect: O. G. Traphagen; *Princess Kaiulani Hotel and Shops (1954), architect: Gardner Dailey. Also of interest nearby: *International Market-Place.

Interesting modern buildings at *University of Hawaii at Manoa, East-West Rd, include: *East-West Center (1963), architect: I. M. Pei; assoc. architects: Young & Henderson; beautiful Japanese garden designed by Kenzo Ogata. At 2913 Pali Hwy, *Queen Emma Summer Palace (about 1847), modest wood-frame example. Also of interest: *Pearl Harbor; *U.S.S. *Arizona* Nat. Mem. Approx. 35 mi N, via St. 63 & 83, LIAE, *Polynesian Cultural Center, interesting reconst. Hawaiian, other Polynesian buildings.

ISLAND OF HAWAII

(Approx. 215 air mi from Honolulu). HILO, *Rev. David Belden Lyman House (1839; later alt.), 276 Haili Rd; once home of early missionary. Also of interest nearby, *Hawaii Volcanoes Nat. Park, including Mauna Loa.

Hilo Vicinity *(NW, via St. 200, 190 & 240).* Approx. 60 mi: KA-MUELA. ●*Mauna Kea Beach Hotel** (1965; later alt. & addit.), Mauna Beach; architects: Skidmore, Owings & Merrill; architects, alt. & addit.: Whisenand, Allison, Tong & Goo; fine modern hotel complex by famous firm; beautiful setting with view of Mauna Kea, active volcano mountain, highest, 13,796 feet, in islands. Approx. 40 mi SW, via St. 190: KAILUA KONA. *Hulihee Palace (1838; rest.), Kailua Village, Alii Dr; summer house of Hawaiian kings; of local woods, lava, coral mortar. Nearby, *Mokuaikaua Church (1837; rest.), built by early missionaries. Also of interest, few miles S: site where famous explorer Capt. James Cook was killed, 1779. Approx. 20 mi S of Kailua, via St. 11 & 16: HON-AUNAU. *City of Refuge, or Pu'uhonua O Hanaunau (c. 1551–1650; rest. 1969), Hawaiian sacred place; reconst. shelters, great figures carved on wood; original stone wall. Not far: *St. Benedict's Roman Catholic Church (1902), Middle Keei Rd; architect: Father John Velghe; also known as Painted Church; for imaginative paintings by Velghe on interior walls, other places.

ISLAND OF KAUAI

(Approx. 100 air mi from Honolulu). From airport at LIHUE, approx. 5 mi N, via St. 56: WAILUA. Reconst. *Holoholoku Heiau, Wailua River State Park, Hawaiian sacred place. Approx. 20 mi farther: HANALEI. *Waioli Mission, includes *Mission House (1836; rest.); *Mission Hall (1841; rest.).

ISLAND OF MAUI

(Approx. 100 air mi from Honolulu). From airport at KAHULUI, approx. 2 mi NW, via St. 340: WAILUKU. *Hale Hoikeike, also known as Edward Bailey House (1833; later alt. & addit.), Iao Rd; once home of early missionary Jonathan Greene. Approx. 34 mi farther: LAHAINA. Interesting buildings include: in Hist. Dist., *Rev. Dwight Baldwin House (1835; later alt. & addit.), Town Square; once home of another early missionary.

Oregon

Early inhabitants Indians of several tribes including Chinook, Paiute, Nez Percé. Spanish believed to have sighted coast, 16th century; Englishman Sir Francis Drake believed to have landed, 1579; Englishman Capt. James Cook visited, 1778. American Robert Gray explored, 1788, as did Englishman George Vancouver, 1792. Americans Meriwether Lewis and William Clark explored, 1805. Russia, Great Britain, Spain and United States all claimed portions of region. American John Jacob Astor established fur-trading post, 1811: Astoria. Settlement by pioneers who travelled Oregon Trail began before mid-19th century. In 1819, S border established by treaty with Spain; in 1846, treaty with Great Britain established N border of United States. Fighting with Indians began with Cayuse War, 1847; continued in later wars with Modoc, other tribes and, in 1877, when Nez Percé, led by Chief Joseph, resisted move to Idaho; wars ended with brief uprisings by Paiute and Bannock tribes, 1878. In 1848, region became Oregon Territory; capital: Oregon City. Became thirty-third state, Feb. 14, 1859. Capital moved to Salem. Today: Important manufacturing and agricultural industries; mining also important.

Land Regions: E to W, Columbia Plateau; Basin and Range Region; Cascade Mountains; Willamette Lowland; Klamath Mountains and Coast Range.

Climate: Mild in W, colder in central and E areas; precipitation very heavy in W, moderate in central, low in E; snowfall minimal in W, moderate elsewhere.

Major Building Materials: Timber, primarily softwoods; bauxite; copper and other metals; perlite; sand; clay.

Architecture: Rich and varied, including some of finest U.S. buildings, especially in Eugene and vicinity; Portland and vicinity.

EUGENE

Interesting buildings include: modern *City Hall (1964), Pearl St bet. 7th & 8th aves; architects: Stafford, Morin & Longwood. At *University of Oregon, Eclectic Second Empire Revival *Deady Hall (1886), architect: W. W. Piper; *Villard Hall (1876; later alt. & addit.), architect: Warren H. Williams. Also of interest, W of city, above COOS BAY, *Oregon Dunes Nat. Recreation Area.

First Presbyterian Church—Modern (Julius Shulman)

Eugene Vicinity *(S, via US I-5).* Approx. 20 mi: COTTAGE GROVE. ●*First Presbyterian Church,** also known as United, (1951), 216 S. 3rd St; architect: Pietro Belluschi; very fine modern example by famous architect. Approx. 45 mi farther: ROSEBURG. *Joseph Lane House (1854; rest.), 554 S.E. Douglas Ave; once home of first territorial governor. Not far: *Douglas Co. Museum (1969; later addit.), architects: Backen, Arragoni & Ross; architects, addit.: WE Group; interesting small, modern example. Nearby, *Douglas Hall (1970), architects: Backen, Arragoni & Ross, sports and exhibit building. Approx. 45 mi farther: WOLF CREEK. *Wolf Creek Tavern (about 1857), wood-frame building, still in use. Approx. 50 mi farther, via US 5 & St. 238, JACKSONVILLE, well-preserved old gold-mining town. Interesting buildings include: in Hist. Dist., on California St, *Beekman Bank (1863; rest.); United States Hotel (1880); *St. Joseph's Roman Catholic Church (1858); *Cornelius C. Beekman House (1890); on 5th St; *Jackson Co. Courthouse, now Jacksonville Museum (1883; later alt. & addit.); *John Wilmer McCully House (1861; later alt. & addit.), once home of first doctor in county; *Table Rock Billiard Saloon (about 1856). Also of interest, NE: *Crater Lake Nat. Park.

PORTLAND

Interesting buildings include: *Union Station (1890; later alt. & addit.), 800 N.W. 6th Ave; architects: Van Brunt & Howe; somewhat Romanesque, somewhat Gothic, Revival. Just across Willamette River, via Broadway Bridge, *Memorial Coliseum (1960), 1401 N.E. Wheeler Ave; architects: Skidmore, Owings & Merrill; fine modern example by famous firm. Nearby, *Lloyd Center (1966 & later), by same firm. Some blocks away: *Central Lutheran Church (1951), 2104 N.E. 21st St; architect: Pietro Belluschi; fine modern example by famous Italian-American architect. Some blocks S of Union Station, at 421 S.W. 6th Ave, ●*Equitable Building, formerly Commonwealth, (1948), architect: Pietro Belluschi; very fine modern office building by famous Italian-American architect; considered one of most important U.S. examples of its era. Next door, *U.S. National Bank (1916), 321 S.W. 6th Ave; architect: A. E. Doyle; fine Eclectic Classic Revival by noted architect for whom Belluschi worked for number of years. Few blocks away: *First Presbyterian Church (1890; later alt. & addit.), 1200 S.W. Alder St; architects: William E. McCaw & Richard Martin, Jr.; fine Gothic Revival. Not far: *Central Library (1913; later alt. & addit.), architects: Doyle & Patterson; Eclectic Georgian Revival. Few blocks away: *The Old Church, originally Calvary Presbyterian Church (1883), 1422 S.W. 11th St; architect: Warren H. Williams; fine wood-frame Gothic Revival. Not far: *Portland Art Museum (1932; later alt. & addit.), S.W. Park Ave & Madison St; architect: A. E. Doyle; one of number of fine buildings designed by Pietro Belluschi while working for Doyle. Few blocks away: *Portland City Hall (1895), 1220 S.W. 5th Ave; architects: Whidden & Lewis; Eclectic Renaissance Revival. Also of interest nearby, *Auditorium Forecourt Fountain (1970), bet. 2nd & 3rd aves, Market & Clay sts; landscape architect: Lawrence Halprin; very fine, delightful array of fountains, cascades, waterfalls, pools, spillways by famous landscape architect. Not far: *Pioneer Post Office (1875; later alt.), 520 S.W. Morri-

**Equitable Building—
Modern** (Morley Baer)

son St; architect: A. B. Mullett; architects, 1973 alt.: Allen, McMath & Hawkins, fine Eclectic Classic Revival; cupola; also used by U.S. courts. Not far: *Bishop's House (1879; later alt.), 219 S.W. Stark St; architect: P. Heurn; Victorian Gothic; once residence of Roman Catholic Archbishop, now offices. Nearby, *New Market Theater (1872; later alt. & addit.), 50 S.W. 2nd Ave; architect: W. W. Piper; Eclectic Renaissance Revival; now garage. Also nearby, *Old Town and *Yamhill Rest. Dist. Not far: *Portland Center (begun 1966), Harrison St & S.W. 1st Ave; modern complex with apartment buildings, shopping center, offices by Skidmore, Owings & Merrill and other architects. Also: very fine *Lovejoy Park and Fountain (1966), landscape architect: Lawrence Halprin. Not far: interesting modern buildings at *Portland State College. Not far: in King's Hill, *Zion Lutheran Church (1952), 1015 S.W. 18th Ave; architect: Pietro Belluschi; fine modern example by famous architect; another of his fine examples in Green Hills area: *St. Thomas More Church (1941), 3525 S.W. Patton Rd; architect: A. E. Doyle; designer: Pietro Belluschi. Two early modern houses, both private: James K. Buell House (1922), 2660 S.W. Vista Ave and William Gray Purcell House (1921), 2635 S.W. Georgian Pl, architect of both: William Gray Purcell. In Arlington Heights area, two interesting, private, modern houses by office of A. E. Doyle; on S. W. Skyline Dr, at no. 1100, Jennings Sutor House (1938), designer: Pietro Belluschi; at no. 1061, A. R. Watzek House (1937), designer: John Yeon; other interesting examples in area. Interesting older houses, not too far away, include: ••**Henry L. Pittock Mansion** (1914), N.W. Pittock Dr; magnificent Eclectic French Renaissance Revival; spectacular hill site overlooking city; once home of founder of *Daily Oregonian* newspaper. At 2035 N.W. Everett St, *Capt. John Andrew Brown House (1898; rest.), Victorian; once home of riverboat and sea captain who developed city's port. Nearby, *Dr. K. A. J. MacKenzie House (1892), 615 N.W. 20th Ave; architects: Whidden & Lewis. Interesting modern buildings: *Portland Community College (begun 1967), 12,000 S.W. 49th Ave; architects: Wolfe, Zimmer, Gunsul, Frasca & Ritter. *Reed College, 3203 S.E. Woodstock Blvd; architects: A. E. Doyle; Pietro Belluschi; Skidmore, Owings & Merrill; Harry Weese; others. Also see: Washington—Vancouver.

Portland Vicinity *(E, via US I-80N/I-84).* Approx. 85 mi, THE DALLES, picturesque town at narrows of Columbia River. Interesting buildings include: at *Ft. Dalles, *Surgeon's Quarters (1857), 1500 Garrison St; architect: Louis Scholl; fine, simple Gothic Revival cottage; last surviving fort building. Also of interest nearby: *Columbia River Gorge; *Bonneville Dam; SW of town: *Mount Hood.

Portland Vicinity *(SE, via US I-205).* Approx. 15 mi: OREGON CITY. Interesting buildings include: in *McLoughlin Park, *Dr.

John McLoughlin House (1846; rest.), once home of chief factor of Hudson's Bay Co., founder of Oregon City; moved here; Nat. Hist. Site; *Dr. Forbes Barclay House (1850; rest.), once home of Ft. Vancouver surgeon; moved here. At 19,195 S. Leland Rd, Greek Revival *Ainsworth House (1851); at 554 Warner Parrott Rd, *Locust Farm, the Gen. Morton Matthew McCarver House (1852; later alt. & addit.), first prefabricated house in state; brought around The Horn from Maine.

Portland Vicinity *(SW, via St. 99W & 18).* Approx. 30 mi: NEW-BERG. *Dr. Henry Minthorn House, also known as Herbert Hoover Boyhood Home (1881; later alt. & addit.), 115 S. River St; Minthorns were foster parents of future president. Approx. 70 mi farther, via St. 99W & 18, US 101: GLENEDEN. Very fine modern *Salishan Lodge (1965), master planners: Skidmore, Owings & Merrill; architect, lodge: John Storrs.

Portland Vicintiy *(NW, via US 30).* Approx. 35 mi: COLUMBIA CITY. *Dr. Charles Green Caples House (1872; later alt. & addit.), once home of pioneer doctor; on grounds: interesting reconst. outbuildings. Approx. 70 mi farther, ASTORIA, founded by John Jacob Astor's trading partners. *Capt. George Flavel Mansion (1884), lavish Victorian. Also of interest nearby: *Ft. Clatsop Nat. Mon.; *End of the Trail Mon. marking final stop, 1805, of Lewis & Clark Expedition.

SALEM

Interesting buildings include: *State Capitol (1937), architects: Francis Kelly, Trowbridge & Livingston and Whitehouse & Church; Art Deco or Moderne; interesting western sculpture, murals. Nearby, *Marion Co. Courthouse (1872), High St, architect: W. W. Piper; Eclectic Baroque Revival. At 302 State St, *U.S. National Bank, Ladd and Bush Branch (1869; later alt. & addit.), architect: John Nestor; architects, 1967 addit.: Skidmore, Owings & Merrill; very fine cast-iron front. *Asahel Bush House (1878; rest.), 600 Mission St SE; architect: William F. Boothby; Italianate; once home of cofounder of Ladd and Bush Bank; on grounds: interesting outbuildings: *Conservatory, or Greenhouse (about 1882; rest.), *Barn, now Bush Barn Art Center. In *Thomas Kay Hist. Park, *Jason Lee House (1841; rest.); *Methodist Parsonage (1841; rest.), moved here. Approx. 20 mi NE of city, via St. 213 & 214: MOUNT ANGEL. Nearby, at *Mount Angel Abbey, *Mount Angel Library (1970), architects: Alvar Aalto and DeMars & Wells; fine modern by famous Finnish architect. Approx. 150 mi SE of city, via St. 22, US 20 & St. 126: PRINEVILLE. In *Pioneer Park, log *Prineville Hist. Museum (1880). Approx. 120 mi E of Prineville, via US 26 & 395: CANYON CITY. *Joaquin Miller Cabin (1864; rest.), Grant Co. Museum, once home of noted poet.

Washington

Early inhabitants Indians of several tribes, including Cayuse, Chinook, Clatsop, Nez Percé, Spokane, Yakima. Spanish believed to have sailed along coast, 16th century. First explorers Spaniards Bruno Heceta and Juan Francisco de la Bodega y Quadra, 1775; claimed region for Spain. Englishman Capt. James Cook sailed along coast, 1778. Englishman Capt. George Vancouver explored, 1792–94; claimed region for British. In same year, American Robert Gray explored, establishing United States claim. Americans Meriwether Lewis and William Clark reached region, 1805. Canadian David Thompson explored, 1807–11. British and American fur traders in area from about 1806. Canadian North West Company founded, 1810: Spokane House, near present-day Spokane. American John Jacob Astor founded first permanent American settlement in what is now Washington State, 1811: Ft. Okanogan. Hudson's Bay Company, led by John McLoughlin, established, 1825: Ft. Vancouver, now Vancouver. In 1846, Great Britain and United States signed treaty establishing 49th parallel as border between British and U.S. regions. Became part of Oregon Territory, 1848; became Washington Territory, 1853. Wars with Indians until 1858. Became forty-second state Nov. 11, 1889. Today: Major manufacturing and agricultural industries.

Land Regions: E to W, Columbia Plateau; Rocky Mountains; Cascade Mountains; Puget Sound Lowland; Olympic Mountains; Coast Range.

Climate: Mild in W, moderate in central and E areas; precipitation heavy in W, minimal in central section, moderate in E; snowfall minimal along coast, heavy in mountains.

Major Building Materials: Timber, primarily softwoods; clay, limestone; sand and gravel; zinc; other metals.

Architecture: Important buildings here, in several places, especially Seattle and vicinity.

OLYMPIA

Interesting buildings include: *Capitol Group, Capitol Way bet. 11th & 14th aves, *Legislative Building (1928), actually capitol; *Insurance Building (1921); *Temple of Justice (1920); architects of all: Wilder & White; all Eclectic Classic Revival with hints of

Art Deco or Moderne. Also: *C. J. Lord House (1923; later alt. & addit.), 214 W. 22nd St; architect: Joseph Wohleb; interesting Eclectic Renaissance and Mediterranean Villa Revival; down street: *Henry McCleary House (1925), architect: Joseph Wohleb; Eclectic Renaissance Revival.

Olympia Vicinity *(S, via US I-5)*. Approx. 5 mi: TUMWATER. *Capt. Nathaniel Crosby House (1860; rest.), once home of grandfather of famous singer and actor Harry Lillis Crosby, more familiarly known as Bing. Approx. 20 mi farther: CHEHALLIS. *John R. Jackson House, also known as Jackson Courthouse (1844), split cedar; used as U.S. district courthouse, 1850.

SEATTLE

Interesting buildings include large number in more than 13 blocks and portions of blocks in *Pioneer Square Hist. Dist., originally called "Skid Roll" because logs were rolled down to water here; later called "Skid Row." At 606 1st Ave, *Pioneer Building (1890; rest.), architect: Elmer Fisher; architect, rest.: Ralph Anderson. *Yesler Building (1895), Yesler Way & 1st Ave S; architect: Elmer Fisher. *L. C. Smith Tower (1914), Yesler Way & 2nd Ave; architects: Gaggin & Gaggin; for many years tallest building, 42 stories, W of Mississippi River; interesting interior details. Not far: *Seattle First National Bank (1969), 1000 4th Ave; architects: Naramore, Bain, Brady & Johanson; consult. architect: Pietro Belluschi; fine modern office building; raised plaza with fine sculpture *Vertebrae* by famous sculptor Henry Moore. At 1218 3rd Ave, *Seattle Tower, originally Northern Life Tower (1929), architects: Albertson, Wilson & Richardson; interesting Art Deco or Moderne. At 2nd Ave & Pine St, *A. E. Doyle Building, originally J. S. Graham Department Store (about 1915; interior remod. 1973), architects: Doyle & Merriam; architect, remod.: Ibsen Nelson; fine Eclectic Renaissance Revival; designed by noted Seattle architect for whom it was renamed. Nearby, *Pike Place Market (1907; later alt. & addit.), 1431 1st Ave, now Hist. Dist. Not far: in *Waterfront Park, at Pier 59 & Elliott Bay, interesting modern *Seattle Public Aquarium (1977); architect: Fred Bassetti. On Seneca St bet. 6th & 8th aves, *Freeway Park (1976), landscape architect: Lawrence Halprin. On Pine St, bet. 4th & 5th aves, entrance to monorail; ride of few blocks to *Seattle Center (1962), originally buildings of 1962 Seattle World's Fair, Century 21; supervising architect: Paul Thiry; interesting buildings by Minoru Yamasaki, others; also: *Space Needle, architect: John Graham, Jr.; now center for music, arts, sports, other activities.

At 1551 10th Ave E, *Eliza Ferry Leary House (1905), impressive Eclectic Gothic Revival; fine wood carving by Belgian artisans; now Episcopal Diocesan House. At Broadway & E. Pine St, fine modern *Seattle Central Community College (1976), architects: Kirk, Wallace & McKinley. Another modern example: *North Seattle Community College (1970), Meridian Ave; architects: Edward & John Mahlum.

Seattle Vicinity *(N, via US I-405 & I-5).* Approx. 15 mi: BOTHELL. *W. A. Hanna House (1893; rest.), 10,222 Main St. Approx. 75 mi farther: BELLINGHAM. *George E. Pickett House (1856), 910 Bancroft St; once home of then captain, U.S. Army, later Confederate general, who led famous charge up Cemetery Ridge during Battle of Gettysburg, 1863. Also of interest E of city: *North Cascades Nat. Park; *Lake Chelan Nat. Recreation Area.

Seattle Vicinity *(SE, via US I-90).* Approx. 105 mi: ELLENSBURG, originally named Robbers' Roost. Nearby, *Samuel Bedient Olmstead Home (1875), Squaw Creek Trail Rd; log cabin, once home of pioneer; interesting outbuildings: wagon shed, granary, barns. Approx. 60 mi N of Ellensburg, via US 97 & 2: CASHMERE. *Willis Carey Pioneer Village, E. Sunset Hwy; reconst. & rest. late 19-century mission, assay office, school, log houses; moved here. Approx. 55 mi S of Ellensburg, via US I-82 & St. 22: TOPPENISH. Nearby, *Ft. Simcoe (1856; rest.), in State Park. Approx. 70 mi SE of Toppenish, via US 12: RICHLAND. Approx. 5 mi via George Washington Way, *Battelle Memorial Institute Pacific Northwest Laboratories (1968), architects: Naramore, Bain, Brady & Johanson; fine modern research complex. Approx. 10 mi farther: PASCO. At *Columbia Basin Community College, *Art, Drama and Music Building (1971), architects: Brooks, Hensley & Creager; very fine modern.

Seattle Vicinity *(S, via US I-5).* Approx. 22 mi: FEDERAL WAY. Nearby, via St. 18, ●*Weyerhaeuser Headquarters (1971), S. 348th St; architects: Skidmore, Owings & Merrill; very fine modern complex by famous architects; very fine landscaping; landscape architect: Hideo Sasaki; number of works of art; considered one of finest buildings of its era. Approx. 18 mi farther: TACOMA. Interesting buildings include: *Union Station (1911), Pacific Ave bet. 17th S & 20th S sts; architects: Reed & Stem; Eclectic Baroque Revival; great copper-covered dome. *Old City Hall (1893; renov. 1970), 7th S St; architects: Heatherton & McIntosh; architect, renov.: Barnett Schorr; Eclectic Renaissance Revival in Hist. Dist.; renov. into shops, restaurants. In *Point Defiance Park, *Ft. Nisqually (1833), built by Hudson's Bay Company. Interesting buildings include: *Factor's House (1845); *Granary (1843); both moved here; remainder of fort reconst. Also of interest, SE of Tacoma, *Mount Rainier Nat. Park. Approx. 6 mi SE of Tacoma, via St. 167: PUYALLUP. *Ezra Meeker Mansion (about 1890), architects: Farrell & Darmer; ornate Victorian; once home of founder of town, who later marked historic Oregon Trail.

Seattle Vicinity *(W & NW, via ferry)*. BREMERTON, location of *U.S.S. *Missouri*. Approx. 25 mi N, via St. 3: PORT GAMBLE. Number of interesting mid-19th century buildings, especially Greek Revival houses, in Hist. Dist. of old sawmill town. Approx. 35 mi NW of Port Gamble, via St. 104 & 20: PORT TOWNSEND. Interesting buildings include: Victorian *Francis Wilcox James House (1889; later alt. & addit.; rest.), Washington St; now inn. Holly Manor, the J. C. Saunders House (1889; later alt. & addit.), architect: Edward A. Batwell; once home of collector of customs. Gothic Revival *George Starrett House (about 1855; rest.), 744 Clay St. Greek Revival *D. C. H. Rothschild House (1868; rest.), Jefferson St; architect: A. H. Tucker. *Manresa Hall, also known as Charles Eisenbeis House (1892; later alt. & addit.), architect: A. S. Whiteway; like castle on Rhine; once home of German immigrant; now inn, restaurant. Via ferry, interesting buildings in Hist. Dist. of COUPEVILLE. Also on Whidbey Island and in San Juan Islands. Also of interest nearby: *Olympic Nat. Park.

SPOKANE

Interesting buildings include: *Spokane Co. Courthouse (1895; later alt. & addit.), 1116 Broadway; architect: Willis A. Ritchie; Eclectic French Renaissance Revival. Modern *Riverpark Center Opera House (1974), Spokane Falls Blvd & Washington St; architects: Walker, McGough, Foultz & Lyerla; also here: exhibition hall. *Grace Campbell House (1898; later alt. & addit.), 2316 1st Ave W; architect: Kirtland K. Cutter. Also of interest, W: *Grand Coulee Dam Nat. Recreation Area.

VANCOUVER

Interesting buildings include: at *Ft. Vancouver, *Grant House (1849), 1106 E. Evergreen Ave; log cabin; once home of Ulysses S. Grant, while serving here as brevet captain. *Commanding Officer's Quarters, now Red Cross Building (1886; later alt. & addit.), 1310 E. Evergreen Ave; Victorian; once quarters of Gen. George C. Marshall. In *LeVerich Park, *Richard Covington House (1848); log cabin; once home of Hudson's Bay Company official; moved here. In *Esther Short Park, *Charles W. Slocum House (about 1867); Victorian; cupola and widow's walk; moved here. Also see: Oregon—Portland.

Vancouver Vicinity *(NW, via US I-5)*. Approx. 40 mi: KELSO. Interesting pioneer exhibits of *Cowlitz Co. Museum. Approx. 75 mi NW of Kelso, via St. 4 & US 101: CHINOOK. *Ft. Columbia, *Commanding Officer's House (1902), now State Park.

Index of Place Names

NEW ENGLAND STATES, 1

MIDDLE ATLANTIC STATES, 45

SOUTHEASTERN STATES, 107

MIDWESTERN STATES, 175

ROCKY MOUNTAIN STATES, 241

SOUTHWESTERN STATES, 261

PACIFIC STATES, 287